Encyclopedia
of Real Estate Forms

Encyclopedia of Real Estate Forms

Jerome S. Gross

Prentice-Hall, Inc.
Englewood Cliffs, N.J.

PRENTICE-HALL INTERNATIONAL, INC., *London*
PRENTICE-HALL OF AUSTRALIA, PTY. LTD., *Sydney*
PRENTICE-HALL OF CANADA, LTD., *Toronto*
PRENTICE-HALL OF INDIA PRIVATE LTD., *New Delhi*
PRENTICE-HALL OF JAPAN, INC., *Tokyo*

Eighth Printing . . . . . October, 1977

This publication is designed to provide
accurate and authoritative information
with regard to the subject matter covered.
It is sold with the understanding that the
publisher is not engaged in rendering legal,
accounting, or other professional advice.
If legal advice or other expert assistance
is required, the services of a competent
professional person should be sought.

> *. . . From a Declaration of Principles jointly
> adopted by a Committee of the American Bar
> Association and a Committee of Publishers and
> Associations.*

Library of Congress Cataloging in Publication Data

Gross, Jerome S
    Encyclopedia of real estate forms.

    1. Real property—United States—Forms.
2. Real estate business—United States—Forms.
I. Title.
KF568.1.G76   346'.73'0437   73-2716
ISBN 0-13-276170-X

To Ev

About the Author

Few men possess a background that blends both the technical and practical aspects of real estate to equal that of Jerome S. Gross. As a practicing licensed real estate broker in both New York and Florida for more than twenty-two years, he has actively engaged in all phases of real estate, including: sales, leasing, management, mortgaging, and appraising. He is President of his own real estate corporation, specializing in the sale and leasing of multi-million dollar commercial and industrial properties, and was formerly Vice President and Director of Keyes National Investors of Miami, Florida.

Mr. Gross is an active member of the National Association of Real Estate Boards (Realtors), and he is also the author of the widely used ILLUSTRATED ENCYCLOPEDIC DICTIONARY OF REAL ESTATE TERMS (Prentice-Hall, Inc., 1969). In addition to these activities, Mr. Gross is on the Board of Directors of Ambucare International, Inc., builders and developers of world health care facilities.

A WORD FROM THE AUTHOR

During almost four years of research while assembling material for this encyclopedia, I sought to include current, representative real estate forms that possessed clarity and sound legal content. If they passed these requisites, they were further studied with a view to practicality, completeness, style, brevity, and effectiveness for the purpose intended. As a consequence, the material finally selected evolved from thousands of court-tested forms in daily use throughout all parts of the country.

The orderly transacting of real estate business today often requires highly specialized instruments. A chapter has been devoted to each familiar type of document as well as those used to a lesser extent. All are defined, briefly discussed, and presented with a choice of forms and clauses within each category to choose from. The chapters are presented alphabetically according to type of form and then numbered within each chapter for easy reference.

Within these pages one will find a single-volume reference work of representative, significant real estate forms. It was my objective to present a handy-to-use, time-saving volume that will prove of lasting value in all facets of real estate.

In addition to legal forms, there are four chapters devoted to Appraisal of Real Estate, Brokerage Agreements, Management of Property and Real Estate Office Forms.

My grateful thanks and acknowledgement is given to the many title companies, brokers, lawyers, real estate boards, and other professional organizations throughout the country who have allowed me to reproduce or adopt their material.

The book was reviewed by my good friend Philip Goodheim, Attorney at Law. His comments and helpful suggestions proved of invaluable assistance to me in fashioning the final manuscript.

JEROME S. GROSS

CONTENTS

Encyclopedia
of Real Estate Forms

1

Acknowledgements, Affidavits and Other Forms of Verification

1

Acknowledgements, Affidavits and Other Forms of Verification

In transacting real estate, the verification of facts or proof of one's signature, actions or intentions is continually required. Legal instruments such as acknowledgements, affidavits, affirmations and certificates are in constant use. Statements have to be notarized and documents attested to (witnessed) and sealed.

All of the types of verification used in modern real estate law will be defined with sample forms and their variations shown.[1]

ACKNOWLEDGEMENTS

An *acknowledgement* is the formal certification of a signature as written evidence before an individual duly authorized to take acknowledgements, that the instrument is his act and deed.

Acknowledgements are required in nearly all states for the recording of real estate instruments. Their purpose is to prove the authenticity of the signatures to the instrument. The form is usually set by statute with such minor variations as custom and court cases may allow. Acknowledgements are taken before officers duly authorized by the state to administer oaths and take acknowledgements, such as Notaries Public, Clerks and Judges of Courts of Record, and Commissioners of Deeds. If the instrument is to be recorded in another state, a certificate must be obtained from the County Clerk of the County where the Notary resides or is authorized to act, certifying as to his power and capacity to act.

Military personnel, their dependents, and civilians attached to military units, may have their acknowledgements taken by any commissioned officer.

Foreign acknowledgements, outside the United States, may be taken before any of the following: Ministers, Consul or Deputy Consul Generals, Charges d'Affaires residing in the foreign country, Judges of that country's court of last resort, Mayors, and others as specified in the statutes of the different countries.

---

1. In some jurisdictions, statutes require that a specific form be used. Those presented here, however, are in general use and acceptance.

Acknowledgements take various forms to meet specific situations, as follows:

No 1–1
ACKNOWLEDGEMENT FOR INDIVIDUAL

STATE OF_____)   On this_____ day of_____,
COUNTY OF_____) ss Nineteen hundred and_____,
before me, the subscriber, personally appeared to me personally known and known to me
to be the same person described in and who executed the within instrument, and he duly
acknowledged to me that he executed the same.

_____
Notary Public

No. 1–2
ACKNOWLEDGEMENT FOR PARTNERSHIP

STATE OF_____)ss:
COUNTY OF_____)
On this_____day of_____, 19_____, before me personally came_____
to me known to be the person who executed the foregoing instrument, and who, being
duly sworn, by me, did depose and say that he is a member of the firm of_____
_____ , a co-partnership,
and that he duly executed the foregoing instrument in the firm name of said co-partnership,
that he is duly authorized to sign the same, and duly acknowledged to me that he executed
the same as the act and deed of said co-partnership, for the uses and purposes mentioned
therein.

_____
Notary Public

No. 1–3
ACKNOWLEDGEMENT
General Form, For An Individual Or A Partnership

State of_____)
) ss
County of_____)
    Before me personally appeared_____to me well
known and known to me to be the person described in and who executed the foregoing
instrument, and acknowledged to and before me that_____
_____executed said instrument for the purposes therein expressed.
    WITNESS my hand and official seal, this_____day of_____

A.D. 19_____.

(Notary Seal)

Notary Public
State of_____
My commission expires

No. 1–4
ACKNOWLEDGEMENT OF HUSBAND AND WIFE WITH SEPARATE ACKNOWLEDGEMENT BY WIFE

State of_____)
) ss
County of_____)

Before me personally appeared_____and_____
_____, his wife, both of whom are to me well known, and known to me to be the individuals described in and who executed the foregoing instrument, and acknowledged to and before me that they executed said instrument for the purposes therein expressed; and the said_____upon a separate and private examination, taken and made separately and apart from her husband, acknowledged to and before me that she executed said instrument freely and voluntarily, without any compulsion, constraint, apprehension or fear of or from her said husband, for the purposes therein expressed.

WITNESS my hand and official seal, this_____day of_____
_____, A.D. 19_____.

(Notary Seal)

Notary Public
State of_____at large
My commission expires_____

No. 1–5
SEPARATE ACKNOWLEDGEMENT BY WIFE

State of_____)
) ss
County of_____)

I HEREBY CERTIFY, that on this day, before me an officer duly authorized in the State aforesaid and in the county aforesaid to take acknowledgements, this day personally appeared_____, to me personally known, acknowledged before me that she freely and voluntarily executed the foregoing instrument. I further certify that said_____, is known to me to be

the wife of_____ , and that she did this day acknowl-
edge before me, separately and apart from her said husband, on a private examination
taken and made by and before me, that she executed said instrument for the purposes of
renouncing, relinquishing and conveying all her right, title and interest, whether dower,
homestead, or of separate property, statutory or equitable, in and to the land and in and
to the personal property described in said instrument and that she executed said instrument
freely and voluntarily and without any compulsion, constraint, apprehension, or fear of
or from her said husband.

      WITNESS my hand and official seal this_____day of_____
_____, A.D. 19_____.

                                      _____

(Notary Seal)   Notary Public
                                   State of_____
                                   My commission expires_____

No. 1–6
ACKNOWLEDGEMENT FOR TRUSTEE, ADMINISTRATOR, EXECUTOR, GUARDIAN OR ANY PERSON ACTING IN A REPRESENTATIVE CAPACITY

State of_____)
) ss
County of_____)

      Before me personally appeared _____ as_____
_____(here insert representative capacity) to me well known
and known to me to be the person described in and who executed the foregoing instrument
and acknowledged to and before me that_____executed said
instrument in the capacity and for the purpose therein expressed.

      WITNESS my hand and official seal, this_____day of_____
_____, A.D. 19_____.

                                          _____

(Notary Seal)   Notary Public
                                   State of_____
                                   My commission expires_____

No. 1–7
ACKNOWLEDGEMENT FOR CORPORATION
Of More Than One Officer

State of_____)

) ss

County of_____)

    Before me personally appeared_____AND_____

_____to me well known, and known to me to be the individuals described in and who executed the foregoing instrument as_____

President and_____Secretary of the above named

_____a Corporation, and severally acknowledged to and before me that they executed such instrument as such President and Secretary, respectively, of said corporation, and that the seal affixed to the foregoing instrument is the corporate seal of said corporation and that it was affixed to said instrument by due and regular corporate authority, and that said instrument is the free act and deed of said corporation.

    WITNESS my hand and official seal, this_____day of_____ ____, A.D. 19_____.

                           _____

                           Notary Public

                           State of_____

                           My commission expires_____

No. 1–8
ACKNOWLEDGEMENT FOR CORPORATION
Of One Officer

STATE OF_____, COUNTY OF_____ss:

On the_____day of_____, 19_____, before me personally came,_____

_____to me known, who, being by me duly sworn, did depose and say that __he resides at No._____

that __he is the_____of_____ the corporation described in and which executed the foregoing instrument, that he knows the seal of said corporation; that the seal affixed to said instrument is such corporate seal; that it was so affixed by order of the board of directors of said corporation, and that he signed his name thereto by like order.

                           _____

                           Notary Public

No. 1–9
INDIVIDUAL FOREIGN ACKNOWLEDGEMENT

UNITED STATES CONSULATE)
City of Rome   ) ss
Republic of Italy   )

  Before the undersigned, the duly appointed Ambassador of the United States of America to the Republic of Italy, on this_____ day of_____ 19_____, personally appeared at the above named consulate_____ _____to me known to be the individual described in who executed the foregoing instrument and acknowledged to me that he executed the same.

  In witness whereof, I have hereunto set my hand and official seal this_____day of _____, 19_____.

(Official Seal)

           _____
           Ambassador of the United States
           of America to the Republic of Italy

No. 1–10
WHEN IN MILITARY SERVICE
BEFORE A MILITARY PERSON AUTHORIZED
TO ADMINISTER OATHS

With the United States Armed Forces
At_____I_____
_____, the undersigned officer, do hereby certify that on this_____day of_____ _____, 19_____, before me, personally appeared_____ _____SN & SSAN[1]_____, whose home address (include zip code) is_____, and who is known to me to be_____, and to be the identical person who is described in, whose name is subscribed to, and who signed and executed the foregoing instrument, and having the first made known to him the contents thereof, he personally acknowledged to me that he signed and sealed the same, on the date it bears as his true, free, and voluntary act and deed, for the uses, purposes, and considerations therein set forth. And I do further certify that I am at the date of the certificate a commissioned officer of the grade, branch of service and organization stated below in the active service of the United States Armed Forces, that by statute no seal is required on this certificate and that the same is executed in my capacity as_____.

---

1. Service Number and Social Security Account Number

_____   _____
Signature of Officer   Service No. & SSAN, grade and
                                 branch of service
_____   _____
Command or organization   Permanent home address

AFFIDAVITS

An *affidavit* is a voluntary, written statement or declaration sworn to before a notary public or other person authorized by law to administer oaths. It is sometimes accepted as proof when the maker of the affidavit (the affiant) cannot appear in person. Affidavits are frequently used in real estate to clarify a question of ownership or the status of a lien on property before title can be transferred.

Statements in an affidavit should be in direct, clear language with no possible ambiguity. The purpose of the affidavit should be stated at the outset.

No. 1–11
AFFIDAVIT
General Form

State of_____)
) ss
County of_____)
    Before me this day personally appeared_____
_____, who, being first duly sworn, deposes and says:
    That (Here insert fact or facts to be affirmed by the affiant)

                                   _____
                                   Signature of person making affidavit

Sworn to and subscribed before
me this_____day of_____
A.D. 19_____.
    (Notary Seal)

_____
Notary Public
State of_____
My commission expires_____

No. 1–12
AFFIDAVIT
In First Person Form

STATE OF_____:

COUNTY OF_____: ss:

CITY OF_____:

_____, being duly sworn, deposes and says:

I reside at_____Street, City of_____, County of
_____, and State of_____.

I make this Affidavit for the following reason and purpose:_____
_____

IN WITNESS WHEREOF, I have hereunto set my name and seal this_____day of
_____, 19_____.

_____

Subscribed and sworn to before me
this_____day of_____, 19_____.

_____
NOTARY PUBLIC
My Commission Expires_____.

When transferring ownership to real property, some states require a sworn statement from the seller guaranteeing the purchaser that the title he is conveying is not defective. The following is a representative form for this purpose.

No. 1–13
AFFIDAVIT OF TITLE

STATE OF_____)

) ss.:

COUNTY OF_____)

_____ being duly sworn, says, that_____

resides at_____and is by occupation
_____; that_____is a citizen of the United States, twenty-one
years of age and upwards; and that_____is now in possession, and the owner in fee
simple of the

(Here describe the property)

this day to be_____ by_____to_____

Deponent further says that the said premises have been held by_____for_____ _____years last past, and that_____possession thereof has been peaceable and undisturbed, and that the title thereto has never been disputed or questioned to_____ knowledge, nor does deponent know of any facts by reason of which said possession or title might be disturbed or questioned, or by reason of which said possession or title might be disturbed or questioned, or by reason of which any claim to said premises, or any part thereof, might arise or be set up adverse to this deponent; and that he is informed and believes that_____grantors held the said premises for more than twenty years prior to the transfer to_____; and that no person has any contract for the purchase of, or claim to or against said premises, except as hereinafter stated; and that the same are now free and clear of all taxes, incumbrances or liens by mortgage, decree, judgment, or by statute, or by virtue of any proceeding in any Court, or filed in the office of the clerk of any County or Court in this State, and of all other liens of every nature of description, save and except

Deponent further says that_____is married to_____who is over the age of twenty-one years, and who is the same person who executed with deponent, the _____the said premises, and that_____has never been married to any other person now living; and that there are no judgments, or decrees, or attachments, or orders of any Court or officer for the payment of money against_____, or to which_____he is a party, unsatisfied or not cancelled of record in any of the Courts, or before any officer of the United States, or of this State, or any suit or proceeding pending anywhere affecting said premises, to_____knowledge, information or belief, and that any judgments found of record against _____are not against deponent, but against another of similar name; and that no proceedings in bankruptcy have ever been instituted by or against deponent, nor has deponent, nor has deponent at any time made an assignment for the benefit of creditors.

Deponent makes this affidavit to induce_____to accept a_____ _____said premises and pay the consideration therefor, knowing that said relies upon the truth of the statement herein contained. Sworn to before me this _____

_____day of_____19_____.

(Form courtesy of Julius Blumberg, Inc., 80 Exchange Place, New York, N.Y. 10004)

Many states require a sworn statement made by the title holder when transferring real estate, that there are no liens, unpaid bills or any other encumbrance against the personal property. The document used is referred to as as Mechanic's Lien Affidavit or Owner's Affidavit Of No Liens.

No. 1–14
MECHANIC'S LIEN AFFIDAVIT

State of _____)
) ss

County of _____)

     BEFORE ME, the undersigned authority, duly authorized to administer oaths and take acknowledgements, this day personally appeared _____

_____ the owner(s) of the following described property, and who, after being first duly sworn, depose(s) and say(s):

     That _____ he _____ the owner(s) of the following described property:

     Affiant(s) state(s) that there are no unpaid bills for labor performed or materials furnished on the improvements on the above described property; that all taxes thereon have been paid except for the current year; and that there are no unpaid liens or encumbrances against the personal property hereinabove described; that no one, other than the undersigned, is entitled to, or claims possession of said above described property.

     Affiant(s) state(s) that the purpose of this Affidavit is to induce _____

_____ into purchasing this property.

     Deponent(s) further state(s) that _____ he _____ familiar with the nature of an oath and with the penalites as provided by the laws of the State of _____ for falsely swearing to statements made in an instrument of this nature.

     Further Affiant(s) Sayeth Not.

SWORN TO AND SUBSCRIBED before

me this _____ day of _____,

_____ 19 _____ .   _____

                                               _____

_____

Notary Public, State of _____

My commission expires _____

AFFIRMATIONS

     An *affirmation* is a formal and solemn declaration or pledge made as a substitute for an oath. It serves the same legal purpose in real estate transactions as an affidavit and is used in instances where a person's religious or personal beliefs (as in the case of Quakers or Seventh Day Adventists) would cause him to object to taking an oath to a supreme being. It usually is notarized and/or witnessed and has the same effect and is just as binding as an oath taken in any other form.

     In preparing an affirmation, it is only necessary to substitute the work "affirm" in place of "swear", as in the sentence, *Do you, John Jones, solemnly affirm that . . . etc.*

CERTIFICATE

A *certificate* is any formal declaration in writing. It may take a wide variety of forms such as in acknowledgements, shares of stock or simply a letter. Its purpose is to authenticate or prove something and it need not follow any prescribed pattern or phraseology.

In real estate, one of the most frequently used certification documents is that of the Estoppel Certificate. Its purpose is to ascertain the exact balance of a mortgage when property is being transferred. It is generally written and signed by the mortgagee at the request of the mortgagor.

No. 1–15
ESTOPPEL CERTIFICATE

Date_____19_____

Re: Mortgage being held by the undersigned relating to the following legally described property:

_____

_____

Gentlemen:

Be it known that we are the owners of a certain indenture of mortgage and bond bearing the date of_____day of_____ , 19_____ , made and executed by_____ to secure the payment of the principal sum of $_____and interest and duly recorded in the office of the County Clerk, County of_____ , State of_____ _____ , in Liber # _____of Mortgages of Section_____page _____ , on the_____day of_____19_____ and covering premises situated in _____County as above legally described. More commonly known as a two-story dwelling at_____Avenue, City of_____ , State of_____ .

The undersigned hereby certifies that the amount now due on said mortgage and bond has been reduced by monthly principal and interest payment of $_____ , and that there is now due upon said mortgage and bond the principal sum of $_____ . with interest thereon at the rate of_____% per annum from_____day of_____19_____ .

_____

_____

NOTARIZING

A *notary* or *notary public* is a properly appointed public officer whose duties are to attest and certify to the authenticity of documents and the signature(s) upon them.

Notarization is required on a great many real estate documents. It generally appears at the end of instruments in the form of a "jurat," which is simply the clause used to evidence what is being authenticated. A typical jurat reads:

Subscribed and sworn to before me this_____ day of_____, 19_____.

Notary Public, State of_____
My commission expires____, 19___.
(NOTARY SEAL)

(Notary Seal)

Notary Public
State of_____
My commission expires_____

SEAL

The centuries-old custom of having documents signed "under seal" is no longer considered as significant in modern law. It represents a formal attesting to. However, certain documents, notably deeds, are still required to be sealed in many states.

The antiquated custom of making a wax impression upon the document has long been surplanted by the word "Seal" or "L. S."[1] at the end of the signature line. Sometimes these words appear in parenthesis, as shown:

_____(Seal)

The embossed impression that serves to formalize a document, such as a corporate seal, or to verify a signature, as used by a notary public, is another way of assuring the authenticity of legal instruments.

---

1. Abbreviation for the Latin "locus sigilli" meaning "the place of the seal" or "under seal."

(CORPORATE SEAL)

WITNESSING

To *witness* or attest to is to observe and authenticate. In the execution of contracts as well as other real estate instruments, one, two, and in some jurisdictions, as many as three witnesses are required for certain documents. Witnessing serves to verify the fact that the principals have signed of their own free will.

The witness should be a disinterested party to the agreement. His signature appears at the end of the document, on the left side of the page, opposite the signature(s) of the principal(s) he is witnessing.

IN WITNESS WHEREOF, the parties hereto
have duly executed this contract
this_____day of_____, A.D. 19_____.
Signed, sealed and delivered
in the presence of:

1._____   By_____(Seal)
                                    (Seller)

2._____
          (As to Seller)

1._____   By_____(Seal)
                                 (Purchaser)

2._____
          (As to Purchaser)

2

Appraisal of Real Estate

2

Appraisal of Real Estate

An appraisal is an evaluation of property by an impartial, fair, disinterested, knowledgable, qualified party, after a careful inspection and study of the subject property and its surroundings.

Sound professional appraisals are arrived at by the use of certain recognized techniques. The three generally accepted approaches to estimating real estate value are:

(a) The Cost Approach, which is calculated by the replacement value of the property;

(b) The Market (Comparison) Approach, that is, comparing it with similar properties and arriving at a conclusion as to what it will sell for on the open market, and

(c) The Income Approach, which primarily is concerned with the net return a property will bring. When this is known, a logical selling price can be determined.

Appraisers often utilize *all three* methods when appraising a given property, then correlate the conclusions to arrive at a comprehensive and knowledgeable single estimate of its value.

Any qualified real estate broker may make appraisals and their opinions are generally considered as valid or even expert in a court of law. However, the appraisal of larger, commercial properties or mass appraisals of whole areas (such as for condemnation) are generally given over to full-time, professional appraisers, [1] whose main or sole source of income is in the fees they receive for this.

An appraisal report generally follows basic recognized forms. 1. It may be a letter of opinion, usually one or two pages in length and written on the appraiser's letterhead. Though informal in nature, an appraisal letter should contain certain necessary basic facts and conclusions. 2. An appraisal certificate, such as a printed form filled in and signed by the appraiser. 3. In the form of an affidavit, subscribed and sworn to before a notary public. 4. The combination of an affidavit and certificate, and 5. A formal, bookbound, comprehensive document containing, in addition to complete facts and conclusions about the property, surveys, plot plans and photos. Examples of each follow:

---

1. Most professional appraisers in the United States hold membership in either the Society of Real Estate Appraisers, the American Institute of Real Estate Appraisers, or the American Society of Appraisers. The Canadian appraisal organization is the Appraisal Institute of Canada.

No. 2–1
APPRAISAL REPORT
In Letter Form

Date_____

Dear Sirs:

I,_____(Appraiser's Name)_____do hereby state that upon the

request of _____(Name of the one ordering the appraisal)_____

_____, I have made an investigation and analysis of the following described property:

(Here follows the legal description and
common known address of the property)

and that I am of the opinion that on_____19_____,

when a detailed inspection of the premises was made, the Market Value of the land and improvements thereon was:

$_____Total

allocated as Land: $_____Improvements $_____

I further state that, to the best of my knowledge and belief, the evaluations contained in this appraisal are correct.

I have no present or contemplated future interest in the property appraised and compensation for making this appraisal is in no manner contingent upon the value reported.

The physical condition of the improvements described herein was based on visual inspection. No liability is assumed for the soundness of structural members since no engineering tests were made of same.

Respectfully submitted,

_____

Appraiser

(Here follows the qualifications of the appraiser. For example: Licensed Real Estate Broker, Member Society of Real Estate Appraisers, V. A. Appraiser 19_____to 19_____, etc.)

No. 2–2
CERTIFICATE OF
APPRAISAL

APPRAISED FOR _____ ADDRESS _____

PROPERTY _____ TYPE _____

SECTION _____ BLOCK _____ LOT _____ VOLUME _____ PAGE _____

19 ASSESSED VALUATION: LAND $ _____ BUILDING $ _____ TOTAL $ _____

SIZE OF LAND _____ AREA _____ SIZE OF BUILDING _____ EXTENSION _____

HEIGHT _____ MATERIALS _____ HEAT _____

CONDITION _____ USE _____

PRESENT MORTGAGE $ _____

THIS IS TO CERTIFY

THAT THE PROPERTY DESCRIBED ABOVE HAS BEEN PERSONALLY EXA-
MINED BY THE INDIVIDUAL WHOSE SIGNATURE APPEARS BELOW AND
WHO ESTIMATES ITS VALUE AS FOLLOWS:

PRESENT MARKET VALUE OF LAND $ _____
PRESENT MARKET VALUE OF BUILDING $ _____ } TOTAL $ _____

RENTAL ESTIMATED AT $ _____

REMARKS

_____ _____
DATE SIGNATURE

No. 2–3
APPRAISAL AFFIDAVIT

State of_____)
) ss:
County of_____)

    Before the undersigned, an officer duly commissioned by the state of_____ _____, on this_____day of_____, 19_____person- ally appeared_____who having been first duly sworn deposes and says: At the request of_____who employed him to appraise the property owned by_____ located at _____, legally described as
_____

that by reason of a careful inspection of the premises that it is his opinion that the Market Value of the land and improvement was

            Land $_____
            Building(s) $_____
            TOTAL $_____

That he has no financial interest in said property whatsoever.

    That his findings are in no way contingent upon the compensation he is to receive for making the appraisal.

    That his qualifications for making said appraisal include being a licensed real estate broker for_____years, being a Federal Housing Administration appraiser for_____ years, being a_____senior member of the Society of Residential Appraisers since 19_____, (etc.)

    IN WITNESS WHEREOF, the said_____has hereunto set his hand and seal.

_____

Sworn to and subscribed before me this_____day of_____, A.D. 19_____

    Notary Public
      Seal Here   _____
                                _____

No. 2–4
AFFIDAVIT AND CERTIFICATE OF APPRAISAL
Combined Form

STATE OF_____ :
COUNTY OF_____ :
    _____, being duly sworn, deposes and says:
    1. I reside at_____Street in the City of_____, County of

_____, and State of_____, I have been duly licensed by the State of_____as a_____
_____. I have an office for the transaction of business at_____
Street, in the City of_____, State of_____.

2. At the request of_____, I have made an investigation and analysis of the following described Real Property:

_____

3. I am of the opinion that on the_____day of_____, 19_____, when I made a detailed inspection of the aforesaid premises, the market value of the land and improvements thereon was as follows: $_____.

$_____, allocated as to land;

$_____, and improvements.

I CERTIFY that to the best of my knowledge and belief, the evaluation contained in this Appraisal is correct.

4. I have no present or contemplated future interest in the property appraised, and the compensation for making this Appraisal is in no manner contingent upon the value reported.

5. The physical condition of the improvements described herein was based solely on visual inspection, and no liability is assumed for the soundness of structural members, since no engineering tests were made of the same.

IN WITNESS WHEREOF, I hereunto set my hand and seal on this_____day of _____, 19_____.

_____
                                                    Appraiser

Subscribed and sworn to before me
this_____day of_____, 19_____.

_____

NOTARY PUBLIC
My Commission Expires:_____.
(NOTARY SEAL)

No. 2–5
APPRAISAL REPORT
Another Form

PARCEL NO._____
Section_____Job_____Road_____
County_____
I,_____do hereby certify that upon request of:
_____ I have made an investigation and

analysis of the following described property: _____

_____ Parcel No. _____

_____ and that I am of the opinion that on _____ ,

19 _____ the Market Value of the land and improvements thereon, including damages to

the remainder, if any, was: _____

_____ $ _____

allocable as: _____

Land $ _____ Improvements $ _____

_____ Damages $ _____

THE MARKET VALUE, SET FORTH ABOVE, IS SUBJECT TO THE FOLLOWING
LIMITING CONDITIONS:

The undersigned appraiser certifies that, to the best of his knowledge and belief, the
statements contained in this appraisal, subject to the limiting conditions set forth below,
are correct; also that this appraisal has been made in conformity with the Rules of Professional Ethics of the American Institute of Real Estate Appraisers of the National
Association of Real Estate Boards.

This property has been appraised as though free of liens and encumbrances, in responsible ownership, and under competent management.

No responsibility is to be assumed for matters legal in nature, nor is any opinion of
title rendered herewith. Good title is assumed.

Both legal descriptions and dimensions are taken from sources thought to be authoritative; however, no responsibility is assumed for either unless a survey, by a competent
engineer, is furnished to me.

Possession of any copy of this report does not carry with it the right of publication,
nor may it be used for any purpose by any but the applicant without the previous written
consent of the appraiser or the applicant and, in any event, only in its entirety.

The appraiser herein, by reason of this report is not required to give testimony in
Court, with reference to the property herein appraised, unless arrangements have been
previously made therefor.

The undersigned appraiser has no present or contemplated future interest in the
property appraised and the compensation for making this appraisal is in no manner contingent upon the value reported.

The physical condition of the improvements described herein was based on visual
inspection. No liability is assumed for the soundness of structural members since no engineering tests were made of same.

_____

Appraiser

No. 2–6
COMPREHENSIVE APPRAISAL REPORT
In Book Form

TABLE OF CONTENTS

Page

(Start a new page)

LETTER OF TRANSMITTAL

_____ 19_____

Mr. John Doe
Attorney at Law
1000 N W. Main St.
Miami, Florida

Re: Estate of James Roe, 500 Collins
Causeway, Miami Beach, Florida.
Legally described as Lots 1–6, Block 62,
Flagler Sub., Plat Book B Page 32,
according to the records of Dade County, Florida.

Dear Mr. Roe:

Pursuant to the request of the Dade County Judge's Court to appraise the above captioned estate for the purpose of estimating its market value, below is my findings as of_____, 19_____,

I have personally inspected the subject property and through information given me and information in my files which I assume to be reliable and accurate; I have formed, in my judgement, the value to be:

$148,900

ONE HUNDRED FORTY EIGHT THOUSAND NINE HUNDRED DOLLARS

Respectfully submitted,

Peter Hoe, S.R.A., A.S.A.

PH/el

(Start a new page)

QUALIFICATION OF

PETER HOE

Resident of the City of Miami, Dade County, Florida—47 years
Registered Real Estate Broker, State of Florida

MEMBERSHIP ASSOCIATIONS

Society of Real Estate Appraisers, S.R.A.
American Society of Appraisers, A.S.A.
Society of Residential Appraisers—Senior Member
City of Miami Planning & Zoning Board—5 years
American Society of Planning Officials
Member of Staff—University of Miami
American Right of Way Association

COURT QUALIFICATIONS

Qualified as an expert witness of matters pertaining to real estate value for and in:

> Metropolitan Dade County, Florida
> Probate Court of Dade County, Florida
> Circuit Court of the Eleventh Judicial
>   Circuit of Florida
> U. S. District Court—Southern Dist. of Florida

Approved Fee Appraiser for:

> Federal Housing Administration
> General Services Administration

EDUCATIONAL COURSES & DEGREE

B.A., University of Florida—1947

Ellwood Course on "Principles of the Ellwood Theory of Capitalization Tables," American Society of Appraisers

Principles and Techniques of Real Estate Appraising, Society of Real Estate Appraisers

Real Estate Appraising and Marketing, University of Miami

Condemnation Course—American Society of Appraisers

Course 1 and 2, American Institute of Real Estate Appraisers

Clients include:

AAA Corporation
BBB Motels of America
CCC Airlines
DDD Lines
(etc.)
City of Miami, Florida
City of Coral Gables, Florida
City of North Miami Beach, Florida
Town of Medley, Florida

AAA National Bank
BBB Savings & Loan Assn.
CCC Mortgage Corp.
DDD Life Insurance Co.
(etc.)
State Road Department—State of Florida
Board of Public Instruction—Dade County, Florida

(Start a new page)

(HERE INCLUDE A FULL PAGE PHOTOGRAPH OF THE PROPERTY)

Purpose of Report

To estimate the Fair Market Value of the subject property as of _____, 19__. The property appraised will be valued as though it were owned in Fee Simple Title and unencumbered by any indebtedness.

Legal Description—Address

Lots 1–6 Block 62, Flagler Subdivision, Plat Book B Page 32, according to the records of Dade County, Florida. More commonly known as a 14 unit apartment house at 500 Collins Causeway, Miami Beach, Florida.

Owner of Record

James Roe and wife Mabel
500 Collins Causeway
Miami Beach, Florida

Assessed Valuation—19__

Total assessed valuation—$97,400
Total Tax Estimate—$2,700
(both County and Miami Beach)
The property is zoned by the City of Miami Beach as "multiple housing."

Utilities Available

All utilities are available to the property and they include: electricity, city water, septic tanks, telephone, paved streets and police and fire protection from the City of Miami Beach.

Location

The subject property is located approximately 2 1/4 miles south of downtown Miami Beach. (See attached location map).

Size and Shape of Land

The subject as improved is located on the 6 lots as legally described and is situated on the N.E. corner of Collins Causeway and 5th Avenue.
Lot 1—35 feet frontage and 100 feet in depth.
Lots 2—6 inclusive are 25 feet frontage and 100 feet in depth.
Total square feet in parcel—16,000
The land is a street grade with sidewalks and curbs and is free from flooding waters under normal conditions.

Highest and Best Use

The property is placed to the highest and best use.

Market Data Information

Land Sales Analysis—Vacant
Sale No. 1
Lots 14–15–16 Block 62, Flabler Sub.

Size: Each lot 25 × 100 = Total 7,500 S. F.
Consideration—$21,000
Grantor: Edgar Koe
Grantee: Mary Loe
Date: September, 19_____
Value assigned = $7,000 per lot or $2.80 per sq. ft.
Zoning—Multiple

Sale No. 2
Legal: Lot 28, Block 58 Flagler Sub.
Size: 54 front feet, 115 feet in depth. Total = 6,210 S. F.
Consideration: $8,500 or $1.37 per sq. ft.
Grantor: Herman Moe
Grantee: Fredrick C. Noe
Date: July, 19_____
Zoning: Multiple
Sale No. 3—etc.
Sale No. 4—etc
Sale No. 5—etc.

Note: Four or five comparable sales in an area are generally sufficient for an appraiser to arrive at a valid conclusion.

Conclusion as to land value:
The basic land value indicates to this appraiser a range from $2.80 per square foot to $1.37 per square foot with the average value indicating approximately $1.75 per square foot. It is therefore in this appraiser's judgement considering the size, location and utility that the value of $1.75 be applied to the subject property.
16,000 S.F. @ $ 1.75 P.S.F. = $28,000

Improved Property Analysis

Sale No. 1
Date: May 19_____
Legal: Lots 25 and 26, Block 60, Flagler Sub.
Consideration: $127,500
Units: 12 (2 story building)
Average price per unit: $10,626 including land
Grantor: Steven Poe
Grantee: Nancy Soe
Address: 721 Collins Causeway

Sale No. 2—etc.
Sale No. 3—etc.
Sale No. 4—etc.

Conclusion as to improved property sales:
The improved sales indicate to this appraiser that on an average unit basis a Fair Value would be $9,300 per unit. The sales listed were selected because of a mixture of 1- and 2-bedroom apartments. Therefore, by Judgment Conclusion a value on a unit basis would be as follows: $9,300 per unit × 16 units = $148,800

(Start a new page)

Income Valuation

In the valuation of the property by the income approach, this appraiser has endeavored to reflect the present income (gross) on a 3-year basis to establish an average income. From this income, deductions are made to reflect the net income to the property. This net income is then capitalized into a gross value representing the total property value. This is generally the value most investors seek as it is the indicator of the present worth. It is also the value before deducting debt service (mortgage payments) as the property is appraised as though it were free and clear. Any other deductions would be for equity value, which is not the purpose of this report.

From information given me (books and records) and from information in my files which I assume to be reliable and accurate, the following is hereby made a part of this income value.

(Start a new page)

Owner's Statement

Total 16 Units

A. Nine (9) 1-bedroom, 1-bath apartments, rent for $125 per month, furnished
B. Two (2) 2-bedroom, 2-bath apartments, rent for $170 per month, furnished
C. One (1) 2-bedroom, 2-bath apartment, rents for $135, unfurnished
D. Three (3) 2-bedroom, 1-bath apartments, rent for $125 per month, unfurnished

Total Rent expected = $2,120 per month.

This gross rent includes owner's apartment which is part of the appraisal.

$2,120 per month × 12 months = $25,440

Gross Rent per Year		$25,440
Less Vacancy Factor—Use 5%		1,270
Effective Gross Income		$24,170
Less:		
Fixed Expenses		
Taxes	$ 2,700	
Other Tax	235	
Operating Expenses		
Water	$ 325	
Electricity	525	
Insurance	625	
Pool Maintenance	250	
Supplies	100	
Gardener	240	
Exterminator	180	
Gas	72	
Miscellaneous	300	
Reserve for Replacement (furnishings)	1,500	
Total Expense estimate		$7,052
Net Income		$17,118
	USE	$17,120

Capitalization of net income into value as follows:
Return expected on investment = 8%
Return expected of investment = 3.5%
(Remaining economic life — 30 years)
Total capitalization Rate = 11.5%
$17,120 @ 11.5% = $148,869

USE   <u>$148,900</u>

(Start a new page)

Description of Improvements

The subject property is improved with a 2-story, 16-unit apartment building constructed approximately 7 years ago. The building as of the date of inspection is in good condition and does not show signs of deferred maintenance. There is also a swimming pool and patio area situated between the two wings of the building.

Description of Units

16 Units as follows:
Nine (9) 1-bedroom, 1-bath units with kitchen, living room and dining room (furnished)
Seven (7) 2-bedroom units with:

    Four (4) units having 2 baths
    Three (3) units having 1 bath

Each unit also has a kitchen, living room and dining room. Two (2) of these units are furnished.
There is ample storage and closets in each apartment.

Additional Improvements

12 units have 2 air condition units.
4 units have 1 air condition unit.
1st floor has room-size carpets.
2nd floor has wall-to-wall carpets.
Paved off-street parking for 30 cars, lawn sprinkler system, extensive outside lighting, sun deck on roof.

Construction Data

Material = Concrete block stucco
Stories = 2
Foundation = Reinforced concrete
Floors = Terrazzo
Sash = Aluminum awning
Roof = Built-up tar and gravel
Plumbing = Modern throughout
Electricity = Modern throughout, BX cabeling

Replacement Cost Estimate

Building contains 10,900 square feet.
COST NEW
10,900 square feet @ $12.50 per square foot = $136,250
Square foot price includes walks & stairway

Add

Swimming Pool	3,500
Concrete slab	500
Estimated Cost New	$140,250
Landscaping—in use value	375
Cost Before Depreciation	$140,625

Less

Physical Depreciation (15%)	21,093
Depreciated Value	$119,532
Add Land Value	28,000
Value by Replacement	$147,532

USE $147,500

Recapitulation—Final Value

Value by Replacement	$147,500
Value by Income	148,900
Value by Market	148,800

By Judgment Conclusion the greatest weight for Fair Market Value is placed on the income and is reported to be:

$148,900

(HERE INCLUDE A FULL PAGE PLOT PLAN OF THE BUILDING)

(HERE INCLUDE A MAP OF THE IMMEDIATE AREA IN WHICH
     THE PROPERTY IS LOCATED)

(HERE INCLUDE A COUNTY MAP SHOWING LOCATION OF
     PROPERTY IN RELATION TO LANDMARKS)

Appraisers generally make field notes on specially prepared data sheets or inspection report forms. By so doing they are assured that nothing of significance is omitted from the hundreds of facts and details that must be assembled and evaluated before a comprehensive and accurate appraisal can be made. Four such typical work sheets follow:

No. 2-7
RESIDENTIAL APPRAISAL REPORT

IBM.

(11) **Residential Appraisal Report**

IBM Confidential

DATE_____

NAME OF OWNER(S)   MAIL ADDRESS   TELEPHONE NO.(S)

ADDRESS	AREA OR SUBDIVISION
CITY	STATE	

PURPOSE OF APPRAISAL

To estimate Market Value in fee simple as of_____

"Current fair market value" is defined as the amount that a buyer would be willing to pay for the property in its present condition and location, after time for negotiation, which is reasonable for the area, and not based on an immediate sale due to pressures on the seller to transact a quick sale."

APPRAISAL SUMMARY

APPRAISED VALUE — LAND .... $ _____

APPRAISED VALUE — IMPROVEMENTS .... $ _____

TOTAL .... $ _____

CERTIFICATION

I do hereby certify that I have made a personal inspection of subject property and an analysis of those factors affecting its value, that I have no interest, present or contemplated, in the property, that neither the employment to make the appraisal nor the compensation, is contingent upon the value of the property reported, and to the best of my knowledge and belief, all statements and information in this report are true and correct, and no important facts have been withheld or overlooked.

_____
APPRAISER'S SIGNATURE

DATE _____   _____
FIRM NAME *(Please Print)*

LIMITING CONDITIONS

This appraisal is subject to the following limiting conditions:

The legal description furnished us is assumed to be correct.

We assume no responsibility for matters legal in character, nor do we render any opinion as to title, which is assumed to be marketable. All existing liens and encumbrances have been disregarded and the property is appraised as though free and clear under responsible ownership and competent management.

The sketch in this report is included to assist the reader in visualizing the property. We have made no survey of the property and assume no responsibility in connection with such matters.

Unless otherwise noted herein, it is assumed that there are no encroachments, zoning violations or restrictions existing in the subject property.

Information, estimates and opinions contained in this report are obtained from sources considered reliable; however, no liability for them can be assumed by the appraiser.

Possession of this report, or a copy thereof, does not carry with it the right of publication, nor may it be used for any purpose by any but the applicant without the previous written consent of the appraiser or the applicant, and in any event only with proper qualification.

We are not required to give testimony or attendance in court by reason of this appraisal, with reference to the property in question, unless arrangements have been made previously therefor.

The division of the land and improvement values estimated herein is applicable only under the program of utilization shown. These separate valuations are invalidated by any other application.

M02-0623-3   PAGE 1

DETAILS OF PROPERTY *(Describe by Marking "X" Where Possible)*

CHECK TYPE OF HOUSE

Spl. Level	Cape Cod	Colonial	Ranch	English	Other—Describe	NO. DWELLING UNITS	NO. STORIES	TOTAL NO. ROOMS	NO. BEDROOMS	NO. BATHS

TYPE OF EXTERIOR

Stone	Brick	Wood Shingle	Asb. Shingle	Clapb'd	Stucco	Other	PLOT SIZE Front	Rear	Side	Side	Year Built

FIRST LEVEL—(LIST EACH ROOM. INCLUDE CENTER HALL, POWDER ROOM, PORCHES, ETC. STATE IF MODERN KITCHEN.)

SECOND LEVEL—(LIST EACH ROOM. STATE IF BATHS ARE TILED—WITH SHOWER.)

THIRD LEVEL—(LIST EACH ROOM. STATE IF ATTIC IS FULL, FINISHED, ETC.)

ADDITIONAL LEVEL(S)

BASEMENT YES | NO	LIST LAUNDRY, PLAYROOM, ETC.	TYPE OF FOUNDATION Stone	Concrete Block	Poured Concrete	Brick	TYPE OF ROOF Compos.	Shingle	Other

PLUMBING Brass | Copper | Iron	INSULATION Yes | No Type—Rockwool, Fiberglass, etc.	SCREENS Yes | No	Aluminum | Copper	Other	STORM WINDOWS Yes | No | Aluminum	Wood

WATER SOURCE Town | Well	SEWAGE SYSTEM Septic Tank	Sewer	HEATING SYSTEM—TYPE Warm Air	Hot Water	Steam	FUEL Gas | Oil	Coal	ELECTRIC WIRING 110V	220V

GARAGE NO. OF CARS	TYPE OF GARAGE Detached	Attached	Built in	Carport	ANNUAL TAXES $

ASSESSMENTS

ANY EVIDENCE OF TERMITES ☐   DRY ROT ☐   DAMPNESS ☐   SETTLEMENT ☐   NO EVIDENCE ☐

CHARACTER OF NEIGHBORHOOD IS —   NEIGHBORHOOD ACTIVITY

	MAJOR STRUCTURES	CONSTRUCTION	TYPICAL CONDITION	BUILT-UP	AGE TYPICAL BLDG.	OWNER OCC.	VACANCY	ZONING	TRANSITION TO —
NEIGH.				%		%	%		
BLOCK				%		%	%		

UTILITIES	AVAIL.	CONNECTED	STREET IMPS.	CONVENIENCES	BLK.	MI.	TYPICAL INFLUENCES	IS SUBJECT TYPICAL OF NEIGHBORHOOD? (DESC.)
WATER			WALKS	G. SCHOOL			OCCUPN.	SUPERIOR ☐ TYPICAL ☐ INFERIOR ☐
SEWER			CURB	H. SCHOOL			INCOME	
GAS			PAVING	STORES			RENTALS	
ELEC.			ALLEYS	CHURCH			VALUES	
SEPTIC TANK			FIRE PROTECTION	TRANSPN.				

REPAIRS *(Show Below ONLY Repairs Necessary To Protect Property and Put in Saleable Condition—DO NOT INCLUDE ESTIMATES IN APPRAISAL)*

EXTERIOR REPAIRS	ESTIMATED COST	INTERIOR REPAIRS	ESTIMATED COST
	$		$
		TOTAL INTERIOR REPAIRS	$
TOTAL EXTERIOR REPAIRS	$	TOTAL EXTERIOR AND INTERIOR REPAIRS	$

NON-REAL ESTATE ITEMS INCLUDED IN THIS APPRAISAL WITH DOLLAR VALUE.

1.	$	5.	$
2.	$	6.	$
3.	$	7.	$
4.	$	8.	$
		TOTAL *(To Be Included in Cost Approach—Page 3)*	$

COST APPROACH TO VALUE*

I.   MAIN BUILDING
      1st Level _____ sq. ft.
      2nd Level _____ sq. ft.
      3rd Level _____ sq. ft.
      4th Level _____ sq. ft.
      _____ sq. ft.
      TOTAL _____ sq. ft. @ $ _____ per ft. $ _____

      IMPROVEMENTS: Porch $ _____
                     Patio   _____
                     Fireplace   _____
                     -----------   _____
                     -----------   _____
                     -----------   _____ $ _____

      NON-REAL ESTATE ITEMS FROM PAGE 2 $ _____

           REPLACEMENT COST NEW........................... $ _____

      LESS DEPRECIATION: Physical $ _____
                       Functional   _____
                       Economic   _____
                       TOTAL DEPRECIATION .... $ _____

           DEPRECIATED VALUE .... $

II. GARAGE-DEPRECIATED VALUE.. $

III. OTHER BUILDINGS—DEPRECIATED VALUE .... $

IV. LAND
      _____ Sq. or Front ft. @ $ _____ per ft. .... $ _____

      IMPROVEMENTS: Driveway and Walks $ _____
                     Landscaping $ _____
                     Other $ _____
           --- $ _____
           --- $ _____
           TOTAL LAND .... $

INDICATED VALUE BY COST APPROACH .... $

MARKET APPROACH TO VALUE*

ADDRESS	- - - - - - - - - - - - - -	+	−	- - - - - - - - - - - - - -	+	−	- - - - - - - - - - - - - -	+	−
DATE SOLD									
LOT SIZE									
STYLE									
CONDITION									
BEDROOMS									
BATHS									
OTHER:									
TOTAL + or −	$ _____			$ _____			$ _____		
SALE PRICES OF COMPARABLES	$ _____			$ _____			$ _____		
INDICATED VALUE(S) BY MARKET APPROACH	$ _____			$ _____			$ _____		

*Enter Your Final Estimate of Value Under "APPRAISAL SUMMARY", Page 1   PAGE 3

(Reproduced with permission of International Business Machine Corp.)

REMARKS — General condition, adequacy of layout and functional utility. Describe any positive or adverse influences that will affect marketability. Include any other comments or helpful information.

PLOT PLAN AND PHOTOGRAPHS OF PROPERTY

Show street names, location of subject property on plot. Show dimensions of lot. Indicate northerly direction.

PASTE UPPER EDGE OF PHOTOGRAPHS HERE ↓
Sketch outline of subject, giving outside dimensions.

No. 2-8
VETERANS ADMINISTRATION APPRAISAL REPORT

Form Approved
Budget Bureau No. 76-R231.13

VETERANS ADMINISTRATION APPRAISAL REPORT

CASE NUMBER

1. MAJOR STRUCTURES

A. CONSTRUCTION   B. TYPICAL CONDITION   C. BUILT-UP   D. AGE TYP. BLDG.   E. OWN. OCCUP.   F. VACANCY   G. ZONING   H. TRANSITION TO

NEIGHBORHOOD   %   %   %   %

BLOCK   %

2. STATUS OF PROPERTY
- A. PROPOSED
- B. EXISTING, NOT PREVIOUSLY OCCUPIED
- C. EXISTING, PREVIOUSLY OCCUPIED
- D. ALTERATIONS, IMPROVEM'TS, OR REPAIRS

3. CONSTRUCTION COMPLETED BEFORE DATE HEREOF
- A. WITHIN 12 CALENDAR MOS.
- B. MORE THAN 12 CALENDAR MOS.

4. TYPE OF PROPERTY
- HOME
- BUSINESS
- FARM

5. NAME AND ADDRESS OF FIRM OR PERSON MAKING REQUEST (Include No., Street or rural route, City or P.O., State and Zip Code)

6. PROPERTY ADDRESS (Include Zip Code)

7. NO. BLDGS.   8. NO. LIVING UNITS   9. LOT DIMENSIONS

10. UTILITIES	PUBLIC	COMM.	INDIV.	11. TYPE OF STREET PAVING
WATER				
GAS				CURB
ELECT.				SIDEWALK
SANIT. SEWER				STORM SEWER

12. DESCRIPTION			COMB. TYPES	CRAWL SPACE		REC. ROOM	CAR GARAGE	CENT. AIR COND.
DETACHED	WOOD SIDING	C. BLOCK	STORIES	YRS. EST. AGE	1/2 BATHS	LIVING RM.	STORAGE RM.	CAR CARPT.	TYPE OF HEATING & FUEL
SEMI-DET.	WOOD SHINGLE	STONE	SPLIT LEVEL	NO. ROOMS	DINING RM.	UTILITY RM.	BUILT-IN	
ROW	ALUM. SIDING	BRICK & BLOCK	% BASEMENT	BEDROOMS	KITCHEN	RM.	ATTACHED	ROOFING DESCRIP.
FRAME	ASB. SHINGLE	STUCCO	SLAB	BATHS	FAMILY RM.	FIRE PLACE	DETACHED	
	BRICK VENEER							

13. LEGAL DESCRIPTION

14. TITLE LIMITATIONS INCLUDING EASEMENTS, RESTRICTIONS, ENCROACHMENTS, ETC.

15. INTERIOR AND EXTERIOR REPAIRS (Show below ONLY repairs necessary to make property conform with applicable MPR's)

$

TOTAL ESTIMATED COST INTERIOR AND EXTERIOR REPAIRS $

16. TRANSACTION OF COMPARABLE PROPERTIES

LOCATION	PRICE	DATE	STORY	S.F. AREA	RMS.	BED-RMS.	BATH	CONSTR.	GAR/CRPT.	AGE/COND	FINANCING	EQ.	SUP.	INF.
	$										$	%	%	%
												%	%	%
												%	%	%

17. REMARKS (Describe: (a) Property comparability; (b) Detrimental influences; (c) Real estate market in community; (d) Highest and best use; (e) Explain depreciation; (f) Building lot, district, violations; (g) Comments on repairs; (h) Comments on any special assessments) (Use supplemental sheet if necessary.)

18. PROPERTY SHOWS EVIDENCE OF (Check)
☐ TERMITE ☐ DRY ROT ☐ DAMPNESS ☐ SETTLE-MENT ☐ NO EVIDENCE

19. ESTATE (Check) ☐ A. FEE SIMPLE ☐ B. LEASE HOLD

20. FUTURE ECONOMIC LIFE (Years)

21. CALCULATIONS

22. DATA	DESCRIPTION	CONDITION	23. EQUIP.	DESCRIPTION	DEPR. VALUE	24. OTHER IMPROVEMENTS	DEPR. VALUE		MAIN	CU. SQ. OTHER
ROOF					$		$	RATE PER FT.	$	
FOUND.								REPLMT. COST	$	
BSMT.								PHYSICAL DEPR.	$	
FLOORS								FUNCTIONAL	$	
INT. WALLS								ECONOMIC	$	
BATH								TOTAL DEPR.	$	
FINISH								DEPR. COST	$	
GUTTERS										

TOTAL DEPR. COST OF IMPR. $
OTHER IMPR. AND EQUIP. $
LAND VALUE $

25. ANNUAL TAXES
GENERAL | SPECIAL | OTHER
TOTAL $

TOTAL $
TOTAL DEPR. COST OF PROP. $

26. DOES PROPERTY CONFORM TO APPLICABLE MINIMUM PROPERTY REQUIREMENTS?
☐ YES ☐ NO (If "No" explain in Item 17)

27. ESTIMATE FAIR MONTHLY RENT TIMES RENT MULTIPLIER
$ × = $

28. CORRELATION
A. COST APPROACH $ | B. CAPITALIZATION $ | C. MARKET APPROACH $

I HEREBY CERTIFY that (a) I have carefully viewed the property described in this report, INSIDE AND OUTSIDE, so far as it has been completed; that (b) it is the same property that is identified by description in my appraisal assignment; that (c) I HAVE NOT RECEIVED, HAVE NO AGREEMENT TO RECEIVE, NOR WILL I ACCEPT FROM ANY PARTY ANY GRATUITY OR EMOLUMENT OTHER THAN MY APPRAISAL FEE FOR MAKING THIS APPRAISAL; that (d) I have no interest, present or prospective in the applicant, seller, property, or mortgage.

29. I ESTIMATE "REASONABLE VALUE"
☐ "AS IS" ☐ "AS REPAIRED" ☐ "AS COMPLETED"

30. ESTIMATED REASONABLE VALUE
$

31. SIGNATURE OF APPRAISER

32. DATE SIGNED

VA FORM 26-1803
MAY 1967
SUPERSEDES VA FORM 26-1803, OCT 1960, WHICH WILL NOT BE USED.

VA FILE COPY 5

No. 2-9
PROPERTY INSPECTION REPORT
Data Sheet

LOCATION _____

Date _____

Section _____
Block _____
Lot _____
Ward _____
Zone _____
Use _____

LAND _____ x _____ Sq. Ft. _____ Landscaping _____
BUILDING _____ x _____ Height _____ Cu. Ft. _____ Stories _____
EXTENSION _____ x _____ Height _____ Cu. Ft. _____ Stories _____

Construction _____	Wash Tubs _____	**ELEVATORS:**
Year Built _____	Public Laundry _____	Mfgr. _____
Condition _____	Pipe Material _____	(P) No. _____ Size ____
D-S.D.-A _____	Insulation _____	Capacity _____
Apts. _____ Rooms ___	Gas _____	Type (Aut. or Man.) _____
Baths _____ Closets ___		(F) No. _____ Size ____
Floors _____		Capacity _____
Walls _____	Sewer _____	Type (Aut. or Man.) _____
Ceilings _____		Door Contacts _____
Trim _____	**HEATING:**	Door Openers _____
Awnings _____	Type _____	Doors _____
Stores _____	Boiler _____	Floors _____
Offices _____	Radiators _____	Shaftway Enclosure _____
Garages _____	Piping _____	
Lofts _____	Insulation _____	Maintenance Contract ___
Other Space _____	Fuel _____	
	Amt. Used _____	**ROOF:** _____
Layout First Floor _____	**HOT WATER:**	
	Mfgr. _____	Skylights _____
Layout Upper Floors _____	Fuel _____	Leaders _____
	Amt. Used _____	Gutters _____
	Storage Tank _____	Cornice _____
CELLAR _____ x _____	Coils in Boiler _____	Flashings _____
Ceiling Height _____		Water Storage Tank _____
Floor _____	Insulation _____	
Walls _____	**ELECTRIC:**	Chimney _____
Incinerator _____	Wire Conduits _____	Clothes Drying Frames ___
Dumbwaiters _____	Base Plugs _____	
PLUMBING:	Door Bells - Openers ____	
Type W. C. _____		
Bath Tubs _____	Fixtures _____	**PUBLIC SPACE:**
Basins _____	Type _____	Halls _____
Urinals _____	Condition _____	Stairs _____
Stall Showers _____	Power Lines _____	Fire-Escapes _____
Sinks _____		
Flushing Apparatus _____		Lobby Equipment _____
	Meter Location _____	
		Sidewalk _____

Form 292 S. S. CLARKSON MFG. CORP. 17 BERGEN ST., B'KLYN, N. Y. 11201   (Over)

(Reproduced with permisssion of S. S. Clarkson Mfg. Corp., Brooklyn, N. Y.)

Curb ....
Paving ....

NEIGHBORHOOD:
Churches ....
Schools ....
Stores ....

Trend ....
TRANSPORTATION:
Subway Line ....
Station ....
Distance ....
Elevated Line ....
Station ....
Distance ....
Surface Line ....
Distance ....

Bus Line ....
Distance ....
Railroad Line ....
Station ....
Distance ....
Other Transportation ....

MISCELLANEOUS:
Easements ....

Setbacks or Restrictions ....

Legal Violations ....

FACTORY-LOFT DATA
Sprinklers ....
Location ....

Supply ....
Tank ....
Fire Lines ....

Railroad Siding ....
Gross Floor Area ....
Net Floor Area ....
Load per Sq. Ft. ....
Remarks ....

Loading Platform ....

RENTAL INCOME

Space	Rms.	Rms.	Rms.	Rms.	Rms.	Rms.
Cellar						
Base'mt.						
1st Fl.						
2nd Fl.						
3rd Fl.						
4th Fl.						
5th Fl.						
6th Fl.						
7th Fl.						
8th Fl.						
9th Fl.						
10th Fl.						
11th Fl.						
12th Fl.						
13th Fl.						
14th Fl.						
15th Fl.						
16th Fl.						
17th Fl.						
18th Fl.						
19th Fl.						
20th Fl.						
Totals						

Complete Total $ ....

Remarks ....
....
....
....

OPERATING EXPENSES

Taxes .... $ ....
Water ....
Payroll ....
Superintendent Apt. ....
Fuel ....
Decorating Apts. ....
Decorate Public Space ....
Gas ....
Electric ....
Liability Insurance ....
Compensat. Insurance ....
Fire Insurance ....
Plate Glass Insurance ....
Elevator Maintenance ....
Refrigerator Mainten. ....
Plumbing ....
Roofing & Waterproof ....
Electrical Repairs ....
Carpentry ....
Misc. Bldg. Repairs ....
Supplies ....
Advertising ....
Legal & Collect. Fees ....
Vacancy Allowance ....
Rental Commissions ....
Management Fees ....
Depreciation ....
....
....

TOTAL $ ....
OWNER ....
ADDRESS ....

PHONE ....
Assessed Value of Land 19 .... $ ....
Assessed Value of Bldg. 19 .... $ ....
TOTAL $ ....

No. 2-10

INSPECTION AND APPRAISAL REPORT

Property Owned By _____

Street & Number _____

City & State _____

By reason of my investigation and by virtue of my experience I have been able to form and have formed an opinion of fair market value of the property, "as is", which is:

LAND	$
IMPROVEMENTS	$
APPLIANCES	$
(NOT COST APPROCH) TOTAL OR F.M.V. * PROB. S.P.	$

* Should agree with the probable selling price (Mortgage Information line 3, page 3) under the most likely type of financing.

The above total fair market value (for a cash sale including brokerage commission) is defined as: "The highest price estimated in terms of money that a willing and well-informed buyer would be warranted in paying and a willing and equally well-informed seller justified in accepting for a property if placed on the market for a reasonable period of time; with both parties acting free of compulsion or duress and with all rights or benefits inherent in or attributable to a property included in said value."

The appraised value has been treated in confidence. Neither it nor any of its contributing items have been disclosed to others.

I, do hereby certify that to the best of my knowledge and belief the statements and opinions contained in this appraisal are correct, subject to the limiting conditions herein set forth; also that neither the employment to make the appraisal nor the compensation is contingent on the amount of the valuation reported; also that I have no interest present or prospective in the said Real Estate appraised.

_____
SIGNATURE   DATE

_____
STREET & NUMBER

_____
CITY & STATE

Real Estate Forms Institute No. 1100

John W. Murray Co. 118 Summer st. Boston

THE COST APPROACH VALUE ARRIVED AT IS ASSUMED TO BE FOR THE PROPERTY IN ITS PRESENT CONDITION. IF SUBMITTED ON ANY OTHER BASIS (E.G. VALUATION INTENDED TO INCLUDE RECONDITIONING OR COMPLETION), DETAILS AND ESTIMATE OF COSTS SHOULD BE CLEARLY SHOWN.

COST APPROACH

1	TOTAL _____ CU. OR SQ. FT. X REPRODUCTION COST $_____ PER FT.	$
2	LESS_____ % FOR DETERIORATION & OBSOLESCENCE	$
3	DEPRECIATED COST OF IMPROVEMENTS (1 - 2)	$
4	DEPRECIATED COST OF GARAGE	$
5	DEPRECIATED COST OF AUXILIARY BUILDINGS	$
6	LOT IMPROVEMENTS (DESCRIBE)	$
7	LAND VALUE - EXCLUDING #6	$
8	APPLIANCES (SEE PAGE 3)	$
9	TOTAL (LINES 3 TO 8)	$

TYPE HOUSE:	AGE:	LOT SIZE:

IF SIZE OF LOT IS NOT COMPARABLE TO OTHERS IN NEIGHBORHOOD, EXPLAIN NATURE OF VARIATION:

IF ANY PORTION OF LAND OR IMPROVEMENT IS USED FOR PROFIT, EXPLAIN NATURE OF USE:

FARM LAND ☐   FARM PRODUCE OR ANIMALS ☐   BUSINESS SPACE ☐
RENTALS ☐   BOARDING HOUSE ☐   OTHER _____ ☐

DESCRIPTION

EXTERIOR		INTERIOR - BASEMENT	SIZE OF ROOMS
SIDING-TYPE & CONDITION		EXCAVATION - (FULL ☐ PORTION ☐)	
ROOF-TYPE & CONDITION		UTILITY	
FOUNDATION-TYPE & CONDITION		LAUNDRY	
OTHER		LAVATORY	
OTHER		RECREATION	
OTHER		TYPE & CONDITION OF WALLS	
OTHER		TYPE & CONDITION OF FLOORS	

INTERIOR - FIRST FLOOR	SIZE OF ROOMS	INTERIOR - SECOND FLOOR	SIZE OF ROOMS
ENTRANCE HALL		BEDROOM	
LIVING ROOM (F.P. - YES ☐ NO ☐)		BEDROOM	
DINING ROOM		BATHS NO._____ (SHOWER ☐ TUB ☐)	
DINETTE		STORAGE	
KITCHEN		OTHER	
PANTRY		INTERIOR - THIRD FLOOR	SIZE OF ROOMS
PORCHES NO._____		BEDROOM	
BEDROOM		BEDROOM	
BEDROOM		BATHS NO._____	
BEDROOM		STORAGE	
BATHS NO._____ (SHOWER ☐ TUB ☐)		OTHER	
TYPE & CONDITION OF WALLS		TYPE & CONDITION OF WALLS	
TYPE & CONDITION OF FLOORS		TYPE & CONDITION OF FLOORS	

ANY EVIDENCE OF DRY ROT_____, DAMPNESS_____, SETTLEMENT_____.
EXPLAIN:

ANY WATER SEEPAGE IN BASEMENT? YES ☐ NO ☐ IF YES, EXPLAIN UNDER "REMARKS" ON LAST PAGE.

LIST REPAIRS, IF NECESSARY, AND ESTIMATED COSTS NECESSARY TO PLACE HOUSE IN GOOD MARKETABLE CONDITION.

APPURTENANCES

GARAGE: NO. CARS____ ATT. ☐ DET. ☐ UNDER ☐	INSUL. TYPE:
HEAT TYPE:	AMOUNT:_____ CAP_____ SIDES
FUEL USED:	UTILITIES
FUEL TANK:_____ GAL.	SEWERAGE
AUX. BLDG.	HOT WATER
OTHER:	SUMP PUMP

NEIGHBORHOOD DATA

TREND: UP ☐ STATIC ☐ DOWN ☐ UNDESIRABLE INFILTRATIONS: YES ☐ NO ☐

DISTANCE TO: SCHOOLS _____ CHURCHES _____ STATION _____ STORES _____

IS SUBJECT PROPERTY TYPICAL OF NEIGHBORHOOD?

SUPERIOR ☐ TYPICAL ☐ INFERIOR ☐

TAX INFORMATION

ASSESSMENT: LAND	$	HAS THERE BEEN A LOCAL IMPROVEMENT, COMPLETED OR IN PROCESS, FOR WHICH A SPECIAL ASSESSMENT HAS BEEN LEVIED OR IS PENDING
BUILDING		
TOTAL	$	YES ☐ NO ☐
TAX RATE	$	
TOTAL TAX	$	IF SO, FURNISH FOLLOWING DETAILS:

VALUE OF IMPROVEMENTS INCLUDED IN FAIR MARKET VALUE	TOTAL ASSESSMENT LEVIED	APPROXIMATE ASSESSMENT PENDING	AMOUNT OF ASSESSMENT UNPAID
$	$	$	$

APPLIANCES

FURNISH SEPARATE VALUE FOR APPLIANCES INCLUDED IN TOTAL FAIR MARKET VALUE. INDICATE WHETHER OR NOT ANY APPLIANCES ARE BUILT-IN UNITS WHERE REMOVAL WOULD DAMAGE PROPERTY. SHOW COST OF BUILDING REPAIR IF REMOVED. * NOT ACQUIRED IF PORTABLE.

	VALUE	PERSONAL PROP.	PART OF REALTY	TRADE NAME/TYPE/REMARKS
KITCHEN RANGE	$			
REFRIGERATOR	$			
WASHER *	$			
DRYER *	$			
ATTIC FANS *	$			
MIRRORS *	$			
NO. OF WINDOW SCREENS	$			
NO. OF SCREEN DOORS	$			
NO. OF WINDOW STORM SASH	$			
NO. OF STORM DOORS	$			
WALL TO WALL CARPETING	$			
OTHER	$			
OTHER	$			

IS THERE EVIDENCE OF TERMITE INFESTATION IF SO, FURNISH DETAILS:

MORTGAGE INFORMATION

IS THERE ANY POSSIBILITY OF THIS PROPERTY BEING SOLD WITHIN THE NEXT SIX MONTHS WITH FINANCING

NOT REQUIRING PAYMENT OF MORTGAGE DISCOUNT BY SELLER? YES ☐ NO ☐

	CONVENTIONAL	F.H.A.	V.A.	OTHER (EXPLAIN)
1. THIS PROPERTY WILL MOST LIKELY SELL WITH ONE OF THE FOLLOWING TYPES OF FINANCING (INDICATE BY 1, 2, 3 AND 4 IN APPLICABLE SPACE.) ⟶				
2. INDICATE IF GOVERNMENT INSURED FUNDS ARE AVAILABLE (YES OR NO)	X X			
3. FURNISH PROBABLE SELLING PRICE FOR EACH TYPE FINANCING AVAILABLE	$	$	$	$
4. FURNISH MAXIMUM MORTGAGE AMOUNT OBTAINABLE FOR EACH TYPE FINANCING AVAILABLE	$	$	$	$
5. PER CENT OF MAXIMUM MORTGAGE PAYABLE BY SELLER FOR APPLICABLE DISCOUNTS AND RELATED FEES TO AID PURCHASER IN FINANCING PROPERTY.				

EXPLANATIONS

RECENT COMPARABLE SALES				
ADDRESS	ROOMS	PRICE	DATE SOLD	REASON FOR DIFF. FROM SUB. PROP.
		$		

REMARKS

SKETCHES
EXTERIOR PLOT — FLOOR PLANS — AUXILIARY BUILDINGS

PHOTOGRAPHS
ATTACH A MINIMUM OF TWO (2) PHOTOGRAPHS SHOWING FRONT AND BOTH SIDE VIEWS OF THE PROPERTY.

LISTING INFORMATION
WE SHOULD LIKE YOUR OPINION OF REALISTIC TOP LISTING PRICE OR THE RANGE IN LISTING PRICES TO BE
ESTABLISHED TO COVER THE SEVERAL TYPES OF MORTGAGE FINANCING.

CONVENTIONAL   F.H.A.   V.A.

(Reproduced with permission of the Real Estate Forms Institute, Boston, Mass.)

3

Assignments

3

Assignments

An assignment is the relinquishment or transfer of valuable right from one person to another. By this instrument, the interest one possessed in property is vested in another. Assignments are concerned with the intangible rights an owner holds, such as contractual and personal ones in connection with the property, and not the property itself.

An assignment may be oral or written. When in writing it can take many forms. No consideration is needed to make it valid, but it must immediately convey that which is assigned.

The assignee obtains only what the assignor has to convey and nothing more. The assignor generally remains liable for the performance of that which he assigned.

To be recorded, an assignment must meet the requirements of recording statutes. In New York, for example, an assignment of a mortgage cannot be recorded unless acknowledged before a notary public. State and local jurisdiction recording methods should be studied.

In the absence of statements to the contrary, contracts, leases and mortgages can be assigned, as can be accounts receivable (to defray a debt), building loan contracts, chattels, businesses, option contracts, and any other asset one possesses. The typical forms of assignments included on the following pages are in frequent use in real estate transactions.

No. 3–1
ASSIGNMENT
General Form

For Value Received I_____, of_____
_____Street, City of_____, State of_____
_____, hereby assign, transfer and set over to _____
_____, of_____Avenue, City of_____, State of
_____, all my right, title and interest in a certain agreement dated_____
____, 19_____, by and between_____
_____and_____,
subject to all the terms and conditions thereof and hereby remise, release and quit claim
unto_____, all my right, title and interest in and to the

said property.

Dated_____, 19_____.

_____

No. 3–2
ASSIGNMENT OF CONTRACT
Annexed To Contract

For Value Received, I_____hereby assign all my rights, title and interest in the certain contract entered into by me with_____ _____ on_____, 19_____, a copy of which is hereto annexed as a part hereof.

In witness whereof I have hereunto set my hand and seal in the city of_____, State of_____, on this_____day of_____, 19_____.

_____

No. 3–3
ASSIGNMENT OF CONTRACT
With the Consideration Stated

KNOW ALL MEN BY THESE PRESENTS, That _____ _____ of_____County, State of_____, party of the first part, in consideration of the sum of_____ ($_____) and other valuable considerations to me in hand paid by_____ _____, of the County of_____, State of_____, party of the second part, at or before the ensealing and delivery of these presents, the receipt whereof is hereby acknowledged, has granted, bargained, sold, assigned, transferred and set over, and by these presents does grant, bargain, sell, assign, transfer and set over unto the aids party of the second part, his heirs and assigns, forever, a certain land contract bearing date of the_____day of_____19_____, made by_____ _____to_____upon the following described piece or parcel of land, situate and being in the County of_____, State of_____, to wit:

(Here include legal description)

A portion of the consideration of this assignment being that the party of the second part herein assume all the obligations and agree to pay all the payments described in said contract now due or to become due, together with all interest specified in said contract.

And upon the performance of all the terms and conditions and the completion of all payments as set forth in said contract, by the said party of the second part,_____ _____heirs and assigns, the party of the first part does hereby authorize the said_____to make, execute and deliver a good and sufficient deed to the property hereinabove described, in like manner as though the original contract had been made and executed by the said_____ _____with the said party of the second part, instead of with _____.

To Have And To Hold the same unto the said party of the second part, heirs and assigns forever.

In Witness Whereof, the said party of the first part has hereunto set his hand and seal this_____day of_____, 19_____.

Signed, sealed and delivered in the presence of:

_____   _____

_____

No. 3–4
ASSIGNMENT
Endorsed On Contract

For Value Received, I_____, do hereby assign the within contract and all my right, title and interest in and to this contract to_____ _____.

_____

No. 3–5
ASSIGNMENT OF RENT
To Assure Mortgage Payments

Whereas_____is indebted to_____ _____in the sum of_____ _____($_____) as evidenced by a note secured by a mortgage upon

(Here describe property)

dated_____19_____, and recorded in Plat Book_____, Page_____ of the records of_____County, State of_____, the undersigned hereby assigns, transfers and sets over to_____all the rents now due and to become due upon the above described property. The proceeds of said rents collected shall first be applied to payments for normal operating expenses of the property such as repair and maintenance, insurance, taxes, utilities, salaries, etc. All of the remaining sum, if any, shall be applied to the principal and interest of the mortgage described herein until the payment of said loan is made in full.

In Witness Whereof:

_____   _____

_____   _____

When transferring title to commercial properties, leases that are still in force are assigned to the new owner. The following are two typical forms to legally effect this transfer.

No. 3–6
ASSIGNMENT OF LEASES

Know All Men By These Presents, that we,_____
_____and_____of_____
City, State of_____, for and in consideration of_____
_____($_____) and other good and
valuable consideration to me in hand paid by_____
_____, the receipt of which is hereby acknowledged, do hereby sell, transfer, assign and
set over to_____, his executors, administrators
and assigns, all of our right, title and interest in and to the following leases:

1. That certain lease dated_____, 19_____, by and between
_____and_____
_____, his wife, and_____, covering the
following described property:

(Here include legal description)

2. That certain lease dated_____, 19_____, by and
between_____and_____
_____, his wife, and_____as Trustee for
_____Corporation, incorporated in the State of_____,
covering the following described property:

(Here include legal description)

The Assignors do hereby warrant that they have the right to sell, transfer, assign and set over the aforesaid described leases, and the assignors further covenant with the assignee, his executors, administrators and assigns, that the assigned premises now are free and clear of any judgments, executions, taxes, assessments and encumbrances whatsoever.

In Witness Whereof, we have hereunto set our hands and seals this_____day of_____, 19_____.

Witness:
_____   _____(L.S.)

Witness:
_____   _____(L.S.)

_____
(Reproduced with permission of Aaron Barken, Attorney, Miami, Fla.)

No. 3–7
ASSIGNMENT OF LEASES
Another Form

Know all Men by These Presents that the undersigned for and in consideration of the sum of $_____ and other good and valuable considerations to us in hand paid by _____ receipt whereof is hereby acknowledged, have sold and do by these presents grant, convey, sell, assign and transfer unto the said_____, all the leases attached hereto made a part hereof, on those certain premises described as follows:

_____

Assignors hereby warrant and represent that the leases attached hereto and made a part hereof are in good standing and that the Assignors have not been put on any notice as to any defense, offset, claim or counter-claim by the Lessees of said leases or any person or entity claiming by or through said Lessees and the Assignors further represent that there is no litigation now pending or threatened against the Assignors (Lessors) interest in and to said leases.

_____

_____

No. 3–8
ASSIGNMENT OF LESSEE'S INTEREST IN LEASE

THIS AGREEMENT, made and entered into at _____, _____ _____County,_____, this_____day of_____, 19_____, by and between_____, as_____ ___, hereinafter called "First Part_____," and_____, as_____, hereinafter called "Second Part_____;"
WITNESSETH:
That the First Part_____, for_____and other good and valuable considerations to them in hand paid simultaneously with the execution and delivery of these presents by the "Second Part_____," the receipt whereof is hereby acknowledged, have granted, bargained, sold, assigned, transferred, set over and delivered, and by these presents do grant, bargain, sell, assign, transfer, set over and deliver unto the Second Part_____, the following described property situate, lying and being in_____ County,_____, to-wit:

_____

TO HAVE AND TO HOLD the same unto the Second Part_____, their heirs, executors, administrators and assigns for the full term of said lease, together with the security deposit held by the Lessors under said Lease pursuant to Article_____thereof, in the sum of $_____.

The First Part_____hereby represent unto the Second Part_____, and they do covenant and agree with the Second Part_____, as follows:

(a) First Part_____are the owners of the Lessee's interest in and to said lease and have full power and lawful authority to effect the sale and transfer thereof as herewith done; and

(b) That the said Lease is outstanding and in full force and effect, and that the within instrument does transfer the ownership of the Lessee's interest in said lease, together with the security deposit aforesaid, unto the second part_____; and

(c) That the term of the said Lease is for_____years, commencing_____ _____, 19_____; and

(d) That the First Part_____, as Lessees under said Lease, are not in default under any of the terms, conditions and provisions contained in said Lease on the part of the Lessees to be kept and performed.

(e) That the premises are encumbered by a first mortgage held by_____ ____by assignment, as originally filed_____under Clerk's File No._____.

Second Part_____expressly accept and assume all of the terms, covenants and conditions in said Lease contained to be kept and performed by the Lessees, from and after the date of this Agreement.

IN WITNESS WHEREOF, the parties have hereto affixed their hands and seals at the place, on the day and year hereinabove written.

_____(SEAL)
                              First Part_____

_____

_____(SEAL)
                              Second Part_____

_____
Witnesses:

No. 3–9
ASSIGNMENTS OF MORTGAGE
With Covenants [1]

KNOW ALL MEN BY THESE PRESENTS, That_____a corporation existing under the laws of the State of_____, of the first part, in consideration of the sum of_____Dollars, lawful money of the United States, to_____in hand paid by_____ _____of the second part, at or before the ensealing and delivery of these presents, the receipt whereof is hereby acknowledged, has granted, bargained, sold, assigned, transferred and set over, and by these presents does grant, bargain, sell, assign, transfer and set over unto the said party_____of the second part a certain indenture of

---

1. When preparing an Assignment of Mortgage *without covenants,* eliminate the paragraph preceding the "To Have And To Hold" clause.

mortgage bearing date the_____ day of_____, 19_____, made by
_____ and recorded in Mortgage Book_____,
page_____, public records of_____County,_____,
upon the following described piece or parcel of land situate and being in_____
County, State of_____, to wit:

(Here include legal description)

Together with the Note_____or obligation_____described in said mortgage, and the money
due and to become due thereon, with interest from the_____day of_____.
19_____.

The party of the first part covenants that there is now owing upon said mortgage, without offset or defense of any kind, the principal sum of_____
_____Dollars, with interest thereon at_____per centum per annum from the_____
day of_____, 19_____.

TO HAVE AND TO HOLD the same unto the said part_____of the second part, and assigns forever.

IN WITNESS WHEREOF, the said party of the first part has caused these presents to be signed in its name by its President, and its corporate seal to be affixed, attested

(Corporate Seal)   by its
                                      the_____day of_____, 19_____

Attest:_____

Signed, sealed and delivered in presence of us:

_____

                                      By_____
                                                President
_____

No. 3–10
ASSIGNMENT
With Guarantee

Know all Men by These Presents, that we the_____Corporation
with its principal place of business at_____Street, City of_____
_____, State of_____, in consideration of the sum_____
_____ ($_____), paid by_____
_____, hereby assign all our right, title and interest in and to a certain
contract between_____Corporation and_____
_____ dated_____, 19_____, to_____
_____. We
guarantee the payment of all monies due and later to become due under the terms and

conditions of the said contract including reasonable attorney's fees that may be charged to enforce any rights of the said contract. We further guarantee the full performance of the terms and conditions of the said contract. In the event of a breach therein we agree to perform all the terms and conditions of the said contract as though we were liable thereon.

In Witness Whereof:

_____   _____

_____

No. 3–11
PARTIAL ASSIGNMENT

Know All Men By These Presents:

That I_____ of_____

_____, in consideration of_____

_____ dollars ($_____), paid to me by_____

_____ of_____, do hereby sell, assign, transfer and set over to said_____

_____, his executors, administrators and assigns, an undivided_____

_____per cent (_____%) of all my rights, title and interest in and to the following described property:_____

_____.

Witness:

_____

_____

CLAUSE PROHIBITING ASSIGNMENT WITHOUT CONSENT

This instrument, as well as any interest therein or any valuable consideration due or to become due shall not be assigned without first obtaining the written consent of _____

_____.

4

Bills of Sale

4

Bill of Sale

A Bill of Sale is an agreement in writing and made under seal, in which one person sells his rights, title and interest in *personal* assets (chattel) to another. The instrument serves as a receipt and is used in real estate transactions only when items other than the real estate itself are transferred with the property.

Personal items such as appliances, furniture, carpets, drapes, air-conditioning units, merchandise, etc., are included in a bill of sale. Also good will, which encompasses trade names and other intangibles as patents and copyrights. While a bill of sale is not necessary in the transferring of title to real property, it nevertheless is a convenient evidence of the transfer of personal property.

No. 4–1
BILL OF SALE (ABSOLUTE)
General Form

KNOW ALL MEN BY THESE PRESENTS, That I,_____
_____of the city of _____, in the County of_____
_____and the State of_____, in consideration of
_____ Dollars ($_____), lawful money
of the United States, to me paid by_____
_____of_____, the receipt whereof is hereby acknowledged, do
hereby grant, bargain, sell, transfer and deliver unto_____
_____the following goods and chattels:

(Itemize)

TO HAVE AND TO HOLD all and singular the goods and chattels to_____
_____and his executors, administrators and assigns to
their own use forever.

And I hereby covenant with the grantee that I am the lawful owner of said goods and chattels; that they are free from all encumbrances; that I have good right to sell the same as aforesaid; and that I will warrant and defend the same against the lawful claims and demands of all persons whomsoever.

IN WITNESS WHEREOF, I,_____, hereunto set
my hand, this_____day of_____, 19_____.
Signed, sealed and delivered
in the presence of us:

_____   _____ (Seal)
_____   _____ (Seal)

A Bill Of Sale can be made conditional upon certain installment payments being made
or other conditions being met. If these conditions, as specified, are not forthcoming, the
sale may be declared null and void. A form to cover this eventuality follows.

No. 4–2
BILL OF SALE (CONDITIONAL)
Of A Business

KNOW ALL MEN BY THESE PRESENTS, THAT_____
Hereinafter designated as the Seller, for and in consideration of the sum of $ _____
_____lawful money of the United States, received by the Seller, and the sum
of $ _____ to be paid in installments as is evidenced by_____
_____promissory notes, more particularly hereinafter set forth, the receipt of the
above is hereby acknowledged, does hereby conditionally grant, and conditionally bargain
and conditionally sell unto_____
_____of _____
_____hereinafter designated as the Buyer, and by these presents does conditionally grant,
conditionally bargain and conditionally sell unto the said Buyer and the Buyer's executors,
administrators and assigns, all the right, title and interest that the Seller has in and to all

_____,
also the good will of the said business and the lease of the premises, and all other chattels
and fixtures now found in_____
_____of the premises now known as No. _____
all of which chattels and fixtures are free and clear from any and all encumbrances.

TO HAVE AND TO HOLD all and singular the business, stock, goods, chattels and
fixtures above conditionally bargained, conditionally granted or intended so to be, unto
the said Buyer and Buyer's executors, administrators and assigns on the following terms
and conditions:

THE CONDITION of the above is such: That if the Buyer shall and do well and truly
pay unto the Seller the just, true and full sum of $_____, lawful money of the
United States, in installments, and which sum of $_____is evidenced by_____
_____promissory notes each bearing even date herewith, made payable in
the sum and manner following:
The first note of $_____to be paid on the_____day of_____
_____, 19_____, then this agreement is to be in full force and effect, otherwise to be
null, void, inoperative and without any effect.

The Buyer covenants and agrees to and with the Seller that in the event default be made in the payment of any of the installments as hereinbefore mentioned, that it shall be lawful for, and the Buyer does hereby authorize and empower the Seller to enter any dwelling house, store or other premises where the said goods and chattels are, or may be found, and to take and carry away said goods and chattels and to sell and dispose of them at public or private sale for the best price that the Seller can obtain, and out of the proceeds of the said sale, retain the amount remaining unpaid, together with any and all charges and expenses that may be incurred by the Seller, rendering the surplus (if any) unto the Buyer.

The Buyer does hereby agree to and with the Seller that in the event default be made in the payment of any of the installments as the same become due, that the amount remaining unpaid shall then, at the option of the Seller, become immediately due and payable after such default; it being understood and agreed between the parties hereto that the lease of the store aforesaid, and the good will, and the right, title and interest in and to the stock, merchandise, and fixtures of said business shall in no event pass unto the Buyer until the Buyer has fully complied with all the conditions herein, and has made the payments mentioned herein, and in accordance with the terms of this agreement, this being a condition precedent before the title to these premises shall pass from the Seller to the Buyer.

The Seller in consideration of the Buyer fully complying with the terms aforesaid, agrees to and with the Buyer, that the Seller will not engage in a business similar to the one mentioned in this agreement, either directly or indirectly, as principal, agent, servant or employee, or act for any other person, firm or corporation whatsoever for a period of
_____ years from the date hereof, and not within a radius of_____
_____ (_____) square blocks from the premises aforesaid.

The Buyer also agrees to keep said business fully insured against loss or damage by fire for the benefit of the Seller, in a sum not less than $_____, and if the Buyer fails to procure or effect such insurance within ten(10) days from date hereof, the Seller may effect such insurance and charge the cost thereof to the Buyer and which charge the Buyer agrees to pay on demand, or upon the failure or refusal of the Buyer to pay said premium, then the Seller may, at Seller's option, take immediate possession of the said business, anything herein contained to the contrary notwithstanding.

The Buyer in consideration of the above, agrees to keep, during the continuance of this agreement, stock in a sum not less than the amount of stock now contained in the aforesaid premises, the value thereof to be not less than $_____, and in the event that the Buyer fails to comply therewith, the balance remaining unpaid shall then, at the option of the Seller, become due and payable, and the possession of the business herein mentioned is to revert back to the Seller, and the Buyer agrees that the Seller may maintain an action to eject the Buyer as trespasser on said premises.

The Buyer in consideration of the sum of one dollar to one Buyer in hand paid by the Seller, the receipt whereof is hereby acknowledged, hereby agrees to and with the Seller, that in the event the Buyer fails to comply with any and all the terms and conditions of this agreement, or in the event the Buyer fails to pay any and all of the installments at the time and in the manner hereinbefore mentioned, then the Buyer authorizes the Seller to re-take possession of said business, stock, chattels, fixtures, and the good will thereof, and any sum of money paid hereunder shall belong to the Seller, as liquidated, fixed and stipulated damages, and not as a penalty because the parties herein cannot ascertain the exact amount of damages sustained by the Seller for a breach of the conditions of this agreement by the Buyer, and the Buyer agrees to and with the Seller, in the event the Buyer shall default in the payment of the installments hereinbefore mentioned, or in the event the Buyer fails to comply with any and all the terms and conditions of this agreement, that the Buyer will not engage in a business similar to the one mentioned in this agreement, either directly or indirectly, as principal, agent, servant, or employee, for any person, firm or corporation whatsoever, neither will the Buyer establish a business of a like nature, nor cause the same to be established, for a period of_____ years from date hereof, within a radius of _____ (____) square blocks from the aforesaid premises, and the parties hereto agree that in the event of a breach of the aforementioned condition, the Seller will be entitled to an injunction restraining the Buyer for violating the terms of the agreement hereinbefore mentioned.

If more than one person joins in the execution of this agreement, and if any be of the feminine sex, or if this agreement is executed by a corporation, the relative words herein shall be read as if written in the plural, or in the feminine or neuter gender, as the case may be.

This agreement may not be changed or terminated orally. This agreement shall bind and enure to the benefit of the parties hereto, their respective heirs, personal representatives, successors and assigns.

IT IS ALSO UNDERSTOOD between the parties hereto, that upon full compliance by the Buyer of all the terms, covenants and conditions herein contained, that the Buyer is to have, hold and enjoy the above business unto Buyer and Buyer's heirs, executors, administrators and assigns forever.

IN WITNESS WHEREOF, the parties hereto have hereunto set their hands and seals this day of_____, 19_____.

In presence of

SCHEDULE OF THE FOREGOING CONDITIONAL BILL OF SALE

(ITEMIZE)

The good will of the business the entire stock of_____

_____including

_____

and all other goods and chattels appertaining to said business now found or which may be hereafter replaced, contained in the store on premises known as No. _____

_____and also a certain lease made and executed on_____

____, 19_____ by and between_____

as Landlord, and_____as

Tenant.

In presence of

_____   _____

_____   _____

(Form by courtesy of Julius Blumberg, Inc., 80 Exchange Place, New York, N.Y. 10004)

UNIFORM COMMERCIAL CODE

In order to achieve uniformity in the filing of liens upon personal property, most states have adopted the Uniform Commercial Code. It provides a simplified form of recording any lien upon personal property. A sample copy of the Financing Statement which is used in Florida is shown on page 000. This particular form gives the name of the debtor, the name of the lien holder, the description or inventory of the property, but none of the details of the lien itself. The filing of this form is usually with the Secretary of State at the capitol of the state in which the property is located, and generally, but not always, in the office of the Recorder or Clerk in the county where the property is located. This means that the purchaser of real estate in which the chattel is included need only have the records in the state capitol searched to determine the existence of a financing statement issued by the seller of the property or his predecessors in title.

If no financing statement is found by such a search, then the purchaser may proceed on the assumption the seller can give good title by Bill of Sale to the personal property involved. If one is found, it is an indication that at some time some of the property was affected by a lien. It is then up to the purchaser to interrogate the seller and the lienholder to determine the amount of the lien, or whether it has, in fact, been paid off and should be satisfied of record.

Forms used in other jurisdictions may vary slightly as may the filing fees. The form shown here is a typical example of one state's Uniform Commercial Code filing requirement.

No. 4–3
STATE OF FLORIDA
UNIFORM COMMERCIAL CODE-FINANCING STATEMENT-FORM UCC-1

Any forms used for filing with the Office of Secretary of State pursuant to the Uniform Commercial Code must be approved by Tom Adams, Secretary of State, State of Florida.

INSTRUCTIONS:

1. PLEASE TYPE this form. Fold only along perforation for mailing.
2. Remove Secured Party and Debtor copies and send other 3 copies with interleaved carbon paper to the filing officer. Enclose filing fee of $2.00.
3. If the space provided for any item(s) on the form is inadequate the item(s) should be continued on additional sheets, preferably $5'' \times 8''$ or $8'' \times 10''$. Only one copy of such additional sheets need be presented to the filing officer with the first three copies of the financing statement. Long schedules of collateral, indentures, etc., may be on any size paper that is convenient for the secured party. Indicate the number of additional sheets attached. Enclose filing fee of $1.00 for each additional sheet.
4. If collateral is crops or goods which are or are to become fixtures, describe generally the real estate and give name of record owner.
5. When a copy of the security agreement is used as a financing statement, it is requested that it be accompanied by a completed but unsigned set of these forms.
6. If acknowledgement of filing is requested indicate so on number three copy and enclose fee of $100.

7. If filing with Clerk of Circuit Court consult Chapter 28, F.S., or local clerk for proper fees.

THIS FINANCING STATEMENT is presented to a filing officer for filing pursuant to the Uniform Commercial Code:

3. Maturity date (if any):

1. Debtor(s) (Last Name First) and address(es)	2. Secured Party(ies) and address(es)	For Filing Officer (Date, Time, Number and filing Office)

4. This financing statement covers the following types (or items) of property:

5. Assignee(s) of Secured Party and Address(es)

6. Check if true ☐ The stamps required by Chapter 201, F. S. have been placed on the promissory instruments secured hereby, and will be placed on any additional and similar instrument that may be so secured.

This statement is filed without the debtor's signature to perfect a security interest in collateral. (Check ☐ if so)
☐ Already subject to a security interest in another jurisdiction when it was brought into this state.
☐ which is proceeds of the original collateral described above in which a security interest was perfected:

Check ☐ if covered: ☐ Proceeds of Collateral are also covered. ☐ Products of Collateral are also covered. No. of additional Sheets presented:

Filed with:

By:_____

Signature(s) of Debtor(s)

By:_____

Signature(s) of Secured Party(ies)

The Bulk Sales Law of the Uniform Commercial Code must be complied with when a going business is transferred with the real estate being only incidental to the sale. The following Bulk Sales Affidavit listing creditors at the time of transfer and the amounts of their claims is a typical form for this purpose.

No. 4-4
BULK SALES AFFIDAVIT
List Of Creditors

State of_____)
) ss.
County of_____)
_____, being first duly sworn, deposes
      (Name)
and says:

That he is the_____(Title)_____of_____Company, transferor, and is authorized to execute this list of creditors.

Set forth below are the names and addresses of all creditors whose claims are acknowledged, with the amounts of their claims.

Name of Creditor	Address	Amount of Claim
1._____	_____	$_____
2._____	_____	$_____
3._____	_____	$_____

That the names and addresses of all persons who are known to him to assert claims against_____Company, transferor, whose claims are disputed or, if partially admitted, the amounts of the claim acknowledged are set forth as follows:

Name of Claimant	Address	Amount of Claim	Amount of Claim Admitted or Denied
1._____	_____	$_____	$_____
2._____	_____	$_____	$_____
3._____	_____	$_____	$_____

Sworn to before me
this_____day of
_____, 19_____ .

For_____Company, Transferor

_____

CLAUSES IN BILLS OF SALE

Agreement By Seller Not To Engage In Similar Business

In consideration of the Buyer complying with the terms and conditions of this agreement, the Seller covenants not to engage, directly or indirectly, in a similar business at any time within_____years from the date hereof, within a radius of_____ miles from the aforesaid premises.

Agreement By Buyer To Pay Seller's Debts

The Buyer, his successors and assigns, agrees to assume and fully discharge all debts, obligations and personal liabilities of the Seller's in connection with the aforesaid business.

Representations By The Seller

As further assurance to the Buyer, I, the Seller represent and covenant:
1. That I am the lawful owner of the aforesaid inventory.
2. That I have the right to sell, transfer and convey the same.
3. That the same is free of any indebtedness whatsoever.
4. That I will warrant and defend the title to said items of inventory against all persons, companies and corporations whatsoever.

5

Bonds

5

Bonds

A Bond is an instrument, generally under seal, that creates evidence of an indebtedness. It obligates the maker, his heirs and assigns, to pay a stipulated sum to another at a specified time. In real estate it is secured by a mortgage or other lien.

In some jurisdictions a bond is required to accompany the mortgage. This bond is not recorded. In the past the penalty of the bond was twice the amount of the money secured, but now it is usually the same amount. In New York State a combined bond and mortgage form is occasionally used. (See page 72). In other jurisdictions, such as Florida, the debt is evidenced by a promissory note instead of a bond.

A properly drawn bond contains a promise to pay a specified amount, at a certain time, to the party named; the conditions, if any; and a testimonium clause (signed, sealed, witnessed and dated). The following sample bond form contains all necessary elements.

    a. (OPENING WORDING)
KNOW ALL MEN BY THESE PRESENTS,
    b. (PARTIES)
    That_____and_____
_____, his wife, residing at_____Street, City
of_____, State of_____, hereinafter designated as obligors, do hereby acknowledge to be justly indebted to the_____Corporation, organized under the laws of the State of_____, having its principal place of business at_____ _____Avenue,_____City, State of_____,
herein designated as obligee,
    c. (AMOUNT OF INDEBTEDNESS & MANNER OF PAYMENT)
    in the sum of_____Dollars ($_____)
lawful money of the United States, which sum said obligors do hereby covenant to pay to obligee, its successors or assigns, with interest as follows:
    The sum of $_____on the first day of_____, 19_____
and a like sum on the first day of each and every month thereafter, until the first day of
_____, 19_____, when the balance of said principal sum shall be due and payable; said payments to be applied first to the interest on said principal sum at the rate of_____
% per annum, computed from the date hereof and the balance on account of principal.

The obligors have the privilege of paying the whole or any part of the principal sum at any time.

d. (WHERE PAYABLE)

All sums under this bond and the mortgage securing this bond are payable at the aforesaid principal office of the obligee in lawful money as aforesaid or at which other place as obligee may later designate in writing.

e. (DEFAULT PROVISIONS)

The whole of the principal sum or any part thereof, and of any other sums of money secured by the mortgage given to secure this bond, shall, forthwith or thereafter, at the option of the obligee, become due and payable if default be made in any payment under this bond or upon the happening of any default which, by the terms of the mortgage given to secure this bond shall entitle the mortgagee to declare the same, or any part thereof, to be due and payable: and all of the covenants, agreements, terms and conditions of said mortgage are hereby incorporated herein with the same force and effect as if herein set forth at length.

If more than one person joins in the execution of this bond, the obligation shall be joint and several.

f. (SIGNED, SEALED, WITNESSED, DATED)

Signed and sealed this_____day of_____, 19_____. In the Presence Of:

_____   _____ (Seal)
_____   _____ (Seal)

No. 5–1
BOND
Single[1]

KNOW ALL MEN BY THESE PRESENTS: That I, _____
_____, residing at_____Road, City of_____,
County of_____, State of_____, do hereby acknowledge
myself to be justly indebted unto_____Bank, a corporation
organized under the laws of the State of_____, having its principal
place of business at_____ _____Avenue,_____
City, County of_____, State of_____, in the sum
of _____($_____)
Dollars, lawful money of the United States, to be paid to said_____
Bank And Trust Company, its successors or assigns, for which payment well and truly to be made, I bind myself, my heirs, executors and administrators, and every of them, firmly by these presents.

Signed and sealed this_____ day of_____, 19____.
In the Presence Of:

_____ (L.S.)

---

1. A bond single is a bond without a condition.

No. 5–2
BOND
By More Than One Obligor

KNOW ALL MEN BY THESE PRESENTS, that we_____
_____of_____, and_____
_____, of_____, (the Obligors), do acknowledge ourselves to be justly indebted unto _____
_____of_____, (the Obligee), in the sum of_____
_____dollars ($_____), lawful money
of the United States to be paid to the said Obligee, his successors or assigns, for which
payment well and truly to be made, we do bind ourselves, our heirs, executors and administrators, jointly and severally firmly by these presents.[1]

    We, the above bound, covenant to pay to the Obligee, his successors or assigns, on
_____, 19_____, with interest to be compounded from_____,
19_____, at the rate of_____% per annum, to be paid on_____,
19_____, and monthly thereafter until paid in full.

    It is hereby expressly agreed that the whole of the said principal sum shall become due
at the option of the Obligee after default in payment of interest for_____days, or
after default in payment of any installment of principal for_____days, or after
default in payment of tax, water rate or assessment for_____days after notice and
demand.

    Signed and sealed this_____day of_____, 19_____. In the presence of

_____   _____(L.S.)

_____   _____(L.S.)

No. 5–3
BOND
Including Additional
Covenants And Aggreements

KNOW ALL MEN BY THESE PRESENTS That,_____
_____, hereinafter designated as the OB-
LIGOR, do_____hereby acknowledge_____to be indebted to
the_____SAVINGS AND LOAN ASSOCIATION, a
savings and loan association, organized and existing under the laws of the UNITED
STATES OF AMERICA, having its office and principal place of business at_____
_____, in the Town of_____
_____, County, _____, hereinafter designated as the OB-
LIGEE, in the sum of_____Dollars
($_____), lawful money of the United States, which sum, with interest at the

---

1. If the heirs are to be bound jointly only, substitute the words "jointly but not severally" for "jointly and severally."

rate of_____per centum (_____%) per annum, from the date hereof, said **OBLIGOR** does hereby covenant and agree to pay to the said Obligee, its successors or assigns, at the Office of the Obligee at_____or such other place as it may designate, in installments as follows:

By payment of_____Dollars, ($_____) on the 1st day of_____, 19____, and thereafter in payments of _____Dollars ($_____) on the 1st day of each and every month thereafter until the whole of the said principal sum and interest shall be fully paid, which interest shall be computed on a monthly basis. The final payment of principal and interest, if not sooner paid, shall be due and payable on the first day of_____.

AND IT IS FURTHER EXPRESSLY COVENANTED AND AGREED AS FOLLOWS:

FIRST: That said installment payments may be applied by the Obligee in the following order: FIRST, to the payment of interest; SECOND, to the payment of all taxes, water rates, assessments, fire insurance premiums and other charges affecting the premises described in the mortgage given to secure this obligation, which the Obligee shall have paid; and THIRD, toward the payment of the aforesaid principal sum.

SECOND: That the whole of the principal sum remaining unpaid, shall become due forthwith, at the option of the Obligee, its successors or assigns, after default in the payment of any monthly installment aforesaid for thirty days, or after default in the payment of any taxes, water rates, assessments, insurance premiums, and/or similar charges affecting the mortgaged premises for thirty days, or upon the happening of any event by which, in any case, under the terms of the mortgage securing this bond, the said principal sum may or shall become due and payable.

THIRD: That the Obligee may pay taxes, water rates, assessments, insurance premiums and/or similar charges affecting the mortgage premises, and that all such payments or advances shall be added to and become a part of the unpaid balance of the indebtedness aforesaid as of the first day of the month in which such payments are made or advanced, and shall be deemed to be secured in like manner.

FOURTH: That the Obligor hereby becomes a member (borrower) of the Obligee (Association) and the Obligor hereby agrees to abide by the terms and provisions of Obligee's charter and by-laws as they are now and as they may be hereafter revised, altered or amended.

FIFTH: That the condition of the above obligation is such that if the above Obligor, or the heirs, executors or administrators of said Obligor shall well and truly pay or cause to be paid to the Obligee, its successors or assigns, the aforesaid just and full sum of_____ _____Dollars ($_____), with interest as hereinbefore stated, and also all taxes, assessments, water rates and insurance premiums hereinbefore mentioned, then the above obligation to be void, otherwise to remain in full force and effect.

SIXTH: That the Obligor together with, and in addition to monthly payments of principal and interest payable under the terms of this bond, on the first of each month, until said bond is fully paid, will pay to the Obligee, an installment of the taxes and special assessments levied, or to be levied, against the premises covered by the mortgage given to secure this bond. Such installments shall be equal to the estimated taxes and assessments next due (as estimated by the Obligee) less all installments already paid therefor, divided by the number of months that are to elapse before one month prior to the date when such taxes and assessments will become due and shall be held in trust by the Obligee to pay such taxes and assessments when due. If the total of such payments made by the Obligor shall exceed the amount actually paid by the Obligee for taxes and assessments, such excess shall be credited by the Obligee on subsequent payments of the same nature to be made by the Obligor. If however, such payments made by the Obligor shall not be sufficient to pay taxes and assessments, when the same shall become due and payable, then the Obligor shall pay to the Obligee any amount necessary to make up the deficiency on or before the date when payment of such taxes and assessments shall be due.

SEVENTH: That all the covenants and agreements made by the Obligor in the mortgage covering the premises therein described and collateral hereto are made part of this instrument.

EIGHTH: A. That in the event any payment shall become over-due for a period in excess of fifteen (15) days but not more than thirty (30) days, a "late charge" not to exceed an amount of four per centum (4%) of any installment so over-due may be charged by the holder hereof for the purpose of defraying the expense incident to handling such delinquent payment. B. That in the event any payment, as herein provided, shall become overdue for a period in excess of 30 days, interest shall be charged at the rate of_____ _____per cent (_____%) per annum on the principal balance then due, until said payment is made. C. The Obligors reserve the privilege of prepaying the debt, in whole or part, with interest to the date of payment, at any time. When the total amount so prepaid in any one year exceeds twenty per centum of the original principal amount of the indebtedness secured by this bond and the accompanying mortgage, the Obligors agree to pay an amount to not more than SIX MONTHS' interest on the excess amount so prepaid for the privilege of such prepayment. D. Notwithstanding any other provision of law, or any other provision contained in the within instrument, the unpaid balance of the loan may be prepaid, in whole or in part, without penalty, on or after three years from the date hereof.

NINTH: That if more than one party joins in the execution of this instrument, the covenants and agreements herein shall be their joint and several obligations and, if any be of other than the masculine sex, the relative words herein shall be read as if written in the plural and/or such other gender accordingly, as the case may be.

SIGNED AND SEALED this_____day of_____ nineteen hundred and _____.
IN PRESENCE OF:

_____   _____(L.S.)
_____   _____(L.S.)

No. 5–4
BOND AND MORTGAGE
Combined Statutory Short Form[1]

THIS BOND AND MORTGAGE, made the_____day of_____, 19_____,
between_____, herein referred to as the mortgagor, and
_____, herein referred to as the mort-
gagee.

WITNESSETH, that the mortgagor, does hereby acknowledge himself to be indebted
to the mortgagee in the sum of_____dollars ($_____
_____), lawful money of the United States, which the mortgagor does hereby agree
and bind himself to repay to the mortgagee, his successors or assigns, on the_____
day of_____, 19_____, with interest thereon to be computed at the rate of
_____% per annum, and to be paid on the_____day of_____
_____next ensuing the date hereof and_____thereafter, and to secure the payment of which the mortgagor hereby mortgages to the mortgagee all that certain

(Here include description)

THE MORTGAGOR covenants with the mortgagee as follows:

1. That the mortgagor will pay the indebtedness as hereinbefore provided.

2. That the mortgagor will keep the buildings on the premises insured against loss by
fire for the benefit of the mortgagee.

3. That no building on the premises shall be removed or demolished without the
consent of the mortgagee.

4. That the whole of said principal sum shall become due after default in the payment
of any installment of principal or of interest for 30 days or after default in the payment of
any tax, water rate or assessment for 30 days after notice and demand.

5. That the holder of this bond and mortgage, in any action to foreclose the mortgage,
shall be entitled to the appointment of a receiver.

6. That the mortgagor will pay all taxes, assessments or water rates, and in default
thereof, the mortgagee may pay the same.

7. That the mortgagor, within 6 days upon request in person or within 30 days upon
request by mail, will furnish a statement of the amount due on this bond and mortgage.

8. That notice and demand or request may be in writing and may be served in person
or by mail.

9. That the mortgagor warrants the title to the premises.

In witness whereof this bond and mortgage has been duly signed and sealed by the
mortgagor. In The Presents Of:

_____ (L.S.)

---

1. Adapted from N.Y. Real Property Law, §258, Sched. N.

No. 5–5
CONTRACTOR'S BID BOND

KNOW ALL MEN BY THESE PRESENTS, that we

as Principal, hereinafter called the Principal, and

a corporation duly organized under the laws of the State of

as Surety, hereinafter called the Surety, are held and firmly bound unto

as Obligee, hereinafter called the Obligee, in the sum of

Dollars ($_____),

for the payment of which sum well and truly to be made, the said Principal and the said Surety, bind ourselves, our heirs, executors, administrators, successors and assigns, jointly and severally, firmly by these presents.

WHEREAS, the Principal has submitted a bid for

NOW, THEREFORE, if the Obligee shall accept the bid of the Principal and the Principal shall enter into a Contract with the Obligee in accordance with the terms of such bid, and give such bond or bonds as may be specified in the bidding or Contract Documents with good and sufficient surety for the faithful performance of such Contract and for the prompt payment of labor and material furnished in the prosecution thereof, or in the event of the failure of the Principal to enter such Contract and give such bond or bonds, if the Principal shall pay to the Obligee the difference not to exceed the penalty hereof between the amount specified in said bid and such larger amount for which the Obligee may in good faith contract with another party to perform the Work covered by said bid, then this obligation shall be null and void, otherwise to remain in full force and effect.

Signed and sealed this   day of   , 19   .

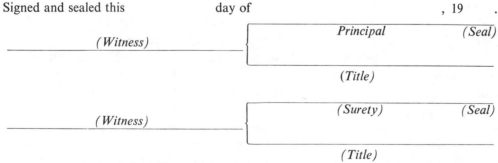

(Reproduced with permission of The American Institute Of Architects. Further reproduction is not authorized.)

No. 5–6
CONTRACTOR'S PERFORMANCE BOND

KNOW ALL MEN BY THESE PRESENTS: that

(Here insert full name and address or legal title of Contractor)

as Principal, hereinafter called Contractor, and,

(Here insert full name and address or legal title of Surety)

as Surety, hereinafter called Surety, and held and firmly bound unto

(Here insert full name and address or legal title of Owner)

as Obligee, hereinafter called Owner, in the amount of

Dollars ($_____),

for the payment whereof Contractor and Surety bind themselves, their heirs, executors, administrators, successors and assigns jointly and severally, firmly by these presents.

WHEREAS,

Contractor has by written agreement dated   19   , entered into a contract with Owner for

in accordance with Drawings and Specifications prepared by

(Here insert full name and address or legal title of Architect)

which contract is by reference made a part hereof, and is hereinafter referred to as the Contract.

NOW, THEREFORE, THE CONDITION OF THIS OBLIGATION is such that, if Contractor shall promptly and faithfully perform said Contract, then this obligation shall be null and void; otherwise it shall remain in full force and effect.

The Surety hereby waives notice of any alteration or extension of time made by the Owner.

Whenever Contractor shall be, and declared by Owner to be in default under the Contract, the Owner having performed Owner's obligations thereunder, the Surety may promptly remedy the default, or shall promptly

1) Complete the Contract in accordance with its terms and conditions, or

2) Obtain a bid or bids for completing the Contract in accordance with its terms and conditions, and upon determination by Surety of the lowest responsible bidder, or, if the Owner elects, upon determination by the Owner and the Surety jointly of the lowest responsible bidder, arrange for a contract between such bidder and Owner, and make available as Work progresses (even though there should be a default or a succession of defaults under the contract or contracts of completion arranged under this paragraph) sufficient funds to pay the cost of completion less the balance of the contract price; but not exceeding, including other costs and damages for which the Surety may be liable hereunder, the amount set forth in the first paragraph hereof. The term "balance of the contract price," as used in this paragraph, shall mean the total amount payable by Owner to Contractor under the Contract and any amendments thereto, less the amount properly paid by Owner to Contractor.

Any suit under this bond must be instituted before the expiration of two (2) years from the date on which final payment under the Contract falls due.

No right of action shall accrue on this bond to or for the use of any person or corporation other than the Owner named herein or the heirs, executors, administrators or successors of the Owner.

Signed and sealed this   day of   , 19

_____   ⎧ _____
        (Witness)   ⎨ (Principal)   (Seal)
                            ⎩ _____
                                            (Title)

_____   ⎧ _____
        (Witness)   ⎨ (Surety)   (Seal)
                            ⎩ _____
                                            (Title)

(Reproduced with permission of The American Institute Of Architects. Further reproduction is not authorized.)

No. 5–7

CONTRACTOR'S LABOR AND MATERIAL PAYMENT BOND

THIS BOND IS ISSUED SIMULTANEOUSLY WITH PERFORMANCE BOND IN FAVOR OF THE OWNER CONDITIONED ON THE FULL AND FAITHFUL PERFORMANCE OF THE CONTRACT

KNOW ALL MEN BY THESE PRESENTS: that

> (Here insert full name and address or legal title of Contractor)

as Principal, hereinafter called Principal, and,

> (Here insert full name and address or legal title of Surety)

as Surety, hereinafter called Surety, are held and firmly bound unto

> (Here insert full name and address or legal title Owner)

as Obligee, hereinafter called Owner, for the use and benefit of claimants as hereinbelow defined, in the amount of

> (Here insert a sum equal to at least one-half of
> the contract price)   Dollars ($_____),

for the payment whereof Principal and Surety bind themselves, their heirs, executors, administrators, successors and assigns, jointly and severally, firmly by these presents.

WHEREAS,

Principal has by written agreement dated   19   , entered into a contract with Owner for

in accordance with Drawings and Specifications prepared by

> (Here insert full name and address or legal title of Architect)

which contract is by reference made a part hereof, and is hereinafter referred to as the Contract.

NOW, THEREFORE, THE CONDITION OF THIS OBLIGATION is such that, if Principal shall promptly make payment to all claimants as hereinafter defined, for all labor and material used or reasonably required for use in the performance of the Contract, then this obligation shall be void; otherwise it shall remain in full force and effect, subject, however, to the following conditions:

1. A claimant is defined as one having a direct contract with the Principal or with a Subcontractor of the Principal for labor, material, or both, used or reasonably required for use in the performance of the Contract, labor and material being construed to include that part of water, gas, power, light, heat, oil, gasoline, telephone service or rental of equipment directly applicable to the Contract.

2. The above named Principal and Surety hereby jointly and severally agree with the Owner that every claimant as herein defined, who has not been paid in full before the expiration of a period of ninety (90) days after the date on which the last of such claimant's work or labor was done or performed, or materials were furnished by such claimant, may sue on this bond for the use of such claimant, prosecute the suit to final judgment for such sum or sums as may be justly due claimant, and have execution thereon. The Owner shall not be liable for the payment of any costs or expenses of any such suit.

3. No suit or action shall be commenced hereunder by any claimant:

a) Unless claimant, other than one having a direct contract with the Principal, shall have given written notice to any two of the following: the Principal, the Owner, or the Surety above named, within ninety (90) days after such claimant did or performed the last of the work or labor, or furnished the last of the materials for which said claim is made, stating with substantial accuracy the amount claimed and the name of the party to whom the materials were furnished, or for whom the work or labor was done or performed. Such notice shall be served by mailing the same by registered mail or certified mail, postage prepaid, in an envelope addressed to the Principal, Owner or Surety, at any place where an office is regularly maintained for the transaction of business, or served in any manner in which legal process may be served in the state in which the aforesaid project is located, save that such service need not be made by a public officer.

(b) After the expiration of one (1) year following the date on which Principal ceased Work on said Contract, it being understood, however, that if any limitation embodied in this bond is prohibited by any law controlling the construction hereof such limitation shall be deemed to be amended so as to be equal to the minimum period of limitation permitted by such law.

c) Other than in a state court of competent jurisdiction in and for the country or other political subdivision of the state in which the Project, or any part thereof, is situated, or in the United States District Court for the district in which the Project, or any part thereof, is situated, and not elsewhere.

4. The amount of this bond shall be reduced by and to the extent of any payment or payments made in good faith hereunder, inclusive of the payment by Surety of mechanics' liens which may be filed of record against said improvement, whether or not claim for the amount of such lien be presented under and against this bond.

Signed and sealed this   day of   , 19

_____ | (Principal) (Seal)
(Witness) |_____
| (Title)

_____ | (Surety) (Seal)
(Witness) |_____
| (Title)

(Reproduced with permission of The American Institute Of Architects. Further reproduction is not authorized.)

No. 5–8
ASSIGNMENT OF BOND

KNOW ALL MEN BY THESE PRESENTS,

That I_____, residing at_____Street, City of_____, State of_____, party of the first part, for and consideration of the sum of_____dollars ($_____), lawful money of the United States, to me in hand paid by_____ _____, residing at_____Avenue, City of _____, State of_____, party of the second part, the receipt whereof is hereby acknowledged, do by these presents bargain, sell and assign unto the said party of the second part, and assigns, a certain written bond or obligation, bearing the date of_____, 19_____, executed by one_____ _____, to me, the said_____, and all sums of money due or to become due, thereon, and I hereby covenant with said party of the second part that there is now due on the said bond or obligation according to the condition thereof, for principal and interest, the sum of_____ _____dollars ($_____), lawful money of the United States.

Dated:_____, 19_____.

_____(Seal)

CLAUSES IN BONDS

Default Provision

It is expressly covenanted and agreed that in the event of default in the payment of any monthly installment for_____days, or after default in the payment of taxes, assessments, insurance premiums, utility charges or similar indebtedness upon the mortgaged premises for_____days, under the terms of the mortgage securing this bond, the principal sum may or shall become due and payable.

Late Charge Provision

Should a payment become past due for a period of_____days but not more than _____days, a late charge of_____% of any installment so overdue shall be charged by the holder hereof. In the event a payment shall become overdue for a period in excess of _____days, interest shall be charged at the rate of_____% per annum on the principal balance then due until said payment is made.

Secured By Mortage

This bond is secured by a mortgage bearing even date and simultaneously executed, in the amount of $ _____, and covering a certain parcel of land situate, lying and being in the city of_____, County of _____ State of_____.

Provision For Installment Payment

The obligor does hereby covenant to pay the obligee, his executors, administrators or assigns, in installments as follows: $_____, on the_____day of_____ _____, 19_____, and a like sum on the_____day of each and every month thereafter until the full amount of said principal sum is paid, and the interest upon the whole sum, or upon so much thereto as shall remain unpaid, to be computed from the_____ day of_____, 19_____, at the rate of_____% per annum. The final payment of principal and interest, if not sooner paid, shall be due and payable on the_____day of _____, 19_____.

6

Brokerage Agreements

6

Brokerage Agreements

GENERAL INFORMATION

A real estate broker or Realtor[1] is a licensed person who,[2] for a fee, acts for another in selling, leasing or managing real property. Unless otherwise provided for, he is generally limited to finding a purchaser or lessee who is ready, willing and able to complete a transaction under the stipulated price and terms.

A broker has a confidential, fiduciary relationship with his principal. Though he acts in the best interest of the one who employs him, he also has a duty and responsibility to deal fairly and honestly with the other party.

A broker may act as the agent for the seller, the purchaser or for *both* parties. When negotiating in a dual employment capacity he is sometimes referred to as a "middleman." His position as such must be made known and then agreed to by both parties. Each party is responsible for the payment of his commission. As a matter of actual practice, however, in the majority of instances, it is the seller of real estate who employs the broker.

As a general rule, a real estate salesman acts in behalf of his employing broker. He is his licensed, authorized representative and to a great extent, the broker is responsible for his actions.

DURATION OF AGENCY

A broker is employed for an express or implied period of time. In the absence of an agreement or understanding as to length of the agency, a reasonable period is substituted. To protect the broker after the term of an agency agreement expires, an extension of time is sometimes agreed to, allowing him to continue negotiating with certain specified parties.

A principal may revoke or withdraw a listing at any time. The broker, however, may be justified in taking legal action to receive his commission. This may occur when revoking the agency is not done in good faith, but rather to avoid paying a commission.

---

1. A Realtor is "A professional in real estate who subscribes to a strict code of ethics as a member of the local and state boards and the National Association of Real Estate Boards." The term Realtor is a service mark registered in the United States Patent Office. Only members of the National Association Of Real Estate Boards and its state and local affiliates may use it and display its seal.
2. Licensed by the state in which he resides and practices.

EMPLOYMENT OF BROKER

Listing real property with brokers follows one of three forms: 1. Open Listing, 2. Exclusive Agency Listing, or 3. Exclusive Right of Sale.

1. Open Listing

The most familiar form of listing in use in real estate offices is the Open Listing. It occurs when an owner lists his property with more than one brokerage firm. It may be implied simply by oral consent or it can be in writing. The first broker to create a meeting of minds (produce a ready, willing and able buyer) under the terms and conditions of an open listing is the procuring cause of the transaction and is the only one entitled to receive a commission. When the sale is consummated it is not necessary for the owner to notify the other listing offices, for the listing is automatically terminated by the sale.

No. 6–1
OPEN LISTING AGREEMENT

In consideration of the services of_____here-
inafter called broker, I hereby list with said broker for a period of_____days from date
hereof, the following described property and at the following described price and terms:

ADDRESS:_____
LEGAL DESCRIPTION:_____
SELLING PRICE: $_____FURN._____UNFURN._____
EXISTING MORTGAGE(S)_____
MORTGAGE COMMITMENTS:_____
MINIMUM CASH REQUIRED:_____

I agree to pay to the broker a commission of_____per cent (_____%)
of the selling price should the broker find a purchaser ready, willing and able to buy at the
above price and terms, or if he sells the property at other price and terms agreeable to me.

It is understood that this listing agreement in no way prohibits me from selling the property direct. I retain the right to sell to any party not first contacted by the broker. I also retain the right to list my property for sale with any other broker or brokers. I also have the right to withdraw the property from the market upon notice to the broker.

Should a sale be made within six months after this authorization terminates to parties with whom the broker may negotiate during the term hereof, and whose name has been disclosed to me, then I agree to pay said commission to said broker.

Should the property be sold, I agree to furnish the purchaser a good and sufficient Warranty Deed, and a complete abstract of title.

Should deposit money paid on account of purchase be forfeited by the purchaser, one half shall be retained by the broker, providing said amount does not exceed the commission.

I hereby acknowledge receipt of a copy of this authorization to sell.
Signed on the_____day of _____, 19_____.

_____   _____(Seal)
Witness   Owner

_____   _____(Seal)
Witness   Owner

In consideration of the foregoing listing and authorization, the undersigned broker agrees to use diligence in procuring a purchaser.

_____
Broker

2. Exclusive Agency

A listing, generally in writing, in which an owner gives it exclusively to only one real estate broker or office to sell or lease for a specified period of time. Should another real estate agent be the procuring cause of the sale, the one possessing the Exclusive Agency is also entitled to collect a commission. The only time the broker is not entitled to compensation upon a sale being made is if the owner sells the property himself.

No. 6–2
EXCLUSIVE LISTING

In consideration of the services of_____hereinafter called broker, I hereby list with said broker, exclusively, for a period of_____days from date hereof, the following described property and at the following described price and terms:

ADDRESS:_____
LEGAL DESCRIPTION_____
SELLING PRICE $_____FURN._____UNFURN. _____
MORTGAGE COMMITMENTS:_____
MINIMUM CASH REQUIRED:_____

I hereby agree to pay said broker as commission_____ (_____) per cent of the selling price should, during the time set forth herein, said property be sold by said broker or by another broker, at the above price and terms agreeable to me.

It is understood that this listing agreement in no way prohibits me from selling the property direct. I retain the right to sell to any party not first contacted by the broker or a co-operating broker.

Should a sale be made within six months after this authorization terminates to parties with whom said broker, or a co-operating broker, may negotiate during the term hereof, and whose name has been disclosed to me, then I agree to pay said commission to said broker.

In case the above described property is sold or disposed of within the time specified, I agree to make the purchaser a good and sufficient warranty deed to the same and to furnish a complete abstract of title brought down to date at my expense. Interests, taxes, rents if any, shall be prorated as of date of closing.

I agree to refer to said broker all other brokers who may contact me directly, and to furnish said broker with their names.

Should a deposit or amounts paid on account of purchase be forfeited, one half may be retained by said broker, providing however, that the broker's share of any forfeited deposit or amounts paid on account of purchase, shall not exceed the commission.

I hereby acknowledge receipt of a copy of this authorization to sell.

Signed on the_____day of_____, 19_____.

_____   _____(Seal)
Witness   Owner

_____   _____(Seal)
Witness   Owner

In consideration of the foregoing listing and authorization the undersigned broker agrees to use diligence in procuring a purchaser.

_____
                                         Broker

By_____

3. Exclusive Right of Sale

A listing agreement, usually in writing, employing a broker for a specified period of time to the exclusion of all others. In this form of exclusive not only is the broker protected in the event of a sale by another broker, but he is also entitled to a commission even if the owner sells the property himself.

An Exclusive Right of Sale can be in the form of a Multiple Listing, that is, given to one broker for the express purpose of his distributing it to others. Many local Real Estate Boards have a central clearing system where such multiple listings are submitted by member brokers. Photos and brochures are printed and sent to participating agents. In this way the client is assured that his property will be getting wide distribution. The commission is shared by the listing and the selling brokers.

No. 6–3
EXCLUSIVE RIGHT OF SALE LISTING AND MULTIPLE LISTING

Date_____

1. In consideration of your agreement to list and to use your efforts to secure a purchaser for the property described as:_____

_____

and your further agreement to advertise the property and list it with other Realtors or real estate brokers, I hereby give you for a period of_____months from this date (and thereafter until this agreement is revoked by ten days' written notice delivered to you), the exclusive right and authority to sell the property at the following price and terms, or at any other price and terms acceptable to me:

Price: _____

Terms: _____

Interest on encumbrances, taxes, insurance and rents shall be adjusted prorata at date of closing. Improvement liens are to be paid by me.

2. In case you secure a purchaser for the property, the usual and customary practice for the examination, curing title and for closing the transaction shall apply. I agree to deliver to the purchaser a good and sufficient warranty deed, free and clear of all liens and encumbrances except encumbrances of record and those which the purchaser shall assume as part of the purchase price and which are especially detailed above.

3. For finding a purchaser for the above property:

  A. I agree to pay the commission of_____ % of the sales price.

  B. I agree to pay you a Special Sales Service fee of_____ % of the sales price in addition to the commission above, for special services to be rendered by you.

  C. The commission and service fee are to be paid whether the Purchaser be secured by you or me, or by any other person, at the price and upon the terms mentioned or at any other price or terms acceptable to me; or if the property is afterwards sold within three (3) months from the termination of this agency, to a purchaser to whom it was submitted by you, or a co-operating broker during the continuance of the agency, and whose name has been disclosed to me.

  D. In any exchange of this property, permission is given you to represent and receive commissions from both parties.

4. In consideration of this exclusive listing, you agree:

  A. To carefully inspect my property and secure complete information regarding it.

  B. To direct the concentrated efforts of your organization in bringing about a sale.

  C. To advertise my property as you deem advisable in the local newspapers or other mediums of merit.

  D. To furnish at all times additional information requested by any Realtor or real estate broker, and to assist co-operating brokers in closing a deal on my property when requested to do so.

  E. To promptly pay any co-operating broker who sells the property for his services.

  F. To keep me informed through the salesman in charge as to the progress being made toward the consummation of a deal.

5. In consideration of the above, I agree to refer to you all inquiries of brokers or others interested in my property.

6. As my agent, you are authorized to accept, receipt for and hold all money paid or deposited as a binder thereon and if such deposit shall be forfeited by the prospective purchaser, you may retain one-half of such deposit, but not exceeding the total amount of your commission, as your compensation.

7. I understand that this agreement does not guarantee the sale of my property, but that it does guarantee that you will make an earnest and continued effort to sell same until

this agreement is terminated.

WITNESS: OWNER:

_____   _____

_____   _____

ACCEPTED BY:

_____   Realtor _____

The words "I," "MY" or "ME" shall be considered plural when applicable.

(Reproduced with permission of the Miami Board of Realtors, Miami, Fla.)

No. 6-4
LISTING AGREEMENT
EXCLUSIVE RIGHT TO SELL
COPYRIGHT 1969—TULSA REAL ESTATE BOARD

This form officially approved by
the Tulsa Real Estate Board

Permission to use this form
is granted to Realtors Only.

ACREAGE FORM

Owners _____ acres _____ $ _____
Location _____ miles _____ of _____ (town)
on _____ Hwy. (Type roads) _____
Mailing address of property _____
Legal Description _____
_____
_____
_____
County: _____ Minerals: _____
Surface Lease $ _____ Yr. _____ Mineral Lease $ _____ Yr. _____
Zoning _____ Topography _____
Water Supply: Drinking _____ Stock _____

Gas _____ Elec _____ Phone _____ Septic _____ Sewer _____
_____ acres pasture. _____ acres cultivation. _____ acres timber
_____ acres other (describe) _____
Total acreage tillable _____ Fences _____
Outbuildings and corrals _____
_____
_____
Houses: _____ BR. _____ bath. Other rooms _____
_____
Taxes: _____ Yr. _____ Hmstd ex. _____ Yr. _____
Loan Bal. $ _____ as of _____ Int. _____ %. Yrs. to go _____
Lender _____ Owner carry _____
Owner's Int. rate _____ Owner's terms _____
How shown _____

Sec. _____ Twp. _____ Rge. _____
Remarks: _____
_____
_____
_____
_____
_____
_____
_____
_____
_____
_____

In consideration of the services to be rendered by the undersigned Realtor, I, the undersigned, herein referred to as "Seller", hereby exclusively list with said Realtor the property described above, and grant to said Realtor the exclusive right to sell said property and to accept a deposit thereon, within the terms of this listing, at the price and on the terms herein stated, or at such other price and terms which shall be acceptable to me. This listing shall be subject to the following terms and conditions:

1. This agreement shall be for a term of six months from the date hereof, terminating (except for the provisions of paragraph 2) at midnight on _____
_____ , 19 ___ .

2. Seller agrees to pay a commission equal to _____ per cent (_____) of the total sale price of the property herein described, as and for the compensation of Realtor, in any of the following events:

    a. The sale or exchange of the property during the term of this agreement, whether procured by Realtor, seller, or a third person.

    b. The sale or exchange of the property within one hundred eighty (180) days after the termination of this agreement, if with any one to whom Realtor has shown the property, or with whom the Realtor has negotiated concerning the property prior to the termination of this agreement; provided that this clause shall not apply if Seller re-lists the property at the termination of this agreement with another member of the Tulsa Real Estate Board.

    c. Seller agrees, in the event of an exchange, that Realtor may also negotiate for and receive a commission from the other party.

3. In the event a contract for sale or exchange is entered into with a purchaser, Seller agrees;

    a. To furnish an abstract of title certified to date showing merchantable title to Seller.

    b. At the time prescribed in the contract of sale, to convey the property by general warranty deed to purchaser, free and clear of all liens and encumbrances, except those specifically reserved in the contract.

    c. Unless otherwise provided in the contract of sale, all ad valorem taxes, interest, rents, and other continuing items be prorated to date of transfer.

4. Realtor's sole duty shall be to use his best efforts to effect a sale of the property during the term of this agreement, in accordance with the Code of Ethics of National Association of Real Estate Boards. Realtor shall not be charged with the custody of the property, its management, maintenance, or repair. Realtor shall be entitled to access to the property for the purpose of showing it to prospects at any reasonable hour.

5. Forfeited earnest money, if any, shall be divided equally between Seller and Realtor, except that Realtor's portion shall in no event exceed his regular commission.

6. The term "Realtor" herein shall include any salesman or sub-agents of the Realtor whose signature appears on this agreement.

7. Realtor shall be authorized to place a "For Sale" sign on the property and to remove all other similar signs.

8. Seller warrants the accuracy of the information provided to Realtor herewith and agrees to hold Realtor harmless from any cost, expense or damage due to any information which is withheld by Seller from Realtor, or which is incorrect.

9. This property is offered without regard to race, religion, color, ancestry, or national origin.

10. Seller acknowledges that he has read this agreement and that he has received a copy thereof. Seller agrees to the terms herein set forth.

ACCEPTED this _____ day of _____ , 19_____

_____
Seller-Owner

_____   _____   _____
Realtor   Phone No.   Seller-Owner

By _____   _____
                                               Mailing Address of Seller-Owner

(Reproduced with permission of the Tulsa Real Estate Board, Tulsa, Okla.)

No. 6–5
EXCLUSIVE AUTHORIZATION AND RIGHT TO SELL
California Real Estate Association Standard Form

In consideration of the services of _____ herein called Broker, I hereby employ Broker, exclusively and irrevocable, for the period beginning _____

_____ , 19_____ and ending at midnight _____ , 19_____ , to sell the property situated

in _____ County of _____ California, described as follows:

and I hereby grant Broker the exclusive and irrevocable right to sell said property within said time for _____ ($_____)

dollars and to accept a deposit thereon _____

Terms:

I hereby agree to pay Broker as commission _____ per cent _____ of the selling price if said property is sold during the term hereof or any extension thereof by Broker or by me or by another broker or through any source. If said property is withdrawn from sale, transferred, or leased during the term hereof or any extension thereof, I agree to pay Broker said per cent of the above listed price.

If a sale, lease or other transfer of said property is made within three (3) months after this authorization or any extension thereof terminates to parties with whom Broker negotiates during the term hereof or any extension thereof Broker notifies me in writing of such negotiations, personally or by mail, during the term hereof or any extension thereof, then I agree to pay said commission to Broker.

Evidence of title shall be a California Land Title Association standard coverage form policy of title insurance to be paid for by_____

If deposits or amounts paid on account of purchase price are forfeited, Broker shall be entitled to one half thereof, but not to exceed the amount of the commission.

I hereby acknowledge receipt of a copy hereof.

Dated_____, 19_____   _____

_____California   _____

_____
    Address of Owner   _____

_____
(City)   (Zone)   (Phone)   Owner

In consideration of the execution of the foregoing, the undersigned Broker agrees to use diligence in procuring a purchaser.

_____   _____
    (Address of Broker)   Broker

_____   By _____
  (City)   (Zone)   (phone)

Size of parcel:_____Taxes: $_____per Year
Loan information_____

         (Reproduced with permission of the California Real Estate Association, Los Angeles, Calif.)

As a Broker and his salesman have certain obligations, responsibilities and duties toward one another, a written employment agreement is frequently entered into.

No. 6–6
CONTRACT BETWEEN BROKER AND SALESMAN

THIS AGREEMENT by and between_____, hereinafter referred to as "broker," and_____, hereinafter referred to as "salesman," for and in consideration of their mutual promises and for their mutual benefits WITNESSETH:

THAT, WHEREAS, the broker is duly registered as a real estate broker, and is duly qualified to, and does, procure the listing of real estate for sale, lease or rental, and prospective purchasers, lessees, and renters therefor, and has and enjoys the good will of, and a reputation for dealing with, the public, and also has and maintains an office, properly equipped and staffed, suitable to serving the public as a real estate broker, and

WHEREAS, the salesman is a duly registered real estate salesman and properly qualified to deal with the public as such, and

WHEREAS, it is deemed to be to the mutual advantage of the broker and salesman to form the association hereinafter agreed to, THEREFORE

1. The broker agrees to make available to the salesman all current listings of the office, except such as the broker may find expedient to place exclusively in the temporary possession of some other salesman, and agrees to assist the salesman in his work by advice, instruction, all full cooperation in every way possible.

2. The broker agrees that the salesman may share with other salesman such facilities as the office may be able to furnish, in connection with the subject matter of this contract.

3. The salesman agrees to work diligently and with his best efforts to sell, lease or rent any and all real estate listed with the broker, to solicit additional listings and customers for said broker, and otherwise promote the business of serving the public in real estate transactions, to the end that each of the parties hereto may derive the greatest profit possible.

4. The salesman agrees to conduct his business and regulate his habits so as to maintain and to increase, rather than diminish, the good will and reputation of the broker, and the parties hereto agree to conform to and abide by all laws, rules, regulations and codes of ethics that are binding upon, or applicable to real estate brokers and salesman.

5. The salesman agrees to maintain at his own cost public liability and property damage insurance in the amount of $_____ indemnifying himself and the broker.

6. The usual and customary commissions shall be charged for any service performed hereunder, unless broker shall advise the salesman of any special contract relating to any particular transaction which he undertakes to handle. When the salesman shall perform any service hereunder, whereby a commission is earned, said commission shall, when collected, be divided between the broker and salesman, in which division salesman shall receive_____per cent, and the broker shall receive the balance. In the event that two or more salesmen participate in such a service, or claim to have done so, the amount of the commission over that accruing to the broker shall be divided between the participating salesmen according to agreement between them, or by arbitration. In no case shall the broker be liable to the salesman for any commission unless the same shall have been collected from the party for whom the service was performed.

7. The broker shall not be liable to the salesman for any expenses incurred by him, or for any of his acts, nor shall the salesman be liable to the broker for office help or expense and the salesman shall have no authority to bind the broker by any promise or representation unless specifically authorized in a particular transaction; but expense for attorney's fees, costs, revenue stamps, abstracts and the like which must, by reason of some necessity, be paid from the commission, or is incurred in the collection of, or the attempt to collect, the commission, shall be paid by the parties in the same proportion as provided for herein in the division of the commissions. Suits for commissions shall, agreeable to the law, be maintained only in the name of the broker, and the salesman shall be construed to be a sub-agent only with respect to the clients and customers for whom services shall be performed, and shall otherwise be deemed to be an independent contractor and not a servant employee, joint adventurer or partner of the broker.

8. This contract, and the association created hereby, may be terminated by either party hereto, at any time upon notice given to the other; but the rights of the parties to any commission, which accrued prior to said notice, shall not be divested by the termination of this contract.

9. The salesman shall not, after the termination of this contract, use to his own advantage, or to the advantage of any other person or corporation, any information gained from the files or business of the broker, relating to property for sale, lease or rental.

IN WITNESS WHEREOF the parties hereto have signed or caused to be signed, these presents, this_____day of_____, 19_____.

Witnesses:

_____
The Broker

_____

_____   _____
The Salesman

(Reproduced with permission of the Florida Association Of Realtors)

No. 6–7
CONTRACT BETWEEN REAL ESTATE CORPORATION
AND SALESMAN

A G R E E M E N T

FOR PROFESSIONAL SERVICES BETWEEN_____,

AN INDIVIDUAL, AND_____A_____CORPORATION

(state)

1. By the signing of this agreement, it shall be known that the above named individual will be performing professional services for the corporation as an independent contractor and that the individual will not be subject to the will and control of the corporation, nor will the corporation have the right to control either the method and the result of the services so performed.

2. Further, it is agreed that the corporation will not be held responsible for the collection and payment of taxes or contributions of any nature on behalf of the individual including, but not by way of limitation, contributions on behalf of the individual for Federal Social Security (F.I.C.A.) for Federal and State Unemployment Compensation, for State Workman's Compensation Insurance, for State Real Estate Commission Registration, for State, County and Municipal Occupational Licensing or for insurance, annuity, or retirement program in which the individual may participate as part of a collective group.

3. The individual will perform professional services to the public as a Registered Real Estate Salesman or Broker-Salesman with the corporation functioning as the Registered Real Estate Broker of the State of_____, and the individual will devote sufficient time and services to the public on behalf of the corporation to accomplish the mutual purposes of the parties.

4. In performing these professional services to the public, the individual will pay all his travel and entertainment expense, and telephone calls (except direct dial calls from the

home offices), and will be reimbursed by the corporation only in accordance with the procedures outlined in the corporation's Procedure Manual as amended from time to time. It shall be understood that all such expense reimbursement received shall be reported to the government as fees paid, and it shall be the burden of the individual to substantiate the fees so received as deductible expense.

5. The individual shall receive as compensation for his public services provided, on all property sales which the individual has listed and sold, an amount equal to_____% of the net cash fees, as and when received by the said corporation, after deducting for any co-broker, referral, or other direct expenses required to complete the transaction, or any expenses, including legal fees, of collecting the commission or defending against any claims thereon; provided, however, that during the initial probationary period of association of the individual with the corporation, which shall be for at least six months after the date of this agreement, the compensation to the individual shall be at_____% of the said net cash fees as and when received by the corporation, after the said deduction, and the individual shall not be reimbursed for his travel and entertainment expense, and telephone calls as set forth in paragraph 4 hereof. In the event the individual performs one of the two functions of listing and selling a property, he shall receive only one-half of the compensation due him as set forth above, and the fellow sales associate who performed the other function shall receive one-half, unless the two sales associates, by written agreement approved by the corporation, shall have agreed on the other division equitably based on the services performed by each.

6. Each of the properties on which the individual shall devote his time and effort shall be assigned an LP (Listed Property) Number by the corporation, and the LP Number shall refer to the property itself and not to the owner or area in which it is located. In order to accomplish the mutual purposes of the parties, the individual shall not devote time and effort on any property which has not been so assigned an LP Number by the corporation.

7. It is agreed by the individual that all LP Numbered sales leads and all leads to prospective buyers are the property of the corporation at all times, and must be returned to the corporation at the time of any termination of the individual's services, or upon demand by the corporation. Further, since the LP Numbered property leads always remain the property of the corporation, the individual, if terminated, will refrain from soliciting business from the principals involved in the property leads, and leads to prospective buyers, and will not reveal any information whatsoever relative to the property leads, or prospective buyer leads, to any other person, associate, employee, agent, or intermediary, for a period of one year following the date of termination.

8. The individual will hold the corporation harmless against all suits, claims, and obligations which the individual may incur in performing his services as an independent contractor, and the individual shall have no right to bind, contract, or obligate the corporation in the performance of his services even though the individual, for purposes of sales promotion only, may use the title of "Vice President" and may be termed as "Sales Associate" by the corporation.

9. It is understood that the individual will abide by all laws, ethical practices and regulations promulgated by the State of_____Real Estate Commission and will adhere to the procedures and policies of the corporation that are currently in force and as they are changed from time to time.

10. It is further understood and agreed that the performance of professional services by the individual as herein set forth may be terminated at any time, without notice. In the event of such termination, the individual shall receive the compensation due him on those properties concerning which a valid contract of purchase and sale has been executed by the principals prior to termination, but for which the corporation receives its commission after such termination. In the event any portion of a commission due the corporation in which the individual is entitled to participate under the terms of paragraph 5 hereof has been deferred by agreement between the corporation and the principal, the individual shall continue to receive his share of such commission as and when received by the corporation, even after such termination.

11. If the Sales Associate is no longer registered with the company, he will receive _____ % of the net commission received by the corporation on any exclusive listing he procured on which a valid contract of sale is executed by both buyer and seller during the period when the exclusive listing is in legal effect between the owner and the corporation. On open listings secured by the Sales Associates that are in legal effect between the company, or on a terminated exclusive listing, the Sales Associate will receive_____ % of the net commission received by the_____corporation if the sales contract is signed within a period extending_____months from the date that the Sales Associate leaves the _____ corporation. After_____months there will be no commission paid under any circumstances on sales made after termination on open or terminated exclusive listings, whether sold to a buyer to whom the sales associate has presented the property previously, or to a new buyer, or under any circumstances whatsoever.

However, the Sales Associate agrees that these sums will be due to him only in the event he complies with paragraph 7 above, and refrains from contacting the owner of the property or otherwise working on the sale, directly or through another, for a period of twelve months from the date he is no longer associated with the_____ _____corporation.

Sales Associate:

_____(SEAL)

Address:_____

Dated_____19_____   _____
Accepted by:
_____, a Corporation

_____

_____

(SEAL)_____
President

No. 6–8
COMMISSION AGREEMENT
In Letter Form

_____, 19_____

Re: The following described property:

_____

_____

Dear Sirs:

This will confirm the commission agreement regarding the sale of the above described property to_____.

The commission shall be_____ % of the selling price, payable in full upon receipt and acceptance of a bona fide offer by the seller.

It is hereby agreed that_____Realty Company is the sole agent to bring about the subject contract of sale and is the only broker entitled to receive the commission.

Very truly yours,

_____

for_____Realty Company

Agreed to and accepted this

_____day of_____, 19_____.

_____ for

_____Corporation

No. 6–9
COMMISSION AGREEMENT
As Part Of Contract

I, or we, agree to sell the above described property on the terms and conditions stated in the foregoing contract, and do hereby approve, ratify and confirm said contract in all respects. The undersigned acknowledges the employment of the broker named herein and agrees to pay said broker_____ % of the purchase price of the said property as a brokerage fee for finding the above signed purchaser. The brokerage fee shall be paid at time of closing of this transaction except as otherwise provided herein.

No. 6–10
COMMISSION AGREEMENT
As Part Of Contract—Another Form

I (We) agree to pay_____Realty Co., as commission for finding the above signed purchaser(s) for the above described property, the sum of_____ _____dollars ($_____) or one-half of all amounts paid under said contract if said amounts are retained as liquidated damages in the event of a default or failure to perform the terms of this contract on the part of the purchaser.

No. 6–11
COMMISSION AGREEMENT
As Part Of Contract—Another Form

The parties agree that_____ brought about this sale and the seller agrees to pay the commission at the rates established or adopted by the established Board of Real Estate Brokers in the locality where the property is situated.

CLAUSES IN BROKERAGE AGREEMENTS

Provision For Paying Commission If Lessee Renews The Lease

Lessor acknowledges that Lessee was procured through the successful efforts of_____
_____Realty Company, and agrees to pay said agent the local Board of Realtors standard commission on such extensions or renewals when made. On month to month extensions, commissions shall be paid monthly or quarterly.

Provision For Paying Commission If Lessee Purchases The Property

If the property of which the premises are a part is sold by the Lessor to the Lessee during the term of his lease, or during the term of any further extension or renewal agreement (any continued occupancy of the premises by the Lessee after the expiration of this lease shall be considered a further extension or renewal agreement), the Lessor will pay said rental agent a commission on the selling price, said commission to be based upon the_____
_____ Board of Realtors schedule of commissions in effect at the time of sale, deducting from such sales commission any unearned leasing commission previously paid by Lessor from date of expiration of lease.

Clause Giving Broker Power To Execute Contract Of Sale For The Seller

I hereby appoint_____ Realty Company as my true and lawful attorneys in fact, with full power to execute contract of sale in my name and bind me by same.

Broker Waiving Commission Until Closing

The commission shall be_____% of the selling price, payable in full when and if title actually closes. If title does not pass from_____Corporation to _____for any reason whatsoever, the broker hereby waives any and all claims or demands for said commission.

Agreement For Commission When Exchanging Real Estate

In Exchanging (Trading) real property if only one broker is concerned, he is generally placed in the position of acting for both parties. He may hold money in escrow for each and usually receives his commission from both sides. A typical agreement (which will apply if either one or more brokers are involved) reads:

Party A agrees to pay his broker (s)_____the sum of $_____ _____, as brokerage commission, which it is agreed shall be earned when this agreement has been signed by the parties hereto.

Liquidated Damages To Broker And Seller Upon Default By Purchaser

It is agreed that in the event this transaction is not completed due to any default or failure on the part of the purchaser, the said purchaser shall in that event become liable to the broker for brokerage commission as hereinafter provided. It is further agreed that in case of default by the purchaser, the seller may at his option take legal action to enforce this contract, in which event the purchaser shall pay reasonable attorney fees and court costs; or else the seller may at his option retain one-half of the deposit paid and the broker retain the other half as consideration for the release of the purchaser by the seller and broker from any and all further obligations under this contract to the seller, which release shall be implied from such act of retention by the seller and the broker.

Commission Payment For Cooperative Sale

It is hereby agreed that_____Realty Company and_____ _____Realtors are the cooperating brokers in bringing about this sale and are the only ones entitled to receive the commission. The commission shall be shared on a 50%— 50% basis.

7

Construction Contracts

7

Construction Contracts

Like all real estate agreements, construction contracts must contain certain basic essentials to be enforceable. However, they are highly specialized instruments containing detailed terms, specifications and provisions that set them apart from other forms of contractual agreements. Construction contracts present a separate study and are being treated as such in this chapter.

The American Institute of Architecture forms that follow enjoy wide use and acceptance throughout the country. It should be noted that they have been prepared for use by the contractor, and are designed to protect his interests.

No. 7–1
AGREEMENT BETWEEN OWNER AND CONTRACTOR
Where The Basis For Payment Is A Stipulated Sum

AGREEMENT made this_____ day of_____in the year of Nineteen Hundred and_____.

BETWEEN _____,
the owner, and_____,
the Contractor.

The Owner and the Contractor agree as set forth below.

ARTICLE 1
THE CONTRACT DOCUMENTS

The Contract Documents consist of this Agreement, Conditions of the Contract (General, Supplementary and other Conditions), Drawings, Specifications, all Addenda issued prior to execution of this Agreement and all Modifications issued subsequent thereto. These form the Contract, and all are as fully a part of the Contract as if attached to this Agreement or repeated herein. An enumeration of the Contract Documents appears in Article 8.

ARTICLE 2
THE WORK

The Contractor shall perform all the Work required by the Contract Documents for
_____ (Insert above the caption descriptive of the Work as used on other Contract Documents.)

ARTICLE 3
ARCHITECT

The Architect for this Project is_____.

ARTICLE 4
TIME OF COMMENCEMENT AND COMPLETION

The Work to be performed under this Contract shall be commenced_____
and completed_____.
(Here insert any special provisions for liquidated damages relating to failure to complete on time.)

ARTICLE 5
CONTRACT SUM

The Owner shall pay the Contractor for the performance of the Work, subject to additions and deductions by Change Order as provided in the Conditions of the Contract, in current funds, the Contract Sum of_____.
(Here state the lump sum amount, unit price, or both, as desired.)

ARTICLE 6
PROGRESS PAYMENTS

Based upon Applications for Payment submitted to the Architect by the Contractor and Certificates for Payment issued by the Architect, the Owner shall make progress payments on account of the Contract Sum to the Contractor as provided in the Conditions of the Contract as follows:

On or about the_____day of each month_____per cent of the proportion of the Contract Sum properly allocable to labor, materials and equipment incorporated in the Work and_____per cent of the portion of the Contract Sum properly allocable to materials and equipment suitably stored at the site or at some other location agreed upon in writing by the parties, up to the_____day of that month, less the aggregate of previous payments in each case; and upon Substantial Completion of the entire Work, a sum sufficient to increase the total payments to_____per cent of the Contract Sum, less such retainages as the Architect shall determine for all incomplete Work and unsettled claims.

(Here insert any provisions made for limiting or reducing the amount retained after the Work reaches a certain stage of completion.)

ARTICLE 7
FINAL PAYMENT

Final payment, constituting the entire unpaid balance of the Contract Sum, shall be paid by the Owner to the Contractor_____days after Substantial Completion of the Work unless otherwise stipulated in the Certificate of Substantial Completion, provided the Work has then been completed, the contract fully performed, and a final Certificate for Payment has been issued by the Architect.

ARTICLE 8
MISCELLANEOUS PROVISIONS

8.1 Terms used in this Agreement which are defined in the Conditions of the Contract shall have the meanings designated in those Conditions.

8.2 The Contract Documents, which constitute the entire agreement between the Owner and the Contractor, are listed in Article 1 and, except for Modifications issued after execution of this Agreement, are enumerated as follows:

(List below the Agreement, Conditions of the Contract [General, Supplementary, and other Conditions], Drawings, Specifications, Addenda and accepted Alternates, showing page or sheet numbers in all cases and dates where applicable.)

This Agreement executed the day and year first written above.

OWNER   CONTRACTOR

_____   _____

(Reproduced with permission of The American Institute Of Architects. Further reproduction is not authorized.)

No. 7-2
AGREEMENT BETWEEN OWNER AND CONTRACTOR
Stipulated Sum For Small Construction Contracts

STIPULATED SUM

AGREEMENT

made this   day of   in the year Nineteen
Hundred and

BETWEEN

the Owner, and

the Contractor.

The Owner and Contractor agree as set forth below.

ARTICLE 1
THE WORK

The Contractor shall perform all the Work required by the Contract Documents for
(Here insert the caption descriptive of the Work as used on other Contract Documents.)

ARTICLE 2
ARCHITECT

The Architect for this project is

ARTICLE 3
TIME OF COMMENCEMENT AND COMPLETION

The Work to be performed under this Contract shall be commenced

and completed

ARTICLE 4
CONTRACT SUM

The Owner shall pay the Contractor for the performance of the Work, subject to additions and deductions by Change Order as provided in the General Conditions, in current funds, the Contract Sum of
(State here the lump sum amount, unit prices, or both, as desired.)

ARTICLE 5
PROGRESS PAYMENTS

Based upon Applications for Payment submitted to the Architect by the Contractor and Certificates for Payment issued by the Architect, the Owner shall make progress payments on account of the Contract Sum to the Contractor as follows:

ARTICLE 6
FINAL PAYMENT

The Owner shall make final payment   days after completion of the Work, provided the Contract be then fully performed, subject to the provisions of Article 17 of the General Conditions.

ARTICLE 7
ENUMERATION OF CONTRACT DOCUMENTS

The Contract Documents are as noted in Paragraph 8.1 of the General Conditions and are enumerated as follows:

(List below the Agreement, Conditions of the Contract (General, Supplementary, and other Conditions), Drawings, Specifications, Addenda and accepted Alternates, showing page or sheet numbers in all cases and dates where applicable.)

GENERAL CONDITIONS

ARTICLE 8
CONTRACT DOCUMENTS

8.1 The Contract Documents consist of this Agreement (which includes the General Conditions), Supplementary and other Conditions, the Drawings, the Specifications, all Addenda issued prior to the execution of this Agreement, all amendments, Change Orders, and written interpretations of the Contract Documents issued by the Architect. These form the Contract and what is required by any one shall be as binding as if required by all. The intention of the Contract Documents is to include all labor, materials, equipment and other items as provided in Paragraph 11.2 necessary for the proper execution and completion of the Work and the terms and conditions of payment therefor, and also to include all Work which may be reasonably inferable from the Contract Documents as being necessary to produce the intended results.

8.2 The Contract Documents shall be signed in not less than triplicate by the Owner and the Contractor. If either the Owner or the Contractor do not sign the Drawings, Specifications, or any of the other Contract Documents, the Architect shall identify them. By executing the Contract, the Contractor represents that he has visited the site and familiarized himself with the local conditions under which the Work is to be performed.

8.3 The term Work as used in the Contract Documents includes all labor necessary to produce the construction required by the Contract Documents, and all materials and equipment incorporated or to be incorporated in such construction.

ARTICLE 9
ARCHITECT

9.1 The Architect will provide general administration of the Contract and will be the Owner's representative during the construction period.

9.2 The Architect shall at all times have access to the Work wherever it is in preparation and progress.

9.3 The Architect will make periodic visits to the site to familiarize himself generally with the progress and quality of the Work and to determine in general if the Work is proceeding in accordance with the Contract Documents. On the basis of his on-site observations as an architect, he will keep the Owner informed of the progress of the Work, and will endeavor to guard the Owner against defects and deficiencies in the Work of the Contractor. The Architect will not be required to make exhaustive or continuous on-site inspections to check the quality or quantity of the Work. The Architect will not be responsible for construction means, methods, techniques, sequences or procedures, or for safety precautions and programs in connection with the Work, and he will not be responsible for the Contractor's failure to carry out the Work in accordance with the Contract Documents.

9.4 Based on such observations and the Contractor's Applications for Payment, the Architect will determine the amounts owing to the Contractor and will issue Certificates for Payment in accordance with Article 17.

9.5 The Architect will be, in the first instance, the interpreter of the requirements of the Contract Documents. He will make decisions on all claims and disputes between the Owner and the Contractor. All his decisions are subject to arbitration.

9.6 The Architect has authority to reject Work which does not conform to the Contract Documents and to stop the Work, or any portion thereof, if necessary to insure its proper execution.

ARTICLE 10
OWNER

10.1 The Owner shall furnish all surveys.

10.2 The Owner shall secure and pay for easements for permanent structures or permanent changes in existing facilities.

10.3 The Owner shall issue all instructions to the Contractor through the Architect.

ARTICLE 11
CONTRACTOR

11.1 The Contractor shall supervise and direct the Work, using his best skill and attention. The Contractor shall be solely responsible for all construction means, methods, techniques, sequences and procedures and for coordinating all portions of the Work under the Contract.

11.2 Unless otherwise specifically noted, the Contractor shall provide and pay for all labor, materials, equipment, tools, construction equipment and machinery, water, heat, utilities, transportation, and other facilities and services necessary for the proper execution and completion of the Work.

11.3 The Contractor shall at all times enforce strict discipline and good order among his employees, and shall not employ on the Work any unfit person or anyone not skilled in the task assigned to him.

11.4 The Contractor warrants to the Owner and the Architect that all materials and equipment incorporated in the Work will be new unless otherwise specified, and that all Work will be of good quality, free from faults and defects and in conformance with the Contract Documents. All work not so conforming to these standards may be considered defective.

11.5 The Contractor shall pay all sales, consumer, use and other similar taxes required by law and shall secure all permits, fees and licenses necessary for the execution of the Work.

11.6 The Contractor shall give all notices and comply with all laws, ordinances, rules, regulations, and orders of any public authority bearing on the performance of the Work, and shall notify the Architect if the Drawings and Specifications are at variance therewith.

11.7 The Contractor shall be responsible for the acts and omissions of all his employees and all Subcontractors, their agents and employees and all other persons performing any of the Work under a contract with the Contractor.

11.8 The Contractor shall furnish all samples and shop drawings as directed for approval of the Architect for conformance with the design concept and with the information given in the Contract Documents. The Work shall be in accordance with approved samples and shop drawings.

11.9 The Contractor at all times shall keep the premises free from accumulation of waste materials or rubbish caused by his operations. At the completion of the Work he shall remove all his waste materials and rubbish from and about the Project as well as his tools, construction equipment, machinery and surplus materials, and shall clean all glass surfaces and shall leave the Work "broom clean" or its equivalent, except as otherwise specified.

11.10 The Contractor shall indemnify and hold harmless the Owner and the Architect and their agents and employees from and against all claims, damages, losses and expenses including attorneys' fees arising out of or resulting from the performance of the Work, provided that any such claim, damage, loss or expense (a) is attributable to bodily injury, sickness, disease or death, or to injury to or destruction of tangible property (other than the Work itself) including the loss of use resulting therefrom, and (b) is caused in whole or in part by any negligent act or omission of the Contractor, any Subcontractor, anyone directly or indirectly employed by any of them or anyone for whose acts any of them may be liable, regardless of whether or not it is caused in part by a party indemnified hereunder. In any and all claims against the Owner or the Architect or any of their agents or employees by any employee of the Contractor, any Subcontractor, anyone directly or indirectly employed by any of them or anyone for whose acts any of them may be liable, the indemnification obligation under this Paragraph 11.10 shall not be limited in any way by any limitation on the amount or type of damages, compensation or benefits payable by or for the Contractor or any Subcontractor under workmen's compensation acts, disability benefit acts or other employee benefit acts. The obligations of the Contractor under this Paragraph 11.10 shall not extend to the liability of the Architect, his agents or employees arising out of (1) the preparation or approval of maps, drawings, opinions, reports, surveys, Change Orders, designs or specifications, or (2) the giving of or the failure to give directions or instructions by the Architect, his agents or employees provided such giving or failure to give is the primary cause of the injury or damage.

ARTICLE 12
SUBCONTRACTS

12.1 A Subcontractor is a person who has a direct contract with the Contractor to perform any of the Work at the site.

12.2 Prior to the award of the Contract the Contractor shall furnish to the Architect in writing a list of the names of Subcontractors proposed for the principal portions of the Work. The Contractor shall not employ any Subcontractor to whom the Architect or the Owner may have a reasonable objection. The Contractor shall not be required to employ any Subcontractor to whom he has a reasonable objection. Contracts between the Contractor and the Subcontractor shall be in accordance with the terms of this Agreement and shall include the General Conditions of this Agreement insofar as applicable.

ARTICLE 13
SEPARATE CONTRACTS

The Owner has the right to let other contracts in connection with the Work and the Contractor shall properly cooperate with any such other contractors.

ARTICLE 14
ROYALTIES AND PATENTS

The Contractor shall pay all royalties and license fees. The Contractor shall defend all suits or claims for infringement or any patent rights and shall save the Owner harmless from loss on account thereof.

ARTICLE 15
ARBITRATION

All claims or disputes arising out of this Contract or the breach thereof shall be decided by arbitration in accordance with the Construction Industry Arbitration Rules of the American Arbitration Association then obtaining unless the parties mutually agree otherwise. Notice of the demand for arbitration shall be filed in writing with the other party to the Contract and with the American Arbitration Association and shall be made within a reasonable time after the dispute has arisen.

ARTICLE 16
TIME

16.1 All time limits stated in the Contract Documents are of the essence of the Contract.

16.2 If the Contractor is delayed at any time in the progress of the Work by changes ordered in the Work, by labor disputes, fire, unusual delay in transportation, unavoidable casualties, causes beyond the Contractor's control, or by any cause which the Architect may determine justifies the delay, then the Contract Time shall be extended by Change Order for such reasonable time as the Architect may determine.

ARTICLE 17
PAYMENTS

17.1 Payments shall be made as provided in Article 5 of this Agreement.

17.2 Payments may be withheld on account of (1) defective Work not remedied, (2) claims filed, (3) failure of the Contractor to make payments properly to Subcontractors or for labor, materials, or equipment, (4) damage to another contractor, or (5) unsatisfactory prosecution of the Work by the Contractor.

17.3 Final payment shall not be due until the Contractor has delivered to the Owner a complete release of all liens arising out of this Contract or receipts in full covering all labor, materials and equipment for which a lien could be filed, or a bond satisfactory to the Owner indemnifying him against any lien.

17.4 The making of final payment shall constitute a waiver of all claims by the Owner except those arising from (1) unsettled liens, (2) faulty or defective Work appearing after Substantial Completion, (3) failure of the Work to comply with the requirements of the Contract Documents, or (4) terms of any special guarantees required by the Contract Documents. The acceptance of final payment shall constitute a waiver of all claims by the Contractor except those previously made in writing and still unsettled.

ARTICLE 18
PROTECTION OF PERSONS AND PROPERTY

The Contractor shall be responsible for initiating, maintaining, and supervising all safety precautions and programs in connection with the Work. He shall take all reasonable precautions for the safety of, and shall provide all reasonable protection to prevent damage, injury or loss to (1) all employees on the Work and other persons who may be affected thereby, (2) all the Work and all materials and equipment to be incorporated therein, and (3) other property at the site or adjacent thereto. He shall comply with all applicable laws, ordinances, rules, regulations and orders of any public authority having jurisdiction for the safety of persons or property or to protect them from damage, injury or loss. All damage or loss to any property caused in whole or in part by the Contractor, any Subcontractor, any Sub-subcontractor or anyone directly or indirectly employed by any of them, or by anyone for whose acts any of them may be liable, shall be remedied by the Contractor, except damage or loss attributable to faulty Drawings or Specifications or to the acts or omissions of the Owner or Architect or anyone employed by either of them or for whose acts either of them may be liable but which are not attributable to the fault or negligence of the Contractor.

ARTICLE 19
CONTRACTOR'S LIABILITY INSURANCE

The Contractor shall purchase and maintain such insurance as will protect him from claims under workmen's compensation acts and other employee benefit acts, from claims for damages because of bodily injury, including death, and from claims for damages to property which may arise out of or result from the Contractor's operations under this Contract, whether such operations be by himself or by any Subcontractor or anyone directly or indirectly employed by any of them. This insurance shall be written for not less than any limits of liability specified as part of this Contract, or required by law, whichever is the greater, and shall include contractual liability insurance as applicable to the Contractor's obligations under Paragraph 11.10. Certificates of such insurance shall be filed with the Owner.

ARTICLE 20
OWNER'S LIABILITY INSURANCE

The Owner shall be responsible for purchasing and maintaining his own liability insurance and, at his op-

tion, may maintain such insurance as will protect him against claims which may arise from operations under the Contract.

ARTICLE 21
PROPERTY INSURANCE

21.1 Unless otherwise provided, the Owner shall purchase and maintain property insurance upon the entire Work at the site to the full insurable value thereof. This insurance shall include the interests of the Owner, the Contractor, Subcontractors and Sub-subcontractors in the Work and shall insure against the perils of Fire, Extended Coverage, Vandalism and Malicious Mischief.

21.2 Any insured loss is to be adjusted with the Owner and made payable to the Owner as trustee for the insureds, as their interests may appear, subject to the requirements of any mortgagee clause.

21.3 The Owner shall file a copy of all policies with the Contractor prior to the commencement of the Work.

21.4 The Owner and Contractor waive all rights against each other for damages caused by fire or other perils to the extent covered by insurance provided under this paragraph. The Contractor shall require similar waivers by Subcontractors and Sub-subcontractors.

ARTICLE 22
CHANGES IN THE WORK

22.1 The Owner without invalidating the Contract may order Changes in the Work consisting of additions, deletions, or modifications, the Contract Sum and the Contract Time being adjusted accordingly. All such Changes in the Work shall be authorized by written Change Order signed by the Owner or the Architect as his duly authorized agent.

22.2 The Contract Sum and the Contract Time may be changed only by Change Order.

22.3 The cost or credit to the Owner from a Change in the Work shall be determined by mutual agreement before executing the Work involved.

ARTICLE 23
CORRECTION OF WORK

The Contractor shall correct any Work that fails to conform to the requirements of the Contract Documents where such failure to conform appears during the progress of the Work, and shall remedy any defects due to faulty materials, equipment or workmanship which appear within a period of one year from the Date of Substantial Completion of the Contract or within such longer period of time as may be prescribed by law or by the terms of any applicable special guarantee required by the Contract Documents. The provisions of this Article 23 apply to Work done by Subcontractors as well as to Work done by direct employees of the Contractor.

ARTICLE 24
TERMINATION BY THE CONTRACTOR

If the Architect fails to issue a Certificate of Payment for a period of thirty days through no fault of the Contractor, or if the Owner fails to make payment thereon for a period of thirty days, the Contractor may, upon seven days' written notice to the Owner and the Architect, terminate the Contract and recover from the Owner payment for all Work executed and for any proven loss sustained upon any materials, equipment, tools, and construction equipment and machinery including reasonable profit and damages.

ARTICLE 25
TERMINATION BY THE OWNER

If the Contractor defaults or neglects to carry out the Work in accordance with the Contract Documents or fails to perform any provision of the Contract, the Owner may, after seven days' written notice to the Contractor and without prejudice to any other remedy he may have, make good such deficiencies and may deduct the cost thereof from the payment then or thereafter due the Contractor or, at his option, may terminate the Contract and take possession of the site and of all materials, equipment, tools, and construction equipment and machinery thereon owned by the Contractor and may finish the Work by whatever method he may deem expedient, and if the unpaid balance of the Contract Sum exceeds the expense of finishing the Work, such excess shall be paid to the Contractor, but if such expense exceeds such unpaid balance, the Contractor shall pay the difference to the Owner.

This Agreement executed the day and year first written above.

OWNER _____   CONTRACTOR _____

No. 7–3
AGREEMENT BETWEEN OWNER AND CONTRACTOR
Cost Of The Work Plus A Fee

AGREEMENT
made this_____day of_____in the year of Nineteen Hundred
and_____
BETWEEN
_____the Owner, and
_____the Contractor.
The Owner and the Contractor agree as set forth below.

ARTICLE 1
THE CONTRACT DOCUMENTS

The Contract Documents consist of this Agreement, Conditions of the Contract (General, Supplementary and other Conditions), Drawings, Specifications, all Addenda issued prior to execution of this Agreement and all Modifications issued subsequent thereto. These form the Contract, and all are as fully a part of the Contract as if attached to this Agreement or repeated herein. An enumeration of all the Contract Documents appears in Article 17. If anything in the General Conditions is inconsistent with this Agreement, the Agreement shall govern.

ARTICLE 2
THE WORK

The Contractor shall perform all the Work required by the Contract Documents for

(Here insert the caption descriptive of the Work as used on other Contract Documents.)

ARTICLE 3
ARCHITECT

The Architect for this Project is

ARTICLE 4
THE CONTRACTOR'S DUTIES AND STATUS

The Contractor accepts the relationship of trust and confidence established between him and the Owner by this Agreement. He covenants with the Owner to furnish his best skill and judgment and to cooperate with the Architect in furthering the interests of the Owner. He agrees to furnish efficient business administration and superintendence and to use his best efforts to furnish at all times an adequate supply of workmen and materials, and to perform the Work in the best and soundest way and in the most expeditious and economical manner consistent with the interests of the Owner.

ARTICLE 5
TIME OF COMMENCEMENT AND COMPLETION

The Work to be performed under this Contract shall be commenced _____

_____

and completed

(Here insert any special provisions for liquidated damages relating to failure to complete on time.)

ARTICLE 6
COST OF THE WORK AND GUARANTEED MAXIMUM COST

6.1 The Owner agrees to reimburse the Contractor for the Cost of the Work as defined in

Article 9. Such reimbursement shall be in addition to the Contractor's Fee stipulated in Article 7.

6.2 The maximum cost to the Owner, including the Cost of the Work and the Contractor's Fee, is guaranteed not to exceed the sum of

_____dollars ($_____); such Guaranteed Maximum Cost shall be increased or decreased for Changes in the Work as provided in Article 8.

(Here insert any provision for distribution of any savings. Delete Paragraph 6.2 if there is no Guaranteed Maximum Cost.)

ARTICLE 7
CONTRACTOR'S FEE

7.1 In consideration of the performance of the Contract, the Owner agrees to pay the Contractor in current funds as compensation for his services a Contractor's Fee as follows:

7.2 For Changes in the Work, the Contractor's Fee shall be adjusted as follows:

7.3 The Contractor shall be paid_____per cent (_____%) of the proportionate amount of his Fee with each progress payment, and the balance of his Fee shall be paid at the time of final payment.

ARTICLE 8
CHANGES IN THE WORK

8.1 The Owner may make Changes in the Work in accordance with Article 12 of the General Conditions insofar as such Article is consistent with this Agreement. The Contractor shall be reimbursed for Changes in the Work on the basis of Cost of the Work as defined in Article 9.

8.2 The Contractor's Fee for Changes in the Work shall be as set forth in Paragraph 7.2, or in the absence of specific provisions therein, shall be adjusted by negotiation on the basis of the Fee established for the original Work.

ARTICLE 9
COSTS TO BE REIMBURSED

9.1 The term Cost of the Work shall mean costs necessarily incurred in the proper performance of the Work and paid by the Contractor. Such costs shall be at rates not higher than the standard paid in the locality of the Work except with prior consent of the Owner, and shall include the items set forth below in this Article 9.

9.1.1 Wages paid for labor in the direct employ of the Contractor in the performance of the Work under applicable collective bargaining agreements, or under a salary or wage schedule agreed upon by the Owner and Contractor, and including such welfare or other benefits, if any, as may be payable with respect thereto.

9.1.2 Salaries of Contractor's employees when stationed at the field office, in whatever capacity employed. Employees engaged, at shops or on the road, in expediting the production or transportation of materials or equipment, shall be considered as stationed at the field office and their salaries paid for that portion of their time spent on this Work.

9.1.3 Cost of contributions, assessments or taxes for such items as unemployment compensation and social security, insofar as such cost is based on wages, salaries, or other remuneration paid to employees of the Contractor and included in the Cost of the Work under Subparagraphs 9.1.1 and 9.1.2.

9.1.4 The proportion of reasonable transportation, traveling and hotel expenses of the Contractor or of his officers or employees incurred in discharge of duties connected with the Work.

9.1.5 Cost of all materials, supplies and equipment incorporated in the Work, including costs of transportation thereof.

9.1.6 Payments made by the Contractor to Subcontractors for Work performed pursuant to subcontracts under this Agreement.

9.1.7 Cost, including transportation and maintenance, of all materials, supplies, equipment, temporary facilities and hand tools not owned by the workmen, which are consumed in the performance of the Work, and cost less salvage value on such items used but not consumed which remain the property of the Contractor.

9.1.8 Rental charges of all necessary machinery and equipment, exclusive of hand tools, used at the site of the work, whether rented from the Contractor or others, including installation, minor repairs and replacements, dismantling, removal, transportation and delivery costs thereof, at rental charges consistent with those prevailing in the area.

9.1.9 Cost of premiums for all bonds and insurance which the Contractor is required by the Contract Documents to purchase and maintain.

9.1.10 Sales, use or similar taxes related to the Work and for which the Contractor is liable imposed by any governmental authority.

9.1.11 Permit fees, royalties, damages for infringement of patents and costs of defending suits therefore, and deposits lost for causes other than the Contractor's negligence.

9.1.12 Losses and expenses, not compensated by insurance or otherwise, sustained by the Contractor in connection with the Work, provided they have resulted from causes other than the fault or neglect of the Contractor. Such losses shall include settlements made with the written consent and approval of the Owner. No such losses and expenses shall be included in the Cost of the Work for the purpose of determining the Contractor's Fee. If, however, such loss requires reconstruction and the Contractor is placed in charge thereof, he shall be paid for his services a Fee proportionate to that stated in Paragraph 7.1.

9.1.13   Minor expenses such as telegrams, long distance telephone calls, telephone service at the site, expressage, and similar petty cash items in connection with the Work.

9.1.14   Cost of removal of all debris.

9.1.15   Costs incurred due to an emergency affecting the safety of persons and property.

9.1.16   Other costs incurred in the performance of the Work if and to the extent approved in advance in writing by the Owner.

ARTICLE 10
COSTS NOT TO BE REIMBURSED

10.1   The term Cost of the Work shall not include any of the items set forth below in this Article 10.

10.1.1   Salaries or other compensation of the Contractor's officers, executives, general manager, estimators, auditors, accountants, purchasing and contracting agents and other employees at the Contractor's principal office and branch offices, except employees of the Contractor when engaged at shops or on the road in expediting the production or transportation of materials or equipment for the Work.

10.1.2   Expenses of the Contractor's Principal and Branch Offices other than the Field Office.

10.1.3   Any part of the Contractor's capital expense, including interest on the Contractor's capital employed for the Work.

10.1.4   Overhead or general expenses of any kind, except as may be expressly included in Article 9.

10.1.5   Costs due to the negligence of the Contractor, any Subcontractor, anyone directly or indirectly employed by any of them, or for whose acts any of them may be liable, including but not limited to the correction of defective Work, disposal of materials and equipment wrongly supplied, or making good any damage to property.

10.1.6   The cost of any item not specifically and expressly included in the items described in Article 9.

10.1.7   Costs in excess of the Guaranteed Maximum Cost, if any, as set forth in Article 6 and adjusted pursuant to Article 8.

ARTICLE 11
DISCOUNTS, REBATES AND REFUNDS

All cash discounts shall accrue to the Contractor unless the Owner deposits funds with the Contractor with which to make payments, in which case the cash discounts shall accrue to the Owner. All trade discounts, rebates and refunds, and all returns from sale of surplus materials and equipment shall accrue to the Owner, and the Contractor shall make provisions so that they can be secured.

(Here insert any provisions relating to deposits by the Owner to permit the Contractor to obtain cash discounts.)

ARTICLE 12
SUBCONTRACTS

12.1   All portions of the Work that the Contractor's organization has not been accustomed to perform shall be performed under subcontracts. The Contractor shall request bids from subcontractors and shall deliver such bids to the Architect. The Architect will then determine, with the advice of the Contractor and subject to the approval of the Owner, which bids will be accepted.

12.2   All Subcontracts shall conform to the requirements of Paragraph 5.3 of the General

Conditions. Subcontracts awarded on the basis of the cost of such work plus a fee shall also be subject to the provisions of this Agreement insofar as applicable.

ARTICLE 13
ACCOUNTING RECORDS

The Contractor shall check all materials, equipment and labor entering into the Work and shall keep such full and detailed accounts as may be necessary for proper financial management under this Agreement, and the system shall be satisfactory to the Owner. The Owner shall be afforded access to all the Contractor's records, books, correspondence, instructions, drawings, receipts, vouchers, memoranda and similar data relating to this Contract, and the Contractor shall preserve all such records for a period of three years after the final payment.

ARTICLE 14
APPLICATIONS FOR PAYMENT

The Contractor shall, at least ten days before each progress payment falls due, deliver to the Architect a statement, sworn to if required, showing in complete detail all moneys paid out or costs incurred by him on account of the Cost of the Work during the previous month for which he is to be reimbursed under Article 6 and the amount of the Contractor's Fee as provided in Article 7, together with payrolls for all labor and all receipted bills for which payment has been received.

ARTICLE 15
PAYMENTS TO THE CONTRACTOR

15.1   The Architect will review the Contractor's statement of moneys due as provided in Article 14 and will promptly issue a Certificate for Payment to the Owner for such amount as he approves, which Certificate shall be payable on or about the _____ day of the month.

15.2   Final payment, constituting the unpaid balance of the Cost of the Work and of the Contractor's Fee, shall be paid by the Owner to the Contractor when the Work has been completed, the Contract fully performed and a final Certificate for Payment has been issued by the Architect. Final payment shall be due _____ days after the date of issuance of the final Certificate for Payment.

ARTICLE 16
TERMINATION OF THE CONTRACT

16.1   The Contract may be terminated by the Contractor as provided in Article 14 of the General Conditions.

16.2   If the Owner terminates the Contract as provided in Article 14 of the General Conditions, he shall reimburse the Contractor for any unpaid Cost of the Work to the date of termination at the rate of the percentage named in Article 7, or (2) if the Contractor's Fee be stated as a fixed sum, such an amount as will increase the payments on account of his Fee to a sum which bears the same ratio to the said fixed sum as the Cost of the Work at the time of termination bears to the adjusted Guaranteed Maximum Cost, if any, otherwise to a reasonable estimated Cost of the Work when completed. The Owner shall also pay to the Contractor fair compensation, either by purchase or rental at the election of the Owner, for any equipment retained. In case of such termination of the Contract the Owner shall further assume and become liable for obligations, commitments and unsettled claims that the Contractor has previously undertaken or incurred in good faith in connection with said Work. The Contractor shall, as a condition of receiving the payments referred to in this Article 16, execute and deliver all such papers and take all such steps, including the legal assignment of his contractual rights, as the Owner may require for the purpose of fully vesting in him the rights and benefits of the Contractor under such obligations or commitments.

ARTICLE 17
MISCELLANEOUS PROVISIONS

17.1   Terms used in this agreement which are defined in the Conditions of the Contract shall have the meanings designated in those Conditions.

17.2   The Contract Documents, which constitute the entire agreement between the Owner and the Contractor, are listed in Article 1 and, except for Modifications issued after execution of this Agreement, are enumerated as follows:

(List below the Agreement, Conditions of the Contract, [General, Supplementary, other Conditions], Drawings, Specifications, Addenda and accepted Alternates, showing page or sheet numbers in all cases and dates where applicable.)

This Agreement executed the day and year first written above.
OWNER   CONTRACTOR

_____   _____

No. 7–4
SUBCONTRACT
Between Contractor And Subcontractor

AGREEMENT
made this_____day of_____in the year Nineteen Hundred
and_____
BETWEEN

_____the Contractor, and
_____the Subcontractor;
for
_____the Project, for
_____the Owner;
Designed by _____the Architect.
The Contractor and Subcontractor agree as set forth below.

ARTICLE 1
THE CONTRACT DOCUMENTS

The Contract Documents for this Subcontract consist of this Agreement and any Exhibits attached hereto, the agreement between the Owner and Contractor dated_____ ,
the Conditions of the Contract between the Owner and Contractor (General, Supplementary and other Conditions), Drawings, Specifications, all Addenda issued prior to execution of the Agreement between the Owner and Contractor, and all Modifications issued subsequent thereto.
All of the above documents, which form the Contract between the Owner and Contractor, are a part of this Subcontract and shall be available for inspection by the Subcontractor upon his request.

ARTICLE 2
THE WORK

The Subcontractor shall furnish all labor, materials and equipment and shall perform all the Work for

(Insert above a precise description of the Work and refer to numbers of Drawings and pages of the Specifications including Addenda and accepted Alternates.)

ARTICLE 3
TIME OF COMMENCEMENT AND COMPLETION

All time limits stated in the Contract Documents are of the essence of this Subcontract. No extension of time will be valid without the Contractor's written consent after claim made by the Subcontractor in accordance with Paragraph. 11.4. Such consent shall not be unreasonably withheld.

(Here insert any information pertaining to notice to proceed or other method of notification for commencement of Work, starting and completion dates, or duration, and any provisions for liquidated damages relating to failure to complete on time.)

ARTICLE 4
THE CONTRACT SUM

The Contractor shall pay the Subcontractor in current funds for the performance of the Work, subject to additions and deductions by Change Order, the total sum of

ARTICLE 5
PROGRESS PAYMENTS

The Contractor shall pay the Subcontractor monthly payments in accordance with Paragraphs 12.2 through 12.5 inclusive of this Subcontract.

(Here insert details on unit prices, payment procedures and date of monthly applications, or other procedure if on other than a monthly basis, consideration of materials and equipment safely and suitably stored at the site or other location agreed upon in writing, and any provisions for limiting or reducing the amount retained after the Work reaches a certain state of completion which should be consistent with the Contract Documents.)

ARTICLE 6
FINAL PAYMENT

Final payment shall be due when the Work described in this Subcontract is fully completed and performed in accordance with the Contract Documents and is satisfactory to the Architect. Such payment shall be in accordance with Article 5 and with Paragraphs 11.9 and 12.2 through 12.5 inclusive of this Contract.

Before issuance of the final payment the Subcontractor, if required, shall submit evidence satisfactory to the Contractor that all payrolls, bills for materials and equipment, and all known indebtedness connected with the Subcontractor's Work have been satisfied.

ARTICLE 7
PERFORMANCE AND LABOR
AND MATERIAL PAYMENT BONDS

(Here insert any requirement for the furnishing of bonds by the Subcontractor.)

ARTICLE 8
TEMPORARY SITE FACILITIES

(Here insert any requirements and terms concerning temporary site facilities such as storage, sheds, water, heat, light, power, toilets, hoists, elevators, scaffoldings, cold weather protection, ventilating, pumps, watchman services, and other applicable facilities.)

ARTICLE 9
INSURANCE

Prior to starting work the required insurance shall be obtained from a responsible insurer, and satisfactory evidence shall be furnished to the Contractor that the Subcontractor has complied with the requirements of this Article 9. The Contractor and Subcontractor waive all rights against each other and against the Owner and all other Subcontractors for damages caused by fire or other perils to the extent covered by property insurance provided under the General Conditions, except such rights as they may have to the proceeds of such insurance.

(Here insert any insurance requirements and Subcontractor's responsibility for obtaining, maintaining and paying for necessary insurance, not less than limits as may be specified in the Contract Documents or required by law. This is to include fire insurance and extended coverage, consideration of public liability; property damage, employer's liability, and workmen's compensation insurance for the Subcontractor and his employees. The insertion should cover provisions for notice of cancellation, allocation of insurance proceeds and other aspects of insurance.)

ARTICLE 10
WORKING CONDITIONS

(Here insert any applicable arrangements concerning working conditions and labor matters for the Project.)

ARTICLE 11
SUBCONTRACTOR'S RESPONSIBILITIES

11.1   The Subcontractor shall be bound to the Contractor by the terms of this Agreement and of the Contract Documents between the Owner and Contractor, and shall assume toward the Contractor all the obligations and responsibilities which the Contractor, by those Documents, assumes toward the Owner, and shall have the benefit of all rights, remedies and redress against the Contractor which the Contractor, by those Documents, has against the Owner, insofar as applicable to this Subcontract, provided that where any provision of the Contract Documents between the Owner and Contractor is inconsistent with any provision of this Agreement, this Agreement shall govern.

11.2   The Subcontractor shall submit to the Contractor applications for payment at such times as stipulated in Article 5 to enable the Contractor to apply for payment.

11.2.1   If payments are made on the valuation of Work done, the Subcontractor shall, before the first application, submit to the Contractor a schedule of values of the various parts of the Work aggregating the total sum of this Subcontract, made out in such detail as the Subcontractor and Contractor may agree upon, or as required by the Owner, and supported by such evidence as to its correctness as the Contractor may direct. This schedule, when approved by the Contractor, shall be used as a basis for Applications for Payment, unless it be found to be in error. In applying for payment, the Subcontractor shall submit a statement based upon this schedule.

11.2.2   If payments are made on account of materials or equipment not incorporated in the work but delivered and suitably stored at the site, or at some other location agreed upon in writing, such payments shall be in accordance with the terms and conditions of the Contract Documents.

11.3   The Subcontractor shall pay for all materials, equipment and labor used in, or in connection with, the performance of this Subcontract through the period covered by previous payments received from the Contractor, and shall furnish satisfactory evidence, when requested by the Contractor, to verify compliance with the above requirements.

11.4   The Subcontractor shall make all claims promptly to the Contractor for additional work, extensions of time, and damage for delays or otherwise, in accordance with the Contract Documents.

11.5   In carrying out his Work the Subcontractor shall take necessary precautions to protect properly the finished work of other trades from damage caused by his operations.

11.6   The Subcontractor shall at all times keep the building and premises clean of debris arising out of the operations of this Subcontract. Unless otherwise provided, the Subcontractor shall not be held responsible for unclean conditions caused by other contractors or subcontractors.

11.7   The Subcontractor shall take all reasonable safety precautions with respect to his

Work, shall comply with all safety measures initiated by the Contractor and with all applicable laws, ordinances, rules, regulations and orders of any public authority for the safety of persons or property in accordance with the requirements of the Contract Documents. The Subcontractor shall report within three days to the Contractor any injury to any of the Subcontractor's employees at the site.

11.8 The Subcontractor shall not assign this Subcontract or any amounts due or to become due thereunder without the written consent of the Contractor, not subcontract the whole of this Subcontract without the written consent of the Contractor, nor further subcontract portions of this Subcontract without written notification to the Contractor when such notification is requested by the Contractor.

11.9 The Subcontractor warrants that all new materials and equipment furnished and incorporated by him in the Project shall be new unless otherwise specified, and that all Work under this Subcontract shall be of good quality, free from faults and defects and in conformance with the Contract Documents. All work not conforming to these standards may be considered defective. The warranty provided in this Paragraph 11.9 shall be in addition to and not in limitation of any other warranty or remedy required by law or by the Contract Documents.

11.10 The Subcontractor agrees that if he should neglect to prosecute the Work diligently and properly or fail to perform any provisions of this Subcontract, the Contractor, after three days written notice to the Subcontractor, may, without prejudice to any other remedy he may have, make good such deficiencies and may deduct the cost thereof from the payments then or thereafter due the Subcontractor, provided, however, that if such action is based upon faulty workmanship or materials and equipment, the Architect shall first have determined that the workmanship or materials and equipment are not in accordance with the Contract Documents.

11.11 The Subcontractor agrees that the Contractor's equipment will be available to the Subcontractor only at the Contractor's discretion and on mutually satisfactory terms.

11.12 The Subcontractor shall furnish periodic progress reports on the Work as mutually agreed, including information on the status of materials and equipment under this Subcontract which may be in the course of preparation or manufacture.

11.13 The Subcontractor shall make any and all changes in the Work from the Drawings and Specifications of the Contract Documents without invalidating this Subcontract when specifically ordered to do so in writing by the Contractor. The Subcontractor, prior to the commencement of such changed or revised work, shall submit promptly to the Contractor written copies of the cost or credit proposal for such revised Work in a manner consistent with the Contract Documents.

11.14 The Subcontractor shall cooperate with the Contractor and other subcontractors whose work might interfere with the Subcontractor's Work, and shall participate in the preparation of coordinated drawings in areas of congestion as required by the Contract Documents, specifically noting and advising the Contractor of any such interference.

11.15 The Subcontractor shall cooperate with the Contractor in scheduling and performing his Work to avoid conflict or interference with the work of others.

11.16 The Subcontractor shall promptly submit shop drawings and samples as required in order to perform his work efficiently, expeditiously and in a manner that will not cause delay in the progress of the Work of the Contractor or other Subcontractors.

11.17   The Subcontractor shall give all notices and comply with all laws, ordinances, rules, regulations and orders of any public authority bearing on the performance of the Work under this Subcontract. The Subcontractor shall secure and pay for all permits, fees and licenses necessary for the execution of the Work described in the Contract Documents as applicable to this Subcontract.

11.18   The Subcontractor shall comply with Federal, State and local tax laws, social security acts, unemployment compensation acts and workmen's compensation acts insofar as applicable to the performance of this Subcontract.

11.19   The Subcontractor agrees that all Work shall be done subject to the final approval of the Architect. The Architect's decisions in matters relating to artistic effect shall be final if consistent with the intent of the Contract Documents.

11.20   The Subcontractor shall indemnify and hold harmless the Contractor and all of his agents and employees from and against all claims, damages, losses and expenses including attorneys' fees arising out of or resulting from the performance of the Subcontractor's Work under the Contract Documents, provided that any such claim, damage, loss, or expense (a) is attributable to bodily injury, sickness, disease, or death, or to injury to or destruction of tangible property (other than the Work itself) including the loss of use resulting therefrom, and (b) is caused in whole or in part by any negligent act or omission of the Subcontractor or anyone directly or indirectly employed by him or anyone for whose acts he may be liable, regardless of whether it is caused in part by a party indemnified hereunder. In any and all claims against the Contractor or any of his agents or employees by any employee of the Subcontractor, anyone directly or indirectly employed by him or anyone for whose acts he may be liable, the indemnification obligation under this Paragraph 11.20 shall not be limited in any way by any limitation on the amount or type of damages, compensation or benefits payable by or for the Subcontractor under workmen's compensation acts, disability benefit acts or other employee benefit acts. The obligations of the Subcontractor under this Paragraph 11.20 shall not extend to the liability of the Architect, his agents or employees arising out of (1) the preparation or approval of maps, drawings, opinions, reports, surveys, Change Orders, designs or specifications, or (2) the giving of or the failure to give directions or instructions by the Architect, his agents or employees provided such giving or failure to give is the primary cause of the injury or damage.

ARTICLE 12
CONTRACTOR'S RESPONSIBILITIES

12.1   The Contractor shall be bound to the Subcontractor by the terms of this agreement and of the Contract Documents between the Owner and the Contractor and shall assume toward the Subcontractor all the obligations and responsibilities that the Owner, by those Documents, assumes toward the Contractor, and shall have the benefit of all rights, remedies and redress against the Subcontractor which the Owner, by those Documents, has against the Contractor, insofar as applicable to this Subcontract, provided that where any provision of the Contract Documents between the Owner and the Contractor is inconsistent with any provision in this Agreement, this Agreement shall govern.

12.2   The Contractor shall pay the Subcontractor within seven days, unless otherwise provided in the Contract Documents, upon the payment of certificates issued under the Contractor's schedule of values, or as described in Article 5. The amount of each progress payment to the Subcontractor shall be equal to the percentage of completion allowed to the Contractor for the Work of this Subcontractor applied to the contract sum of this Subcontract, plus the amount allowed for materials and equipment suitably stored by the Subcontractor, less the percentage retained from payments to the Contractor.

12.3   The Contractor shall permit the Subcontractor to obtain directly from the Architect evidence of percentages of completion certified on his account.

12.4   The Contractor shall pay the Subcontractor, on demand, a progress payment computed as provided in Paragraph 12.2 at the time the payment should be made to the Subcontractor if the Architect fails to issue the Certificate for Payment for any cause not the fault of the Subcontractor, unless otherwise provided herein.

12.5   The Contractor agrees that if he fails to make payments to the Subcontractor as herein provided for any cause not the fault of the Subcontractor, within seven days from the Contractor's receipt of payment or from the time payment should be made as provided in Paragraph 12.4, then the Subcontractor may, upon seven days' written notice to the Contractor, stop work without prejudice to any other remedy he may have.

12.6   The Contractor shall not give instructions or orders directly to employees or workmen of the Subcontractor except to persons designated as authorized representatives of the Subcontractor.

12.7   The Contractor shall make no demand for liquidated damages or penalty for delay in any sum in excess of such amount as may be specifically named in this Subcontract, and no liquidated damages shall be assessed against this Subcontractor for delays or causes attributed to other Subcontractors or arising outside the scope of this Subcontract.

12.8   The Contractor agrees that no claim for services rendered or materials and equipment furnished by the Contractor to the Subcontractor shall be valid unless written notice thereof is given by the Contractor during the first ten days of the calendar month following that in which the claim originated.

12.9   The Contractor shall permit the Subcontractor to be present and to submit evidence in any arbitration proceeding involving his rights.

12.10   The Contractor shall permit the Subcontractor to exercise whatever rights the Contractor may have under the Contract Documents in the choice of arbitrators in any dispute, if the sole cause of the dispute is the Work, materials, equipment, rights or responsibilities of the Subcontractor; or if the dispute involves the Subcontractor and any other Subcontractor or Subcontractors jointly, the Contractor shall permit them to exercise such rights jointly.

ARTICLE 13
ARBITRATION

All claims, disputes and other matters in question arising out of, or relating to, this Contract, or the breach thereof, shall be decided by arbitration in the same manner and under the same procedure as provided in the Contract Documents with respect to disputes between the Owner and the Contractor except that a decision by the Architect shall not be a condition precedent to arbitration.

This Agreement executed the day and year first written above.

CONTRACTOR   SUBCONTRACTOR

_____   _____

No. 7–5
SUBCONTRACT
Another Form

THIS AGREEMENT made this_____day of_____, 19_____, by and between_____

of_____ hereinafter described as Contractor; and_____

of_____ hereinafter described as Subcontractor, the said parties for the considerations hereinafter mentioned hereby agree to the following:

1. The Subcontractor agrees to provide all the materials and perform all the work for the following described parts and divisions of work and materials specified in a certain contract between the Contractor and_____ _____ described therein as Owner, in accordance with the terms, conditions and covenants of said contract as far as the same are applicable to the work and materials hereinafter mentioned, and as shown on the drawings and as set forth in the specifications mentioned in said contract prepared by_____ _____hereinafter described as Architect as far as the same are applicable to the work hereinafter mentioned, which said contract and said drawings and specifications therein mentioned are identified by the signatures of the respective parties hereto and are made and form a part of this contract:

2. The several portions of said work mentioned in this contract shall be finished at the times hereinafter stated, to wit:

and the entire work embraced in this agreement shall be complete on or before the day of _____, 19_____and if the said work is not completed by the said date last mentioned the said Contractor shall be entitled to receive as damages from the said Subcontractor for any such delay, in the absence of any legal ground or justification therefor, the sum of _____dollars per_____, it being understood and agreed between said parties hereto that the said sum fixed as liquidated damages is a reasonable sum, considering the damages that the Owner will sustain in the event of any such delay, and said amount is herein agree upon and fixed as liquidated damages, because of the difficulty of ascertaining the exact amount of damages that may be sustained by such delay.

If, however the said Subcontractor is delayed in the performance or completion of said work by any act or neglect of the Contractor, or of the Owner, or of the Architect, or of any other Subcontractor employed by this Contractor or of any Contractor employed by the Owner, or by changes ordered in the work, or by labor strikes, lockouts, unavoidable casualties or other causes beyond the control of the said Subcontractor, then the time of the performance or completion of said work shall be extended for such period as the said Contractor or the said Architect may decide, but no such extension for a period covering more than seven days shall be valid, unless the same is in writing signed by said Contractor or by said Architect.

3. The Contractor agrees to pay to the Subcontractor for the work to be done and the materials to be furnished under this agreement the sum of_____

_____dollars, subject to additions and deductions for changes that may be agreed upon and to make payments on account thereof as follows:
but said payments shall be made only upon certificates signed by_____,

_____, and the final payment shall be made within_____days after the completion of the said work embraced in this contract and after the issuance of the Architect's certificate to that effect. No certificate, however, given by said Architect, or payment made under this contract, shall be conclusive evidence of the full performance of this contract by the Subcontractor, either wholly or in part, and no payment shall be considered to be an acceptance of defective work or improper materials.

4. The said Subcontractor agrees to assume towards the Contractor all the obligations and responsibilities in so far as the same may be applicable to the work and materials mentioned in this contract, as the said Contractor assumes towards the Owner.

5. The Contractor agrees to be bound to the Subcontractor by all the obligations that the Owner assumes to the Contractor under the contract between them hereinbefore mentioned, and by the drawings and specifications mentioned thereunder, and by all the provisions thereof, as far as the same may be applicable to the work and materials mentioned in this contract.

6. The Contractor agrees to pay the Subcontractor a just share of any fire insurance money that may be received by the Contractor under and pursuant to the provisions of said contract existing between the Contractor and the Owner.

7. The said Contractor agrees in the event of any arbitration involving the work and materials mentioned in this contract under the terms and provisions of said contract between the Contractor and the Owner, to give the Subcontractor an opportunity to be present and submit evidence in reference thereto and to name as arbitrator the person named by the said Subcontractor, if the sole cause of controversy is the work and materials, rights or responsibilities of the Subcontractor; or, if of the Subcontractor and any other Subcontractor jointly, to name as such arbitrator the person upon whom they agree.

The terms Subcontractor, Owner, Contractor and Architect shall be read as if in the plural, or in the feminine gender, wherever appropriate.
IN WITNESS WHEREOF, the parties hereto have executed this agreement the day and year first above written. In presence of

(Form by courtesy of Julius Blumberg, Inc., 80 Exchange Place, New York, N.Y. 10004)

No. 7–6
BUILDER'S CONTRACT
To Erect A Private Residence

Date_____

_____HOMES, INC., hereinafter referred to as the Seller, hereby acknowledges receipt of the sum of:_____

DOLLARS ($_____) from_____

and his wife_____hereinafter referred to as the PURCHASER, as a deposit, on account of the purchase price of the following described property according to the terms and conditions hereinafter set forth:

DESCRIPTION OF PROPERTY: Lot_____ Block_____, Subdivision _____ as per plat thereof, recorded in Plat Book_____, Page_____, of the Public Records of_____County,_____together with a dwelling building to be erected thereon at:

Address:_____

The SELLER agrees to deliver the house below described within_____days of issuance of mortgage credit approval, and issuance of building permit, or as soon as practicable subject to the availability of labor and supplies and in accordance with the plans and specifications of file with_____County. In the event the below described home is not completed within said time, the purchaser shall at his option, be given a refund in the full amount of deposit receipted and this contract shall be null and void. The Purchase price shall include the following:

_____
_____
_____

_____

Purchase Price _____	$	_____
Closing Costs_____	$	_____
Total Cost to Purchaser_____	$	_____
Mortgage (_____)_____	$	_____
Approximate Down Payment_____	$	_____

TERMS AND CONDITIONS OF SALE:

_____
_____
_____

_____

The Purchaser agrees to make a mortgage loan application within five days of the signing of this contract, at a lending institution designated by the Seller, and to execute all necessary papers for such loan. In the event the application for loan is rejected by the lender, all monies receipted for, less cost of credit report, will be returned to the Purchaser and this contract will be null and void.

The PURCHASER agrees to pay all escrow payments as authorized by the lending institution together with any amount remaining due the SELLER at the time of the closing. In the event the PURCHASER fails or refuses to execute all the documents required of him promptly and when requested by the SELLER, or fails or refuses to pay the closing costs or such other sums as may be required, as set forth above, or fails or refuses to close within five days after written notification of closing date, then and in the event any of the aforementioned conditions are not complied with by the PURCHASER, all monies paid by the PURCHASER to the SELLER shall be retained by the SELLER as the agreed to or liquidated damages suffered by the SELLER.

Taxes, insurance and interest shall be pro-rated at the time of the closing. Property to be subject to restrictions, limitations and easements of record. Pending liens to be paid by PURCHASER, certified liens to be paid by SELLER.

It is agreed to by the PURCHASER and SELLER that the approval of the construction as evidenced by the final inspection report and issuance of a Certificate of Occupancy by _____County shall constitute conclusive evidence of the completion of the house and other improvements as provided for in the plans and specifications.

SELLER agrees to deliver title, good, marketable and/or insurable, and agrees to furnish individual abstract.

SELLER agrees to furnish PURCHASER a builder's warranty in accordance with the form used and accepted by the National Association of Home Builders.

Title insurance will be available to PURCHASER at closing as an option.

The PURCHASER does hereby agree not to interfere with or molest any workman during working hours and that all matters pertaining to the construction will be taken up by said PURCHASER with the Sales Office.

I (We) have read the foregoing instrument and agree to all terms, conditions and provisions hereinabove set forth.

Witnessed by_____

_____

_____ (PURCHASER)   (SEAL)

_____ (PURCHASER)   (SEAL)

Witnessed by_____   _____HOMES, INC.

BY_____

(Reproduced with permission of William Raskin, Caraval Quality Homes, Inc., Miami, Fla.)

Form 7-7
ESTIMATE
With Acceptance

Date_____, 19_____

Job Name_____
Job Address_____
Submitted To_____
Address_____ Phone_____

_____

We hereby submit specifications and estimates for:

(Here include full details of material to be used and work to be done)

_____

We propose to furnish labor and materials, complete in accordance with the above specifications, for the sum of_____

dollars ($_____), with payments to be made as follows:_____

_____

Material used is guaranteed to be as specified. All work to be completed in a workmanlike manner according to standard practices. Any alteration or deviation from above specifications involving extra costs will be executed only upon written orders, and will become an extra charge over and above this estimate. All agreements are contingent upon strikes, accidents or delays beyond our control. This estimate is subject to acceptance by_____
_____, 19_____ or is void thereafter at the option of the undersigned.

_____
Authorized Signature
Address_____
Phone_____

_____

ACCEPTANCE: The above estimate is hereby accepted. You are authorized to commence work as specified. Payment will be made as outlined above.

_____
Authorized Signature

Date_____, 19_____ _____
Authorized Signature

8

Condominiums

8

Condominiums

One of the oldest forms of real estate ownership dating back to biblical times, the condominium concept is today experiencing its widest use and acceptance throughout the free world. The word condominium is from the Latin meaning "ownership together." It differs from cooperative ownership in that each owner possesses a marketable deed to his specific part of the premises. He pays his taxes independently of the others and may buy, sell, mortgage, lease, option or will his part of the building as he sees fit.

The public areas of the building such as the halls, basement, lobby, elevators, incinerator, roof foundation, storage areas, etc., as well as the land itself are owned jointly with others. All types of real estate including residential apartments, offices, industrial buildings, shopping centers, etc. lend themselves to condominium possession.

Because of the legal ramifications that this form of ownership can involve, a specific set of forms, in many ways completely distinctive from those used in any other type of real estate transaction, are necessary.

Within the past decade, nearly every state has enacted their own condominium legislation. Though they follow generally similar guidelines, it is wise to check one's own state statutes when preparing condominium documents. Those that follow are in general use and acceptance.

The purpose of a Declaration Of Condominium is to set forth in detail the intentions, conditions, covenants and restrictions for which the condominium project is created. Its provisions must comply with state condominium requirements in those states that have enacted laws regulating offerings made to condominium buyers. In like manner, the Declaration Of Condominium must comply with federal standards and regulations when under FHA auspices.

No. 8–1
DECLARATION OF CONDOMINIUM

I.

SUBMISSION STATEMENT

The undersigned, being the holder of title of record to the real property situate, lying and being in_____County, State of_____, the legal description of which is attached hereto, and made a part hereof, and labelled "Exhibit A," hereby states and declares that the land described herein is submitted to condominium ownership, pursuant to Chapter_____, State of_____Statutes, 19_____, the Condominium Act (hereinafter referred to as the "Condominium Act"), the provisions of which said Act are hereby incorporated by reference, and included herein thereby, and does herewith file for record this Declaration.

Definitions of terms used herein are as follows:

1. Condominium Act means Chapter_____, State of_____Statutes, 19_____.

2. Declaration means the Declaration for the Creation of this Condominium, pursuant to the Condominium Act.

3. Corporation means_____Condominium Apartments, Inc., the non-profit Corporation which operates the Condominium property under this Declaration.

4. Unit means those parcels of the Condominium property designated at the Exhibits attached to the Declaration, which are subject to private ownership.

5. Common Elements means the portions of the Condominium property not included in the units, and shall include the personal property required for the maintenance and operation of the Condominium, even though owned by the Association. Limited Common Elements means those common elements which are reserved for the use of a certain unit to the exclusion of all others.

6. Condominium Parcel means a unit, together with the undivided share in the common elements, which is appurtenant to the unit.

7. Unit Owner means the owner of a condominium parcel.

8. Common Expenses means expenses for which the unit owners are liable to the Corporation. A common expense assessed against the individual unit owners, but not shared proportionately, shall be the sum due pursuant to that certain agreement entitled "Restrictions and Covenants Running with Land" which are recorded in Official Records Book_____, at page_____and Official Records Book #_____, at page_____, all in the Public Records of_____County, State of_____. The Association shall collect the social membership fee of $_____per annum, semi-annually in advance, from those unit owners obligated to pay same under the terms of the said recorded restrictions and such sum together with the proportionate assessments referred to in this Declaration of Condominium shall constitute the unit assessment as contemplated by this article.

9. Assessment means a share of the funds required for the payment of common expenses which from time to time are assessed against the unit owners by the Board of Directors.

a. The social membership fee of $_____per annum pursuant to the aforesaid "Restrictions and Covenants Running with Land" shall be an assessment chargeable only to those unit owners that are obligated to pay this membership fee under the terms of the said recorded agreement.

10. Condominium Property means and includes the land described in the Declaration, and all improvements thereon, and all easements and rights appurtenant thereto intended

for use in connection with the Condominium.

   11. Institutional Mortgagee means a Bank, a Federal and Savings Loan Association, a Savings and Loan Association chartered by the State of_____ , Pension Fund, or a Life Insurance Company (the Mortgage may be placed through a Mortgage or Title Company).

   12. DEVELOPER means_____Corporation, State of _____corporation, qualified to do business in the State of _____ .

II
NAME

The name by which this Condominium is to be identified is: _____CONDOMINIUM APARTMENTS, INC.

III
IDENTIFICATION OF UNITS: SURVEY: SHARES IN COMMON ELEMENTS: PROPORTIONS OF COMMON EXPENSES

A.   The improvements on the land described consist of:

   a) #_____Unit Building being numbered Unit Nos._____to_____, inclusive, Unit No._____and Unit Nos._____to_____inclusive, Unit Nos._____to_____, inclusive, Unit Nos._____to_____, inclusive, Unit Nos._____to_____, inclusive, Unit Nos._____to_____, inclusive, Unit Nos._____to_____, inclusive, and Unit Nos._____to_____, inclusive, as shown on the attached Exhibits. The building has been constructed substantially in accordance with the plans and specifications prepared by _____ and identified as a_____ Unit, _____Story Apartment Building for_____ a State of_____corporation, qualified to do business in the State of_____ _____. There is also attached hereto as Exhibit_____, a Plot Plan and Survey, showing the location of the building and the remainder of the Condominium property.

   1. The unit owner shall not be deemed to own the undecorated and/or unfinished surfaces of the perimeter walls, floors and ceilings surrounding the respective "Condominium Unit," nor shall the owner be deemed to own pipes, wires, conduits, or other public utility lines running through said respective "Condominium Unit," which are utilized for or serve more than one "Condominium Unit," which items are by these presents hereby made a part of the "Common Elements." Said owner, however, shall be deemed to own the walls and partitions which are contained in said owner's respective "Condominium Unit," and also shall be deemed to own the inner decorated and/or finished surfaces of the perimeter walls, floors and ceilings, including plaster, paint, wallpaper, etc.

   2. If any portion of a Condominium Unit or Common Element encroaches upon another, a valid easement for the encroachment and the maintenance of same, so long as it stands, shall and does exist. In the event the multifamily structure is

partially or totally destroyed, and then rebuilt, encroachments of parts of the "Common Elements" or "Condominium Units," as aforedescribed, due to construction, shall be permitted, and a valid easement for said encroachments and the maintenance thereof shall exist.

3. In connection with the floor plans and Plot Plan, identified as Exhibit_____, the legend and notes thereon contained are incorporated herein, and made a part hereof by reference, and the said plans have been certified in the manner required by the Condominium Act.

B. The undivided share in the land and other Common Elements, including balconies and parking spaces and in the common surplus which is appurtenant to each apartment are shown on Exhibit_____which is attached hereto.

C. The Common Elements include parking areas for automobiles of Unit Owners. Parking areas will be available for use pursuant to the regulations of the Association, which regulations shall provide that the owners of each unit shall be entitled to a designated parking space for one automobile.

D. All the Balconies on the building which are used for ingress and egress to all of the units located on each floor are and shall remain a part of the Common Elements.

1. The balconies shown and graphically described in the Floor Plans and Plot Plan, identified as Exhibit_____, annexed hereto, are limited common elements appurtenant to each of the apartments as shown. These limited common elements are reserved for the use of the apartments appurtenant thereto, to the exclusion of other apartments, and there shall pass with an apartment, as appurtenant thereto, the exclusive right to use the limited common elements so appurtenant.

2. There are_____enclosed patio areas which are appurtenant to Units_____, _____,_____,_____, and_____. They are exclusively for the use and enjoyment of the respective units. These_____enclosed patio areas are designated as limited common elements, and shall be used exclusively by the unit owner of the unit to which they are attached.

3. Expenses of maintenance and repair relating to the interior surfaces of the limited common elements referred to in paragraph Nos._____and 2, immediately above, shall be borne by and assessed against the individual apartment owner. Any expense of maintenance, repair or replacement relating to the exterior surfaces of such limited common elements or involving structural maintenance, repair or replacement shall be treated as and paid for as a part of the common expenses of the Association.

IV
VOTING

Subject to the provisions and restrictions set forth in the By-Laws of the Corporation responsible for the operation of this Condominium, each unit owner is entitled to one vote for each unit owned by him.

V
METHOD OF AMENDMENT OF DECLARATION

This Declaration may be amended at any regular or special meeting of the unit owners of this Condominium, called in accordance with the By-Laws, by the affirmative vote of a majority of the unit owners. Such amendment shall be evidenced by a Certificate executed with the formalities of a Deed, and shall include the recording data identifying this Declaration, and said Certificate shall be signed and acknowledged by any officer of the Corporation responsible for the operation of this Condominium. This Certificate shall become effective upon its being recorded in the Public Records of_____County,_____ _____.

No amendment shall change any Condominium unit, nor its undivided share of the Common Elements, nor a Condominium Unit's proportionate share of the common expenses or common surplus, nor the voting rights pertinent to any unit, unless the record owners thereof and all record owners of liens thereon shall join in the execution of the amendment, and provided further that said amendment shall be voted on, and evidenced and recorded in the same manner as all other amendments to this Declaration.

No amendment shall change the provisions of this Declaration with respect to mortgagees without the written approval of all institutional mortgagees of record.

VI
BY-LAWS

The operation of the condominium property shall be governed by By-Laws which are set forth in a document entitled "BY-LAWS OF_____ CONDOMINIUM INC." and which is annexed to this Declaration, and incorporated herein by reference. No modification or other amendment to the By-Laws shall be valid, unless set forth in, or annexed to, a duly recorded amendment to this Declaration. The By-Laws shall be amended in the same manner as this Declaration is amended.

VII
MISCELLANEOUS CONDITIONS, COVENANTS AND RESTRICTIONS

A. Assessments:

The Corporation, through its Board of Directors, shall have the power to make and collect assessments, and to lease, maintain, repair and replace the common elements, as provided for by the Condominium Act.

B. Maintenance:

The Board of Directors of the Corporation may enter into a contract with any firm, person or corporation for the maintenance and repair of the condominium property, and may join with other condominium corporations in contracting with the same firm, person or corporation for maintenance and repair.

C. Liens:

The Corporation shall have a lien on each condominium parcel for any unpaid assessments, and interest thereon, against the unit owner of such condominium parcel, which lien shall be effective as and in the manner provided for by the Condominium Act, and shall have the priorities established by said Act. The lien of the Corporation for unpaid assessments shall also secure reasonable attorneys' fees incurred by the Corporation incident to the collection of such assessments reinforcement of such lien. Nothing herein shall deprive a first mortgagee of his prior lien.

D. Occupancy and Use:

The unit owner, or owner of a unit, shall occupy and use his condominium parcel as a private dwelling for himself and the adult members of his family and social guests, and for other purposes. No children under_____ years old shall be permitted to permanently reside in any of the units or rooms thereof in this condominium. The unit owner shall not permit or suffer anything to be done or kept in his unit which will increase the rate of insurance on the condominium property, or which will obstruct or interfere with the rights of other unit owners or annoy them by unreasonable noises or otherwise; nor shall the unit owner commit or permit any nuisance, immoral or illegal act in or about the condominium property. A unit owner may keep any pet or animal on the condominium property so long as such pet or animal does not constitute a nuisance and unreasonably interfere with the quiet enjoyment of the premises by the other condominium owners. No clotheslines or similar devices shall be allowed on any portion of the condominium property, except in area designated as "Laundry and Storage Room."

E. Re-sale:

In the event of re-sale or renting or leasing of said unit, the Board of Directors of the Corporation has the option to purchase, rent or lease the same on the same conditions as offered by the said unit owner to any third person. Any attempt to re-sell or rent or lease said unit without prior offer to the Board of Directors shall be deemed a breach of this Declaration, and shall wholly be null and void, and shall confer no title or interest whatsoever upon the intended purchaser, tenant or lessee.

F. Mortgages:

No apartment owner may mortgage his apartment or any interest therein without the approval of the Corporation, except to an institutional mortgagee. The approval of any other mortgage may be granted upon conditions determined by the Corporation, or may be arbitrarily withheld. This provision shall not be construed so as to prevent the Developer or Corporation from accepting a Purchase Money Mortgage as a part of the purchase price of an apartment, nor prevent an apartment owner from accepting a purchase Money Mortgage from an approved purchaser.

G. Offer to Sell:

Should the unit owner wish to sell, lease or rent his condominium parcel (which means the unit, together with the undivided share in the common elements, and the right to use limited common elements, if applicable, which are appurtenant thereto) he shall, before making or accepting any offer to sell, purchase, lease or rent his condominium parcel, deliver to the Board of Directors, at the office of the Corporation, a written notice of his intent to sell, lease or rent, which notice shall contain the terms of the offer he has received, which he wishes to accept, or the terms of the offer he is prepared to make, and the name and address of the prospective purchaser or tenant. The Board of Directors, within_____(____) days after receiving such notice, shall either consent to the transaction specified in said notice, or, by written notice to be delivered to the unit owner's unit, designate that the Corporation, one or more persons then unit owners, or any other person or persons satisfactory to the Board of Directors is willing to purchase, lease or rent upon the said terms as those specified in the unit owner's notice. Thereupon, the unit owner shall either accept such offer or withdraw and/or reject the offer specified in his notice to the Board of Directors. The stated designee of the Board of Directors shall have_____ (_____) days to close from the date of the notice sent by the Board of Directors upon the same terms specified in the unit owner's notice. Failure of the Board of Directors to designate such person or persons within said_____day period, or failure of such person or persons to close within said second_____day period, shall be deemed consent by the Board of Directors to the transaction specified in the unit owner's notice, and the unit owner shall be free to make or accept the offer specified in his notice, and sell, lease or rent said interest pursuant thereto to the prospective purchaser or tenant named therein within_____ (_____) days after his notice was given. The Board of Directors shall give to the apartment owner an instrument in recordable form showing the consent of the Board of Directors of the Corporation to the transfer of ownership in the apartment. The unit owner shall have no right to sell, lease or rent his interest, or any part thereof, except as expressly provided for herein. The sub-leasing or sub-renting of said interest shall be subject to the same limitations as are applicable to the leasing or renting thereof. The liability of the unit owner under these covenants shall continue notwithstanding the fact that he may have leased or rented said interest as provided herein. Every purchaser, tenant or lessee shall take, subject to this Declaration and the By-Laws of the Corporation, and the provisions of the Condominium Act. The provisions of paragraphs "E" and "G" of this Article shall be operative until the _____day of_____, 19_____, and shall be automatically extended for successive periods of_____years unless an amendment to this Declaration, signed by a majority of the then unit owners, has been recorded, amending this Declaration, so as to delete the provisions of paragraphs "E" and "G" of this Article.

H. Mortgaged Units:

Should any condominium unit or parcel at any time become subject to an institutional mortgage given as security, the holder thereof, upon becoming the owner of such interest through whatever means, shall have the unqualified right to sell, lease or otherwise dispose of said unit or parcel, including the fee ownership thereof, without offer to the Board of

Directors, notwithstanding the provisions of Paragraphs "E" and "G" above, provided, however, that in all other respects, the provisions of the Condominium Act, shall be applicable thereto; and provided, further, that nothing herein contained shall be deemed to allow or cause a severance from the condominium unit of the share of the common elements or other appurtenances of said unit. All provisions of a real property mortgage in favor of an institutional mortgagee shall take precedence over the provisions of this Declaration— particularly in terms of right to receive insurance proceeds and right to approve of companies on which insurance is written, as well as the Condominium Act requirements concerning the non-effect of prior assessments in the event of foreclosure by said institutional mortgagee.

I. Developer's Units and Privileges:

The provisions of Paragraphs "E" and "G" of this Article shall not be applicable to the Developer who is irrevocably empowered to sell, lease or rent condominium units to any purchaser approved by it. The said Developer shall have the right to transact any business necessary to consummate sales of units, including but not limited to the right to maintain models, have signs, employees in the offices, use the elevators and common elements, and to show apartments. Sales office, signs and all items pertaining to sales shall not be considered common elements, and remain the property of the Developer. In the event there are unsold parcels, Developer retains the right to be the owner of unsold parcels under the same terms and conditions as all other parcel owners in said condominium, and Developer, as parcel owner, shall contribute to the common expenses in the same manner as other parcel owners, provided, however, if the Developer retains any of said parcels, it may rent them on any basis, notwithstanding anything to the contrary which may be contained in this Declaration of Condominium.

J. Insurance:

The insurance which shall be carried upon the condominium property and the property of the unit owners shall be governed by the following provisions:

1) *Authority to purchase*—All insurance policies upon the condominium property shall be purchased by the Corporation for the benefit of the unit owners and their mortgagees, as their interest may appear in the company, triple "A"—best rating or better, and provisions shall be made for the issuance of Certificates of Mortgagee Endorsements to the Mortgagees of condominium parcels. Such policies and endorsements shall be deposited with the Insurance Trustee. Unit owners may obtain insurance coverage at their own expense upon their personal property, and for their personal liability and living expense.

2) *Coverage*—

(a) *Casualty*—All buildings and improvements upon the land and all personal property included in the condominium property shall be insured in an amount equal to the maximum insurable replacement value, excluding foundation and excavation costs, as determined annually by the Board of Directors of the Corporation. Such coverage shall afford protection against:

(i) Loss or damage by fire and other hazards covered by a standard extended-coverage endorsement;

(ii) Such other risk as from time to time shall be customarily covered with respect to buildings similar in construction, location, and use, including, but not limited to, vandalism and malicious mischief.

(b) *Public Liability*—in such amounts and with such coverage as shall be required by the Board of Directors of the Corporation, with cross-liability endorsements to cover liability of the unit owners as a group to a unit owner.

(c) *Workmen's Compensation*—as shall be required to meet the requirements of the law.

(d) Each individual unit owner shall be responsible for the purchasing of liability insurance for accidents occurring in his own unit. The owner of a unit shall have no personal liability for any damages caused by the Corporation, or in connection with the use of the common elements. A unit owner shall be liable for injuries or damages resulting from an accident in his own unit to the same extent and degree that the owner of a house would be liable for an accident occuring within the house.

3) *Loss Payable*—All casualty insurance policies purchased by the Corporation hereunder shall provide that all proceeds covering casualty losses shall be paid to any bank or trust company in_____County as Trustee, or to any other Bank in_____ County, in the State of_____, with powers as may be designated by the Board of Directors of the Corporation, and approved by a majority of the Mortgagees of the units in the condominium property (the term "majority" meaning the holders of debts secured by first mortgages, the unpaid balance of which is more than one-half the unpaid principal of all first mortgages on said units). Said Trustee is herein referred to as the "Insurance Trustee." The Insurance Trustee shall not be liable for the payment of premiums or the sufficiency of premiums, nor for the failure to collect any insurance proceeds. The Insurance Trustee shall be responsible only for monies which come into its possession, and only for its willful misconduct, bad faith or gross negligence. The duty of the Insurance Trustee shall be to receive such proceeds as are paid to it, and to hold the same in trust pursuant to the terms of the Trust Agreement between the Corporation and the Insurance Trustee, which shall not be inconsistent with any of the provisions herein set forth.

4) *Payment of Premiums—Trustee's Expenses and Collection:* The Board of Directors shall collect and pay the premiums for all insurance and all fees and expenses of the Insurance Trustee as a part of the common expenses for which assessments are levied.

5) *Mandatory Repair*—Unless there occurs substantial damage to or destruction of all or a substantial part of the condominium property, as hereinafter defined, and subject to the provisions hereinafter provided, the Corporation and the unit owners shall repair, replace and rebuild the damage caused by casualty loss, and pay the costs of the same in full. The Corporation shall levy assessments in the event insurance proceeds are insufficient for the purpose of repairing, replacing and rebuilding the damage caused by casualty loss.

6) *Determination of Damage and Use of Proceeds:*

(a) Immediately after a casualty causing damage to any part of the condominium property, the Board of Directors shall obtain reliable and detailed estimates of the cost necessary to repair and replace the damaged property to a condition as good as the condition that existed prior to the casualty loss; provided, however, that if a casualty causing damage is limited to a single unit, then it shall be the responsibility of that unit owner to obtain estimates of the cost of replacement as aforesaid. If the net proceeds of insurance are insufficient to pay the estimated cost of reconstruction and repair, the Board of Directors shall promptly, upon determination of deficiency, levy a special assessment against all unit owners for that portion of the deficiency related to common elements, in accordance with the percentages set forth in Article III of this Declaration, and against the individual unit owners for that portion of the deficiency related to individual damage units; provided, however, that if, in the opinion of the Board of Directors, it is impossible to accurately and adequately determine the portion of the deficiency relating to individual damaged units, the Board of Directors shall levy the special assessment for the total deficiency against each of the unit owners, according to the percentages set forth in Article III of this Declaration.

(b) Unless there occurs substantial damage to or destruction of all or a substantial portion of the condominium property, and the unit owners elect not to rebuild and repair, as provided in Paragraph 7 below, the Insurance Trustee shall use the net proceeds and the funds collected by the Board of Directors from the assessments hereinabove set forth to repair and replace any damage or destruction of property, and shall pay any balance remaining to the unit owners and their mortgages, as their interests may appear, and the proceeds of insurance, and the funds collected by the Board of Directors from the assessments as hereinabove provided shall be held by the Insurance Trustee in trust for the use and purposes herein provided.

7) *Total Destruction:*   As used in this Declaration, and in any other connection or context dealing with this Condominium, the term "substantial damage to or destruction of all or a substantial portion of the Condominium property" shall mean that three-fourths (3/4) or more of the apartment units are rendered untenantable by casualty loss or damage. Should there occur substantial damage to or destruction of all or a substantial part of the condominium property, the condominium project shall not be reconstructed, unless three-fourths (3/4) of the unit owners agree thereto, in writing, within sixty (60) days after the casualty loss or damage occurs. It is understood and agreed that in the event a mortgagee should require the payment of the proceeds to it, that sum shall be paid to the said mortgagee, and the unit owner shall then be obliged to deposit the funds necessary for his unit towards his share of the rebuilding costs. In the event such reconstruction is not approved, as aforesaid, the Insurance Trustee is authorized to pay proceeds of the insurance to the unit owners and their mortgagees, as their interests may appear, and the Condominium property shall be removed from the provisions of the Condominium Act with the results provided for by Section 16 of the Condominium Act. The determination not to reconstruct after casualty shall be evidenced by a certificate, signed by one of the officers of the Corporation, stating that the said sixty (60) day period has elapsed, and that the Corporation has not received the necessary writings from three-fourths (3/4).

8) *Corporation as Agent:*   The Corporation is hereby irrevocably appointed Agent for each unit owner to adjust all claims arising under insurance policies purchased by the Corporation.

K.   Alterations:

There shall be no material alterations, door or color changes, enclosing of Balconies, or substantial additions to the common elements, except the same are authorized by the

Board of Directors, and ratified by the affirmative vote of a majority of the unit owners. No unit owner shall block, hamper, or otherwise interfere with the common elements of the property to the operation thereof.

L. Owners:

1) That no owner of a "Condominium Parcel" may exempt himself from liability for his contribution towards the common expenses by waiver of the use and enjoyment of any of the "common elements," or by the abandonment of his "Condominium Unit."

2) The owners of each and every "Condominium Parcel" shall return the same for the purpose of ad valorem taxes with the Tax Assessor of_____County,_____, or such other future legally authorized governmental officer or authority having jurisdiction over the same.

For the purpose of ad valorem taxation, the interest of the owner of a "Condominium Parcel" in his "Condominium Unit," and in the "common elements" shall be considered as a unit. The value of said unit shall be equal to the percentage of undivided shares in common elements of the entire Condominium, including land and improvements as has been assigned to said unit in Paragraph III of this Enabling Declaration. The total of all of said percentage equals 100% of the value of all of the land and improvements thereon.

The percentage assigned above shall be binding upon all owners for all purposes, including ad valorem taxation, at all times in the future, and may not be amended or changed.

M. Termination:

The provisions for termination set forth in Article VII J. 7 of this Declaration shall be in addition to the provisions for voluntary termination, as provided for by Section 16 of the Condominium Act.

N. Severability:

If any provision of this Declaration, or of the By-Laws attached hereto, or the Condominium Act, is held invalid, the validity of the remainder of this Declaration, or of the By-Laws attached hereto, or of the Condominium Act, shall not be affected thereby.

O. Titles:

Article and paragraph titles inserted throughout this Declaration are intended only as a matter of convenience and for reference, and in no way define, limit, or in any way affect this Declaration.

P. Notices:

Whenever notices are required to be sent hereunder, the same shall be sent to the unit owners by Certified Mail, at their place of residence in the Condominium building, and to the Corporation, by Certified Mail, at_____,
and to the undersigned at_____

All notices shall be deemed and considered sent when mailed. Any party may reserve the right to change the place of notice to him, or it, by written notice, in accordance with the terms and provisions of this paragraph.

IN WITNESS WHEREOF, the undersigned have executed this Declaration of Condominium this _____ day of _____, 19 _____.

IN THE PRESENCE OF: _____ CONDOMINIUM APARTMENTS, INC.

_____   By: _____
                                                                        President

_____   Attest: _____
                                                                         Secretary

(Corporate Seal)

No. 8–2
CONDOMINIUM BY-LAWS

The operation of the condominium property of the condominium described and named in the Declaration to which these By-Laws are attached shall be governed by these By-Laws.

ARTICLE I: CORPORATION MEMBERS: MEETINGS

Section 1. *Member and Voting Rights*. Each unit owner shall be a member of the Corporation. The membership of the Corporation shall consist of all of the unit owners. Each unit owner shall be entitled to one vote for each unit owned by him.

Section 2. *Transfer of Membership*. The Corporation shall not issue stock. Membership in the Corporation may be transferred only as an incident to the transfer of title to a unit as and in the manner provided for by the Declaration of these By-Laws, and, upon compliance with all of the terms thereof, shall become effective if in accordance with the aforegoing, upon the recordation of a deed of conveyance to the said unit.

Section 3. *Annual Meeting*. The annual meeting of the unit owners shall be held on the first Monday in the month of _____ of each year beginning on the first Monday in the month of _____, 19 _____, and each and every year thereafter at _____ o'clock _____. M. at such location on the condominium property as the President or a majority of the Board of Directors shall specify in writing to the unit owners, or at such other place in _____ County, _____, as the President or a majority of the Board of Directors shall designate. Should the date for said annual meeting fall on a holiday, the meeting shall be held on the next succeeding business day.

Section 4. *Special Meetings*. A special meeting of the unit owners may be called at any time by the President or by a majority of the Board of Directors, and shall be held at such place as is designated by the President or a majority of the Board of Directors, and stated in a written notice. No special meeting shall be called unless the Secretary of the Corporation shall have mailed to or served upon all of the owners written notice of the said meeting at least_____( ) days prior to the date of said meeting. A special meeting shall also be called by the President upon written demand of a majority of the unit owners, and in the event such demand is made, then and in that event, the President shall direct the Secretary to mail to or serve upon all of the unit owners written notice of the said meeting at least_____ ____ ( ) days prior to the date of the meeting. All notices shall be mailed to or served at the address of the unit owner as it appears on the books of the Corporation.

Section 5. *Qualifications of Officers*. Until the election to be held on_____, 19_____, an officer need not be a unit owner; thereafter, at least two of the officers shall be unit owners. No unit owner shall be eligible for election as an officer if he is more than _____ ( ) days delinquent in the payment of his assessment. Commencing with the officers elected at the meeting of unit owners to be held on_____ _____, 19_____, a transfer of title of his unit by an officer who is a unit owner shall automatically operate as his resignation as an officer, and as a member of the Board of Directors.

Section 6. *Removal and Vacancies*. After_____, an officer or director may be removed from office upon the affirmative vote of a majority of the unit owners for any reason deemed by the unit owners to be detrimental to the best interests of the condominium. In the event of any removal, resignation or vacancy in any of the offices, the remaining members of the Board of Directors shall elect a person to serve as a successor to the removed, resigned or vacant office, who shall hold office for the balance of the unexpired term, and shall succeed to a membership in the Board of Directors for the same term. The election held for the purpose of filling said vacancy may be held at any regular or special meeting of the Board of Directors.

Section 7. *Annual Meetings*. The annual meeting of the Board of Directors shall be held at such place in_____County,_____, as may be agreed upon by the Board of Directors immediately following the adjournment of the annual meeting of the owners. The Board of Directors may establish a schedule of regular meetings to be held at such place as the Board of Directors may designate, in which event, no notice shall be required to be sent to the said Board of Directors of said regular meetings once said schedule has been adopted.

Section 8. *Special Meetings*. Special meetings of the Board of Directors may be called by the President, and in his absence, by the Vice-President, or by a majority of the members of the Board of Directors, by giving_____ ( ) days' notice, in writing, to all of the members of the Board of Directors of the time and place of said meeting, said notice to be mailed to or personally served on each member of the Board of Directors by the Secretary of the Corporation. By unanimous consent of the Board of Directors, a special meeting of the Board of Directors may be held without notice at any time or place. All notices of special meeting shall state the purpose of the meeting.

Section 9. *Quorum*. A quorum for the transaction of business at any regular or special meeting of the Board of Directors shall consist of a majority of the members of the Board; but a majority of those present at any annual, regular or special meeting shall have the power to adjourn the meeting to a future time, provided that written notice of the new time, date and place shall be mailed to or personally served on each member of the Board of Directors by the Secretary of the Corporation at least_____( ) days prior to the time fixed for said meeting.

Section 10. *Compensation*. The officers of this Corporation shall serve without compensation.

ARTICLE II. OFFICERS: POWERS AND DUTIES

Section 1. *The President*. He shall be the Chief Executive officer of the Corporation; he shall preside at all meetings of the unit owners and of the Board of Directors. He shall have executive powers and general supervision over the affairs of the Corporation and other officers. He shall sign all written contracts of the Corporation, and shall perform and have the powers necessary to perform all of the duties incident to his office and that may be delegated to him from time to time by the Board of Directors.

Section 2. *The Vice-President*. He shall perform all of the duties of the President in his absence and such other duties as may be required of him from time to time by the Board of Directors.

Section 3. *The Secretary-Treasurer*.

(A) He shall issue notices of all Board of Directors meetings and all meetings of the unit owners; he shall attend and keep the Minutes of the same; he shall have charge of all of the Corporation books, records and papers.

(B) He shall have the custody of the Corporation funds and securities and shall keep full and accurate accounts of receipts and disbursements in books belonging to the Corporation, and shall deposit all moneys and other valuable effects in the name and to the credit of the Corporation in such depositories as may be designated from time to time by the Board of Directors.

(C) He shall disburse the funds of the Corporation as may be ordered by the Board in accordance with these By-Laws, making proper vouchers for such disbursements, and shall render to the President and Board of Directors at the regular meeting of the Board of Directors, or whenever they may require it, an account of all of his transactions as Treasurer and of the financial condition of the Corporation.

(D) He shall collect the assessments and shall promptly report the status of collections and of all delinquencies to the Board of Directors.

(E) He shall also give status reports to potential transferees, on which reports the transferees may rely. The liability of the owners shall continue until the transfers have been approved and all such transferees shall be deemed liable for past due assessments (other than institutional mortgages or purchases at institutional mortgage foreclosure sales).

Section 4. *Bond*. The Secretary-Treasurer, and all officers who are authorized to sign checks, must be bonded in an amount equal to the total anticipated assessments for a full year.

ARTICLE III: POWER OF THE CORPORATION

The Corporation, acting through the Board of Directors, shall have the following powers:

Section 1. *Declaration.* All of the powers specifically set forth in the Declaration and all of the powers incidental thereto.

Section 2. By-Laws. All of the powers specifically set forth in the By-Laws and all of the powers incidental thereto.

Section 3. *Condominium Act.* All of the powers specifically set forth in the Condominium Act and all powers incidental thereto.

Section 4. *Miscellaneous Powers.*

(A) To use and expend the assessments collected to carry out the purposes and powers of the Corporation.

(B) To employ attorneys, accountants and other professionals as the need arises.

(C) To employ workmen, janitors, gardeners, and such other agents and employees to carry out the powers of the Corporation, and to purchase supplies and equipment therefor.

ARTICLE IV: FINANCE AND ASSESSMENTS

Section 1. *Depository.* The funds of the Corporation shall be deposited in a bank in _____ _____ County, _____ , designated by the Board of Directors, in an account for the Corporation under resolutions approved by the Board of Directors, and shall be withdrawn only upon checks and demands for money signed by any of the officers of the Corporation. All notes of the Corporation shall be signed by any two of the officers of the Corporation.

Section 2. *Fiscal Year.* The fiscal year for the Corporation shall begin on the 1st day of January of each year; provided, however, that the Board of Directors is expressly authorized to change to a different fiscal year in accordance with the provisions and regulations from time to time prescribed by the Internal Revenue Code of the United States of America at such time as the Board of Directors deems it advisable.

Section 3. *Determination of Assessments.*

(A) The Board of Directors of the Corporation shall fix and determine from time to time the sum or sums necessary and adequate for the common expenses of the condominium property. Common expenses shall include expenses for the operation, maintenance, repair, or replacement of the common elements, costs of carrying out the powers and duties of the Corporation, all insurance premiums and expenses relating thereto, taxes until separately assessed, and any other expenses designated as common expense from time to time by the Board of Directors of the Corporation. Also included in the common expenses is the semi-annual assessment in that certain Agreement entitled "Restrictions and Covenants Running with Land," recorded in Official Records Book # _____ , at page # _____ .

The Board of Directors is specifically empowered on behalf of the Corporation to make and collect assessments, and to lease, maintain, repair and replace the common elements of the condominium. Funds for the payment of common expenses shall be assessed against the unit owners in percentage proportions to the size units they own. Said assessment shall be paid monthly, in advance, as ordered by the Board of Directors. In addition to the proportionate payment of the common expenses, each unit shall pay $_____ per month as their portion of the charges in that certain Agreement entitled "Restrictions and Covenants Running With Land" referred to above. Special Assessments should such be required by the Board of Directors, shall be levied and paid in the same manner as hereinbefore provided for regular assessments.

The Board of Directors is specifically empowered, on behalf of the Corporation, to make and collect assessments, and to lease, maintain, repair, and replace the common elements of the condominium. Funds for the payment of common expenses shall be assessed against the unit owners in the proportions or percentages of sharing common expenses provided in the Declaration. Said assessments shall be payable monthly, in advance, as ordered by the Board of Directors. Special assessments, should such be required by the Board of Directors, shall be levied, and paid in the same manner as hereinbefore provided for regular assessment.

(B) When the Board of Directors has determined the amount of any assessment, the Secretary-Treasurer of the Corporation shall mail or present a statement of the assessment to each of the owners. All assessments shall be payable to the Secretary-Treasurer of the Corporation and upon request, the Secretary-Treasurer shall give a receipt for each payment made to him.

Section 4. *Delinquent Assessments*. In the event an assessment is not paid within_____ days of the date it is due and payable, the Corporation, through its Board of Directors, may proceed to enforce and collect the said assessment and interest at the rate of_____ % per annum against the unit owner owing the same in any manner provided for by the Condominium Act.

Section 5. *Collection and Enforcement*. In connection with assessment, the Corporation shall have all of the powers, rights and privileges and legal remedies provided for by the Declaration and the Condominium Act in and about collecting and enforcing assessments. Further, in this connection, each unit owner shall be liable for his assessment in the same manner provided for by the Declaration of Condominium Act, and shall likewise be responsible for reasonable attorneys' fees, interest and costs incurred by the Corporation incident to the collection of such assessment or enforcement of any lien held by the Corporation for unpaid assessments.

ARTICLE V: MAINTENANCE AND REPAIRS

Section 1. *Access*. Any officer of the Corporation, or any agent of the Board of Directors, shall have irrevocable right to have access to each unit from time to time during reasonable hours that may be necessary for the inspection, maintenance, repair or replacement of any common element therein or accessible therefrom, or for making emergency repairs therein to prevent damage to the common elements, or to another unit or units.

Section 2. *Maintenance and Repair*. The Board of Directors may enter into a contract with any firm, person or corporation for the maintenance and repair of the condominium property, and may join with other condominium associations in contracting with the same firm, person or corporation for maintenance and repair. The Board of Directors may, by contract, empower and grant to such firms, person or corporation, the right of access, as set forth in Section 1 of this Article.

Section 3. *Unit Owners.* Every unit owner must perform promptly all maintenance and repair work within his own unit which, if omitted, would affect the condominium property, and the condominium project in its entirety, or in a part, belonging to other owners, being expressly responsible for the damages and liabilities that his failure to do so may engender.

Section 4. *Prohibition.* No unit owner shall make any alteration in the portions of the improvements of a condominium which are to be maintained by the Corporation, or remove any portion thereof, or make any additions thereto, or do any work which would jeopardize the safety or soundness of the building containing his unit or impair any easement. No unit owner may enclose the Balcony area adjacent to his unit.

Section 5. *Material Alterations.* There shall be no material alterations or substantial additions to the common elements, except as the same are authorized by the Board of Directors, and ratified by the affirmative vote of a majority of the unit owners present at any regular or special meeting of the unit owners.

ARTICLE VI: VIOLATIONS

Section 1. In the event of a violation (other than the non-payment of an assessment) by the unit owner in any of the provisions of the Declaration, these By-Laws, or the applicable portions of the Condominium Act, the Corporation, by direction of its Board of Directors, may notify the unit owner by written notice of such breach, transmitted by Registered or Certified Mail, Return Receipt Requested, and if such violation shall continue for a period of_____ days from the date of this notice, the Corporation, through its Board of Directors, shall have the right to treat such violation as an intentional and inexcusable and material breach of the Declaration, the By-Laws, or the pertinent provisions of the Condominium Act, and the Corporation may then, at its option, have the following elections: (i) An action at law to recover for its damage on behalf of the Corporation or on behalf of the other unit owners; (ii) an action in equity to enforce performance on the part of the unit owner; or (iii) an action in equity for such equitable relief as may be necessary under the circumstances, including injunctive relief. Failure on the part of the Corporation to maintain such an action at law or in equity within_____days from date of a written request, signed by a unit owner, sent to the Board of Directors, shall authorize any unit owner to bring an action in equity or suit at law on account of the violation, in the manner provided for by the Condominium Act. Any violations which are deemed by the Board of Directors to be a hazard to public health may be corrected immediately as an emergency matter.

ARTICLE VII: ACQUISITION OF UNITS

Section 1. *Voluntary Sale or Transfer.* Upon receipt of a unit owner's written notice, described in Paragraph 6 of Article VII of the Declaration, the Board of Directors may, with the authorization and approval of a majority of the unit owners present at any regular or special meeting of the unit owners, acquire and/or rent and/or lease a condominium parcel in the name of the Corporation or a designee.

Section 2. *Acquisition on Foreclosure.* At any judicial sale of a unit, the Board of Directors may, with the authorization and approval of a majority of the unit owners present at any regular or special meeting of the unit owners, acquire a condominium parcel in the name of the Corporation or its designee. The term "judicial" as used in this Section shall include any foreclosure of any lien, including a lien for assessments. The power of the Board of Directors to acquire at any judicial sale shall never be interpreted as any requirement or obligation on the part of the Board of Directors, or of the Corporation, to acquire at any judicial sale, the provisions hereof being permissive in nature and for the purpose of setting forth the power in the Board of Directors to so acquire should the requisite approval of the unit owners be obtained.

ARTICLE VIII: NOTICE

Section 1. Whenever notices are required to be sent hereunder, the same shall be sent to the unit owners by Certified Mail, at their place of residence in the condominium building, and to the Corporation, by Certified Mail, at_____ . All notices shall be deemed and considered sent when mailed. Any party may reserve the right to change the place of notice to him or it by written notice, in accordance with the terms and provisions of this Article.

ARTICLE IX: AMENDMENTS TO THE BY-LAWS

Section 1. These By-Laws may be amended in the same manner as the Declaration may be amended, and in accordance with the provisions of the Condominium Act. No modification or amendment shall be valid unless set forth in, or annexed to, a duly recorded Amendment to the Declaration. Until_____, 19_____, these By-Laws may not be amended, however, without also having a Resolution requesting said Amendment from the Board of Directors.

ARTICLE X: RULES AND REGULATIONS

Section 1. The Board of Directors may, from time to time, adopt and amend previously adopted administrative rules and regulations covering the details of the operation and use of the common elements of the condominium; provided, however, that no such rules and regulations shall conflict with the Declaration, these By-Laws, or the provisions of the Condominium Act, and in the event of any conflict between the said rules and regulations and the foregoing, the latter shall prevail. The Board of Directors shall, from time to time, post in a conspicuous place on the condominium property a copy of the Rules and Regulations adopted, from time to time, by the Board of Directors.

APPROVED AND DECLARED AS
BY-LAWS OF_____
CONDOMINIUM, INC., by the
Undersigned

By: _____
President

(Corporate Seal)

ATTEST:_____
                    Secretary

No. 8–3
ARTICLES OF CONDOMINIUM INCORPORATION

The UNDERSIGNED hereby associate themselves for the purpose of forming a corporation not for profit under Chapter_____,_____State Statutes, and certify as follows:

ARTICLE I

The name of the corporation shall be_____CONDOMINIUM APARTMENTS, INC., and shall hereinafter be referred to as the "Corporation."

ARTICLE II

1. A condominium known as_____Condominium Apartments, Inc. has been constructed on certain land located in_____ County, State of _____, more particularly described as:

(Here include legal description)

hereinafter called the "Land." The Corporation is organized to provide a means of administering the condominium by the owners thereof.

2. The documents creating the condominium are to be recorded in the Public Records of_____County, State of_____.

3. The Corporation shall make no distributions of income to its members, directors or officers.

ARTICLE III

The powers of the Corporation shall be governed by the following provisions:

1. The Corporation shall have all the common law and statutory powers of a corporation not for profit which are not in conflict with the terms of these Articles.

2. The Corporation shall have all the powers granted to the "Association" by Chapter_____,_____State Statutes 19_____.

3. The Corporation shall have all of the powers granted to it in the Declaration of Condominium of_____ Condominium Apartments, Inc., when said Declaration is recorded in the Public Records of_____ County, State of_____.

ARTICLE IV
MEMBERS

The qualifications of members, the manner of their admission and voting by such members shall be as follows:

1. All unit owners shall be members of the Corporation and no other person or entities shall be entitled to membership.

2. Members in the Corporation shall be established by recording in the Public Records of_____County, State of_____, of a deed or other instrument establishing a change of record title to a condominium parcel in the condominium and the notification in writing to the Corporation of the recording information, the new owner designated by such instrument thereby becoming a member of the Corporation. The membership of the prior owner shall thereby terminate.

3. The share of a member in the funds and assets of the Corporation cannot be assigned, pledged or transferred in any manner except as an appurtenance to the individual condominium unit.

4. Members of the Corporation shall be entitled to one vote for each unit owned by such member. Voting rights will be exercised in the manner provided by the By-Laws of the Corporation.

ARTICLE V
DIRECTORS

1. The affairs of the Corporation will be managed by a Board of not less than_____ nor more than_____directors, as shall be determined by the By-Laws.

2. Directors of the Corporation shall be appointed or elected at the annual meeting of the members in the manner set out in the By-Laws. Directors may be removed and vacancies of the Board of Directors shall be filled as set out in the By-Laws.

3. The names and addresses of the members of the first Board of Directors, who shall hold office until their successors are elected and have qualified, are as follows:

(Here list names and addresses of Board members)

ARTICLE VI
OFFICERS

The affairs of the Corporation shall be administered by officers elected by the members of the Corporation at the annual meeting of the members of the Corporation. The names and addresses of the officers who shall serve until their successors are elected, are as follows:

(Here list names and addresses of Officers)

ARTICLE VII
INDEMNIFICATION

Every director and officer of the Corporation shall be indemnified by the Corporation against all expenses and liabilities, including counsel fees, reasonably incurred by or imposed upon him in connection with any proceeding to which he may be a party, or in which he may become involved, by reason of his being or having been an officer or director of the Corporation, or any settlement thereof, whether or not he is a director or officer at the time such expenses are incurred, except in such cases wherein the director or officer is adjudged guilty of willful misfeasance or malfeasance in the performance of his duties, provided that in the event of a settlement the indemnification herein shall apply only when Board of Directors approves such settlement and reimbursement as being for the best interest of the Corporation. The foregoing right of indemnification shall be in addition to and not exclusive of all other rights to which such directors or officers may be entitled.

ARTICLE VIII
BY-LAWS

The By-Laws of the Corporation shall be those By-Laws set forth in the aforesaid Declaration of Condominium and may be altered, amended or rescinded in the manner provided by the said By-Laws.

ARTICLE IX
AMENDMENTS

Amendments to the Articles of Incorporation shall be adopted in the following manner:

These Articles of Incorporation may be amended at any regular or special meeting of the members of the Corporation, called in accordance with the By-Laws by the affirmative vote of a majority of the members. Each member shall have the number of votes specified in Article IV of these Articles.

ARTICLE X
TERM

The term of the Corporation shall be the life of the condominium unless the Corporation is terminated sooner by the unanimous action of its members. The Corporation shall be terminated by the termination of the condominium in accordance with the condominium documents.

ARTICLE XI
SUBSCRIBERS

The names and residences of the subscribers to these Articles of Incorporation are:

(Here list names and addresses of Subscribers)

IN WITNESS WHEREOF, the subscribers hereto have affixed their signatures this _____ day of _____, 19_____.

_____

_____

_____

(Notarized)

No. 8–4
CONDOMINIUM CONTRACT

FHA FORM NO. 3279
Rev. January 1967

U.S. DEPARTMENT OF HOUSING AND URBAN DEVELOPMENT
FEDERAL HOUSING ADMINISTRATION

_____

MODEL FORM OF SUBSCRIPTION AND PURCHASE AGREEMENT*
(Section 234, National Housing Act)

*(To be executed in triplicate, one copy with indicated
attachments to be retained by the Subscriber.)*

Application No._____

Family Unit No._____

Project_____

Date_____

WHEREAS,_____ (here-
inafter called Seller) is the owner of [or proposes to construct] a multifamily housing project
known as

_____located at_____
_____ and WHEREAS, the said project is
proposed to be converted to a Condominium; And

WHEREAS, 80 percent of the total value of the family units in the project (or such
lesser precent as may be approved by the Federal Housing Administration [hereinafter
referred to as the FHA]) must be sold to purchasers approved by the FHA before its
insurance of individual mortgages under Section 234 (c) of the National Housing Act; and

WHEREAS, it will be necessary to establish an association of owners for the operation
and regulation of the "common areas and facilities" of the Condominium;

BE IT AGREED AS FOLLOWS:

1. Subscription and Purchase Amount

I/We_____, in consideration of the
mutual promises of other subscribers and other good and valuable considerations, and
having a bona fide intention to reside in a unit in the above-referred-to project, hereby

_____

*This form is required in cases where subscriber seeks an insured mortgage under Section 234.

subscribe for participation in_____

(hereinafter called Association) and hereby agree to purchase the above-numbered family unit and the_____percentage undivided interest in the common areas and facilities** for the price of $_____, payable as follows: $_____ upon signing this agreement; $_____ within_____days after date hereof and the balance at time of conveyance as provided in paragraph 3, hereof.

Seller hereby agrees that all sums received on account of the purchase of the family unit shall be held in trust and shall be placed in an escrow account with_____

_____Bank under an escrow agreement, the terms of which are acceptable to the FHA. The escrow agreement shall provide that Seller shall not be entitled to receive any sums in the escrow until conveyance of title.

I/We hereby subscribe to the Plan of Apartment Ownership, Association By-Laws and Regulatory Agreement, copies of which are attached hereto and receipt of which is hereby acknowledged. I/We hereby agree that, in addition to the purchase price above mentioned, I/We will be liable for our proportionate share of the Association assessments as outlined in the By-Laws. I/We also agree that in addition to the above-mentioned purchase price we will pay to the Association at or before conveyance of title the sum of $_____ _____, representing our proportionate share of the Association's required working capital.

2. Plan and Purpose

The Association will be established for the purpose of operating and maintaining the common areas and facilities of the Condominium. Each owner of a family unit in the Condominium will be a member of the Association and will be subject to the by-laws and regulations thereof. As set forth in the Plan of Apartment Ownership, the vote of each member will be based on the ratio of the value of the family unit(s) which he owns to the total value of the entire project.

The affairs of the Association will be conducted by a Board of Directors as provided for in the By-Laws.

3. Conveyance of Title

In consideration of this subscription the Seller agrees to convey to Subscriber good and marketable title to said family unit. Subscriber agrees to purchase said family unit from the Seller within thirty (30) days after Seller has notified Subscriber it is prepared to tender title and possession thereof to him for an amount equal to the purchase price. It is contemplated that the unpaid purchase price will be secured by an individual mortgage on the family unit insured by the FHA under Section 234. Subscriber may, however, pay this

_____

**References hereinafter made to "family unit" shall include the undivided interest in the common areas and facilities.

amount in cash or may elect to finance under a conventional uninsured mortgage. It is understood that Subscriber will, at the time title is conveyed to him, pay such closing costs as are customarily paid by the purchaser of comparable real estate in this jurisdiction and taxes, assessments and insurance will be adjusted to the date of closing. The FHA estimate of value of the above-described family unit is $_____.

4. Location of Project

The above-referred-to housing project will be located at_____
_____ in the City of _____.
Nearest public transportation in the form of (bus, streetcar, subway, train service)*** is available at the following points:

_____.

Churches, schools, shopping centers, playgrounds and other community facilities available to members of the project are located as follows:

_____
_____
_____

5. Priority of Mortgage Lien

This Agreement and all rights hereunder are and at all times shall be subject and subordinate to the lien of the mortgage and accompanying documents to be executed by the Subscriber to a lending institution and to be insured under Section 234 of the National Housing Act; and to any and all modifications, extensions, and renewals thereof; and to any mortgage or deed of trust made in place thereof.

6. Cancellation Rights

In the event Subscriber shall have died prior to his acquisition of title to the family unit, the Seller reserves the right to return such amount or amounts to Subscriber's estate or legal representative, and thereupon all rights of Subscriber shall cease and terminate without further liability on the part of the Seller.

It is understood that Subscriber's credit is subject to approval by the Federal Housing Administration. In the event the FHA determines that Subscriber does not meet its credit requirements for participation in this project or Subscriber is unable to obtain an FHA-insured mortgage thereupon within_____days from date hereof, seller shall have privilege of withdrawal from this contract and the Seller shall return to Subscriber all of the sums paid hereunder and this Agreement shall be deemed null and void and all of Subscriber's and Seller's rights shall cease and terminate without further liability on the part of either party.

*** Strike out inappropriate reference

If Subscriber within five (5) days after the execution of this Agreement notifies the Seller in writing that Subscriber wishes to withdraw from this Agreement, the amounts theretofore paid by him under this Agreement will be returned to him and thereupon all rights and liabilities of Subscriber hereunder shall cease and terminate. The right of the Subscriber to withdraw shall, however, expire unless exercised within such five-(5) day period, except that if title to the family unit is not conveyed to the Subscriber in accordance with FHA requirements on or before_____, the Subscriber and the Seller shall have the right to withdraw from this agreement, in which event Seller shall return to Subscriber all sums paid hereunder and Subscriber's and Seller's rights shall cease and terminate without further liability on the part of either party.

If the subscriber shall default in any of the payments or obligations called for in this Agreement, and such default shall continue for fifteen (15) days after notice sent by registered mail by the seller to the subscriber at the address given below, then, forthwith at the option of the seller, the subscriber shall lose any and all rights under this Agreement, and any amount paid toward the purchase price may be retained by the seller as liquidated damages, or may at the option of the seller be returned less the subscriber's proportionate share of expenses to be determined solely by the seller.

The Seller, may, at its option, release the obligations of Subscriber under this Agreement in the event Subscriber shall secure another subscriber who is satisfactory to the Seller and to the Federal Housing Administration. This agreement is not otherwise assignable.

7. Function of FHA in Connection with this Project

The FHA as insurer of the individual mortgage loan covering a family unit does not insure Subscriber against loss. The validity of title is the responsibility of the Seller and the parties to the mortgage transaction and not of the FHA. FHA has not examined or approved any advertising or informational material in connection with this project other than that contained in this Subscription and Purchase Agreement.

8. Oral Representation Not to be Relied Upon

This Agreement will supersede any and all understandings and agreements and constitutes the entire agreement between the parties and no oral representations or statements shall be considered a part hereof.

9. Types of Dwelling Units Available

Attached hereto as Exhibit "A" is a listing of the various family units in connection with this project, showing types, cash down payment requirements, estimated monthly assessments by the Association and estimated monthly mortgage payments, inclusive of deposits for mortgage insurance premiums and taxes, which will be applicable in the event individual mortgages are insured under Section 234 of the National Housing Act.

10. <u>Interim Occupancy on Rental Basis</u>

You as a subscriber may, if you desire, move into the completed dwelling unit prior to conversion of the project to condominium ownership, provided the proposed Seller permits you to do so and the FHA approves such interim occupancy. If you do so, however, you should be mindful of the fact that prior to passage of title you will be occupying the premises merely as a tenant of the proposed Seller and you are therefore advised not to expend any sums for improvements without a written agreement and authority from the proposed Seller satisfactory to you as to the manner in which compensation or adjustments will be made for such expenditures in the event the conversion to condominium ownership does not ultimately materialize.

WITNESS:

_____   _____
                                                    (Subscriber)

                                             _____
                                                    (Subscriber)

                                             _____
                                                    (Address)

                                             _____
                                                    (Telephone)

                                             _____
                                                 (Name of Corporation)

                                             _____
                                                    (Address)

                                             _____
                                                    (Telephone)

                                             _____
                                             (President or other Corporate Officer)

                                             _____
                                                    (Address)

                                             _____
                                                    (Telephone)

No. 8–5
CLAUSES IN CONDOMINIUM MORTGAGE

The forms that may be used for mortgaging condominium property are, as a rule, similar to those in use for other forms of real estate ownership.[1]

---

1. See Chapter __15__, Mortgages.

The description of the property should clearly state that portion of the property being mortgaged, as follows:

Condominium apartment unit # _____ , of _____ Condominium, Inc., all as set forth in the Declaration of Condominium and the exhibits annexed thereto and forming a part thereof, recorded in Official Records Book _____ , at page _____ of the Public Records of _____ County, State of _____ . Together with all of the appurtenances thereto, including an undivided _____ % interest in and to the common elements of said condominium.

All of the foregoing condominium apartment unit is situated on a portion of Lot _____ , Block _____ in _____ Subdivision, according to the Public Records of _____ County, State of _____ . A more detailed meets and bounds description that the said condominium apartment unit is situated on is set forth in the said Declaration of Condominium.

In addition to the above, a condominium mortgage should contain a reference clause to the Declaration of Condominium, as follows:

This is a mortgage on an apartment in a condominium together with appurtenances thereto. The failure of the mortgagor to pay any assessments required to be paid pursuant to the Declaration of Condominium or to otherwise comply with any of the terms, covenants or conditions of said Declaration shall constitute a default under this mortgage; and the mortgagee may, at its option, immediately or thereafter, declare the indebtedness secured hereby due and payable.

No. 8–6
WARRANTY DEED
For Condominiums

THIS INDENTURE, made this _____ day of _____ , 19 _____ , between _____ , a corporation existing under the laws of the State of _____ , having its principal place of business in the County of _____ , State of _____ , as Grantor, and _____ _____ , as Grantee(s), whose address is _____ _____ .

WITNESSETH: That the Grantor, for and in consideration of the sum of $ _____ _____ , and other good and valuable considerations, to it in hand paid by the Grantee(s), the receipt whereof is hereby acknowledged, has granted, bargained and sold to the Grantee(s), his heirs and assigns forever, the following described real property located, situate, lying and being in the County of _____ , and State of _____ , to wit:

Condominium Unit No. _____ of _____ Condominium Apartments, Inc., according to the Declaration of Condominium thereof, recorded in Official Records Book _____ , Page _____ , of the public records of _____ County, State of _____ , together with all appurtenances thereto, including the undivided interest in the common elements of said Condominium.

This conveyance is subject to the following:

1. Taxes and assessments for the year 19_____, and subsequent years thereto.

2. Conditions, restrictions, limitations, covenants running with the land, and easements appearing of record.

3. Zoning ordinances of _____County, State of_____.

4. The Declaration of Condominium and exhibits attached thereto and the Articles of Incorporation and By-Laws of _____ Condominium Apartments, Inc.

The said Grantor does hereby fully warrant the title to said real property and will defend the same against the lawful claims of all persons whomsoever.

IN WITNESS WHEREOF, the said Grantor has caused these presents to be signed in its name by its proper officers, and its corporate seal to be affixed, attested by its secretary, the day and year above written.

(Corporate Seal)

Attest:_____   _____ Condominium
                          Secretary   Apartments, Inc.
Signed, sealed and delivered
in the presence of:

_____   By:_____
                                                   President

_____

9

Cooperatives

9

Cooperatives

In a cooperative form of group ownership, each tenant of a building is a stockholder in a corporation that owns the real estate. Members of the cooperative are jointly and severally responsible for the obligations and actions of the corporation.

The members possess a percentage portion of the corporation, and are periodically assessed (usually monthly or quarterly) a fixed amount that goes toward the payment of taxes, mortgages, salaries, repairs, as well as all other operational expenses.

Unlike condominium ownership, the tenant-stockholder does not possess any specific area. He can sell his interest in the structure, but is guided in this as well as other corporate related acts by the terms and conditions of the project's Articles of Incorporation and By-Laws.

As well as for the purpose intended, the Federal Housing Administration's model forms reproduced within this chapter are readily adaptable for use in private cooperative projects.

Those preparing Cooperative forms should bear in mind the necessity of fulfilling local statute requirements. These should be complied with and included with the forms presented here.

No. 9–1
MODEL FORM OF
CERTIFICATE OF INCORPORATION*

(For Sales Type Cooperative Corporations Organized on a Stock Basis under Section 213 Involving Community Facilities and One or More Project Mortgages)

This is to certify:

That we, the subscribers:_____,

(Name)

whose post office address is_____

_____, whose post office address is

(Name)

---

*Should be drawn in a format to conform to laws of jurisdiction in which filed.

_____ ; and

_____ , whose post office adddress is
                    (Name)
_____ , all being of full legal age, do,
under and by virtue of the general laws of the State of_____ , authorizing
the formation of corporations, associate ourselves with the intention of forming a Corporation pursuant to the following:

ARTICLE I-NAME

The name of the Corporation is_____ .

ARTICLE II-PURPOSES

The purpose for which the Corporation is formed and the business and objects to be
carried on and promoted by it are as follows:

(a) to create a corporation to provide housing on a cooperative basis and to provide
on a cooperative basis the community facilities as described in Appendix A hereof
and such additions or changes thereto as are approved by the Preferred Stockholders, to be regulated by the Federal Housing Commissioner (hereinafter
called the "Commissioner") as to sales, charges, capital structure, and methods
of operation in the manner and for the purposes provided in Section 213 of Title II
of the National Housing Act, as amended, (hereinafter called the "Act") and the
Administrative Regulations thereunder; to enable the financing of such housing
and community facilities with the assistance of mortgage insurance under the Act,
as amended, in accordance with the provisions of any state or local laws pro-
hibiting discrimination in housing on the basis of race, color, creed, or national
origin, and with the Regulations of the Federal Housing Administration providing for nondiscrimination and equal opportunity in housing, on the understanding that failure or refusal to comply with any such provisions shall be a
proper basis for the Commissioner to take any corrective action he may deem
necessary including, but not limited to the rejection of future applications for
FHA mortgage insurance and the refusal to enter into future contracts of any kind
with which the corporation, corporate officers, directors, trustees, managers or
stockholders are identified; and as such housing corporation, to acquire any real
estate or interest or rights therein or appurtenant thereto and any and all personal
property in connection therewith. So long as any of the dwellings or property listed
and described in Appendix B hereof is owned by this corporation or by a share-
holder of this corporation or is encumbered by a Mortgage or Deed of Trust
insured under the Act or held by the Commissioner, or so long as any such property
dwelling is owned by the Commissioner, the corporation shall engage in no other
business than the construction and operation of a housing development and the
described community facilities, all on a non-profit cooperative basis.

(b) to construct, operate, maintain and improve, and to sell, convey, assign, mortgage
or lease any real estate and any personal property necessary to the operation of

such development and community facilities;

(c) to borrow money and issue evidence of indebtedness in furtherance of any or all of the objects of its business; to secure the same by mortgage, deed of trust, pledge or other lien;

(d) to enter into, perform and carry out contracts of any kind necessary to, or in connection with, or incidental to the accomplishment of any one or more of the purposes of the corporation; and

(e) to make patronage refunds to stockholders, occupants of living units, or others as provided for in the by-laws.

ARTICLE III-ADDRESS

The Post Office address of the place at which the principal office of the Corporation in this State will be located is _____ .
The resident agent of the Corporation on whom process may be served is _____
_____ , whose Post Office address is _____
_____ .

ARTICLE IV-DIRECTORS AND OFFICERS

The number of directors of the corporation shall be as provided in the by-laws. The directors shall be elected by the regular members except as herein otherwise provided, and shall act as such until their successors are duly chosen and qualified. Officers shall be elected as provided for in the by-laws.

ARTICLE V-CAPITAL STOCK

The total amount of the capital stock of the Corporation shall be _____
shares, of which 5 shares having a par value of $20.00 per share shall be designated as Preferred stock*, and _____ shares having a par value of $ _____ per share shall be designated as Common Stock**.

Section 1. Provision of Preferred Stock Power and Authority of Holders Thereof

Subsection 1. Upon insurance by the Commissioner of a certain Mortage or Deed of Trust (herein after called the Mortage) said Preferred Stock shall be issued to the Federal Housing Administration (hereinafter called the "Administration") or to its designated representatives, and delivered to the Commissioner in order that the Commissioner, in connection with the insurance of said Mortage under the Act, may regulate and restrict the Corporation as to rents or sales, charges, capital structure, rate of return and methods of

---

* This stock must be registered in the name of the Federal Housing Administration; it must be par stock; the value and number of shares (not less than 5) may vary from that designated herein but the consideration paid for it will always be $100. The certificate should contain a statement of the rights, privileges and restrictions pertaining to this stock.

** The "common stock" may be par or no par and may provide for such classes or preferences as are deemed appropriate. The total number of shares of common stock should equal the total number of units covered by the commitment.

operation as provided in this Certificate of Incorporation and to enable the Commissioner to protect the contingent liability of the Administration as insurer of such mortgage or of subsequent insured mortgages covering any of the dwellings or property described in Appendix B. So long as any mortgage insurance pertaining to any of the said dwelling units or property shall be in effect, or any mortgage covering any of said dwelling units or property shall be held by the Commissioner, or any of said dwelling units or property shall be owned by the commissioner, said Preferred Stock shall be held by the Commissioner or his successors and shall be registered upon the books of the Corporation in the name of the Administration or its nominees. During such period the Corporation shall not be required to recognize any persons other than the Administration, or representatives of the Administration, as the holders of the Preferred Stock.

Subsection 2. The Preferred Stock at any time outstanding may be redeemed by the Corporation at par, provided, however, that such stock shall not be redeemed (1) if any of the dwellings or property described in Appendix B is covered by an FHA insured mortgage, (2) if the Commissioner is the holder of a mortgage on any of said dwellings or property, or (3) if the Commissioner is the owner of any of said dwellings or property. Notwithstanding the above provisions, the Preferred Stock shall be redeemed by the Corporation at par when the request for same has been received from the Preferred Stockholder. Preferred Stock, so redeemed, shall be retired or cancelled.

Section 2. Rights in Case of Default

In the event of any default by the Corporation, as hereinafter defined, and during the period of such default or at any time during the period between initial and final endorsement of any mortgage executed by the Corporation for mortgage insurance by the Commissioner whether or not a default has occurred, the holder or holders of the Preferred Stock, voting as a class and for the purpose of making effective the regulation and restriction set forth in this Certificate of Incorporation, and to protect the interest of the Administration, shall be entitled to remove all existing directors of the Corporation and to elect a new board of directors in their stead consisting of three members, through either of the following procedures:*

Subsection 1. The president or the secretary, or either of them, as may be required by law, shall, at the request in writing of the holders of record of a majority of shares of the Preferred Stock, addressed to him at the office of the Corporation and stating the purpose of the meeting, forthwith call a special meeting, to take place within ten days after such call, of the Preferred Stockholders for the purpose of removal of existing directors and officers and the election of new directors and officers. If such officer shall fail to issue a call for such meeting within three days after the receipt of such request, then the holders of a majority of the shares of the Preferred Stock may do so by giving notice as provided by law, or, if not so provided, then by giving ten days' notice of the time, place and object of the meeting by advertisement inserted in any newspaper published in the county or city in which the principal office of the Corporation is situated;

---

*   In Insurance Upon Completion cases, delete the phrase "or at any time during the period between initial and final endorsement for mortgage insurance by the Commissioner whether or not a default has occurred."

OR

Subsection 2. Such meeting may be called pursuant to the statutes of the jurisdiction under which the Corporation was organized, or pursuant to the Statutes of the Jurisdiction in which the property described in Appendix B is situated;

OR

Subsection 3. Notwithstanding either of the foregoing Subsection 1 or 2, the holders of the Prefered Stock may, by waiver of notice, or by three days' notice by registered mail given on behalf of the Commissioner, call and hold a meeting either in the offices of the Administration in Washington, D.C., or in the offices of the Insuring Office in the state in which the property described in Appendix B is situated.

Subsection 4. At the meeting held pursuant to such notice or call, without regard to whether such call is issued pursuant to the provisions of Subsection 1, 2 or 3 of this Section, the holders of the Preferred Stock shall proceed to elect three new directors (the number being limited to three under either of said provisions), any or all of whom may be Preferred Stockholders, but one of whom, at the discretion of the Preferred Stockholders, may be a Common Stockholder.

Subsection 5. When such default shall have been cured, and the Commissioner shall have so advised the former president or secretary to that effect, and shall have advised either of them that satisfactory evidence has been submitted to the effect that any further defaults of a similar nature will not be permitted again to recur, if within the power of the officers or stockholders to prevent the same, or if there has been no default when the mortgage note has been finally endorsed for mortgage insurance, then the right again to elect directors of their own choosing shall be vested in the holders of the Common Stock who shall proceed to give notice to the holders of both the Common and the Preferred Stock of their intention to hold a meeting, stating the date and place of such meeting, for the purpose of removing existing directors and electing new directors.

Section 3. Powers, Duties and Rights of Holders of Common Stock

Subsection 1. Except as otherwise provided by law or as set forth in this Certificate of Incorporation, all voting rights shall be vested in the holders of the Common Stock.

Section 4. Dividends

Unless otherwise required by law no dividend shall be paid at any time upon any class of stock issued by the Corporation.

Section 5. Rights on Dissolution

In the event of any voluntary or involuntary liquidation or dissolution of the Corporation, the holders of the Preferred Stock shall be entitled to receive for each share held, out of the assets of the Corporation available for distribution to its stockholders, whether from capital, surplus or earnings, an amount equal to the par value of each share held, before any distribution of such assets shall be made to the holders of the Common Stock.

ARTICLE VI-REQUIRED RESERVES

Section 1. Reserve Fund or Funds for Replacements

Commencing on the date of the first payment toward amortization of the principal of any FHA-insured mortgage executed by this Corporation unless a later date is approved in writing by the holders of the Preferred Stock, a Reserve Fund for Replacements for any such mortgage shall be established and maintained by the Corporation by the allocation thereto of an amount equal to 1/12 of the annual reserve required by the FHA commitment applicable to any such FHA-insured mortgage and a like amount monthly thereafter. At the election of the Corporation, any such Fund may be maintained in the form of cash or may be invested in obligations of, or fully guaranteed as to principal by the United States of America. Any such Fund shall be maintained in a separate account with the mortgagee (or in the case of a deed of trust, with the beneficiary) or under the control of the mortgagee in a safe and responsible depository designated by the mortgagee, and shall at all times be under the control of the mortgagee. Any such Fund shall be for the purpose of effecting the replacement of structural elements and mechanical equipment of the property covered by the respective mortgage and for such other purposes as may be agreed to in writing by the holders of the Preferred Stock. Disbursements from any such Fund may be made only after receiving the consent in writing of the holders of the Preferred Stock: Provided, however, that upon the payment in full of the respective FHA-insured mortgage executed by the Corporation, the Corporation shall cease to be obligated to make monthly payments to the respective Reserve Fund for Replacements and disbursements from the respective Reserve Fund for Replacements shall be only for such purposes as may be agreed to in writing by the holders of the Preferred Stock. Upon completion of the community facilities as approved by the FHA and with the prior written consent of the holders of the Preferred Stock, the amount remaining in any Reserve Fund for Replacements shall be transferred to a new Reserve Fund for Replacements designated as the Community Facility Reserve Fund for Replacements which shall be under the control of the Corporation in such manner as the Corporation shall prescribe.

Section 2. Operating Reserve or Reserves

Commencing at occupancy of any of the dwelling units listed and described in Appendix B which are covered by an FHA-insured mortgage executed by the Corporation, a General Operating Reserve shall be established and maintained for the dwelling units covered by any such mortgage by allocation and payment thereto monthly of an amount equivalent to not less than 3% of the monthly amount otherwise chargeable to the members pursuant to their occupancy agreements. Such reserve shall remain in a special account and may be in the form of a cash deposit or invested in obligations of, or fully guaranteed as to principal by, the United States of America, and shall at all times be under the control of the Corporation. Such cumulative reserve or reserves are intended to provide a measure of financial stability during periods of special stress and may be used to meet deficiencies from time to time as a result of delinquent payment by individual cooperators, to provide funds for the re-purchase of stock of withdrawing members and other contingencies. Disbursements totaling in excess of 20% of the total balance of any such reserve as of the close of the preceding annual period may not be made during any annual period without the consent of the holders of the Preferred Stock. Reimbursements shall be made to any such account upon payment of delinquencies or sale of stock for which funds were withdrawn from the respective reserve: Provided, however, that upon payment in full of the respective FHA-insured mortgage executed by the Corporation, the Corporation shall cease to be obligated to make payments to the respective General Operating Reserve; and upon the completion of the community facilities as appproved by the FHA and with the prior consent of the Preferred Stockholders, the amount remaining in any General Operating Reserve shall be transferred to a new General Operating Reserve designated as the Community Facility Operating Reserve, which shall be under the control of the Corporation in such manner as it shall prescribe.

ARTICLE VII-RULES FOR CONDUCT OF AFFAIRS

The following provisions are hereby adopted for the conduct of affairs of the Corporation and in regulation of the powers of the Corporation, the directors and stockholders:

Section 1. Limitations on Alienation, Encumbrances, Remodeling, Occupancy,
Changing Corporate Structure, Disposition of Excess Mortgage Funds.

The Corporation shall not without prior approval of the holders of the Preferred Stock, given in writing, (a) sell, assign, transfer, rent, lease, dispose of or encumber any real or personal property; (b) remodel, reconstruct, demolish or subtract from any property owned by the Corporation; (c) permit the occupancy of any of the dwelling accommodations of the Corporation except at the charges fixed by the schedule of charges provided for hereinafter; (d) permit occupancy of any of the dwelling accommodations of the Corporation except by a tenant-stockholder of the Corporation; (e) consolidate or merge the Corporation into or with any other Corporation; go into voluntary liquidation; carry into effect any plan of reorganization of the Corporation; cancel any of its shares of Preferred Stock, or effect any changes whatsoever in its capital structure; alter or amend this Certificate of Incorporation; or amend its by-laws; (f) fail to establish and maintain the Fund or Funds for Replacements and General Operating Reserve or Reserves or any other fund or reserve as set forth in this Certificate of Incorporation; (g) incur liabilities (direct or contingent) with respect to the particular dwellings and property covered by any mortgage executed by the Corporation which will exceed in the aggregate 1% of the FHA commitment amount applicable to the particular dwellings and property covered by any such mortgage, provided that this requirement shall be applicable only so long as any such mortgage executed by the Corporation is insured or held by the FHA; (h) fail to provide in a manner approved by the holders of the Preferred Stock for the management of any dwelling units or property covered by an FHA-insured mortgage or by a mortgage held by FHA and executed by the Corporation; (i) invest any funds of the Corporation in any property, real, personal or mixed, except obligations of, or fully guaranteed as to principal by, the United States of America as provided in this Certificate of Incorporation provided this requirement shall be applicable only so long as any mortgage executed by the Corporation is insured or held by the FHA.

Section 2. Limitations on Carrying Charges

Monthly carrying charges charged to members during the initial occupancy period shall be made by the Corporation in accordance with a schedule of charges filed with and approved in writing by the holders of the Preferred Stock prior to the opening of the development for occupancy. Such charges shall be in an amount sufficient to meet the FHA estimate of cooperative management expense, operating expense and maintenance expense, debt service, taxes, special assessments and ground rents, if any, reserves and all other expenses of the Corporation. Subsequent to the initial occupancy period, charges made by the Corporation for its accommodations shall be in accordance with a schedule of charges filed with and approved in writing by the holders of the Preferred Stock and shall be in amounts sufficient to meet the Corporation's estimate of expenses set forth in an operating budget which shall be prepared and submitted to the FHA sixty days prior to the beginning of each fiscal year. The operating budget shall set forth the anticipated income of the development and a sufficiently detailed estimate of expenses which will include separate estimates for administration expense, operating expense, maintenance expense, utilities, hazard insurance, taxes and assessments, ground rent, interest and amortization, mortgage insurance premium, replacement reserve and operating reserve. The Corporation shall not permit occupancy of its accommodations except in accordance with a schedule of charges approved by the holders of the Preferred Stock and such schedule shall not be changed except with the written approval of the Preferred Stockholders; nor shall occupancy be permitted by the Corporation except upon the execution of an occupancy agreement in a form approved by the holders of the Preferred Stock. The property of the Corporation shall not be rented as an entirety.

Section 3. Limitation on Payments

During the period between initial and final endorsement for mortgage insurance by the Administration, no compensation or fee shall be paid nor obligation therefor incurred by the Corporation except with the prior written approval of the holders of the Preferred Stock. Thereafter* no compensation or fee shall be paid by the Corporation except for necessary services and except at such rate as is fair and reasonable in the locality for similar services, nor, except with the prior written approval of the holders of the Preferred Stock, shall any compensation be paid by the Corporation to its officers, directors or stockholders, or to any person, or corporation, for supervisory or managerial services; nor shall any compensation be paid by the Corporation to any employee in excess of $4,000 per annum, except with such prior written approval. No officer, director, stockholder, agent, or employee of the Corporation shall in any manner become indebted to the Corporation, except on account of approved occupancy charges: Provided, however, that upon the payment in full of all FHA-insured mortgages covering the property described in Appendix B and executed by the Corporation, the limitations herein shall not be applicable.

---

* In Insurance Upon Completion cases, delete the first sentence of this section, the word "Thereafter," and begin the section with the words "No compensation . . ."

Section 4. Maintenance Requirements

The Corporation shall maintain its property, the grounds, buildings and equipment appurtenant thereto, in good repair and in such condition as will preserve the health and safety of its members.

Section 5. Requirements as to Corporate Property and Records

The Corporation, its property, equipment, buildings, plans, office, apparatus, devices, books, contracts, records, documents and papers shall be subject to inspection and examination by the holders of the Preferred Stock or their duly authorized agent at all reasonable times.

Section 6. Uniform Record System Required

The books and accounts of the Corporation shall be kept in accordance with the Uniform System of Accounting prescribed by the holders of the Preferred Stock. The Corporation shall file with the holders of the Preferred Stock and the mortgagee the following reports verified by the signature of such officers of the Corporation as may be designated and in such form as may be prescribed by the holders of the Preferred Stock.

(a) monthly or quarterly operating reports, when required by the holders of the Preferred Stock;

(b) semi-annual financial statement within sixty days after the semi-annual period when required by the holders of the Preferred Stock;

(c) annual reports prepared by a certified public accountant or other person acceptable to the holders of the Preferred Stock, within sixty days after the end of each fiscal year, when required by the holders of the Preferred Stock;

(d) specific answers to questions upon which information is desired from time to time relative to the operation and condition of the property and the status of any mortgage;

(e) copies of minutes of all stockholders' meetings certified to by the secretary of the Corporation within thirty days after such meetings, and copies of minutes of director's meetings, when required by the holders of the Preferred Stock.

Section 7. Limitations Against Racial Restrictions

The Corporation shall not execute or file for record any instrument which imposes a restriction upon the sale, leasing, occupancy, or use of the property described in Appendices A & B, or any part thereof, on the basis of race, color or creed.

ARTICLE VIII-CONTRACTUAL POWERS

No contract or other transaction between this Corporation and any other corporation, and no act of this Corporation, shall in any way be affected or invalidated by the fact that any of the directors or officers of this Corporation are pecuniarily or otherwise interested in, or are directors or officers of, such other corporation; any directors individually, or any firm of which any director may be a member, may be a party to, or may be pecuniarily or otherwise interested in, any contract or transaction of this Corporation, provided the fact that he or such firm is so interested, shall be disclosed on the minutes of this Corporation; and any director of this Corporation who is also a director or officer of such other corporation or who is so interested may be counted in determining the existence of a quorum at any meeting of the board of directors of this Corporation, which shall authorize any such contract or transaction, provided, however, such director may not vote threat to authorize any such contract or transaction.

ARTICLE IX–EVENTS OF DEFAULT

The happening of any of the following events shall constitute a default within the meaning of that word as used in this Certificate of Incorporation: (1) the failure of the Corporation to have dismissed within thirfy days after commencement of any bankruptcy, receivership, or any petition for reorganization filed by or against the Corporation under the provisions of any State insolvency law or under the provisions of the Bankruptcy Act of 1898, as amended, or upon the making by the Corporation of an assignment for the benefit of its creditors, unless said action is previously approved in writing by the holders of the Preferred Stock; (2) the failure of the Corporation to pay the principal, interest, or any other payment due on any note, bond, or other obligation executed by it, as called for by the terms of such instrument; (3) the failure of the Corporation to establish and maintain the Reserve Fund or Funds for Replacements and General Operating Reserve or Reserves or any other fund or reserve as provided in Article Sixth hereof or the use of such reserves except as permitted in said Article; (4) execution or filing for record by the Corporation of any instrument which imposes a restriction upon sale, leasing, occupancy, or use of the property or any part thereof, on the basis of race, color or creed; (5) the violation of any of the terms of this Certificate of Incorporation, or the failure of the Corporation to perform any of the covenants, conditions or provisions required by it to be performed by this Certificate, the By-laws of the Corporation, of any FHA-insured Mortgage or mortgage held by the FHA, and executed by the Corporation, or any contract to which the Corporation and the Commissioner shall be parties, or the failure to carry out in full the terms of any agreement whereby the loan covered by any FHA-insured Mortgage executed by the Corporation is to be advanced or the project is to be constructed and operated; (6) the attempt by the Corporation, its officers, directors or stockholders to accomplish by indirect methods that which they are not permitted by the terms hereof to do directly; (7) the failure of the Corporation to report to the holders of the Preferred Stock any changes in its officers and directors or in its official address to which mail is to be directed or notices sent; (8) the failure of the Corporation to complete the community facilities described in Appendix A within the time provided for in the FHA Commitment.

ARTICLE X-DURATION

The duration of the Corporation shall be _____ .*

(To be appropriately executed and Acknowledged)

---

* In those states where the statutes do not permit corporations to have a perpetual duration, a clause substantially as follows should be added: "Six months prior to the period heretofore mentioned, this Corporation shall take the necessary steps to extend the life of this Certificate of Incorporation for such additional period of time as the FHA directs. Failure of the Corporation to extend the life of the Corporation for such additional period shall be considered an event of default in addition to the events enumerated in the preceding Article."

No. 9–2
COOPERATIVE BY-LAWS
Prepared For FHA Use In Section 213, 221, and 236 Cases

ARTICLE I
NAME AND LOCATION OF CORPORATION

Section 1. The name of this Corporation is _____
_____. Its principal office is
located at _____,
_____.

ARTICLE II
PURPOSE

Section 1. The purpose of this Corporation is to provide its members* with housing and community facilities, if any, on a nonprofit basis consonant with the provisions set forth in its Certificate of Incorporation.

ARTICLE III
MEMBERSHIP

Section 1. *Eligibility.* Any natural person approved by the Board of Directors shall be eligible for membership, provided that he or she executes a Subscription Agreement and Occupancy Agreement in the usual form employed by the Corporation covering a specific unit in the housing project.**

Section 2. *Application for Membership.* Application for membership shall be presented in person on a form prescribed by the Board of Directors, and all such applications shall be acted upon promptly by the Board of Directors.

Section 3. *Subscription Funds.* *** All subscription funds (except funds required for credit reports) received from applicants prior to the endorsement of the mortgage note by the Federal Housing Administration (hereinafter sometimes referred to as the "Administration") shall be deposited promptly without deduction in a special account or accounts of the Corporation as escrowee or trustee for the Subscribers to Membership, which monies shall not be corporate funds, but shall be held solely for the benefit of the Subscribers until transferred to the account of the Corporation as hereinafter provided. Such special account or accounts shall be established with _____

---

* In corporations organized on a stock basis, change the word "members" to "stockholders" and add thereafter the following parenthetical clause: "(hereinafter referred to as 'members')."

** In corporations organized on a stock basis, change the word "membership" to "stock ownership" and add thereafter the following parenthetical clause: "(hereinafter referred to as 'membership')."

*** In view of the fact that certain sponsoring groups such as labor unions, veterans' organizations, chruch groups, cooperative sponsoring organizations, may wish to use some other method of handling subscriptions or subscriptions funds, this section may be altered, subject to prior approval of the Administration.

(name of institution) located at_____ ,
whose deposits are insured by an agency of the Federal Government. Such account or
accounts may be interest bearing, with the interest earned to be retained and owned by the
Corporation. Such funds shall be subject to withdrawal, or transfer to the account of the
Corporation or disbursed in a manner directed by the Corporation only upon certification
by the President and Secretary of the Corporation to the above-named institution or in-
stitutions that:

(a) The Subscription Agreement of a named applicant has been terminated pursuant to
its terms and such withdrawal is required to repay the amount paid by him under
such agreement; or

(b) Applicants for_____* dwelling units have not been procured within
the effective period of the FHA Commitment, or any extension thereof, and such
withdrawal is required to repay to the applicants the amounts paid by them; or

(c) Applicants for_____* dwelling units (or such lesser number as may
be approved by the Administration) have signed Subscription Agreements, have
been approved as to their credit by the Administration, and have paid the subscription price in full. If these requirements have been met and the mortgage loan
has been scheduled for closing with the approval of the Administration, the entire
amount of the funds in the subscription escrow account may be transferred to
the corporation, at which time the corporation shall issue and deliver membership
certificates to all members.

If more than one mortgage is to be executed by the corporation, this section shall be deemed
to be applicable to the specific subscription fund received from applicants with respect to the
specific dwelling units to be covered by each mortgage and to require the creation of separate
and specific escrow accounts with respect to each mortgage.

Section 4. *Members.* The members shall consist of the incorporators and such subscribers as have been approved for membership by the Board of Directors and who have paid
for their membership and received membership certificates. The status of the incorporators
as members shall terminate at the first annual meeting of members unless they have executed
Subscription Agreements and, where required by the Administration, Occupancy Agreement. The authorized membership of the Corporation shall consist of_____
regular memberships.**

Section 5. *Membership Certificates.* Each membership certificate shall state that the
Corporation is organized under the laws of the State of _____ ,
the name of the registered holder of the membership represented thereby, the Corporation
lien rights as against such membership as set forth this Article, and the preferences and
restrictions applicable thereto, and shall be in such form as shall be approved by the Board
of Directors. Membership certificates shall be consecutively numbered, bound in one or
more books, and shall be issued therefrom upon certification as to full payment. Every

---

*   Insert number required by the applicable FHA Commitment.
**   In cases where FHA control is via ownership of preferred stock, add "and_____preferred
memberships."

membership certificate shall be signed by the President or Vice President, and the Secretary, and shall be sealed with the corporate seal.

Section 6. *Lost Certificates.* The Board of Directors may direct a new certificate or certificates to be issued in place of any certificate or certificates previously issued by the corporation and alleged to have been destroyed or lost, upon the making of an affidavit of that fact by the person claiming the share certificate to be lost or destroyed. When authorizing such issuance of a new certificate or certificates, the Board of Directors may, in its discretion, and as a condition precedent to the issuance thereof, require the registered owner of such lost or destroyed certificate or certificates, or his legal representative, to advertise the same in such manner as the Board of Directors shall require and to give the Corporation a bond in such sum as the Board of Directors may require as indemnity against any claim that may be made against the Corporation.

Section 7. *Lien.* The Corporation shall have a lien on the outstanding regular memberships in order to secure payment of any sums which shall be due or become due from the holders thereof for any reason whatsoever, including any sums due under any occupancy agreements.

Section 8. *Transfer of Membership.* Except as provided herein, membership shall not be transferable and, in any event, no transfer of membership shall be made upon the books of the Corporation within ten (10) days next preceding the annual meeting of the members. In all transfers of membership the Corporation shall be entitled to a fee it deems appropriate to compensate it for the processing of the transfer.

(a) *Death of Member.* If, upon death of a member, his membership in the Corporation passes by will or intestate distribution to a member of his immediate family, such legatee or distributee may, by assuming in writing the terms of the Subscription Agreement and Occupancy Agreement, where required by the Administration, within sixty (60) days after member's death, and paying all amounts due thereunder, become a member of the Corporation. If member dies and an obligation is not assumed in accordance with the foregoing, then the Corporation shall have an option to purchase the membership from the deceased member's estate in the manner provided in paragraph (b) of this Section, written notice of the death being equivalent to notice of intention to withdraw. If the Corporation does not exercise such option, the provisions of paragraph (c) of this Section shall be applicable, the references to "member" therein to be construed as references to the legal representative of the deceased member.

(b) *Option of Corporation to Purchase.* If the member desires to leave the project, he shall notify the Corporation in writing of such intention and the Corporation shall have an option for a period of thirty (30) days commencing the first day of the month following the giving of such notice, but not the obligation, to purchase the membership, together with all of the member's rights with respect to the dwelling unit, at an amount to be determined by the Corporation as representing the transfer value thereof, less any amounts due by the member to the Corporation under the Occupancy Agreement, and less the cost or estimated cost of all deferred maintenance, including painting, redecorating, floor finishing, and such repairs and replacements as are deemed necessary by the Corporation to place the dwelling unit in suitable condition for another occupant. The purchase by the Corporation of the membership will immediately terminate the member's rights and the member shall forthwith vacate the premises.

(c) *Procedure Where Corporation Does Not Exercise Option.* If the Corporation waives in writing its right to purchase the membership under the foregoing option, or if the Corporation fails to exercise such option within the thirty (30) day period, the member may sell his membership to any person who has been duly approved by the Corporation as a member and occupant.

If the Corporation agrees, at the request of the member, to assist the member in finding a purchaser, the Corporation shall be entitled to charge the member a fee it deems reasonable for this service. When the transferee has been approved for the membership and has executed the prescribed Occupancy Agreement, the retiring member shall be released of his obligations under his Occupancy Agreement, provided he has paid all amounts due the Corporation to date.

(d) *Transfer Value.** Whenever the Board of Directors elects to purchase a membership, the term "transfer value" shall mean the sum of the following:

(1) The consideration (i.e. down payment) paid for the membership by the first occupant of the unit involved as shown on the books of the Corporation;

(2) The value, as determined by the Directors, of any improvements installed at the expense of the member with the prior approval of the Directors, under a valuation formula which does not provide for reimbursement in an amount in excess of the typical initial cost of the improvements; and

(3) The amount of principal amortized by the Corporation on its mortgage indebtedness and attributable to the dwelling unit involved as paid by the member involved and previous holders of the same membership.** However, the amount of principal paid by the Corporation for a period of three (3) years after the Corporation has made its first principal payment on the mortgage shall not be included in this computation.

Section 9. *Termination of Membership for Cause.* In the event the Corporation has terminated the rights of a member under the Occupancy Agreement, the member shall be required to deliver promptly to the Corporation his membership certificate and his Occupancy Agreement, both endorsed in such manner as may be required by the Corporation. The Corporation shall thereupon at its election either (1) repurchase said membership at its transfer value (as hereinabove defined) or the amount the retiring member originally paid

---

*   If desired, a provision may be added to the effect that the transfer value otherwise applicable may be increased and decreased pursuant to fluctuations in the economy as evidenced by a Cost of Living Index or a Construction Cost Index. The language of such provision must be cleared with the FHA.

**   In Section 221 below market interest rate cases and in Section 236 cases the sentence following the asterisks should be added. (A limitation which further restricts the amount payable to the retiring member in such cases may be imposed subject to the approval of FHA).

for the acquisition of his membership certificate, whichever is the lesser, or (2) proceed with reasonable diligence to effect a sale of the membership to a purchaser and at a sales price acceptable to the Corporation. The retiring member shall be entitled to receive the amount so determined, less the following amounts (the determination of such amounts by the Corporation to be conclusive):

(a) any amounts due to the Corporation from the member under the Occupancy agreement;

(b) the cost or estimated cost of all deferred maintenance, including painting, redecorating, floor finishing, and such repairs and replacements as are deemed necessary by the Corporation to place the dwelling unit in suitable condition for another occupant; and

(c) legal and other expenses incurred by the Corporation in connection with the default of such member and the resale of his membership. In the event the retiring member for any reason should fail for a period of 10 days after demand to deliver to the Corporation his endorsed membership certificate, said membership certificate shall forthwith be deemed to be cancelled and may be reissued by the Corporation to a new purchaser.

*Section 10. *Sales Price.* Memberships may be sold by the Corporation or the member only to a person approved by the Board of Directors in accordance with the requirements of the Regulatory Agreement, and the sales price shall not exceed the transfer value as provided in this Article, except that in sales effected by the Corporation a service charge not in excess of $100 may be charged by the Corporation. Where the sale is accomplished by a member, a certificate in form approved by the FHA as to the price paid shall be executed by the seller and purchaser and delivered to the Corporation.

ARTICLE IV
MEETINGS OF MEMBERS

Section 1. *Place of Meetings.* Meetings of the membership shall be held at the principal office or place of business of the Corporation or at such other suitable place convenient to the membership as may be designated by the Board of Directors.

Section 2. *Annual Meetings.* The first annual meeting of the Corporation shall be held on_____. (Date) Thereafter, the annual meetings of the Corporation shall be held on the_____(1st, 2nd, 3rd, 4th)_____ (Monday, Tuesday, Wednesday, etc.) of_____ (Month) each succeeding year. At such meeting there shall be elected by ballot of the members a Board of Directors in accordance with the requirements of Section 3 of Article V of these By-Laws. The members may also transact such other business of the Corporation as may properly come before them.

Section 3. *Special Meetings.* It shall be the duty of the President to call a special meeting of the members as directed by resolution of the Board of Directors or upon a petition signed by twenty (20) percent of the members having been presented to the Secretary, or at

---

* Omit in Section 213 cases and market interest rate cases under Section 221 (d) (3).

the request of the Federal Housing Commissioner or his duly authorized representative. The notice of any special meeting shall state the time and place of such meeting and the purpose thereof. No business shall be transacted at a special meeting except as stated in the notice unless by consent of four-fifths of the members persent, either in person or by proxy.

Section 4. *Notice of Meetings.* It shall be the duty of the Secretary to mail a notice of each annual or special meeting, stating the purpose thereof as well as the time and place where it is to be held, to each member of record, at his address as it appears on the membership book of the Corporation, or if no such address appears, at his last known place of address, at least_____ but not more than_____days prior to such meeting (the number of days notice to comply with state statute). Service may also be accomplished by the delivery of any such notice to the member at his dwelling unit or last known address. Notice by either such method shall be considered as notice served. Notices of all meetings shall be mailed to the Director of the local insuring office of the Federal Housing Administration.

Section 5. *Quorum.* The presence, either in person or by proxy, of at least_____ * percent of the members of record of the Corporation shall be requisite for, and shall constitute a quorum for the transaction of business at all meetings of members. If the number of members at a meeting drops below the quorum and the question of a lack of quorum is raised, no business may thereafter be transacted.

Section 6. *Adjourned Meetings.* If any meeting of members cannot be organized because a quorum has not attended, the members who are present, either in person or by proxy, may, except as otherwise provided by law, adjourn the meeting to a time not less than forty-eight (48) hours from the time the original meeting was called, at which subsequent meeting the quorum requirement shall be_____ * percent.

Section 7. *Voting.*** At every meeting of the regular members, each member present, either in person or by proxy, shall have the right to cast one vote on each question and never more than one vote. (Note—If desired, a provision may be included to the effect that where a husband and wife are joint members, each shall be entitled to cast a one-half vote.) The vote of the majority of those present, in person or by proxy, shall decide any question brought before such meeting, unless the question is one upon which, by express provision of statute or of the Certificate of Incorporation or of these By-Laws, a different vote is required, in which case such express provision shall govern and control. No member shall be eligible to vote or to be elected to the Board of Directors who is shown on the books or

---

*   The figure to be inserted will vary with the size of the cooperative, as follows:

Number of Memberships	Quorum percentage to be inserted in Article IV, Sec. 5	Quorum percentage applicable to adjourned meetings to be inserted in Article IV, Sec. 6
20 or less	50	25
21–150	25	15
151–300	20	10
301–500	15	10
501 or more	10	5

** There will be no objection to including a provision permitting voting by mail, and this may be desirable in the larger cooperatives.

management accounts of the Corporation to be more than 30 days delinquent in payments due the Corporation under his Occupancy Agreement.

Section 8. *Proxies.* A member may appoint as his proxy only a member of his immediate family (as defined by the Board of Directors) except that an unmarried member may appoint any other member as his proxy. In no case may a member cast more than one vote by proxy in addition to his own vote. Any proxy must be filed with the Secretary before the appointed time of each meeting.

Section 9. *Order of Business.* The order of business at all regularly scheduled meetings of the regular members shall be as follows:

(a) Roll Call.
(b) Proof of notice of meeting or waiver of notice.
(c) Reading of minutes of preceding meeting.
(d) Reports of Officers.
(e) Report of committees.
(f) Election of inspectors of election.
(g) Election of directors.
(h) Unfinished business.
(i) New Business.

In the case of special meetings, items (a) through (d) shall be applicable and thereafter the agenda shall consist of the items specified in the notice of meeting.

If present, a representative of the Administration will be given an opportunity to address any regular or special meeting.

ARTICLE V
DIRECTORS

Section 1. *Number and Qualification.* The affairs of the Corporation shall be governed by a Board of Directors composed of_____ persons*, a majority of whom shall be members of the Corporation.

Section 2. *Powers and Duties.* The Board of Directors shall have all the powers and duties necessary for the administration of the affairs of the Corporation and may do all such acts and things as are not by law or by these By-Laws directed to be exercised and done by the members. The powers of the Board of Directors shall include but not be limited:

(a) To accept or reject all applications for membership and admission to occupancy of a dwelling unit in the cooperative housing project, either directly or through an authorized representative;

(b) Subject to the approval of the Administration, to establish monthly carrying charges as provided for in the Occupancy Agreement, based on an operating budget formally adopted by such Board;

(c) Subject to the approval of the Administration, to engage an agent or employees for the management of the project under such terms as the Board may determine;

---

* Any convenient number of Directors (not less than three nor more than nine) may be provided.

(d) To authorize in their discretion patronage refunds from residual receipts when and as reflected in the annual report;*

(e) To terminate membership and occupancy rights for cause;

(f) To promulgate such rules and regulations pertaining to use and occupancy of the premises as may be deemed proper and which are consistent with these By-Laws and the Certificate of Incorporation; ** and

(g) ***Pursuant to a plan approved by the Administration, to prescribe additional monthly carrying charges to be paid by families whose incomes exceed the limitations for continuing occupancy established from time to time by the Administration; or, at the Board's option, to terminate the membership and occupancy of such families.

Section 3. *Election and Term of Office.* The term of the Directors named in the Certificate of Incorporation shall expire when their successors have been elected at the first annual meeting or any special meeting called for that purpose. At the first annual meeting of the members the term of office of two Directors shall be fixed for three (3) years. The term of office of two Directors shall be fixed at two (2) years, and the term of office of one Director shall be fixed at one (1) year. At the expiration of the initial term of office of each respective Director, his successor shall be elected to serve a term of three (3) years. The Directors shall hold office until their sucessors have been elected and hold their first meeting. (If a larger Board of Directors is contemplated, the terms of office should be established in a similar manner so that they will expire in different years.)

Section 4. *Vacancies.* Vacancies in the Board of Directors caused by any reason other than the removal of a Director by a vote of the membership or by the vote of the preferred members**** shall be filled by vote of the majority of the remaining Directors, even though they may constitute less than a quorum; and each person so elected shall be a Director until a successor is elected by the members at the next annual meeting to serve out the unexpired portion of the term.

Section 5. *Removal of Directors.* At any regular or special meeting duly called, any Director may be removed with or without cause by the affirmative vote of the majority of the entire regular membership of record and a successor may then and there be elected to fill the vacancy thus created. Any Director whose removal has been proposed by the members shall be given an opportunity to be heard at the meeting. The term of any Director who becomes more than 30 days delinquent in payment of his carrying charges shall be automatically terminated and the remaining Directors shall appoint his successor as provided in Section 4, above.

Section 6. *Compensation.* No compensation shall be paid to Directors for their services as Directors. No remuneration shall be paid to a Director for services performed by him for

---

   *   Delete in Section 236 cases.

  **   Add "and the Regulatory Agreement" where Regulatory Agreement is executed by the Corporation.

 ***   Include this provision only in Section 221 below market rate cases.

****   Delete "or by a vote of the preferred members" where Corporation has executed Regulatory Agreement.

the Corporation in any other capacity, unless a resolution authorizing such remuneration shall have been unanimously adopted by the Board of Directors before the services are undertaken. No remuneration or compensation shall in any case be paid to a Director without the approval of the Administration. A Director may not be an employee of the Corporation.

Section 7. *Organization Meeting.* The first meeting of a newly elected Board of Directors shall be held within ten (10) days of election at such place as shall be fixed by the Directors at the meeting at which such Directors were elected, and no notice shall be necessary to the newly elected Directors in order legally to constitute such meeting, providing a majority of the whole Board shall be present.

Section 8. *Regular Meetings.* Regular meetings of the Board of Directors may be held at such time and place as shall be determined, from time to time, by a majority of the Directors, but at least four such meetings shall be held during each fiscal year. Notice of regular meetings of the Board of Directors shall be given to each Director, personally or by mail, telephone or telegraph, at least three (3) days prior to the day named for such meeting.

Section 9. *Special Meetings.* Special meetings of the Board of Directors may be called by the President on three days' notice to each Director, given personally or by mail, telephone or telegraph, which notice shall state the time, place (as hereinabove provided) and purpose of the meeting. Special meetings of the Board of Directors shall be called by the President or Secretary in like manner and on like notice on the written request of at least three Directors.

Section 10. *Waiver of Notice.* Before or at any meeting of the Board of Directors, any Director may, in writing, waive notice of such meeting and such waiver shall be deemed equivalent to the giving of such notice. Attendance by a Director at any meeting of the Board shall be a waiver of notice by him of the time and place thereof. If all the Directors are present at any meeting of the Board, no notice shall be required and any business may be transacted at such meeting.

Section 11. *Quorum.* At all meetings of the Board of Directors, a majority of the Directors shall constitute a quorum for the transaction of business, and the acts of the majority of the Directors present at a meeting at which a quorum is present shall be the acts of the Board of Directors. If, at any meeting of the Board of Directors, there be less than a quorum present, the majority of those present may adjourn the meeting from time to time. At any such adjourned meeting, any business which might have been transacted at the meeting as originally called may be transacted without further notice.

Section 12. *Fidelity Bonds.* The Board of Directors shall require that all officers and employees of the Corporation handling or responsible for corporate or trust funds shall furnish adequate fidelity bonds. The premiums on such bonds shall be paid by the Corporation.

Section 13. *Safeguarding Subscription Funds.* It shall be the duty of the Board of Directors to see to it that all sums received in connection with membership subscriptions prior to the closing of the mortgage transaction covering the housing project of the Corporation, are deposited and withdrawn only in the manner provided for in Article III, Section 3 of these By-Laws.

ARTICLE VI
OFFICERS

Section 1. *Designation*. The principal officers of the Corporation shall be a President, a Vice President, a Secretary, and a Treasurer, all of whom shall be elected by and from the Board of Directors. The Directors may appoint an assistant treasurer, and an assistant secretary, and such other officers as in their judgment may be necessary. (In the case of a corporation of one hundred members or less the offices of Treasurer and Secretary may be filled by the same person).

Section 2. *Election of Officers*. The officers of the Corporation shall be elected annually by the Board of Directors at the organization meeting of each new Board and shall hold office at the pleasure of the Board.

Section 3. *Removal of Officers*. Upon an affirmative vote of a majority of the members of the Board of Directors, any officer may be removed, either with or without cause, and his successor elected at any regular meeting of the Board of Directors, or at any special meeting of the Board called for such purpose.

Section 4. *President*. The President shall be the chief executive officer of the Corporation. He shall preside at all meetings of the members and of the Board of Directors. He shall have all of the general powers and duties which are usually vested in the office of president of a corporation, including but not limited to the power to appoint committees from among the membership from time to time as he may in his discretion decide is appropriate to assist in the conduct of the affairs of the Corporation.

Section 5. *Vice President*. The Vice President shall take the place of the President and perform his duties whenever the President shall be absent or unable to act. If neither the President nor the Vice President is able to act, the Board of Directors shall appoint some other member of the Board to so do on an interim basis. The Vice President shall also perform such other duties as shall from time to time be imposed upon him by the Board of Directors.

Section 6. *Secretary*. The Secretary shall keep the minutes of all meetings of the Board of Directors and the minutes of all meetings of the members of the Corporation; he shall have the custody of the seal of the Corporation; he shall have charge of the stock transfer books and of such other books and papers as the board of Directors may direct; and he shall, in general, perform all the duties incident to the office of Secretary.

Section 7. *Treasurer*. The Treasurer shall have responsibility for corporate funds and securities and shall be responsible for keeping full and accurate accounts of all receipts and disbursements in books belonging to the Corporation. He shall be responsible for the deposit of all moneys and other valuable effects in the name, and to the credit, of the Corporation in such depositaries as may from time to time be designated by the Board of Directors.

ARTICLE VII
RIGHTS OF FEDERAL HOUSING ADMINISTRATION

Section 1*. The management, operation and control of the affairs of the Corporation shall be subject to the rights, powers, and privileges of the Federal Housing Administration pursuant to a Regulatory Agreement between the Corporation and the Federal Housing Administration. The Corporation is bound by the provisions of the Regulatory Agreement which is a condition precedent to the insurance of a mortgage of the Corporation on the project.

ARTICLE VIII
AMENDMENTS

Section 1. These By-Laws may be amended by the affirmative vote of the majority of the entire regular membership of record at any regular or special meeting, provided that no amendment shall become effective unless and until it has received the written approval of the Administration. Amendments may be proposed by the Board of Directors or by petition signed by at least twenty (20) percent of the members. A description of any proposed amendment shall accompany the notice of any regular or special meeting at which such proposed amendment is to be voted upon.

ARTICLE IX
CORPORATE SEAL

Section 1. *Seal.* The Board of Directors shall provide a suitable corporate seal containing the name of the Corporation, which seal shall be in charge of the Secretary. If so directed by the Board of Directors, a duplicate of the seal may be kept and used by the Treasurer or any assistant secretary or assistant treasurer.

ARTICLE X
FISCAL MANAGEMENT

Section 1. *Fiscal Year.* The fiscal year of the Corporation shall begin on the_____ day of_____every year, except that the first fiscal year of the Corporation shall begin at the date of incorporation. The commencement date of the fiscal year herein established shall be subject to change by the Board of Directors should corporate practice subsequently dictate, but not without the prior written approval of the Administration.

Section 2. *Books and Accounts.* Books and accounts of the Corporation shall be kept under the direction of the Treasurer and in accordance with the Uniform System of Ac-

---

* Delete the language of this section where FHA regulation is exercised through ownership of preferred stock rather than by Regulatory Agreement and substitute the following:

"**Section. 1.** *Rights of Federal Housing Administration.* The rights and privileges of the regular memberships of the Corporation and the management, operation and control of the affairs of the Corporation shall be subject to the rights, powers and privileges of the preferred memberships of the Corporation registered in the name of the Federal Housing Administration as provided in the Certificate of Incorporation."

counts prescribed by the FHA Commissioner. That amount of the carrying charges required for payment on the principal of the mortgage of the Corporation or any other capital expenditures shall be credited upon the books of the Corporation to the "Paid-In Surplus" account as a capital contribution by the members.

Section 3. *Auditing.* At the closing of each fiscal year, the books and records of the Corporation shall be audited by a Certified Public Accountant or other person acceptable to the Administration, whose report will be prepared and certified in accordance with the requirements of the Administration. Based on such reports, the Corporation will furnish its members with an annual financial statement including the income and disbursements of the Corporation. The Corporation will also supply the members, as soon as practicable after the end of each calendar year, with a statement showing each members's pro rata share of the real estate taxes and mortgage interest paid by the Corporation during the preceding calendar year.

Section 4. *Inspection of Books.* Financial reports such as are required to be furnished to the Administration and the membership records of the Corporation shall be available at the principal office of the Corporation for inspection at reasonable times by any members.

Section 5. *Execution of Corporate Documents.* With the prior authorization of the Board of Directors, all notes and contracts, including Occupancy Agreements, shall be executed on behalf of the Corporation by either the President or the Vice President, and all checks shall be executed on behalf of the Corporation by (1) either the President or the Vice President, and countersigned (2) by either the Secretary or Treasurer.

ARTICLE XI*
COMMUNITY FACILITY PROVISIONS

Section 1. *Applicable Provisions.* Notwithstanding any provision herein to the contrary, upon the payment in full of each FHA-insured mortgage executed by the Corporation and the release of the dwelling units included therein to the respective members, the following provisions of these By-Laws shall not be applicable to such members:

(a) Article III; and

(b) Sections 2 and 13 of Article V; and

in lieu thereof the following provisions shall apply to such members, and to all members upon payment in full of all FHA-insured mortgages executed by the Corporation:

Section 2. *Membership.*

(a) *Members.* Members shall consist of the owners of the dwelling units listed in Appendix B of the Articles of Incorporation, a copy of which is attached hereto, who have been approved for membership by the Board of Directors, and who have paid for their membership and received membership certificates, and such other persons to whom memberships have been transferred as provided herein.

---

* This Article to be included only in Sales Type projects where community facilities are to be owned by the Corporation.

(b) *Transfer of Membership.* Except as herein provided, memberships are not transferable or assignable:

1. The Board of Directors shall determine the membership value (hereinafter called the "Membership Fee") at which same may be transferred.

2. Subject to the prior approval of the Board of Directors, memberships may be permanently transferred by members to any of the following, in the order listed:

   a. To the purchaser or lessee of the member's home if same is listed in Appendix B of the Articles of Incorporation.

   b. To the owner or lessee of any of the other houses listed in Appendix B of the Articles of Incorporation who does not already own a membership.

   c. To the applicant for membership at the top of a waiting list maintained by the Board of Directors, who is a resident of the area, the confines of which shall be as determined by the Board of Directors.

   d. To a non-resident of the area.

(c) *Temporary Transfers.* Subject to the prior approval of the Board of Directors, a member may temporarily assign his membership to his lessee for a designated period of time provided, however, that the member making the temporary assignment remains obligated to the Corporation for the payment of all assessments and other charges approved by the membership, and for the payment of the lessee's dues. Any delinquency in payment of dues, assessment and such other charges shall be subject to the provisions of paragraph (d) hereof.

(d) *Termination of Membership.* Any member failing to pay annual dues, assessments or other charges duly approved by the Board of Directors within thirty (30) days after notification of delinquency has been mailed to him at the address appearing on the records of the Corporation shall be suspended by the Board of Directors. Any person thus suspended shall be notified promptly in writing by the Secretary of his suspension, and if the amounts due and payable are not paid within fifteen (15) days after the sending of such notice he shall cease to be a member of the Corporation and shall not be entitled to the privileges accorded to members. The Corporation shall be obligated, after reassignment and sale of said membership to return the Membership Fee less amounts due. (The Board of Directors, in its discretion, may reinstate any member upon request and payment of all amounts in arrearage.) The Board of Directors, at its discretion, may cancel the membership of any member upon the return of the Membership Fee provided, however, that the member may be reinstated upon appeal and approval of reinstatement by the majority of the members present at a regular or special meeting. The Corporation shall not be obligated to refund any membership fee to any member except as provided herein.

Section 3. *Directors.* The Board of Directors shall have the powers and duties necessary for the administration of the affairs of the Corporation and may do all such acts and things as are not by law or by these By-Laws directed to be exercised and done by the members. The powers of the Board of Directors shall include but not be limited:

(a) To promulgate such rules and regulations pertaining to the use and operation of the community facilities which are consistent with these By-Laws and the Certificate of Incorporation.

(b) To establish the annual dues, assessments and charges for the operation and maintenance of the community facilities and any other property, real or personal, owned by the Corporation.

No. 9-3

FHA FORM NO. 3241-D
February 1969

U. S. DEPARTMENT OF HOUSING AND URBAN DEVELOPMENT
FEDERAL HOUSING ADMINISTRATION

MODEL FORM OF INFORMATION BULLETIN
For Prospective Members

NOTE: This Bulletin is designed to furnish the information that applicants for membership generally desire. Any information not included in this Model Form should, of course, be furnished applicants upon request. The Bulletin is to be followed verbatim with only such deletions and additions as will conform to the facts of the proposed project. The actual form to be used must be cleared by the FHA prior to public solicitation.

TO APPLICANTS FOR MEMBERSHIP IN

_____
Name of Cooperative Corporation
(hereinafter called the "Cooperative")

Date _____

1. <u>INTRODUCTION.</u>

A subscription for membership in a housing cooperative is more than an application for a place to live. It lends to your participation in the cooperative ownership and operation of a housing project. There has been a sharp increase in cooperative ownership of housing in the United States during recent years. Much of this increase in cooperatively-owned units has been attributed to cooperatives whose mortgages have been insured by the Federal Housing Administration. The reasons for this increase in popularity of cooperatives in the housing field are many and varied. The cooperative approach to housing instills a pride of ownership resulting in a deeper interest in maintaining the property and participating in civic affairs. A cooperative is operated on a democratic basis. It gives the residents a greater insight and appreciation of the democratic process in general. Cooperative residents normally occupy the premises for longer terms than renters. The members thus become better acquainted with their fellow residents and learn to work together for the over-all betterment of the project and the community. This working together makes for better understanding between individuals of different backgrounds and income levels.

Cooperative housing offers the following financial benefits:

(1) The absence from the monthly housing cost of the owner's profit inherent in most rental projects.
(2) Tax benefits as described later in this Bulletin.
(3) Rental schedules usually include an allocation for vacancy loss. In a cooperative, the monthly charges usually include only such income losses, if any, as have actually been incurred.
(4) Maintenance costs in a well-operated cooperative are minimized since experience has shown that owners take better care of their property. Cooperative members frequently handle the redecoration of their units on a "do-it-yourself" basis, thus eliminating this as a project expense.
(5) A cooperative is operated on a nonprofit basis. Thus, increases in the monthly housing cost are limited to actual increases in operating costs.
(6) If a cooperative is successfully operated, a modest equity accrued upon resale may result, subject to limitations set forth in the By-Laws.

Your cooperative is receiving the benefit of special financing which Congress provided in Section 236 of the National Housing Act to assist families of lower income and displaced families in meeting their housing needs. Because of the purposes of this program, certain income limitations are necessary, as described later in this Information Bulletin.

This Bulletin is intended to provide general information concerning the above cooperative which will be found useful when read in conjunction with the Articles of Incorporation, Regulatory Agreement, By-Laws, Occupancy Agreement and Subscription Agreement*, copies of which you have received or will receive at the time you sign a Subscription Agreement.

_____

* Insert "Cooperative Agency Agreement" in cases where the cooperative has retained an organizing agent.

The Subscription Agreement is the document in which you apply for membership in the cooperative; the Occupancy Agreement describes the terms and conditions under which you will occupy one of the dwelling units therein; the Articles of Incorporation and By-Laws set forth the authority and methods of operation of the cooperative; and the Regulatory Agreement is the agreement by the cooperative to be regulated and restricted in certain respects by the FHA as provided by law. ⌈In cases where a Cooperative Agency Agreement is used, add, "and the Cooperative Agency Agreement spells out the relationship between the cooperative and the organization which is forming the cooperative and soliciting memberships."⌉ It is strongly urged that you read these documents.

2. COOPERATIVE METHOD OF OPERATION.

The cooperative has been incorporated as a nonprofit cooperative housing corporation for the purpose of acquiring, owning, and operating a housing project consisting of (an apartment house-apartment houses-individual homes-town houses-semidetached houses)* the permanent occupancy of which will be restricted to (members-stockholders), in the cooperative. If your subscription is accepted by the cooperative and approved by the FHA, you will become a member of the cooperative. The cooperative will deliver to you the stock or membership certificate representing your interest in the cooperative not later than the time of initial mortgage closing, provided your cash equity investment has been paid in full in accordance with the terms of the Subscription Agreement. Each member of the cooperative, regardless of the dollar amount of his investment, will have one vote.

The affairs of the cooperative will be conducted by a Board of Directors. Until the first membership election, the Board of Directors will consist of the following named individuals;** _____ , _____ _____ , _____ . The first annual stockholders' meeting will be held on _____ _____ .

It is contemplated that the cooperative will enter into an agreement for management of the project with _____ _____ for an initial term of _____ (months) (years) at a fee computed and payable monthly in an amount equivalent to _____ _____ .

One of the most important functions the members will be called upon from time to time to perform is the selection of qualified directors. The cooperative functions through its Board of Directors, which acts on behalf of the member. The Board performs important duties such as engaging a management agent acceptable to the mortgagee and to the FHA for the operation of the project; establishing eligibility standards for admission to membership; determining the degree and type of maintenance and service; promulgating rules and regulations pertaining to use and occupancy of the premises; and adopting an operating budget subject to the approval of the FHA which must reflect carrying charges adequate to meet the costs of operation. Thus the voting right means that the member participates through his elected representatives in the management of the project's affairs. Each member should bear in mind that the management agent takes its assignments from the President of the Board of Directors, speaking for the Board, and not from individual members. A cooperative that harbors irresponsible factions which are at odds creates an undesirable image. Property values could be adversely affected in a project known for its irresponsible actions. The elected Board of Directors should receive the full support of all the members. Full support does not preclude constructive criticism. If necessary, any Board member who is not properly fulfilling his duties may be removed by a vote of the members as prescribed in the By-Laws.

3. FINANCING THE PROJECT.

This cooperative housing development is being constructed in _____ sections (numbered _____) each of which will be separately financed through an FHA-insured mortgage. This Information Bulletin relates to the _____ sections only, but it is contemplated that as each section is constructed, title will vest in a single cooperative corporation. The management and operation of all _____ sections will be combined; one Board of Directors will be elected by the members to govern the entire housing development; and the mortgage notes and mortgages will become the obligation of the single cooperative corporation. The carrying charges under Occupancy Agreements will require the residents of each section to pay an amount at least sufficient to retire the mortgage indebtedness covering that section, including principal, interest, and required deposits into the Reserve for Replacements and General Operating Reserve. The cooperative will be responsible for its notes and mortgages on all sections owned by it and will collect sufficient carrying charges to meet all of its obligations.***

The funds provided by your subscription and the subscription of other members will constitute the equity investment and are intended to furnish the cost of acquiring the project over and above the mortgage proceeds and to provide working capital funds in the amount of _____ required by the FHA. It is anticipated that a mortgage loan in the approximate amount of $_____ , will be obtained by the cooperative from _____ _____ , a private lending institution, covering all the property of the cooperative and providing for amortization over a period of _____ years with interest at _____ %.**** This loan will be insured by the FHA only after construction of the project has been completed. The estimated cost of the project as indicated by the anticipated mortgage amount plus the amount scheduled to be collected from the members (exclusive of working capital requirements) equals $_____ . The FHA for its own purposes in determining the maximum insurable mortgage amount has estimated the replacement cost of this project at $_____ .

The cooperative's members are in effect their own landlord. They pay monthly carrying charges to their cooperative in accordance with the Occupancy Agreement. The cooperative corporation holds title to the property and executes a blanket mortgage. The individual member signs no note or mortgage and has no personal obligation thereunder.

---

* Strike out inappropriate references.
** Brief description of background and business affiliations of each should be given. The relationship, if any, between such directors and the sponsoring group or other having any interest in the undertaking should be specified.
*** Include this paragraph only in cases where one over-all cooperative is being developed in sections.
**** Include the following sentence only in insurance upon completion projects.

4. <u>FUNCTION OF FHA IN CONNECTION WITH THIS PROJECT</u>.

If the terms of the FHA Insurance Commitment are complied with, the FHA under Section 236 of Title II of the National Housing Act will insure the lending institution against loss by reason of any default of the cooperative in its obligations under the mortgage. The FHA as insurer of such mortgage loan does not insure a member of the cooperative against loss. It is contemplated that the amounts paid by an applicant for his membership subscription will be handled in accordance with the provisions of the By-Laws. Such funds will not be deposited with or be otherwise under the control or responsibility of the FHA.

While the FHA is authorized to furnish technical advice and assistance to sponsoring groups in the organization of cooperatives, such advice and assistance are of an advisory nature only. The FHA does not select the contractor, is not a party to the construction contract, and does not act as the architect of the cooperative. During the construction period the FHA will assign inspectors for the purpose of determining that the project is an acceptable security for the insurance liability assumed under the insurance contract with the lending institution.

As described in more detail in Paragraph 9 below and in the Regulatory Agreement, the FHA will make monthly payments to the mortgagee which will reduce the payments by the cooperative which would otherwise be required on the project mortgage.

5. <u>CONSTRUCTION OF PROJECT</u>.

The construction of the project will be performed by _____ , a general contractor. The performance of the contract by the general contractor will be assured in such manner as is acceptable to the cooperative, the mortgagee and the FHA. All construction must meet local building code requirements and be acceptable to the cooperative, the mortgagee and the FHA. It is difficult to predict at this time with any degree of certainty when the project will be completed. While it is in the interests of all concerned to complete the project as speedily as possible, in any construction operation there are many factors which may bring about delays. The cooperative will give you a thirty (30) day notice of the date when your dwelling unit will be available for occupancy.

The Officers and Directors of the Cooperative will authorize and execute such agreements and documents as they find necessary or advisable for the construction of the project and related facilities; purchase of the land, architectural supervision; Mortgage Notes; Mortgages; Building Loan Agreements; Regulatory Agreements; Cost Certification Agreements; acceptance or granting of easements; and other instruments required to enable the Cooperative to obtain FHA-insured mortgage loans, complete the Project and otherwise carry out the purposes of the Cooperative.

6. <u>LOCATION OF PROJECT</u>.

The above referred to housing project will be located at _____ , in the City of _____ . Nearest public transportation in the form of (bus, streetcar, subway, train service)* is available at the following points: _____ _____ . Churches, schools, shopping centers, playgrounds and other community facilities available to members of the project are located as follows: _____ _____ _____

7. <u>DESCRIPTION OF STRUCTURES</u>.

(Describe generally the type of structure or structures to be erected, the number of dwelling units, number of rooms in each, the interior and finish of the dwelling units, provision for garages, storage space, laundry rooms, children's play areas, and any other community facilities which will be owned and operated by the cooperative. It is suggested that this Bulletin be accompanied by an architect's sketch of the structures, plot layout, and sketches of floor plans or dwelling unit layouts.)

8. <u>OWNERSHIP OF REAL ESTATE</u>.

The land upon which the structures will be built consists of an area of approximately _____ (acres, square feet)*, in which the cooperative will own a (fee simple, leasehold)* estate, subject to a mortgage as hereinabove mentioned. Inasmuch as this is a cooperative project the title to the property will be held by the cooperative and not by the individuals who are members of the cooperative. **The ground lease will run for a term of _____ years and will provide for a monthly payment by the cooperative of $ _____ based upon a _____% per annum return on the FHA valuation of $ _____ .

---

* Strike out inappropriate references.
** Include the following statement only in leasehold project.

9. SCHEDULE OF DOWN PAYMENTS AND MONTHLY CARRYING CHARGES FOR EACH TYPE DWELLING UNIT.
(Changes Shown Are Estimates Based On Full Occupancy And Are Subject To Change)

1. Dwelling Unit Designation	2. Value Allocated to Unit by Sponsorship *	3. Proportionate Factor of Unit Valuation to Total Valuation **	4. Required Cash Down Payment	5. Estimated Initial Monthly Charge to be Paid to Cooperative		6.*** Estimated Monthly Personal Benefit Expense	7.*** Estimated Total Monthly Housing Expense	
				(a) Not Less Than	(b) Not More Than		(a) Not Less Than	(b) Not More Than
_____	$_____	_____	_____	_____	_____	_____	_____	_____
_____	_____	_____	_____	_____	_____	_____	_____	_____
_____	_____	_____	_____	_____	_____	_____	_____	_____
_____	_____	_____	_____	_____	_____	_____	_____	_____
_____	_____	_____	_____	_____	_____	_____	_____	_____

TOTAL VALUATION $_____

To bring the monthly carrying charges down to a level which lower income families can afford, the FHA will make an assistance payment to the mortgagee on behalf of the cooperative each month during the term of the mortgage which will reduce the payments on the project mortgage from the amount which would otherwise have been required for principal, interest and mortgage insurance premiums to the amount that would have been required for principal and interest if the mortgage had borne an interest rate of 1 percent.

The actual initial monthly carrying charges to be paid by individual members to the cooperative will be not less than the amount shown in Column 5(a) nor more than the amount shown in Column 5(b). The exact amount required will depend upon the family size and adjusted annual income of the subscribers. This amount will be made known tentatively to each subscriber after processing by the cooperative's sales agent, but the figure is subject to approval by the FHA as indicated in the Subscription Agreement.

Since the formula used to compute the individual carrying charge for each member is based on the member's income the income must be certified prior to occupancy and it must be recertified every two years, and the carrying charge of the member adjusted, where appropriate at such intervals.

_____ , a Management Agent, independent of the general contractor and landowner, has made a study of the foregoing projections and has submitted its (his) written opinion to the effect that the estimated carrying charges set forth above will be adequate to meet all expenses for the first and subsequent years of operation based on costs reasonably foreseeable as of _____ , the date of its (his) opinion. ****The detailed Operating Budget on which these carrying charges are predicated may be examined by prospective members at the address listed at the end of this Bulletin.

*****Column 6, above, does not represent any money to be paid to the cooperative. It represents an estimate of the monthly amount a member will need to pay to maintain his own unit in proper state of repair and includes estimates for monthly payment of the following utilities:_____
_____
_____ .

The amount required to maintain his unit depends to a degree upon the care and attention given by the member to his unit.

******Replacement of the kitchen range and refrigerator is a responsibility of the (individual member) (cooperative)******* and (the personal benefit expense estimate includes an amount for this purpose) (the monthly carrying charge paid to the cooperative includes an allocation for this purpose which will be deposited by the cooperative in a replacement reserve account).*******

The figures shown in columns 5(a) and 5(b) are estimated on the basis of full occupancy. Any vacancy or collection losses may require an increase in such charges. An increase may also be necessary in cases where taxes are raised, the costs of utilities furnished by the cooperative are increased or where supplies and labor costs rise. The cooperative will operate on a nonprofit basis and will collect monthly carrying charges in an amount sufficient to meet all operating costs including payments on its mortgage. The cost of amortizing the mortgage will normally remain constant since the mortgage payments have been computed in equal monthly installments covering the full term of the mortgage.

Part of the monthly carrying charge payment is deposited by the cooperative in the Reserve Fund for Replacements for the purpose of defraying at least in part the cost of replacement when it become necessary of structural components and mechanical equipment.

---

*The total of all units should equal the indicated project cost.
**Item 9(a) of the Uniform System of Accounts for Housing Cooperatives (FHA No. 4405.1) describes the procedure to determine this factor.
***Delete in cases where the monthly payment to the cooperative includes all utilities except telephone. Utilities must be handled as a corporate expense unless master-metering is not legally permissible or is not consistent with utility company requirements or general practice in the area.
****If the Management Agent is not of the opinion that such carrying charges will be adequate, his opinion on this subject should be set forth in full in the Information Bulletin. In his projections, the Management Agent should contemplate a typical year of operation and must, therefore, discount any beneficial circumstances that might apply to the first year of operation, such as tax benefits or availability of special funds or other advantages which would not apply to operations in subsequent years.
*****Include this subparagraph only where column 6 is included in the tabulation.
******If included in mortgage proceeds, replacement of kitchen ranges and refrigerators must be included in the corporate replacement reserve and not treated as a personal benefit expense.
*******Strike out inappropriate references.

Three percent of the monthly carrying charge payment is deposited in another reserve known as the General Operating Reserve, which is intended to be available for unforeseen contingencies and to finance resales of memberships, etc.

By paying the monthly carrying charges promptly as they become due, the member will save the penalty for the late payment of his charges which will otherwise be assessed against him.

10. INCOME TAX ADVANTAGES.*

(a) In computing his over-all housing cost, the member may wish to consider the benefit of the federal income tax deductions allowed to tenant-stockholders of cooperative housing corporations under the provisions of Section 216 of the Internal Revenue Code. Under this provision, provided 80 percent of the income of the cooperative consists of carrying charges received from its members, the members are entitled to deduct from their gross income their proportionate share of real estate taxes and mortgage interest paid by the cooperative. At the end of each year the cooperative will advise each member of his proportionate share of the total amounts paid by the corporation for mortgage interest and real estate taxes This will be of significance to those members whose status is such that it is in their financial interest to itemize deductions on their income tax returns. The actual amount of any tax benefit will depend upon the income of the taxpayer, as well as his deductions and tax bracket.

(b) A member of a cooperative has available to him the same basic federal income tax advantages available to a home owner who sells his home and purchases a new one. Residence has been defined by the Internal Revenue Service to include a cooperative apartment. If a person sells or exchanges his principal residence at a gain, the gain is taxable. However, if within the year before or the year after the sale, the seller buys and occupies another residence, the gain is not taxed at the time of the sale if the cost of the new residence equals or exceeds the adjusted sales price of the old residence. More complete information about this can be obtained from a booklet entitled "Selling Your Home" (Publication 523), which is available from the Internal Revenue Service.

11. RIGHT OF APPLICANT TO WITHDRAW AFTER SIGNING SUBSCRIPTION AGREEMENT.

For a period of five days after signing the Subscription Agreement, an applicant may withdraw and obtain a return of his deposit, provided he notifies the cooperative in writing to this effect. (See Subscription Agreement.)

12. MEMBER'S SUBSCRIPTION SUBJECT TO ACCEPTANCE BY COOPERATIVE AND FHA.

Your membership is not assured unless and until your application and subscription has been accepted by the cooperative and your credit and family income have been found acceptable by the FHA.

13. FAMILY INCOME AND OCCUPANCY LIMITATIONS.

To be eligible for assisted admission in a Section 236 project as a member who cannot afford the full carrying charge, a family must have an adjusted annual income which is not greater than the amounts listed below. Adjusted annual income means the total annual income during the preceding 12 months of all the members of the family who will live in the unit, without deduction for taxes and withholding, except that there will be excluded the following: (1) 5 percent of such income; (2) Unusual or temporary income; (3) The earnings of each family member who is under 21 years of age and who is living with the family; and (4) $300 for each family member who is under 21 years of age and who is living with the family.

The current income limitations are set forth below:

Eligible one person Households	Families of 2 Persons	Families of 3 and 4 Persons	Families of 5 and 6 Persons	Families of 7 or more Persons

The foregoing income limitations are subject to change from time to time by the FHA to reflect increases or decreases in construction costs and levels of income in the area.

In addition to income, initial occupancy is restricted to families and certain single persons. A "family" is defined as two or more persons related by blood, marriage, or operation of law who occupy the same unit. Single persons who are elderly or handicapped are also eligible. To qualify as "elderly" a single person must be 62 years of age or older. To qualify as "handicapped" a single person must have a physical impairment which is expected to be of long continued and indefinite duration, substantially impedes his ability to live independently, and is of such nature that his ability to live independently could be improved by more suitable housing conditions. Single persons meeting the income requirements who are not elderly are eligible to the extent of 10% of the dwelling units in the project.

Preference for occupancy will be given to those families or persons displaced from their homes by urban renewal government action, or national disaster determined by the President.

Persons or families who have incomes which exceed the foregoing income limitations are also eligible for membership. However, they will be required to pay full carrying charges and will not receive the benefit of FHA assistance payments.

* The income tax laws of some States also accord tax advantages to members of housing cooperatives. A statement to this effect, subject to approval by the FHA, can be included under this paragraph where the project is located in such States.

To achieve the purposes of the Section 236 program and to make certain that it is being used to its highest advantage, the following occupancy limitations will be observed. These limitations are distinct and separate from the maximum income limits above and are designed to provide for varying needs without under-utilization or over-crowding of housing accommodations.

Number of Bedrooms	Number of Persons	
	Minimum	Maximum
0	1	2
1	1*	2
2	2	4
3	4	6
4	6	8

Certain modifications of these occupancy limitations may be permitted IF APPROVED BY THE FHA when justified because of varying factors of age, health, etc. of the residents.

The Regulatory Agreement sets forth in more detail the requirements of the FHA concerning family income and occupancy limitations.

14. TRANSFERS FROM THE PROJECT.

If after taking occupancy you wish to move from the project, you may sell your interest, giving the cooperative the first option to purchase your stock in accordance with the terms of the By-Laws. If the cooperative fails to exercise its option, you may sell your stock and right of occupancy to a purchaser approved by the cooperative. Where the sale is accomplished by a member, a certificate in form approved by the FHA as to the price paid shall be executed by the seller and purchaser and delivered to the cooperative.

15. THIS BULLETIN IS THE ONLY INFORMATIONAL LITERATURE WHICH HAS BEEN APPROVED BY THE FHA.

The other documents listed in paragraph 1, above, have also been approved as to form by the FHA. However, these forms of documents, until the loan is endorsed for insurance, are subject to change to reflect policies and requirements adopted or approved by the FHA. The FHA has not examined nor approved any advertising or other informational material in connection with this project.

16. ADDITIONAL INFORMATION.

In this Bulletin the cooperative has endeavored to summarize pertinent facts concerning its undertaking. There may be other points which have not been covered here. If you wish to obtain further information, please feel free to communicate with:

Name _____

Address _____

Tele. No. _____

(NAME OF CORPORATION)

(STREET ADDRESS - CITY - STATE)

(Telephone No. _____)

_____
PRESIDENT
(or other corporate officer)

---

* Only if no single rooms or efficiencies are available.

HUD-Wash., D. C.

No. 9–4
SUBSCRIPTION AGREEMENT

1. Subscription Amount

    I,_____ , a legal resident of the State of_____ ,
hereinafter called the "Subscriber", in consideration of the mutual promises of other
subscribers and other good and valuable considerations, hereby subscribe for_____
_____ ( ) shares of capital stock in said corporation having a par value of $_____
per share. I hereby agree to pay the subscription price of $_____ , as follows:

    $_____ upon signing this agreement;

    $_____ on written demand by the corporation.

(Such demand will constitute notification of subscriber's acceptability for membership.)

    I hereby ratify the provisions contained in the Certificate of Incorporation, By-laws, In-
formation Bulletin, and Occupancy Agreement, copies of which are attached hereto and
receipt of which is hereby acknowledged.

2. Priority of Mortgage Lien

    This agreement and all rights hereunder are and at all times shall be subject and sub-
ordinate to the lien of the mortgage and accompanying documents to be executed by the
corporation to a lending institution and to be insured under Section 213 of the National
Housing Act; and to any and all modifications, extensions, and renewals thereof; and to any
mortgage or deed of trust made in place thereof; and to any mortgage or deed of trust which
may at any time thereafter be placed on the property of the corporation or any part thereof.

3. Occupancy Agreement

    The subscriber, if approved for membership, will be entitled to occupancy of the above
numbered dwelling unit under provisions of the above mentioned Occupancy Agreement.
It is estimated that the initial carrying charge per month for said unit will not exceed $_____ ,
but it is to be emphasized that this is only an estimate, subject to fluctuations as provided
for in the Occupancy Agreement. Subscriber agrees to execute the Occupancy Agreement
on demand and to comply with all the terms thereof.

4. Cancellation Rights

    The corporation reserves the right at any time before it has notified the subscriber of his
acceptability for membership, for reasons deemed sufficient by the corporation, to return the
amount paid by the subscriber under this agreement, or in the event the subscriber shall have
died prior to becoming a stockholder, the corporation reserves the right to return same
to subscriber's estate or legal representative, and thereupon all rights of the subscriber
shall cease and terminate without further liability on the part of the corporation.

    It is understood that the subscriber's credit is subject to approval by the Federal
Housing Administration. In the event the Federal Housing Administration determines that
the subscriber does not meet FHA credit requirements for participation in this project,
thereupon, upon return to the subscriber of the sums paid hereunder, this agreement shall

be deemed null and void and all of the subscriber's rights shall cease and terminate without further liability on the part of the corporation.

If the subscriber within_____days after the execution of this subscription agreement notifies the corporation in writing that he wishes to withdraw from the agreement, the amounts theretofore paid by him under this agreement will be returned to him and thereupon all rights and liabilities of the subscriber hereunder shall cease and terminate. The right of the subscriber to so withdraw shall, however, terminate unless exercised within such_____period, except that if membership is not fully achieved and construction of the project has not commenced within one year from the date of execution of this agreement, subscriber shall again have the right to withdraw and obtain such refund.

If the subscriber shall default in any of the obligations called for in this agreement, and such default shall continue for_____days after notice sent by registered mail by the corporation to the subscriber at the address given below, then, forthwith at the option of the corporation, the subscriber shall lose any and all rights under this agreement, and any amount paid toward the subscription price may be retained by the corporation as liquidated damages, or may at the option of the corporation be returned less the subscriber's proportionate share of expenses incurred by the corporation, such proportionate share of expenses to be determined solely by the corporation. The corporation may, at its option, release the obligations of the subscriber under this agreement in the event the subscriber shall secure an assignee of this agreement who has assumed the obligations herein contained and is satisfactory to the corporation and the Federal Housing Administration. This agreement is not otherwise assignable.

5. Oral Representations Not to be Relied Upon

This agreement will supersede any proper understandings and agreements and constitutes the entire agreement between us, and no oral representations or statements shall be considered a part hereof.

(Signatures)

_____(Set out additional disclosures required under federal Truth and Lending Act or under similar state laws.)

Subscriber's Address:_____

No. 9–5
SUBSCRIPTION AND PURCHASE AGREEMENT
PROPOSED PROJECT

Application No._____

Dwelling Unit No._____

_____, 19_____

1. Subscription Amount

I _____ , a legal resident of the State of_____, hereinafter called the "Subscriber," in consideration of the mutual promises of other subscribers and other good and valuable considerations, and having a bona fide intention to reside in the above referred to dwelling unit hereby subscribe for membership in_____, hereinafter called the "Corporation," and hereby subscribe for_____shares of capital stock in said corporation having a par value of $_____per share. I hereby agree to pay the subscription price of $_____as follows:

$_____upon signing this agreement;

$_____on written demand by the corporation.

Such demand will constitute notification of subscriber's acceptability as a stockholder and purchaser.

I hereby subscribe to the plan set forth in the Certificate of Incorporation, By-laws, and Information Bulletin, copies of which are attached thereto and receipt of which is hereby acknowledged.

2. Agreement to Purchase Individual Property

As indicated in the Information Bulletin the corporation will cause a housing project to be erected on the lots owned or to be acquired by it. This housing project will consist to _____single-family dwellings, one of which is the single-family dwelling to be erected on lot _____block_____in the City of_____, State of_____, and more conveniently identified in the caption hereof as dwelling unit_____.

Upon completion of construction of all the dwellings comprising the housing project and final endorsement of the blanket mortgage for insurance under section 213 of the National Housing Act (12 USC 1715e) and upon payment to the corporation of all sums required to be paid under this agreement, the corporation agrees to convey to the subscriber good and marketable title to said dwelling unit.

Subscriber agrees to purchase said dwelling unit from the corporation within_____ days after the corporation has notified subscriber it is prepared to tender title and possession thereof to him, for an amount equal to that portion of the blanket mortgage covering the housing project as a whole which is allocated to the captioned dwelling unit, which amount is estimated to be approximately $_____.

It is understood that subscriber will, at the time title is conveyed to him, pay such closing costs as are customarily paid by the purchases of real estate in this jurisdiction and taxes, assessments and insurance will be adjusted to the date of closing.

The FHA estimate of the replacement cost of the above described unit is $_____.

3. Financing of Purchase Price

Subscriber may wish to finance the purchase price by means of an individual mortgage made by a private lending institution and insured by the Federal Housing Administration, or he may, of course, pay the purchase price without financing if he desires to do so, or he may elect to finance the purchase price under a conventional uninsured mortgage.

4. Interim Occupancy on Rental Basis

In the event said dwelling unit becomes available for occupancy prior to completion of the housing project as a whole, subscriber shall, if requested by the corporation to do so, take possession of said dwelling unit as lessee from the corporation within _____ days after receipt of such request, at such rental as may be specified by the corporation with the approval of the FHA, it being specifically understood that any period of occupancy prior to the transfer of title to the subscriber shall be only as a tenant of the corporation.

All rental amounts paid to the corporation shall be considered as corporation income to be used for appropriate corporation purposes and will not be credited to the amount which the undersigned subscriber is to pay the purchase price for the above described dwelling unit.

In the event of interim occupancy, the corporation and the subscriber agree to execute prior to such occupancy an Interim Occupancy Agreement in such form as may be approved by the FHA.

5. Priority of Mortgage Lien

This agreement and all rights hereunder are and at all times shall be subject and subordinate to the lien of the mortgage and accompanying documents to be executed by the corporation to a lending institution and to be insured under Section 213 of the National Housing Act (12 USC 1715e); and to any and all modifications, extensions, and renewals thereof; and to any mortgage or deed of trust made in place thereof; and to any mortgage or deed of trust which may at any time thereafter be placed on the property of the corporation or any part thereof.

6. Cancellation Rights

The corporation reserves the right at any time before it has notified the subscriber of his acceptability for reasons deemed sufficient by the corporation, to return the amount or amounts paid by the subscriber under this agreement or, in the event the subscriber shall have died prior to becoming a stockholder, the corporation reserves the right to return same to subscriber's estate or legal representative, and thereupon all rights of the subscriber shall cease and terminate without further liability on the part of the corporation.

It is understood that the subscriber's credit is subject to approval by the Federal Housing Administration. In the event the Federal Housing Administration determines that the subscriber does not meet FHA credit requirements for participation in this project, thereupon, upon return to the subscriber of the sums paid hereunder, this agreement shall be deemed null and void and all of the subscriber's rights shall cease and terminate without further liability on the part of the corporation.

If the subscriber within_____days after the execution of this agreement notifies the corporation in writing that he wishes to withdraw from the agreement, the amounts theretofore paid by him under this agreement will be returned to him and thereupon all rights and liabilities of the subscriber hereunder shall cease and terminate. The right of the subscriber to withdraw shall, however, terminate unless exercised within such _____ day period, except that if membership is not fully achieved within_____from the date of execution of this agreement, subscriber shall again have the right to withdraw and obtain such refund.

If the subscriber shall default in any of the payments or obligations called for in this agreement, and such default shall continue for_____days after notice sent by registered mail by the corporation to the subscriber at the address given below, then, forthwith at the option of the corporation, the subscriber shall lose any and all rights under this agreement, and any amount paid toward the subscription price may be retained by the corporation as liquidated damages, or may at the option of the corporation be returned less the subscriber's proportionate share of expenses to be determined solely by the corporation.

The corporation may, at its option, release the obligations of the subscriber under this agreement in the event the subscriber shall secure an assignee of this agreement who has assumed the obligations herein contained and is satisfactory to the corporation and the Federal Housing Administration. This agreement is not otherwise assignable.

7. Certification re Other Mortgages

Subscriber certifies that he is not presently the mortgagor under any mortgage insured under Section 213 of the National Housing Act (12 USC 1715e) and that he is not presently the mortgagor of a mortgage or mortgages covering more than_____dwelling units insured under the National Housing Act.

8. Oral Representations Not to be Relied Upon

This agreement will supersede any and all prior understandings and agreements and constitutes the entire agreement between us, and no oral representations or statements shall be considered a part hereof._____(Set out additional disclosures required under federal Truth in Lending Act or under similar state laws.)

(Signatures)

(Courtesy of Federal Housing Administration, Washington 25, D. C.)

No. 9–6
U.S. DEPARTMENT OF HOUSING AND URBAN DEVELOPMENT
FEDERAL HOUSING ADMINISTRATION

MODEL FORM OF OCCUPANCY AGREEMENT

THIS AGREEMENT, made and entered into this_____day of_____, 19_____by and between_____ (hereinafter referred to as the Corporation), a corporation having its principal office and place of business at_____and _____(hereinafter referred to as Member).

WHEREAS, the Corporation has been formed for the purpose of acquiring, owning and operating a cooperative housing project to be located at_____ _____, with the intent that its members [in stock corporations change "members" to "stockholders" and add the following parenthetical clause "(hereinafter called members)"] shall have the right to occupy the dwelling units thereof under the terms and conditions hereinafter set forth; and

WHEREAS, the Member is the owner and holder of a certificate of membership [or _____shares of common capital stock] of the Corporation and has a bona fide intention to reside in the project;

     WHEREAS, the Corporation proposes to develop the property in_____ sections which will involve a total of approximately_____ dwelling units, with Section_____ _____thereof involving_____ of such dwelling units. (Section_____ is hereinafter referred to as the 'Project.')

     *****WHEREAS,** the Member has certified to the accuracy of the statements made in his application and family income survey and agrees and understands that family income, family composition and other eligibility requirements are substantial and material requirements of his initial and of his continuing occupancy;

     NOW, THEREFORE, in consideration of One Dollar ($1.00) to each of the parties paid by the other party, the receipt of which is hereby acknowledged, and in further consideration of the mutual promises contained herein, the Corporation hereby lets to the Member, and the Member hereby hires and takes from the Corporation, dwelling unit number_____located at _____ ;

     TO HAVE AND TO HOLD said dwelling unit unto the Member, his executors, administrators and authorized assigns, on the terms and conditions set forth herein and in the corporate Charter and By-laws of the Corporation and any rules and regulations of the Corporation now or hereafter adopted pursuant thereto, from the date of this agreement, for a term terminating on_____, 19_____, **renewable thereafter for successive three-year periods under the conditions provided for herein.

ARTICLE 1. MONTHLY CARRYING CHARGES

     Commencing at the time indicated in **ARTICLE 2** hereof, the Member agrees to pay to the Corporation a monthly sum referred to herein as "Carrying Charges", equal to one-twelfth of the Member's proportionate share of the sum required by the Corporation, as estimated by its Board of Directors to meet its annual expenses pertaining to the Project and to the community of other facilities which the Member is entitled to utilize, including but not limited to the following items:

(a) The cost of all operating expenses of the project and services furnished.

(b) The cost of necessary management and administration.

(c) The amount of all taxes and assessments levied against the project of the Corporation or which it is required to pay, and ground rent, if any.

(d) The cost of fire and extended coverage insurance on the project and such other insurance as the Corporation may effect or as may be required by any mortgage on the project.

(e) The cost of furnishing water, electricity, heat, gas, air-conditioning, garbage and trash collection, and other utilities, if furnished by the Corporation.

(f) All reserves set up by the Board of Directors pertaining to the project.

(g) The estimated cost of repairs, maintenance and replacements of the project property to be made by the Corporation.

---

*   Required only in Sec. 236 cases and in Sec. 221 below market interest rate cases.

**   The termination date to be inserted should be three years from the date of the Occupancy Agreement.

(h) The amount of principal, interest, mortgage insurance premiums, if any, and other required payments on the hereinafter-mentioned insured mortgage.

(i) Any other expenses of the Corporation approved by the Board of Directors, including operating deficiencies, if any, for prior periods.

The Board of Directors shall determine the amount of the Carrying Charges annually, but may do so at more frequent intervals, should circumstances so require. No member shall be charged with more than his proportionate share thereof as determined by the Board of Directors. That amount of the Carrying Charges required for payment on the principal of the mortgage of the Corporation or any other capital expenditures shall be credit upon the books of the Corporation to the "Paid-In Surplus" account as a capital contribution by the members.

*Notwithstanding the above provisions it is understood and agreed by the Member and the Corporation that where the annual family income of the Member is such that he is entitled to the benefit of the interest reduction payment made by the FHA to the mortgagee, the monthly Carrying Charges for the member shall be reduced to the extent required by the FHA as set forth in the Regulatory Agreement.

Until further notice from the Corporation the Monthly Carrying Charges for the above mentioned dwelling unit shall be $ _____ .

*It is understood and agreed that if the annual family income of the Member is hereafter increased, his monthly Carrying Charges will be increased to the extent required by the FHA as set forth in the Regulatory Agreement.

**The Member agrees, however, that if during the term of this agreement the total income of his family exceeds the limitations for occupancy which may be established from time to time by the Federal Housing Adminisration, he will pay to the Corporation, at the option of the Corporation and upon 60 days' written notice, additional Monthly Carrying Charges in an amount commensurate with the amount of his family income in excess of the FHA income limitations, pursuant to a plan previously developed by the Corporation and approved by the Federal Housing Administration. In no event shall the total Monthly Carrying Charge, including such additional charges for excess income, exceed that which would have been applicable had the mortgage of the Corporation borne interest at the rate of 6 percent per annum and a mortgage insurance premium of $\frac{1}{2}$ of 1 percent been required.

*The Member agrees that his family income, family composition and other eligibility requirements are substantial and material conditions with respect to the amount of monthly carrying charges he will be obligated to pay and with respect to his continuing right of occupancy. The Member agrees to make a recertification of his income to the Corporation at least every two years from the date of this Agreement so long as he is receiving the benefit of interest reduction payments made by the FHA to the mortgagee. The Member further agrees that the monthly carrying charges are subject to adjustment by the Corporation to reflect income changes which are disclosed on any of the Member's recertifications, as required by the Regulatory Agreement. Immediately upon making such adjustment, the Corporation

---

*   Required only in Section 236 cases.

**   Required only in Sec. 221 below market interest rate cases.

agrees to give 30 days written notice to the Member stating the new amount the Member will be required to pay, which, until further notice shall then be the Member's monthly carrying charge.

ARTICLE 2. WHEN PAYMENT OF CARRYING CHARGES TO COMMENCE

After thirty days' notice by the Corporation to the effect that the dwelling unit is or will be available for occupancy, or upon acceptance of occupancy, whichever is earlier, the Member shall make a payment for Carrying Charges covering the unexpired balance of the month. Thereafter, the Member shall pay Carrying Charges in advance on the first day of each month.

*ARTICLE 3. PATRONAGE REFUNDS

The Corporation agrees on its part that it will refund or credit to the Member within ninety (90) days after the end of each fiscal year, his proportionate share of such sums as have been collected in anticipation of expenses which are in excess of the amount needed for expenses of all kinds, including reserves, in the discretion of the Board of Directors.

ARTICLE 4. MEMBER'S OPTION FOR AUTOMATIC RENEWAL

It is covenanted and agreed that the term herein granted shall be extended and renewed from time to time by and against the parties hereto for further periods of three years each from the expiration of the term herein granted upon the same covenants and agreements as herein contained unless: (1) notice of the Member's election not to renew shall have been given to the Corporation in writing at least four months prior to the expiration of the then current term, and (2) the Member shall have on or before the expiration of said term (a) endorsed all his (stock) (membership certificate) for transfer in blank and deposited same with the Corporation, and (b) met all his obligations and paid all amounts due under this agreement up to the time of said expiration, and (c) vacated the premises, leaving same in good state of repair. Upon compliance with provisions (1) and (2) of this Article, the Member shall have no further liability under this agreement and shall be entitled to no payment from the Corporation.

ARTICLE 5: PREMISES TO BE USED FOR RESIDENTIAL PURPOSES ONLY

The Member shall occupy the dwelling unit covered by this agreement as a private dwelling unit for himself and/or his immediate family and for no other purpose, and may enjoy the use in common with other members of the corporation of all community property and facilities of the entire cooperative community so long as he continues to own a [membership certificate] [share of common stock] of the Corporation, occupies his dwelling unit, and abides by the terms of this agreement. Any sublessee of the Member, if approved pursuant to Article 7 hereof, may enjoy the rights to which the Member is entitled under this Article 5.

The Member shall not permit or suffer anything to be done or kept upon said premises which will increase the rate of insurance on the building, or on the contents thereof,

---

*   Omit in Section 236 cases.

or which will obstruct or interfere with the rights of other occupants, or annoy them by unreasonable noises or otherwise, nor will he commit or permit any nuisance on the premises or commit or suffer any immoral or illegal act to be committed thereon. The Member shall comply with all of the requirements of the Board of Health and of all other governmental authorities with respect to the said premises. If by reason of the occupancy or use of said premises by the Member the rate of insurance on the building shall be increased, the Member shall become personally liable for the additional insurance premiums.

ARTICLE 6. MEMBER'S RIGHT TO PEACEABLE POSSESSION

In return for the Member's continued fulfillment of the terms and conditions of this agreement, the Corporation covenants that the Member may at all times while this agreement remains in effect, have and enjoy for his sole use and benefit the dwelling unit hereinabove described, after obtaining occupancy, and may enjoy in common with all other members of the Corporation the use of all community property and facilities of the entire cooperative community.

ARTICLE 7. NO SUBLETTING WITHOUT CONSENT OF CORPORATION

The Member hereby agrees not to assign this agreement nor to sublet his dwelling unit without the written consent of the Corporation on a form approved by the Federal Housing Administration. The liability of the Member under this Occupancy Agreement shall continue notwithstanding the fact that he may have sublet the dwelling unit with the approval of the Corporation and the Member shall be responsible to the Corporation for the conduct of his sublessee. Any unauthorized subleasing shall, at the option of the Corporation, result in the termination and forfeiture of the members's rights under this Occupancy Agreement. Nonpaying guests of the Member may occupy Member's unit under such conditions as may be prescribed by the Board of Directors in the rules and regulations.

ARTICLE 8. TRANSFERS

Neither this agreement nor the Member's right of occupancy shall be transferrable or assignable except in the same manner as may now or hereafter be provided for the transfer of memberships in the By-Laws of the Corporation.

ARTICLE 9. MANAGEMENT, TAXES AND INSURANCE

The Corporation shall provide necessary management, operation and administration of the project; pay or provide for the payment of all taxes or assessments levied against the project; procure and pay or provide for the payment of fire insurance and extended coverage, and other insurance as required by any mortgage on property in the project, and such other insurance as the Corporation may deem advisable on the property in the project. The Corporation will not, however, provide insurance on the Member's interest in the dwelling unit or on his personal property.

ARTICLE 10. UTILITIES

The Corporation shall provide water, electricity, gas, heat and air-conditioning in amounts which it deems reasonable. (Strike out any of the foregoing items in this Article which are not applicable.) The Member shall pay directly to the supplier for all other utilities.

ARTICLE 11. REPAIRS

(a) *By Member:* The Member agrees to repair and maintain his dwelling unit at his own expense as follows:

    (1) Any repairs or maintenance necessitated by his own negligence or misuse;

    (2) Any recordation of his own dwelling unit; and

    (3) Any repairs, maintenance or replacements required on the following items:

      (Insert the items desired, subject to FHA approval.)

(b) *By Corporation.* The Corporation shall provide and pay for all necessary repairs, maintenance and replacements, except as specified in clause (a) of this Article. The Officers and employees of the Corporation shall have the right to enter the dwelling unit of the Member in order to effect necessary repairs, maintenance, and replacements, and to authorize entrance for such purposes by employees of any contractor, utility company, municipal agency, or others, at any reasonable hour of the day and in theve ent of emergency at any time.

(c) *Right of Corporation to Make Repairs at Member's Expense.* In case the Member shall fail to effect the repairs, maintenance or replacements specified in clause (a) of this Article in a manner satisfactory to the Corporation and pay for same, the latter may do so and add the cost thereof to the Member's next month's Carrying Charge payment.

ARTICLE 12. ALTERATIONS AND ADDITIONS

The Member shall not, without the written consent of the Corporation, make any structural alterations in the premises or in the water, gas or steampipes, electrical conduits, plumbing or other fixtures connected therewith, or remove any additions, improvements, or fixtures from the premises.

If the Member for any reason shall cease to be an occupant of the premises he shall surrender to the Corporation possession thereof, including any alterations, additions, fixtures and improvements.

The Member shall not, without the prior written consent of the Corporation, install or use in his dwelling unit any air conditioning equipment, washing machine, clothes dryer, electric heater, or power tools. (Strike out any of the foregoing items which are not applicable.) The Member agrees that the Corporation may require the prompt removal of any such equipment at any time, and that his failure to remove such equipment upon request shall constitute a default within the meaning of Article 13 of this agreement.

ARTICLE 13. DEFINITION OF DEFAULT BY MEMBER AND EFFECT THEREOF

It is mutually agreed as follows: At any time after the happening of any of the events specified in clauses (a) to (i) *of this Article the Corporation may at its option give to the Member a notice that this agreement will expire at a date not less than ten (10) days thereafter. If the Corporation so proceeds all of the Member's rights under this agreement will

---

* Change "(i)" to "(k)" in Section 236 and Section 221 below market interest rate cases.

expire on the date so fixed in such notice, unless in the meantime the default has been cured in a manner deemed satisfactory by the corporation, it being the intention of the parties hereto to create hereby conditional limitations, and it shall thereupon be lawful for the Corporation to re-enter the dwelling unit and to remove all persons and personal property therefrom, either by summary dispossess proceedings or by suitable action or proceeding at law or in equity or by any other proceedings which may apply to the eviction of tenants or by force or otherwise, and to repossess the dwelling unit in its former state as if this agreement had been made:

(a) In case of any time during the term of this agreement the Member shall cease to be the owner and legal holder of a membership [or share of the stock] of the Corporation.

(b) In case the Member attempts to transfer or assign this agreement in a manner inconsistent with the provisions of the By-Laws.

(c) In case at any time during the continuance of this agreement the Member shall be declared a bankrupt under the laws of the United States.

(d) In case at any time during the continuance of this agreement a receiver of the Member's property shall be appointed under any of the laws of the United States or of any State.

(e) In case of any time during the continuance of this agreement the Member shall make a general assignment for the benefit of creditors.

(f) In case of any time during the continuance of this agreement any of the stock membership of the Corporation owned by the Member shall be duly levied upon and sold under the process of any Court.

(g) In case the Member fails to effect and/or pay for repairs and maintenance as provided for in Article 11 hereof.

(h) In case the Member shall fail to pay any sum due pursuant to the provisions of Article 1 or Article 10 hereof.

(i) In case the Member shall default in the performance of any of his obligations under this agreement.

*(j) In case at any time during the term of this agreement the limitations for oc-cupancy which may be established from time to time by the Federal Housing Administration are exceeded.

*(k) In case at any time during the term of this agreement, the Member fails to comply promptly with all requests by the Corporation or the Federal Housing Commissioner for information and certifications concerning the income of the Member and his family, the composition of the Member's family and other eligibility requirements for occupancy in the project.

The Member hereby expressly waives any and all right of redemption in case he shall be dispossessed by judgment or warrant of any Court or judge; the words "enter," "re-enter," and "re-entry," as used in this agreement are not restricted to their technical legal meaning, and in the event of a breach or threatened breach by the Member of any of the covenants or provisions hereof, the Corporation shall have the right of injunction

---

*   Required only in Section 236 cases and Section 221 below market interest rate cases.

and the right to invoke any remedy allowed at law or inequity as if re-entry, summary proceedings, and other remedies were not herein provided for.

The Member expressly agrees that there exists under this Occupancy Agreement a landlord-tenant relationship and that in the event of a breach or threatened breach by the Member of any covenant or provision of this Agreement, there shall be available to the Corporation such legal remedy or remedies as are available to a landlord for the breach or threatened breach under the law* by a tenant of any provision of a lease or rental agreement.

The failure on the part of the Corporation to avail itself of any of the remedies given this agreement shall not waive nor destroy the right of the Corporation to avail itself of such remedies for similar or other breaches on the part of the Member.

ARTICLE 14. MEMBER TO COMPLY WITH ALL CORPORATE REGULATIONS

The Member covenants that he will preserve and promote the cooperative ownership principles on which the Corporation has been founded, abide by the Charter, By-Laws, rules and regulations of the Corporation and any amendments thereto, and by his acts of cooperation with its other members bring about for himself and his co-members a high standard in home and community conditions. The Corporation agrees to make its rules and regulations known to the Member by delivery of same to him or by promulgating them in such other manner as to constitute adequate notice.

ARTICLE 15. EFFECT OF FIRE LOSS ON INTERESTS OF MEMBER

In the event of loss or damage by fire or other casualty to the above-mentioned dwelling unit without the fault or negligence of the Member, the Corporation shall determine whether to restore the damaged premises and shall further determine, in the event such premises shall not be restored, the amount which shall be paid to the Member to redeem the (membership) (common stock) of the Member and to reimburse him for such loss as he may have sustained.

If, under such circumstances, the Corporation determines to restore the premises, Carrying Charges shall abate wholly or partially as determined by the Corporation until the premises have been restored. If one the other hand the Corporation determines not to restore the premises, the Carrying Charges shall cease from the date of such loss or damage.

ARTICLE 16. INSPECTION OF DWELLING UNIT

The Member agrees that the representatives of any mortgagee holding a mortgage on the property of the Corporation, the officers and employees of the Corporation, and with the approval of the Corporation the employees of any contractor, utility company, municipal agency or others, shall have the right to enter the dwelling unit of the Member and make inspections thereof at any reasonable hour of the day and at any time in the event of emergency.

---

* In some States it may be desirable to include reference to a particular State statute on this subject.

ARTICLE 17. SUBORDINATION CLAUSE

The project, of which the above-mentioned dwelling unit is a part, was or is to be con-structed or purchased by the Corporation with the assistance of a mortgage loan advanced to the Corporation by a private lending institution with the understanding between the Corporation and the lender that the later would apply for mortgage insurance under the provisions of the National Housing Act. Therefore, it is specifically understood and agreed by the parties hereto that this agreement and all rights, privileges and benefits hereunder are and shall be at all times subject to and subordinate to the lien of a first mortgage and the accompanying documents executed by the Corporation under date of_____

_____, (or to be executed by the Corporation) payable to_____

_____in the principal sum of $_____ with

interest at_____per centum, and insured or to be insured under the provi-sions of the National Housing Act, and to any and all modifications, extensions and rene-wals thereof and to any mortgage or deed of trust made in replacement thereof and to any mortgage or deed of trust which may at any time hereafter be placed on the property of the Corporation or any part thereof. The Member hereby agrees to execute, at the Corpora-tion's request and expense any instrument which the Corporation or any lender may deem necessary or desirable to effect the subordination of this agreement to any such mortgage, or deed of trust, and the Member hereby appoints the Corporation and each and every officer thereof, and any future officer, his irrevocable attorney-in-fact during the term hereof to execute any such instrument on behalf of the Member. The Member does hereby ex-pressly waive any and all notices of default and notices of foreclosure of said mortgage which may be required by law.

In the event a waiver of such notices is not legally valid, the Member does hereby con-stitute the Corporation his agent to receive and accept such notices on the Member's behalf.

ARTICLE 18. LATE CHARGES AND OTHER COSTS IN CASE OF DEFAULT

The Member covenants and agrees that, in addition to the other sums that have be-come or will become due, pursuant to the terms of this Agreement, the Member shall pay to the Corporation a late charge in an amount to be determined from time to time by the Board of Directors for each payment of Carrying Charges, or part thereof, more than 10 days in arrears.

If a Member defaults in making a payment of Carrying Charges or in the performance or observance of any provision of this Agreement, and the Corporation has obtained the the services of any attorney with respect to the defaults involved, the Member covenants and agrees to pay to the Corporation any costs or fees involved, including reasonable attorney's fees, notwithstanding the fact that a suit has not yet been instituted. In case a suit is institut-ed, the Member shall also pay the costs of the suit, in addition to other aforesaid costs and fees.

ARTICLE 19. NOTICES

Whenever the provisions of law or the By-Laws of the Corporation or this agreement require notice to be given to either party hereto, any notice by the Corporation to the Member shall be deemed to have been duly given, and any demand by the Corporation upon the Member shall be deemed to have been duly made if the same is delivered to the Member at his unit or to the Member's last known address; and any notice or demand by the Member to the Corporation shall be deemed to have been duly given if delivered to an officer of the Corporation. Such notice may also be given by depositing same in the United States mails addressed to the Member as shown in the books of the Corporation, or to the President of the Corporation, as the case may be, and the time of mailing shall be deemed to be the time of giving of such notice.

ARTICLE 20. ORAL REPRESENTATION NOT BINDING

No representations other than those contained in this agreement, the Charter and the By-Laws of the Corporation shall be binding upon the Corporation.

IN WITNESS WHEREOF, the parties hereto have caused this agreement to be signed and sealed the day and year first above written.

_____
Corporation

By _____ (SEAL)

_____

_____
Member and Stockholder

No. 9-7
MODEL FORM OF MANAGEMENT AGREEMENT
For Cooperative Housing

FHA FORM NO. 3238
Rev. November 1964

U. S. DEPARTMENT OF HOUSING AND URBAN DEVELOPMENT
FEDERAL HOUSING ADMINISTRATION

For Cooperative Housing Projects Under
Sections 213 and 221(d)(3)

Agreement made this_____day of _____ , 19__, between_____
_____ , a corporation organized and existing under the laws of
_____ , having its principal office at_____
_____ , hereinafter called the "Owner", and_____ ,
having its principal office at _____ , hereinafter called
the "Agent",

WITNESSETH:

In consideration of the terms, conditions, and covenants hereinafter set forth, the parties hereto mutually agree as follows:

FIRST. (a) The Owner hereby appoints the Agent, and the Agent hereby accepts appointment, on the terms and conditions hereinafter provided, as exclusive managing agent of the development known as_____
_____ , located in the County of_____State of_____
_____ , and consisting of_____dwelling units, which property is also designated as FHA Project No._____ , and together with the land on which erected, is hereinafter referred to as the "Project".

(b) The Agent fully understands that the Owner is a non-profit cooperative ownership housing corporation, providing accommodations in the Project principally for residential use by its stockholders, hereinafter referred to as "Members", and the Agent agrees, notwithstanding the authority given to the Agent in this Agreement, to confer fully and freely with the Owner in the performance of its duties as herein set forth. The Agent agrees to keep himself informed on cooperative housing and FHA policies relative thereto and to encourage whenever possible the principles of cooperative effort among the Members and to attend stockholders' and directors' meetings at any time or times requested by the Owner.

SECOND. In order to facilitate efficient operation, the Owner shall inform the Agent with regard to standards to be kept and furnish the Agent with a set of community or house rules and a complete set of the plans and specifications of the Project as finally approved by the Federal Housing Administration. With the aid of these documents and inspection made by competent personnel, the Agent will inform itself with respect to the layout, construction, location, character, plan and operation of the lighting, heating, plumbing, and ventilating systems, as well as elevators, if any, and other mechanical equipment in the Project. Copies of guarantees and warranties pertinent to the construction of the Project and in force at the time of the execution of this Agreement shall be furnished to the Agent. From the Agent's predecessor, the Owner shall procure and provide the Agent a set of books and financial reports complying with the FHA Uniform System of Accounts for Cooperative Housing Projects.

THIRD. The Agent shall hire in its own name all managerial personnel including the resident manager where necessary for the efficient discharge of the duties of the Agent hereunder. Compensation for the services of such employees shall be the responsibility of the Agent. The agent directly and those employees of the Agent who handle or are responsible for the handling of the Owner's monies shall, without expense to the Owner, be bonded by a fidelity bond acceptable both to the Agent and the Owner, in an amount and company acceptable to the Agent, the Owner and the Mortgagee. The Owner shall be the obligee under such bond.

FOURTH. Under the personal and direct supervision of one of its principal officer, the Agent shall render services and perform duties as follows:

(a) On the basis of an operating schedule, job standards, and wage rates previously approved by the Owner on the recommendation of the Agent or resulting from wage negotiations, investigate, hire, pay, supervise, and discharge the personnel necessary to be employed in order properly to maintain and operate the Project. Such personnel shall in every instance be in the Owner's and not in the Agent's employ. Compensation for the services of such employees (as evidenced by certified payrolls) shall be considered an operating expense of the Project.

(b) Immediately ascertain the general condition of the property, and if the accommodations there afforded have yet to be occupied for the first time, establish liaison with the general contractor to facilitate the completion by him of such corrective work, if any, as is yet to be done; also, cause an inventory to be taken of all furniture, office equipment, maintenance tools and supplies, including a determination as to the amount of fuel on hand.

(c) Coordinate the plans of Members for moving their personal effects into the Project or out of it, with a view towards scheduling such movements so that there shall be a minimum of inconvenience to other Members.

(d) Maintain businesslike relations with Members whose service requests shall be received, considered and recorded in systematic fashion in order to show the action taken with respect to each. Complaints of a serious nature shall, after thorough investigation, be reported to the Owner with appropriate recommendations. As part of a continuing program to secure full performance by the Members of all items and maintenance for which they are responsible, the Agent shall make an annual inspection of all dwelling units and report its findings to the Owner and to the consenting parties.

(e) Collect all monthly carrying charges due from Members, all rents due from users of garage spaces and from users or lessees of other non-dwelling facilities in the Project; also, all sums due from concessionaires. The Owner hereby authorizes and directs the Agent to request, demand, collect, receive, and receipt for any and all charges or rents which may at any time be or become due to the Owner, and to take such legal action as necessary to evict members delinquent in payment of monthly carrying charges for 30 days or more. As a standard practice, the Agent shall furnish the Owner with an itemized list of all delinquent accounts immediately following the tenth day of each month.

(f) Cause the buildings, appurtenances and grounds on the Project to be maintained according to standards acceptable to the Owner, including but not limited to interior and exterior cleaning, painting, and decorating, plumbing, steam fitting, carpentry, and such other normal maintenance and repair work as may be necessary, subject to any limitations imposed by the Owner in addition to those contained herein. With the exception of payments required under the mortgage, taxes, insurance, utilities and Owner-approved contractual obligations, no disbursement shall be made in excess of _____* unless specifically authorized by the Owner; excepting, however, that emergency repairs, involving manifest danger to life or property, or immediately necessary for the preservation and safety of the property, or for the safety of the Members, or required to avoid the suspension of any necessary service to the Project, may be made by the Agent irrespective of the cost limitation imposed by this paragraph. Notwithstanding this authority as to emergency repairs, it is understood and agreed that the Agent will, if at all possible, confer immediately with the Owner regarding every such expenditure and its effect on the budget. The Agent shall not incur liabilities (direct or contingent) which will at any time exceed the aggregate of _____**, or any liability maturing more than one year from the creation thereof, without first obtaining the approval of the Owner.

(g) Take such action as may be necessary to comply promptly with any and all orders or requirements affecting the premises placed thereon by any federal, state, county, or municipal authority having jurisdiction thereover, subject to the same limitation contained in Paragraph (f) of this Article in connection with the making of repairs and alterations. The Agent, however, shall not take any action under this Paragraph (g) so long as the Owner is contesting, or has affirmed its intention to contest any such order or requirement. The Agent shall promptly, and in no event later than 72 hours from the time of their receipt, notify the Owner in writing of all such orders and notices of requirements.

---

* From $100 to $500, depending upon the size of the project.

** From $1,000 to $5,000 depending upon the size of the project, but not exceeding the amount specified in Owner's Articles of Incorporation or Regulatory Agreement.

(h) Subject to approval by the Owner, make contracts for water, electricity, gas, fuel oil, telephone, vermin extermination, and other necessary services, or such of them as the Owner shall deem advisable. Also, place purchase orders for such equipment, tools, appliances, materials and supplies as are necessary properly to maintain the Project. All such contracts and orders shall be made in the name of the Owner and shall be subject to the limitations set forth in Paragraph (f) of this Article. When taking bids or issuing purchase orders, the Agent shall act at all times under the direction of the Owner, and shall be under a duty to secure for and credit to the latter any discounts, commissions, or rebates obtainable as a result of such purchases.

(i) Obtain recommendations and prices from at least three different insurance companies and cause to be placed and kept in force all forms of insurance needed adequately to protect the Owner (or as required by law), including, where appropriate, workmen's compensation insurance, public liability insurance, boiler insurance, fire and extended coverage insurance, and burglary and theft insurance. All of the various types of insurance coverage required for the benefit of the Owner shall be placed with such companies, in such amounts, and with such beneficial interests appearing therein as shall be acceptable to the owner and the consenting parties, and otherwise be in conformity with the requirements of the mortgage. The Agent shall promptly investigate and make a full written report as to all accidents or claims for damage relating to the ownership, operation and maintenance of the Project including any damage or destruction to the Project, the estimated cost of repair, and shall cooperate and make any and all reports required by any insurance company in connection therewith.

(j) From the funds collected and deposited in the special account hereinafter provided, cause to be disbursed regularly and punctually (1) salaries and any other compensation due and payable to the employees of the Owner, and the taxes payable under Paragraph (k) of this Article; (2) the single aggregate payment required to be made monthly to the mortgagee, including the amounts due under the mortgage for premium charges under the contract of insurance, ground rents if any, taxes and assessments, fire and other hazard insurance premiums, interest on the mortgage, amortization of the principal of the mortgage, and the amount specified in the Certificate of Incorporation or Regulatory Agreement for allocation to the Fund for Replacements; and (3) sums otherwise due and payable by the Owner as operating expenses authorized to be incurred under the terms of this Agreement, including the Agent's commission. After disbursement in the order herein specified, any balance remaining in the special account may be disbursed or transferred from time to time, but only as specifically directed by the Owner in writing, but such balance must be within the limits of the fidelity bond which shall be in an amount equal to at least the amount of each gross monthly collection.

(k) Working in conjunction with an accountant, prepare for execution and filing by the Owner all forms, reports, and returns required by law in connection with unemployment insurance, workman's compensation insurance, disability benefits, Social Security, and other similar taxes now in effect or hereafter imposed, and also requirements relating to the employment of personnel.

(l) Maintain a comprehensive system of office records, books, and accounts in a manner satisfactory to the Owner and to the consenting parties, which records shall be subject to examination by their authorized agents at all reasonable hours. As a standard practice, the Agent shall render to the Owner by not later than the tenth of each succeeding month a statement of receipts and disbursements, a schedule of accounts receivable and payable, and a reconciled bank statement as of the end of the preceding month. He shall render a comparison quarterly of income and expense to the budget.

(m) On or about _____ and thereafter at least 60 days before the beginning of each new fiscal year, prepare with the assistance of an accountant, if need be, an operating budget setting forth an itemized statement of the anticipated receipts and disbursements for the new fiscal year based upon the then current schedule of monthly carrying charges, and taking into account the general condition of the Project and the cooperative's objectives for the ensuing year. Each such budget, together with a statement from the Agent outlining a plan of operation and justifying the estimates made in every important particular, shall be submitted to the Owner in final draft at least 30 days prior to the commencement of the annual period for which it has been made, and following its adoption by the Owner, copies of it shall be made available, upon request, for submission to the consenting parties. The budget shall serve as a supporting document for the schedule of monthly carrying charges proposed for the new fiscal year. It shall also constitute a major control under which the Agent shall operate, and there shall be no substantial variances therefrom, except such as may be sanctioned by the Owner. By this is meant that no expenses may be incurred or commitments made by the Agent in connection with the maintenance and operation of the Project in excess of the amounts allocated to the various classifications of expense in the approved budget without the prior consent of the Owner, except that, if necessary because of an emergency or lack of sufficient time to obtain such prior consent, an overrun may be experienced, provided it is brought promptly to the attention of the Owner in writing.

(n) Maintain a current list of prospective Members and make such record changes as are appropriate in connection with all transfers of memberships approved by the Owner. It (shall) (shall not) * be the duty of the Agent to use his best efforts to cause available memberships held by the Owner to be sold. (In cases where a membership is being sold by an individual member and not by the Owner, the Agent shall not be required to assist such individual member in connection with the sale unless the Agent and the individual member separately so contract.) The Agent shall actively handle the renting of any garage spaces or other non-dwelling accommodation, arranging for the execution of such leases or permits as may be required.

(o) It shall be the duty of the Agent at all times during the term of this Agreement to operate and maintain the Project according to the highest standards achievable consistent with the overall plan of the Owner and the interests of the consenting parties. Full compliance by the Members with the terms and conditions of their respective Occupancy Agreements shall be secured, and to this end the Agent shall see that all Members are informed with respect to such rules, regulations and notices as may be promulgated by the Owner from time to time. The Agent shall be expected to perform such other acts and deeds as are reasonable, necessary and proper in the discharge of its duties under this Agreement.

FIFTH. Everything done by the Agent under the provisions of Article FOURTH shall be done as Agent of the Owner, and all obligations or expenses incurred thereunder shall be for the account, on behalf, and at the expense of the Owner, except that the Owner shall not be obligated to pay the overhead expenses of the Agent's office. Any payments to be made by the Agent hereunder shall be made out of such sums as are available in the special account of the Owner, or as

---

* Delete inappropriate clause.

may be provide d by the Owner. The Agent shall not be obliged to make any advance to or for the account of the Owner or to pay any sum, except out of funds held or provided as aforesaid, nor shall the Agent be obliged to incur any liability or obligation for the account of the Owner without assurance that the necessary funds for the discharge thereof will be provided.

SIXTH. The Agent shall establish and maintain, in a bank whose deposits are insured by the Federal Deposit Insurance Corporation and in a manner to indicate the custodial nature thereof, a separate bank account as Agent of the Owner for the deposit of the monies of the Owner, with authority to draw thereon for any payments to be made by the Agent to discharge any liabilities or obligations incurred pursuant to this Agreement, and for the payment of the Agent's fee, all of which payments shall be subject to the limitations in this Agreement.

SEVENTH. The sole compensation which the Agent shall be entitled to receive for all services performed under this Agreement shall be a fee computed and payable monthly in an amount equivalent to _____(%) of gross collections, exclusive of all surcharges.**

EIGHTH.(a) Unless cancelled pursuant to section (b), (c), or (d) of this Article, this Agreement shall be in effect from _____ to _____ , provided that in no event shall it be of any force and effect until there is endorsed hereon the consent of the consenting parties.

(b) This Agreement may be terminated by mutual consent of the parties as of the end of any calendar month, but not without prior written notice to the consenting parties.

(c) In the event a petition in bankruptcy is filed by or against either Owner or Agent, or in the event that either shall make an assignment for the benefit of creditors or take advantage of any insolvency act, either party hereto may terminate this Agreement without notice to the other, but prompt advice of such action shall be given to the consenting parties.

(d) It is expressly understood and agreed by and between the parties hereto that the Federal Housing Administration or the Mortgagee shall have the right to terminate this Agreement at the end of any calendar month, with or without cause, on 30 days' written notice to the Owner and the Agent of its intention so to do, except that in case a default of the owner has occurred under its Articles of Incorporation, or under the obligation of the mortgage, the Federal Housing Administration or the Mortgagee shall have the right to terminate this Agreement immediately upon the issuance of a notice of cancellation to the Owner and the Agent. It is further understood and agreed that no liability shall attach to the Federal Housing Administration or the Mortgagee in the event of termination of this Agreement pursuant to this section.

(e) Upon termination, the Agent shall submit Financial Statements pursuant to the Uniform System of Accounts for Cooperative Housing Projects, and after the contracting parties have accounted to each other with respect to all matters outstanding as of the date of termination, the Owner shall furnish the Agent security, satisfactory to the Agent, against any outstanding obligations or liabilities which the Agent may have incurred hereunder.

NINTH. As used in this Agreement:

(a) The term "mortgage" shall mean that certain indenture of mortgage dated the _____day of_____, 19____by and between the Owner, as mortgagor, and the _____ _____, as mortgagee, which mortgage is insured by the Federal Housing Administration pursuant to the authority contained in Title II, Section 213 or 221 (d)(3) of the National Housing Act and the regulations promulgated thereunder.

(b) The term "mortgagee" shall mean_____ , or any other holder of said mortgage.

(c) The term "consenting parties" shall mean (i) the mortgagee as herein defined, and (ii) the Federal Housing Administration acting through its Commissioner or his duly authorized representatives.

(d) The term "Occupancy Agreements" shall mean those certain forms of agreement between the Owner and its stockholder Members (and any renewals thereof) under the terms of which said stockholder Members are entitled to enjoy possession of their respective dwelling units.

(e) The term "carrying charges" shall mean those monthly rates which stockholder Members are bound to pay to the Owner pursuant to the terms of their respective Occupancy Agreements.

(f) The term "gross collections" shall mean all amounts actually collected by the Agent, either as carrying charges or as rents.

** If desired, a flat fee may be inserted in lieu of the percentage arrangement. Also, if desired, the following clause may be added: "except that the Agent shall also be entitled to receive the sum of $ for each membership sold by him on behalf of the Owner, and a service charge of $15 for each transfer of membership processed by him regardless of by whom it was sold."

TENTH. (a) This Agreement, which is made subject and subordinate to all rights of the Federal Housing Administration as insurer of the mortgage, shall inure to the benefit of and constitute a binding obligation upon the contracting parties, their respective successors and assigns; and to the extent that it confers rights, privileges, and benefits upon the consenting parties, the same shall be deemed to inure to their benefit, but without a liability to either, in the same manner and with the same force and effect as though the mortgagee and the Federal Housing Administration were signatories to this Agreement.

(b) This Agreement shall constitute the entire Agreement between the contracting parties, and no variance or modification thereof shall be valid and enforceable, except by supplemental agreement in writing, executed and approved in the same manner as this Agreement.

(c) For the convenience of the parties, this Agreement has been executed in several counterparts, which are in all respects similar and each of which shall be deemed to be complete in itself so that any one may be introduced in evidence or used for any other purpose without the production of the other counterparts. Immediately following endorsement of the consenting parties, counterparts will be furnished to the consenting parties so that each may be advised of the rights, privileges, and benefits which this Agreement confers.

IN WITNESS WHEREOF, the parties hereto have executed this Agreement the day and year first above written.

_____
(Cooperative)

By _____

_____
(Agent)

By _____

_____ hereby consents to the foregoing Management Agreement and the Managing Agent designated therein.

DATE: _____   _____
                                                          (Mortgagee)

By _____

The Federal Housing Administration hereby consents to the foregoing Management Agreement and the Managing Agent designated therein.

DATE: _____   _____
                                                          (Federal Housing Commissioner)

By _____
                                                          (Authorized Agent)

143627-P Rev. 11/64   HUD—Wash., D. C.

No. 9–8
MONTHLY FISCAL REPORT

FHA PROJECT CASE NUMBER_____

DATE OF THIS REPORT_____

REPORT COVERING MONTH ENDING_____

1. Cumulative income from beginning of fiscal year to end of month covered by this report . . . .$_____

2. Cumulative expenses from beginning of fiscal year to end of month covered by this report. . . . .$_____

3. 100% of potential monthly income from dwelling units, garages and commercial space . . . .$_____

4. Actual income from dwelling units, garages and commercial space this month $_____

5. Accounts receivable at end of month covered by this report . . . .$_____

6. Accounts receivable at end of last preceding month . . . .$_____

7. Accounts payable at end of month covered by this report . . . .$_____

8. Accounts payable at end of last preceding month . . . .$_____

9. Number of occupant accounts deliquent at end of last preceding month. . . .$_____

10. Number of occupant accounts deliquent at end of the month covered by this report . . . .$_____

11. Cumulative deposits to General Operating Reserve required from beginning of this fiscal year to end of month covered by this report. . . . .$_____

12. Actual cumulative deposits to General Operating Reserve from beginning of this fiscal year to end of month covered by this report . . . .$_____

Carrying Charge delinquencies of over two months:

Name	Unit No.	From	To	Amount
_____	_____	_____	_____	_____
_____	_____	_____	_____	_____
_____	_____	_____	_____	_____

I certify this is a true and
correct report.

_____

Title: _____

10

Deeds

10

Deeds

A deed is a legal instrument signed by the grantor that transfers title to real property from one to another. To be valid, a deed must be made between competent parties, contain a valuable consideration, that which is conveyed by the deed must be legal in nature, accurately state what is being conveyed, and be properly signed, sealed, and then delivered to the grantee.

The contents of all deeds should include certain essentials. The following shows the structural make up of a typical deed with sample phraseology.

    a. (OPENING WORDING AND DATE)

        THIS INDENTURE[1] made in the city of_____, the_____ day of_____ nineteen hundred and _____.

    b. (PARTIES)

        BETWEEN_____, residing at No._____, Avenue, City of_____, State of_____, herein called the party of the first part and _____, residing at No._____, Street, City of_____, State of_____, herein called the party of the second part.

    c. (CONSIDERATION AND INTENT TO CONVEY)

        WITNESSETH that in consideration of_____ dollars lawful money of the United States, to him in hand paid by the party of the second part, the party of the first part does hereby grant and convey unto the party of the second part, the heirs and assigns forever.

    d. (DESCRIPTION)

    All that certain plot, piece or parcel of land, with the building and improvements thereon erected, situate, lying and being in the

(Insert legal description)

---

1. In less frequent use is the form referred to as a "poll deed." It begins with the words, "KNOW ALL MEN BY THESE PRESENTS," and is written in the first person singular. When this style is used the date generally appears at the end of the body of the deed, before the signature line.

1. a. The words, "THIS DEED" are frequently used in place of, "THIS INDENTURE."

Together with the woods, ways, streets, alleys, passages, waters, water courses, rights, liberties, privileges, tenements, hereditaments and appurtenances thereto belonging,

e.   (EXTENT OF WHAT IS BEING TRANSFERRED)

TO HAVE AND TO HOLD THE premises herein granted, together with the appurtenances, unto the party of the second part, his heirs, and assigns, to and for his and their own use, benefit, and advantage forever.

f.   (ENCUMBRANCES ON PROPERTY)

That the premises are free from all encumbrances except as herein otherwise stated:

Subject to a purchase money first mortgage given by the grantee to the grantor.

Subject to taxes for the year 19____and all subsequent years.

Subject to conditions, restrictions, easements and zoning ordinances of record.

g.   (RESTRICTIONS, EASEMENTS OR ENCROACHMENTS)

That the party of the second part, his heirs and assigns shall not erect or permit to be erected any building other than a single family dwelling not more than two stories in height.

h.   (GRANTOR'S RIGHT TO CONVEY)

That the party of the first part is lawfully seized of a good, absolute and indefeasible estate in fee simple and has good right, full power and has lawful authority to convey the same by this indenture.

i.   (QUIET ENJOYMENT)

That the party of the second part, his heirs and assigns, shall peaceably and quietly have, hold, use, occupy, possess and enjoy the said premises.

j.   (WARRANTIES BY THE GRANTOR)

That the party of the first part shall execute or procure any further necessary assurance of the title to said premises and that he will forever warrant[1] and defend the title to said premises.

k.   (GRANTOR'S SIGNATURE AND WITNESSES)

IN WITNESS WHEREOF, the party of the first part has duly executed this deed the day and year first above written.

In the presence of:

_____   _____ (SEAL)

_____

TYPES OF DEEDS

There are deeds for many purposes, such as those that create life estates, co-tenancies or to correct a prior deed.[2] There are others that are used when one acts in a representative capacity, such as Administrator or Executor Deeds, Guardian Deed, Referee's Deed, Sheriff's Deed and Trust Deed. Some other miscellaneous deeds and their uses include:

---

1.   This phraseology is used in warranty deeds only.
2.   Variously known as a correction deed, reformation deed, or deed of confirmation.

Cemetery Plot Deed—Conveying a cemetery plot.

Cession Deed[1]—Conveying street rights of privately owned property to a municipality.

Committee Deed—When a court appoints more than one person to act for a minor or incompetent.

County Deed—Conveying county-owned property.

Deed In Lieu of Foreclosure—Conveying property to a mortgagee to prevent a foreclosure action.

Deed of Release—To release property, or some portion of it, from the lien of a mortgage.

Deed of Surrender—Creating an estate for life or for years.

Deed of Trust—When a third party acts as escrow agent by holding the deed until an obligation (such as a mortgage) is satisfied.

Gift Deed—When conveying property free of charge or when only a token payment is involved.

Grant Deed—This deed warrants that the property is free of encumbrances only while the grantor was the owner. (Used extensively in California).

Mineral Deed—For conveying mineral rights to one's property.

Quit Claim Deed—To remove all claims and interest in ownership by the grantor at the time of conveyance. It does not warrant the quality or validity of the title. It is used to remove a cloud, claim or ambiguity by the grantor in a prior deed.

Support Deed—When the consideration is that the grantee will support the grantor for life.

Deeds mentioned above are primarily for specific situations, but the forms in general use for conveying most properties are warranty deeds,[2] and bargain and sales deeds.

For an example of a Condominium Deed, see Chapter 8 , Condominiums, page 153.

A Warranty Deed guarantees that the grantor is giving good title free of all encumbrances. He warrants the title forever. It is the best form of a deed a grantee can receive. The grantor warrants that he will defend the title against all claimants. In a full covenant Warranty Deed the grantor further agrees to execute or procure any further necessary assurances of title.

A Bargain and Sale Deed is one that conveys fee simple possession to property for a monetary consideration. It may contain a covenant by the grantor that the property is not encumbered in any way. Unlike the warranty deed in which title is warranted forever, such covenants are personal assurances of the grantor only and do not run with the land.

No. 10–1
WARRANTY DEED
Statutory Short Form[3] Full Covenants—Individual

THIS INDENTURE, made in the City of_____,State of_____

_____, on the____day of_____, nineteen hundred and_____

BETWEEN _____, party of

---

1. Also referred to as a Dedication Deed.
2. Also referred to as Full Covenant and Warranty Deeds, or General Warranty Deeds.
3. This statutory short form is adapted from New York Real Property Law, §258, Schedule B.

the first part and_____, party of the
second part.

WITNESSETH, that the party of the first part, in consideration of_____
_____ dollars, lawful money of the United States, paid by the party of the second
part, does hereby grant and release unto the party of the second part, his heirs and assigns
forever,

ALL that certain plot, piece or parcel of land

(Insert legal description)

together with the buildings and improvements thereon and all the estate and rights of the
party of the first part in and to said property.

TO HAVE AND TO HOLD the premises herein granted unto the party of the second
part, his heirs and assigns forever,

And the party of the first part covenants as follows:

FIRST—That the party of the first part is seized of the said premises in fee simple, and
has good right to convey the same.

SECOND—That the party of the second part shall quietly enjoy the said premises.

THIRD—That the premises are free of encumbrances.

FOURTH—That the party of the first part will execute or procure any further necessary
assurances of the title to said premises.

FIFTH—That the party of the first part will forever warrant the title to said premises.

SIXTH—THE GRANTOR, in compliance with Section 1–3 of the Lien Law of the
State of New York, covenants that the grantor will receive the consideration for this
conveyance and will hold the right to receive such consideration as a trust fund to be applied
for the purpose of paying the cost of the improvement before using any part of the total of
the same for any other purpose.[1]

IN WITNESS WHEREOF, the party of the first part has hereunto set his hand and
seal the day and year above written.
In presence of:

_____(SEAL)

No. 10–2
WARRANTY DEED
Statutory Short Form Full Covenants—Corporation

*The contents of this form are the same as the foregoing Warranty Deed for Individuals ex-
cept for the following changes in the second and closing clauses:*

BETWEEN_____, Incorporated, a corporation, duly
created, organized and existing under, and by virtue of, the laws of the State of_____
_____, and having its principal office at_____ Street,

---

1. Clause applicable in New York State only.

City of_____, State of_____, party of the first part
and _____, party of the second part.

****

IN WITNESS WHEREOF, the party of the first part has caused its corporation seal to be hereunto affixed, and these presents to be signed by its duly authorized officer, the day and year first above written.

(Corporate Seal goes here)

Attest:

_____, Inc.

_____   By_____
               Secretary   President

No. 10–3
BARGAIN AND SALE DEED
With Covenants Against Grantor's Acts

THIS INDENTURE, made the_____day of_____;nineteen hundred and

_____.

BETWEEN_____, residing at No.
_____Street, City of_____, State of
_____, herein called the party of the first part and_____
_____residing at No._____ _____
Avenue, City of_____, State of_____ ,
herein called the party of the second part.

WITNESSETH, that the party of the first part, in consideration of_____
_____dollars ($_____) lawful money of the United States, paid by the party of the second part does hereby grant and release unto the party of the second part, the heirs or successors and assigns of the party of the second part forever.

ALL that certain plot, piece, or parcel of land with the buildings and improvements thereon erected, situate, lying and being in the

(Insert legal description)

TOGETHER with the buildings, improvements, woods, ways, streets, alleys, passages, waters, water course, rights, liberties, privileges, tenements, hereditments and appurtenances thereto belonging.

TOGETHER with the appurtenances and all the estate and rights of the party of the first part in and to said property.

TO HAVE AND TO HOLD the premises herein granted together with the appurtenances unto the party of the second part his successors and assigns forever.

AND THE SAID party of the first part covenants that he has not done or suffered anything whereby the premises have been encumbered in any way whatsoever.[1]

---

1. The contents of a Bargain and Sale Deed, *without* covenants against grantor's acts differs only in that this clause is omitted.

THE GRANTOR, in compliance with Section 13 of the Lien Law of the State of New York, covenants that the grantor will receive the consideration for this conveyance and will hold the right to receive such consideration as a trust fund to be applied first for the purpose of paying the cost of the improvement and that the grantor will apply the same first to the payment of the cost of the improvement before using any part of the total of the same for any other purpose.[1]

IN WITNESS WHEREOF, the party of the first part has hereunto set his hand and seal the day and year first above written. In the presence of:

_____   _____ (SEAL)
                                                                    Grantor

_____

No. 10–4
QUIT CLAIM DEED
Individual or Corporation

THIS DEED, made the_____ day of_____, 19___, BETWEEN _____ of No._____ _____ Street, City of_____, State of_____, party of the first part, and_____ of No._____ _____ Avenue, City of_____, State of_____, party of the second part,

WITNESSETH, that the party of the first part, in consideration of $_____, lawful money of the United States, paid by the party of the second part, does hereby remise, release and quitclaim unto the party of the second part, the heirs, successors and assigns of the party of the second part forever.

ALL that certain plot, piece or parcel of land, with the buildings and improvements thereon erected, situate, lying and being in the

(Here include legal description)

TOGETHER with all right, title and interest, if any, of the party of the first part in and to any streets and roads abutting the above described premises to the center lines thereof; together with the appurtenances and all the estate and rights of the party of the first part in and to said premises.

TO HAVE AND TO HOLD the premises herein granted unto the party of the second part, the heirs or successors and assigns of the party of the seond part forever.

IN WITNESS WHEREOF, the party of the first part has duly executed this deed the day and year first above written.

_____

1. Clause applicable in New York State only.

In Presence of:

_____

Grantor

_____

_____

****

No. 10–5
EXECUTOR'S DEED
Individual or Corporation

THIS DEED, made the_____day of_____, 19_____, between_____ of No._____ _____Street, City of_____, State of_____, party of the first part, and_____of No._____ _____Avenue, City of_____, State of_____, party of the second part,

WITNESSETH, that the party of the first part, by virtue of the power and authority given in and by said last will and testament, and in consideration of_____ _____dollars ($_____), lawful money of the United States, paid by the party of the second part, does hereby grant and release unto the party of the second part, the heirs or successors and assigns of the party of the second part forever.

ALL that certain plot, piece or parcel of land, with the buildings and improvements thereon erected, situate, lying and being in the

(Here include legal description)

TOGETHER with all right, title and interest, if any, of the party of the first part in any streets and roads abutting the above described premises to the center lines thereof. Together with the appurtenances, and also all the estate which the said decedent had at the time of decedent's death in said premises, and also the estate therein, which the party of the first part has or has power to convey or dispose of, whether individually, or by virtue of said will or otherwise.

TO HAVE AND TO HOLD the premises herein granted unto the party of the second part, the heirs or successors and assigns of the party of the second part forever.

AND the party of the first part covenants that the party of the first part has not done or suffered anything whereby the premises have been incumbered in any way whatsoever, except as aforsaid.

IN WITNESS WHEREOF, the party of the first part has duly executed this deed the day and year first above written.

In Presence of:
                           _____(Seal)
                                         Grantor

_____

_____

To avoid unnecessary repetition, only those portions of a specific type deed that vary from the usual phraseology are included below. The rest of the deed form is omitted.

No. 10–6
DEED FOR LIFE OF GRANTOR

WITNESSETH, that the party of the first part, in consideration of_____ _____dollars, does hereby grant and release unto the party of the second part, his heirs and assigns, for and during the term of the remainder of the natural life of the party of the first part, all that certain lot, piece or parcel of land, with the buildings thereon erected, situate, lying and being in the County of_____, State of_____ , to wit:

(Here include legal description)

TO HAVE AND TO HOLD the premises herein granted unto said party of the second part, his heirs and assigns, for and during the term of the remainder of the natural life of the party of the first part.

No. 10–7
DEED FOR LIFE OF GRANTEE

WITNESSETH, that the party of the first part, in consideration of_____ _____dollars, paid by the party of the second part, does hereby grant and release unto the party of the second part, his heirs and assigns, for and during the term of the remainder of the natural life of the party of the second part, all that certain lot, piece or parcel of land, with the buildings thereon erected, situate, lying and being in the County of_____ _____ , State of_____ , to wit:

(Here include legal description)

TO HAVE AND TO HOLD the premises herein granted unto said party of the second part, his heirs and assigns, for and during the term of the remainder of the natural life of the party of the second part.

*****

No. 10–8
DEED CORRECTING ERROR IN PRIOR DEED

Whereas, in order to correct a defect in the description of the aforesaid deed, the party of the first part is desirous and willing to have conveyed to the party of the second part, all that certain lot, piece or parcel of land with the buildings and improvements thereon erected, situate, lying and being in the

(Here include *corrected* legal description)

No. 10–9
DEED CREATING TENANCY IN COMMON

WITNESSETH, that the party of the first part, in consideration of the sum of_____ _____dollars, paid by the party of the second part, does hereby grant and release to the parties of the second part and their respective heirs and assigns forever, as tenants in common, and not as joint tenants, all that certain lot, piece or parcel of land with the buildings and improvements thereon erected, situate, lying and being in the

(Here include legal description)

Together with the appurtenances and all the estate and rights of the party of the first part in and to said premises.

*****

No. 10–10
DEED CREATING JOINT TENANCY
With Right Of Survivorship

WITNESSETH, that the said party of the first part, in consideration of the sum of _____dollars, to him in hand paid by the parties of the second part, does hereby grant and release unto the parties of the second part as joint tenants, with right of survivorship, and to their survivors, and to the heirs and assigns of such survivors, the following described land, situate, lying and being in the County of_____, State of _____, to wit:

(Here include legal description)

Together with the appurtenances and all the estate and rights of the party of the first part in and to said premises.

*****

No. 10–11
DEED CREATING ESTATE BY THE ENTIRETY
For Taking Title By Husband And Wife

WITNESSETH, that the said party of the first part, for and in consideration of the sum of_____dollars, to him in hand paid by the parties of the second part, the receipt of which is hereby acknowledged, does hereby grant and release unto the parties of the second part, as tenants by the entirety, and to the survivors of them, assigns of such survivors forever, the following described land, situate, lying and being in the County of_____, and State of_____, to wit:

(Here include legal description)

TO HAVE AND TO HOLD the premises herein granted unto the parties of the second part, as tenants by the entirety, and to the survivors of them, and to the heirs and assigns of such survivors forever.

No. 10–12
CESSION DEED[1]
For Dedicating Land To A Municipality

THIS INDENTURE, made the_____ day of_____, nineteen hundred and_____, between_____, residing at No._____ _____Street, Town of_____, State of_____, party of the first part, and the Incorporated Town of_____ _____, State of_____, party of the second part.

WHEREAS, the party of the first part is the owner of the above described land, and is willing to cede and dedicate said property to the Incorporated Town of_____ _____, in pursuance of the acquisition provisions contained in Chapter_____, Section _____, Paragraph_____, of the laws of the State of_____.

TOGETHER with the appurtenances and all the estates and rights of the party of the first part in and to said premises, it being the intention of the party of the first part to convey all land for access roadway purposes and all the estate therein that it may own.

****

No. 10–13
REFEREE'S DEED IN FORECLOSURE

THIS INDENTURE, made the_____ day of_____, nineteen hundred and_____,

BETWEEN_____, duly appointed referee in the subject foreclosure action, residing at No._____ _____Street,_____ _____City, State of_____, as grantor, and_____ _____, residing at No._____ _____Avenue,_____ _____City, State of_____, grantee.

WITNESSETH, that the grantor, duly appointed as the referee in a foreclosure action entered at_____Court, County of_____, State of_____ _____, between_____, plaintiff, and_____, defendant, does hereby grant and convey unto the grantee all that certain plot, piece or

_____

1. Also referred to as a Dedication Deed.

parcel of land, with the buildings and improvements thereon erected, situate lying and being in the

(Here include legal description)

IN CONSIDERATION of_____ dollars, lawful money of the United States, which sum represents the highest bid at the foreclosure sale held in pursuance of a judgment entered at_____Court, County of_____ _____, State of_____, on the_____ day of_____ _____, 19_____.

****

No. 10–14
REFEREE'S DEED IN PARTITION

THIS INDENTURE, made the_____ day of_____, nineteen hundred and _____,

BETWEEN _____ , duly appointed as referee in the subject partition action, residing at No._____ _____Street, _____City, State of_____, as grantor, and_____ _____, residing at No._____ _____Avenue, _____City, State of_____, grantee.

WITNESSETH, that the grantor, duly appointed as referee in a partition action between_____ , plaintiff, and_____ , defendant, does hereby grant and convey unto the grantee all that certain plot, piece or parcel of land, with the buildings and improvements thereon erected, situate, lying and being in the

(Here include legal description)

IN CONSIDERATION of_____ dollars, lawful money of the United States, which sum represents the highest bid at public sale under said judgment entered at_____Court, County of_____ , State of_____, on the_____ day of_____ _____, 19_____.

****

CLAUSES IN DEEDS

In Consideration of Love and Affection

Witnesseth, that in consideration of his natural love and affection, the party of the first part hereby grants and releases to the party of the second part, his heirs and assigns forever all that certain plot, piece or parcel of land with the building and improvements thereon, situate, lying and being in the

(Insert legal description)

Restricting Property to Residential Use

The party of the second part convenants and agrees that the land herein granted shall be used for residential purposes only and that no building or structure of any kind shall be constructed other than a single family, one- or two- story dwelling house.

Right of Way Easement

It is expressly agreed that the party of the first part and to their successors and assigns shall forever have the right to use the adjoining eight (8) feet wide driveway running the length of the northern boundary line of the above described premises for purposes of ingress and egress. Said driveway shall be kept open and passable perpetually for the free use of the owners and tenants. Title to said eight (8) feet driveway shall be held in common ownership with the owners of the lots lying north of the subject driveway and adjoining it at the said southern border.

Relinquishment of Dower and Homestead Rights

The said grantor hereby relinquishes all dower and homestead rights in and to the above described premises.

11

Easements

11

Easements

An easement is a nonprofitable, limited right or privilege one is given for the use of land belonging to another. It can be permanent or temporary in nature. It is a right bestowed to travel on, over or through another's land or to use it for a specific purpose.

An easement must be created by a grant. To be valid or enforceable it cannot exist by merely an oral agreement. Unless prohibited by deed restrictions, easements generally transfer with the land when sold.

Easements can be categorized in various forms and distinctions. Those frequently encountered are the following:

An *Easement In Gross* is the granting of a personal interest in real property, rather than a right to the land itself. Such an easement is generally not assignable or inheritable. The right to use the outside wall of a building as a billboard is an example.

A *Negative Easement* is one that acts to curtail the complete use of the property. It relinquishes some valuable right or rights of the property. Building codes that limit the use of the land, and covenants preventing certain types of structures on a given lot, are examples.

Other types of easements include *Avignon Easements,* permitting aircraft to fly over one's land at certain elevations; *Sub-Surface Easements,* permitting use of land below the surface; and *Overflow Easements,* the right to backwater or submerge another's land. Also in modern real estate practice such grants as rights to *Party Wall* usage, *Light and View,* and *Lateral Support* are in general use.

No specific wording is prescribed when preparing an easement agreement. The intentions of the parties clearly and unambiguously stated, and an accurate description of the land are the basic requisites.

Easements should be recorded so that future owners of the property are given constructive notice of their existence.

No. 11–1
EASEMENT
General Form

This Agreement, made in the City of _____ , State of _____ ,
on _____ , 19_____ , by _____ ,

residing at _____ , party of the first part and_____
_____residing at_____,
herein called party of the second part.

Whereas, the party of the first part represents and warrants that he owns and has fee
simple title to that certain parcel of real estate located in the City of_____,
County of_____, State of_____, more particularly
bounded and described as follows:

(Here include legal description)

Whereas, the party of the second part desires to use said property for

(Here describe nature and type of easement desired)

Now, therefore, it is mutually agreed as follows:

The party of the first part does hereby grant, assign and set over to the party of the
second part

(Here describe nature and type of easement granted)

Except as herein granted, the party of the first part shall continue to have the full use
and enjoyment of the property.

The party of the second part shall bear full responsibility for the use and enjoyment of
the property and shall hold the party of the first part harmless from any claim of damages to
person or premises resulting from the use, occupancy and possession thereof by the party of
the second part.

To have and to hold the said easement unto the party of the second part and unto his
successors and assigns forever.

In witness whereof, the parties hereto have duly executed this agreement.

_____   _____

_____

_____   _____

_____

No. 11–2
EASEMENT
Creating Right Of Way[1]

This Agreement made on the_____day of_____, 19_____, by and
between _____ of_____

---

1. In a right of way Easement, title usually remains with the grantor.

City,_____, party of the first part, and_____

_____, of_____City,_____, party of the second part.

Witnesseth, that the party of the first part, for himself, his heirs and assigns, grants and conveys unto the party of the second part, his heirs and assigns, an easement in, to, upon and over all that paved portion of a certain roadway situated

(Here give detailed description)

Said easement is given for the sole purpose of ingress and egress and it is agreed and understood that it is not to be construed as an easement given to the exclusion of the party of the first part, his heirs and assigns, or to others later granted a similar right.

The party of the second part, his heirs or assigns, covenants with the party of the first part, his heirs and assigns, to at all times maintain and make necessary repairs, at his or their own expenses, should the roadway require same for its proper upkeep and maintenance.

To have and to hold the said right of way easement unto the party of the second part for a period of_____years.

In witness whereof, the parties hereto have duly executed this agreement.

_____   _____

_____   _____

_____

No. 11–3
EASEMENT
For Electrical Power Lines

KNOW ALL MEN BY THESE PRESENTS that_____

_____

of the County of_____ and State of_____
in consideration of the sum of One Dollar ($1.00) and other valuable considerations, receipt of which is hereby acknowledged, do_____hereby grant to the_____Power And Light Company, a corporation organized and existing under the laws of the State of _____, whose address is_____, and to its successors and assigns, an easement forever for a right-of-way_____feet in width to be used for the construction, operation and maintenance of one or more electric transmission and distribution lines, including wires, poles, "H" frame structures, towers, anchors, guys, telephone and telegraph lines and appurtenant equipment, in, over, upon and across the following described lands of the Grantor_____, situated in the County of_____
_____and State of_____and more particularly described as follows:

(Here include legal description)

together with the right and privilege to reconstruct, inspect, alter, improve, remove or re-locate such transmission and distribution lines on the right-of-way above described, with all rights and privileges necessary or convenient for the full enjoyment or the use thereof for the above mentioned purposes, including the right to cut and keep clear all trees and un-dergrowth and other obstructions within said right-of-way and all trees of such height on lands of Grantor____adjoining said right-of-way that may interfere with the proper con-struction, operation and maintenance of said electric transmission and distribution lines, and also including the right of ingress and egress over adjoining lands of Grantor____for the purpose of exercising the easement herein granted.

The Grantor____, however, reserve___ the right and privilege to use the above des-cribed right-of-way for agriculture and all other purposes except as herein granted or as might interfere with Grantee's use, occupation or enjoyment thereof, or as might cause a hazardous condition; and provided further by way of illustration and not of limitation to the grant herein made, no portion of the right-of-way shall be excavated or altered without written permission of the Grantee and no building, structure or obstruction shall be located or constructed on said right-of-way by the Grantor____, _____successors, heirs or assigns.

IN WITNESS WHEREOF, the Grantor_____ha_____ executed this agreement this _____day of_____ , 19_____.

Signed, sealed and delivered
in the presence of:

_____   _____ (Seal)

_____   _____ (Seal)

_____   _____ (Seal)

_____   _____

(Reproduced with permission of the Florida Power & Light Company)

No. 11–4
RIGHT-OF-WAY EASEMENT
For Telephone Lines

In consideration of the sum of money hereinafter set out and other good and valuable consideration, the adequacy and receipt of which is hereby acknowledged from the Southern Bell Telephone and Telegraph Company, the undersigned, owner(s) of the premises de-scribed below, do hereby grant to the Southern Bell Telephone and Telegraph Company its licensees, agents, successors, assigns, and allied and associated companies, a right of way easement to construct, operate, maintain, add or remove such lines or systems of communi-cations or related services as the grantee may require, consisting of:

(1) poles, guys, anchors, aerial cables and wires;

(2) buried cables and wires, cable terminals, markers, splicing boxes and pedestals;

(3) conduits, manholes, markers, underground cables and wires;

(4) and other amplifiers, boxes, appurtenances or devices

upon, over and under a strip of land_____ feet wide across the following lands in____
_____ County, State of_____ generally described as follows:

and, to the fullest extent the undersigned has the power to grant, if at all, over, along and under the roads, streets or highways adjoining or through said property.

The following rights are also granted: to allow any other person or company to attach wires or lay cable or conduit within the right of way for communications or electric power transmission or distribution; ingress and egress to said premises at all times; to clear the land and keep it cleared of all trees, undergrowth or other obstructions within the easement area; to trim and cut and keep trimmed and cut all dead, weak, leaning or dangerous trees or limbs outside of the easement area which might interfere with or fall upon the lines or systems of communications or power transmission or distribution.

The receipt of_____ and_____ 100 Dollars ($_____) is hereby acknowledged by the undersigned.

To have and to hold the above granted easement unto Southern Bell Telephone and Telegraph Company, its successors and assigns forever.

IN WITNESS WHEREOF, the undersigned ha_____ signed and sealed this document
caused this instrument to be executed by
its duly authorized agent

on_____, 19_____.
Signed, sealed and delivered
in the presence of:

_____ L.S.

_____ L.S.

_____
Witness

_____   _____
                                                   Name of Corporation

Attest:

_____   By: _____
Corporate officer   Title:

(Reproduced with permission of Southern Bell Telephone And Telegraph Co.)

12

Exchange Agreements

12

Exchange Agreements

An exchange or trade of real estate is the mutual transfer of property for property. In recent years, exchanging real estate has become increasingly popular. It has proven a practical method of transacting real property when little or no cash is available.

Under the Internal Revenue Code no gain or loss is recognized if property held for productive use or investment is exchanged solely for property of like nature. For example, if a Virginia farmer can dispose of his property for one of equal value in Texas, he is not subject to a tax for the trade. In like manner, an apartment house owner who might otherwise be assessed a large capital gains tax if he sold in the conventional manner, can accomplish a tax-free transfer by exchanging his building for another of equal value.

Specifically worded forms are necessary to properly effect dual sales of this nature.

No. 12–1
EXCHANGE AGREEMENT

CALIFORNIA REAL ESTATE ASSOCIATION STANDARD FORM

_____

_____

hereinafter called first party, hereby offers to exchange the following described property, situated in _____ , County of_____ , California;

(Here include description)

For the following described property of_____

_____ hereinafter called second party, situated in_____ , County of _____ , California.

(Here include description)

TERMS AND CONDITIONS OF EXCHANGE:

_____

_____

_____

_____

The parties hereto shall execute and deliver, within_____days from the date this offer is accepted, all instruments, in writing, necessary to transfer title to said properties and complete and consummate this exchange. Each party shall supply Preliminary Title Reports for their respective properties. Evidences of title shall be California Land Title Association standard coverage form policies of title insurance showing titles to be merchantable and free of all liens and encumbrances, except taxes and those liens and encumbrances as otherwise set forth herein. Each party shall pay for the policies of Title insurance for the property to be acquired_____conveyed_____.

If either party is unable to convey a marketable title, except as herein provided, within three months after acceptance hereof by second party, or if the improvements on any of the herein named properties be destroyed or materially damaged prior to transfer of title or delivery of agreement of sale, then this agreement shall be of no further effect, except as to payment of commissions and expenses incurred in connection with examination of title, unless the party acquiring the property so affected elects to accept the title the other party can convey or subject to the conditions of the improvements.

Taxes, insurance premiums (if policies be satisfactory to party acquiring the property affected thereby), rents, interest and other expenses of said properties shall be pro-rated as of date of transfer of title or delivery of agreement of sale, unless otherwise provided herein.

_____ of _____ Calif._____
       Broker   Address   Phone Number

is hereby authorized to act as broker for all parties hereto and may accept commission therefrom. Should second party accept this offer, first party agrees to pay said broker commission for services rendered as follows: _____

_____

Should second party be unable to convey a marketable title to his property then first party shall be released from payment of any commission, unless he elects to accept the property subject thereto. First party agrees that broker may cooperate with other brokers and divide commissions in any manner satisfactory to them.

This offer shall be deemed revoked unless accepted in writing within_____days after date hereof, and such acceptance is communicated to first party within said period. Broker is hereby given the exclusive and irrevocable right to obtain acceptance of second party within said period.

Time is of the essence of this contract, but Broker may, without notice, extend for a period of not to exceed one month the time for the performance of any act hereunder, except the time for the acceptance hereof by second party.

All words used herein in the singular shall include the plural, and the present tense shall include the future, and the masculine gender shall include the feminine and neuter.

_____

_____

                                              _____

                                              _____

Dated_____19_____   _____

ACCEPTANCE

Second party hereby accepts the foregoing offer upon the terms and conditions stated and agrees to pay commission for services rendered, to:

_____ of_____ Calif._____
Broker   Address   Phone No.

as follows: _____

_____

Second party agrees that broker may act as broker for all parties hereto and may accept commission therefrom, and may cooperate with other brokers and divide commissions in any manner satisfactory to them.

Should first party be unable to convey a marketable title to his property then second party shall be released from payment of any commission, unless he elects to accept the property of first party subject thereto.

_____

_____

_____

_____

Dated_____19_____   _____

(Reproduced with permission of the California Real Estate Association)

No. 12–2
DEPOSIT RECEIPT

REAL ESTATE TRADE AGREEMENT

Date of Offer (Date signed by TRADER A):_____, 19_____

Date of Acceptance (Date signed by TRADER B):_____, 19_____

Date of Closing:_____, 19_____

Name of TRADER A:_____

Name of TRADER B:_____

Escrow Agent: (Name)_____

(Address)_____

Property Given by TRADER A:

(Here include description)

Property Given by TRADER B:

(Here include description)

WITNESSETH:

In consideration of the mutual covenants hereinafter contained and based upon the foregoing names, descriptions, parties and information, the parties hereto covenant and agree as follows:

1. Each TRADER shall convey to the other all real estate by general warranty deed, any personal property by good bill of sale, and pay the cash due by cash, cashier's check or certified check, the property above described, at the office of the ESCROW AGENT, at closing date, free and clear of all liens or encumbrances except as above described.

2. TRADER A agrees to pay to his broker_____ the sum of $ _____ and TRADER B agrees to pay to his broker_____ _____ the sum of $_____ , as brokerage commission, which it is agreed shall be earned when this agreement has been signed by both TRADERS hereto.

3. Taxes based upon current year's assessments, insurance, interest, rents and other expenses or revenue of all properties shall be prorated as of closing date. All certified liens shall be paid by the conveying TRADER and all pending liens shall be assumed by the receiving TRADER. Each property is subject to zoning restrictions of record, which zoning restrictions each TRADER acknowledges that he has heretofore investigated. Any differences in mortgage balances from the amounts set forth herein shall be appropriately adjusted as of closing date.

4. All property above described shall include all improvements permanently affixed to the realty, including all heating, lighting, gas and water supply apparatus and fixtures, window screens and awnings now thereon, and shall be subject to present leases and tenancies, which each TRADER hereby acknowledges that he has heretofore investigated.

5. If improvements on any of the property to be conveyed are destroyed or substantially damaged by fire, windstorm or other casualty before the closing date, the TRADER entitled to conveyance of said property shall have the option of either cancelling this agreement or enforcing this agreement, in which latter case the party entitled to conveyance shall be entitled to the insurance proceeds due as a result of said destruction or damage.

6. Each TRADER shall, within 10 days from the date of acceptance, deliver to the ESCROW AGENT complete abstracts of title to his presently owned property, brought to date, showing his title to be good, marketable and/or insurable, and either TRADER not delivering an abstract within said time hereby authorizes his above named BROKER to have an abstract made at said TRADER's expense and delivered to the ESCROW AGENT.

7. Each TRADER shall have 20 days from the date of said abstract delivery for examination thereof and within which to report in writing at the office of the ESCROW AGENT defects therein, if any. Thereafter the TRADER whose property has a defective title shall use reasonable diligence to make said title good and marketable and/or insurable and shall have 60 days to do so, in default of which, the other TRADER may either elect to have the trade consummated and accept title in its then-existing condition, or may elect to declare this agreement inoperative, in which event all instruments and monies shall be returned to the TRADER by whom furnished or deposited.

8. Each TRADER hereto has deposited herewith with the ESCROW AGENT the sums of: Trader A $_____ , Trader B $_____ to be returned to the TRADER by whom deposited upon performance by him of this agreement; the ESCROW AGENT being authorized, however, to apply any part thereof towards any payment due under this agreement from the TRADER by whom deposited. If either TRADER fails to comply with this agreement on his part as herein provided, then his deposit shall be paid over and forfeited to the TRADER not in default as agreed and liquidated damages, and thereafter this agreement shall be operative or inoperative at the election of the TRADER not in default.

9. This agreement shall be binding upon all parties, their heirs, personal representatives and assigns when this agreement shall have been signed by both TRADERS. Each TRADER acknowledges that he has made his own independent investigation of the property he is to receive, and that there are no oral agreements or other provisions of this agreement except as contained hereinabove and except as follows:

IN WITNESS WHEREOF, the parties hereto subscribe their names the day and year first above written.

WITNESSES:

_____

_____   _____ (SEAL)
As to TRADER A   ESCROW AGENT

ESCROW AGENT

_____ (SEAL)

_____ (SEAL)
TRADER A

_____   _____ (SEAL)

_____   _____ (SEAL)
As to TRADER B   TRADER B

(Reproduced with permission of the Miami Board Of Realtors, Miami, Fla.)

No. 12–3
EXCHANGE AGREEMENT
Another Form

Date_____   _____ , Florida

The undersigned, as First Party (1)_____

_____

does agree to transfer and convey to, as Second Party (2)_____

_____

the following described property (show Legal of (1))

(show mortgages and amounts, if any)

and (pay) (accept) $_____upon

closing in consideration of the transfer and conveyance of the following described property

to him or his assigns (show legal of (2))
(show mortgages and amounts, if any)

TERMS AND CONDITIONS

The parties hereto shall execute and deliver within_____days from the date of acceptance, all instruments, in writing, necessary to transfer title to said properties and complete this exchange. Conveyance shall be by warranty deed. Abstracts_____ _____shall be furnished by the owners showing their titles to be insurable in the usual form subject to easements and restrictions common to the subdivision. Liens of governmental agencies for work authorized or not completed at time of closing and the mortgages shown above which shall be_____, taxes, insurance, interest and rents shall be prorated to date of closing.

First Party agrees that the Real Estate Broker representing him in this exchange is:
_____of_____Fla._____
        Broker(s)   Address   Phone No.

First party agrees that Broker may cooperate with other Brokers and divide commissions in any manner satisfactory to them. The above Broker or (Brokers) is (are) authorized to act as Broker for all parties hereto and may accept commission therefrom. Should second party accept this offer, first party agrees to pay said Broker commission for services rendered as follows:

_____

_____

This offer shall be deemed revoked unless accepted in writing within_____days after date hereof and such acceptance is communicated to first party within said period. Broker is hereby given the exclusive and irrevocable right to obtain acceptance of second party within said period.

Time is of the essence of this contract, but Broker may, without notice, extend for a period of not to exceed one month the time for the performance of any act hereunder, except the time for the acceptance hereof by second party.

_____

Signed, sealed and delivered in
presence of:

_____   _____(Seal)

_____   _____(Seal)
                                     First Party or Parties

Dated_____, 19_____.   Accepted:
                              Broker:_____

                              By_____

ACCEPTANCE

Second party hereby accepts the foregoing offer upon the terms and conditions stated and agrees to pay commission for services rendered to:

_____ of _____ Fla. _____
          Broker   Address   Phone No.

as follows: _____

_____

Second party agrees that Broker may act as Broker for all parties hereto and may accept commission therefrom, and may co-operate with other Brokers and divide commission in any manner satisfactory to them.

_____

_____

Signed, sealed and delivered in
presence of:

_____   _____ (Seal)

_____   _____ (Seal)
                                              Second Party or Parties
Dated _____ 19 _____   Accepted:

                                   Broker: _____

                                   By _____

(Copyright form of the Florida Association Of Realtors used with its permission in this publication and not for reprinting)

No. 12–4
EXCHANGE AGREEMENT
Another Form

The undersigned (1) _____ does agree to
transfer and convey to (2) _____
_____ the following described property

(Here include legal description of (1))

Subject to

(Here include mortgages and amounts, if any)

any (pay) (accept) _____
_____ dollars ($ _____) upon closing, in consideration of the transfer
and conveyance of the following described property to him or his assigns

(Here show legal description of (2))

Subject to

(Here include mortgages and amounts, if any)

Both parties agree: Conveyance shall be by_____deed. Abstract shall be furnished by the owners showing their titles to be insurable in the usual form subject to easements and restrictions common to the subdivision, liens of governmental agencies for work authorized or not completed at time of closing and the mortgages shown above which shall be assumed. Taxes, insurance, interest and rents shall be prorated to date of closing. Commissions shall be paid as agreed. Closing shall be on or before_____, 19_____.

(Here include special terms and conditions, if any)

In witness whereof the parties hereto have set their hands and seals the dates indicated.
Signed, sealed and delivered in presence of: Signed_____ 19_____.

_____   By_____(SEAL) 1.

_____   By_____(SEAL) 1.

Received this offer on_____, 19_____, and if not accepted by_____
M. on_____, 19_____, the offer shall be returned.

_____(Broker)

Accepted_____M._____, 19_____

The undersigned agrees to transfer and convey his above described property as agreed.
Signed, sealed and delivered in presence of:

_____   By_____(SEAL) 2.

_____   By_____(SEAL) 2.

No. 12–5
EXCLUSIVE AUTHORIZATION TO EXCHANGE PROPERTY
California Real Estate Association Standard Form

This listing expires_____, 19_____.

_____

_____

(Owner) hereby irrevocably employs_____

(Realtor) as Owner's exclusive agent for a period beginning_____, 19_____,
and ending_____, 19_____, at midnight, to solicit offers to exchange for other real property acceptable to Owner the property of the Owner described as follows:
SUBJECT TO:

Owner reserves the right to accept or reject any offer of property, but shall specify to Realtor the reason why any offer to exchange presented by Realtor is not satisfactory to Owner. In consideration of the services to be rendered by Realtor hereunder, Owner agrees to pay Realtor a fee of_____upon the occurrence of any of the following:

(a) The presentation by Realtor to Owner of a written offer to exchange for the property of Owner other property acceptable to Owner and the completion of the contemplated exchange. If the Owner accepts the offer but the exchange is not completed through his fault, the fee is nevertheless payable.

(b) The sale, lease or exchange of the property of Owner during the term of this Authorization and any extension hereof, whether the sale, lease or exchange is effected by Owner with or without the assistance of Realtor.

(c) The sale, exchange or lease of said property, within one year after termination of this Authorization and all extensions hereof, to parties with whom Realtor has negotiated before the termination, if Realtor before the said termination has notified Owner in writing personally or by mail of the negotiations and the identity of the parties to them.

Owner agrees that Realtor may act as agent for all parties to any transactions in connection with the above described property and may accept from any or all parties to consummated transactions fees for services rendered, may cooperate with other brokers, and divide with other brokers fees for services in any manner satisfactory to them.

I acknowledge receipt of a copy of this Authorization.

Dated_____, 19_____.

_____

_____

_____
Owner

_____
Address of Owner

_____
City   Phone

In consideration of the execution of the foregoing, the undersigned Realtor agrees to use diligence in effecting an exchange.

_____   _____
Address of Realtor   Realtor
_____   By _____
City   Phone

(Reproduced with permission of the California Real Estate Association)

No. 12–6
EXCLUSIVE EXCHANGE LISTING

Date _____

_____

_____

In consideration of your agreement to list the property described as:

_____

_____

_____

to advertise it in such manner as you may deem advisable and to use your efforts to secure an acceptable trade and to notify all members of the_____ Board of Realtors by means of a Photo Listing Brochure, I hereby give you for a period of_____ months from this date, the exclusive right and authority to find a trade for the property at the value hereinafter set forth, or at any other value and terms acceptable to me.

I agree to furnish a complete Abstract of Title to the property brought to date showing a marketable and/or insurable title thereto. In case you secure a purchaser for the property, the usual and customary practice for the examination, curing title and for closing the transaction shall apply. I agree to execute and deliver to the purchaser a good and sufficient warranty deed with dower rights, if any, released, free and clear of all liens and encumbrances except those which the purchaser shall assume as part of the trade and which are specifically detailed below.

I grant you the exclusive right to install a sign on the property and agree to refer to you all inquiries which I may receive during the continuance of this listing.

For finding a trade for the above property I agree to pay you the regular_____ _____ Board of Realtors commission of_____ % of the gross trade value, whether the trade be secured by you or me, or by any other person; or if the property is afterwards sold or exchanged within three (3) months from the termination of this listing to a party to whom it was submitted by you or a cooperating broker during the continuance of the agency, and whose name has been disclosed to me.

In the trade of this property, permission is given you to represent and receive commissions from both parties.

The Gross PRICE for which this property is to be traded is $_____, subject to the following encumbrances:_____

_____

_____

Interest on encumbrances, taxes, insurance premiums and rents shall be adjusted prorata as of date of closing. Improvement liens are to be paid by me.

As my agent you are authorized to accept, receipt for and hold all money paid or deposited as a binder thereon, and if total amount of your commission, as your compensation.

Singular pronouns of the first person shall be read as plural when the agreement is signed by two or more persons.

WITNESS_____hand_____and seal_____this the_____day of_____, 19_____.

WITNESSES, as of Owner:

_____(SEAL)

_____(SEAL)

Owner or Owners

WITNESSES as to   ACCEPTED:
Listing Realtor:

                                                      _____

_____   Listing Realtor

_____   By_____

No. 12–7

COMMISSION AGREEMENT FOR EXCHANGE OF REAL ESTATE

RE: EXCHANGE OF PROPERTY AT

_____

_____

_____

I hereby agree to pay_____

for the services rendered in the exchange of my property at the above address the sum of

_____when exchange is completed and deeds are passed

according to the contract I have signed dated_____for the property

located at_____

_____.

SIGNATURES:

_____

_____

_____

_____

No. 12–8

EXCHANGE LISTING FORM

Owner's Name_____

Address_____Phone_____

Legal Of Property To Be Exchanged _____

Price $_____

Terms_____

No. of Lots_____Zoned_____Taxes, City_____

Size of Lots_____Taxes, County_____

Paved Street_____Sidewalks_____Sewers_____

Equity_____Will Add Cash_____Needs Cash_____

1st Mortgage $_____Payments $_____Interest_____%

2nd Mortgage $_____Payments $_____Interest_____%

Property Desired_____

Reason For Trading_____

Remarks_____

_____

13

Leases

13

Leases

A lease is a contract for the temporary use or occupancy of land and/or the improvements upon it. Lease agreements need not follow a prescribed form and can be for most any duration—from a day to 99 years or more. To be enforceable, leases for one year or over should be in writing. As further evidence and protection, leases are sometimes recorded.

When preparing a lease, the following essentials should be included. (Sample wording is shown for clarity).

  a. (DATE)

    This lease agreement entered into this_____day of_____, A.D. 19_____,

  b. (PARTIES)

    by and between_____hereinafter referred to as the Lessor and_____ hereinafter referred to as the Lessee.

  c. (DESCRIPTION OF THE DEMISED PREMISES)

    Witnesseth that in consideration of the rental below specified and of the covenants hereinafter stipulated, the Lessor agrees to lease the following described premises situated at No._____ _____Avenue,_____City,_____ County, State of_____, legally described as:

(Here include full legal description)

  d. (TERM)

    To have and to hold the demised premises unto the lessee, his successors and assigns for the term of_____years, commencing the_____day of_____, A.D., 19___ and ending the_____day of_____, A.D., 19_____.

  e. (RENT)

    The rent for the term of this lease is $_____, payable without demand or notice in equal monthly installment of $_____ on the_____day of each and every month of the term hereof beginning on the_____day of_____, A.D., 19_____. Receipt is hereby acknowledged by the Lessor of the first month's rental in advance and $_____ as security deposit.

  f. (USE)

    The use of the premises shall be for _____ _____and for no other purpose except with the written consent of the Lessor.

g.   (ASSIGNMENT)

The Lessee may not assign this lease or to sublet any part of said premises without the written consent of the Lessor.

h.   (LESSOR'S MAINTENANCE RESPONSIBILITIES)

The Lessor hereby agrees to keep the entire exterior portion of the premises in good repair and maintenance. The Lessee shall give written notice to the Lessor of necessary repairs and the Lessor shall have a reasonable time to make same.

i.   (LESSEE'S MAINTENANCE RESPONSIBILITIES)

The Lessee agrees to maintain the interior portion of the premises in good repair at all times. However, alterations, additions or structural improvements made to the premises must have the written consent of the Lessor. Said alterations, additions or structural improvements shall remain a part of the premises at the conclusion of the term of this lease.

j.   (INSURANCE)

The Lessee agrees to carry adequate public liability insurance with a bona fide insurance company maintaining sufficient protection against any injuries or damages sustained by individuals while upon the demised premises for which the Lessor and Lessee may become liable.

k.   (DEFAULT REMEDIES)

The said Lessee hereby convenants and agrees that if a default shall be made in the payment of rent or if the Lessee shall violate any of the covenants of this lease, then said lessee shall become a tenant at sufference, hereby waiving all right of notice, and the Lessor shall be entitled immediately to re-enter and retake possession of the demised premises.

l.   (TERMINATION)

The Lessee agrees to quit and deliver up said premises at the end of said term in good condition as they are now, ordinary wear and tear excepted.

m.   (OPTION)

The Lessee has the option to renew this lease for a further term of_____ years beginning_____ and ending_____ for a total rental of $_____ payable $_____ per month. All other terms and conditions of this lease agreement shall remain in full force and effect.

n.   (QUIET ENJOYMENT)

As long as the Lessee performs all of the covenants and conditions of this lease and abides by the rules and regulations he shall have peaceful and quiet enjoyment of the demised premises for the term of this lease.

o.   (SIGNATURES AND WITNESSES)

In witness whereof, the Lessor and Lessee have executed this lease the day and year first above written.

Witness:

_____   By_____
                                                        Lessor

_____

_____   By_____ _____
                                                        Lessee

_____

No. 13–1
APARTMENT HOUSE LEASE

This LEASE made this_____ day of_____, 19_____ by and between
_____hereinafter called "LANDLORD," and _____
_____hereinafter called "TENANT;"

WITNESSETH:

LANDLORD leases to TENANT and TENANT rents from LANDLORD, for use and occupation as a private residence for TENANT and his immediate family, Apartment No._____in the building known as_____at_____ on the following terms and conditions:

LEASE TERM: The term of this lease commences_____, 19_____, unless sooner terminated.

RENT: The rent for the term is $_____payable in advance without demand or notice, in equal monthly installments of $_____on the first day of each and every month during the term, at the office of _____ _____at_____.

SECURITY: Landlord acknowledges receipt from Tenant of the sum of $_____as security deposit, which shall not bear interest, need not be kept separately, and shall be returned to Tenant within_____days of the peaceful termination of the full term of this lease and surrender of possession, less the cost of any repairs which shall have been made necessary by acts of the tenant.

OCCUPANCY AND USE: The premises shall be used solely as a private dwelling for Tenant and his immediate family and for no others except with written permission of Landlord. Tenant agrees not to use or permit the use of the premises for unlawful or immoral purposes. Tenant agrees to keep the premises clean, sanitary and in good order, and agrees not to hamper, disturb or interfere with other tenants in the building, nor to create or suffer any nuisances in the premises affecting the rights of others, and agrees to comply with all laws, ordinances, rules, regulations and directions of governmental authorities and the Board of Fire Underwriters. Upon termination of this lease, Tenant agrees to surrender possession in as good condition and repair as when received, ordinary wear and tear excepted.

EQUIPMENT: The premises are furnished by the Landlord with a range, refrigerator, disposal and dishwasher, among other mechanical installations. Tenant agrees to use and maintain all such equipment, and plumbing fixtures and all other equipment with which apartment is furnished, in accordance with manufacturers' specifications and the regulations of the Landlord now or hereafter provided, and to be responsible for all repairs and any damage to the apartment brought about by misuse or neglect of such equipment by the Tenant. All repairs to equipment furnished by Landlord shall be made by licensed persons approved by Landlord. Should Tenant fail or refuse to make repairs after reasonable notice from Landlord, Landlord may cause same to be done and the cost thereof shall be additional rent immediately due from Tenant to Landlord.

ALTERATIONS, ADDITIONS OR IMPROVEMENTS: Tenant agrees not to make any alterations, additions, improvements or changes in the premises, interior or exterior, or to the equipment and fixtures provided by landlord or to install any major appliances in the premises without written consent of the Landlord.

UTILITIES: Tenant agrees to pay all charges for electricity, telephone service and____ _____ when and as they become due.

ASSIGNMENT: No assignment or sub-lease of the apartment shall be binding upon the Landlord or confer any rights on the proposed assignee or sub-lessee without the written consent of Landlord. No assignment or sub-lease shall release Tenant from the obligations of this lease.

INTERRUPTION OF SERVICE: Interruption or failure of any service maintained in the building in which the apartment is located, if due to causes beyond Landlord's control, shall not entitle Tenant to any claim against Landlord or to any reduction in rent, and shall not constitute constructive eviction unless Landlord shall fail to take such measures as may be reasonable in the circumstances to restore the service without undue delay.

DELAY IN TENDERING POSSESSION: If Landlord is unable to give possession on the commencement date, rent shall abate until possession is given, and Tenant shall pay a fractional part from date of possession up to first day of the next month following date of possession. Tenant waives all damages by reason of Landlord's failure to give possession on the commencement date. Delay in tendering possession shall not extend the termination date of this lease.

RELEASE OF LIABILITY: The Tenant assumes all risk of any damage to person or property that may occur by reason of water or the bursting or leaking of any pipes or waste about said premises or from any act of negligence of any co-tenants or occupants of the building or of any other person, or fire or hurricane or other act of God or from any cause whatsoever, provided that Landlord shall make necessary repairs to prevent further damage with reasonable diligence after notice given to it, and the Tenant agrees to give the Landlord prompt written notice of any accident to or defect in the water pipes, electricity or of any plumbing, heating or cooling apparatus or device.

SUBORDINATION: This lease shall always be subordinate to any mortgage now or hereafter placed against the property in which the apartment is located, and the Tenant agrees to execute such documents as are necessary to complete such subordination, or in lieu thereof, Tenant appoints Landlord Tenant's agent irrevocably to execute such documents as are necessary to complete such subordination.

TENANT'S PROPERTY: If, upon the termination of this lease or abandonment of the premises by Tenant, Tenant abandons or leaves any property in the apartment, Landlord shall have the right, without notice to Tenant, to store or otherwise dispose of the property at Tenant's cost and expense, without being liable in any respect to the Tenant.

PARKING: Tenant shall use only that parking space designated for his use by the Landlord, and the Tenant shall see to it that Tenant's guests use only the parking space provided for guest parking.

LANDLORD'S RIGHT OF ENTRY: Landlord shall have the right to enter the apartment at all times which are necessary to make needed repairs, and this right shall exist whether or not Tenant or other occupant shall be on premises at such time. During the last_____ days of the term of the lease, Landlord shall have the right to enter the apartment at reasonable hours to show the same to prospective tenants.

POSSESSION: Taking of possession of the apartment by Tenant shall be conclusive evidence against Tenant that he received the premises in good condition.

FIRE AND CASUALTY: If the premises are damaged by fire or other casualty, Landlord may cause the damage to be repaired and the rent will be abated for such period of time as premises remain untenantable, but if the premises are destroyed or so damaged that Landlord shall decide that it is inadvisable to repair same, this lease shall cease and terminate, and rental shall be adjusted to the date when such fire or casualty occurred. Tenant agrees to release Landlord from any and all claims for loss, damage or inconvenience arising from such fire or casualty.

RULES AND REGULATIONS: There are attached hereto certain Rules and Regulations which are made a part of this lease. Tenant agrees to comply with all current rules and regulations, together with any subsequent reasonable rules and regulations which may be adopted by the Landlord for the general benefit of all tenants in the building. Any violation of these rules or any one of them shall be cause for termination of this lease at the option of the Landlord.

DEFAULT CLAUSE: If the Tenant shall fail to pay the rent or any other charge required to be paid by the Tenant, or if the Tenant shall breach any of the terms of this lease or the rules attached hereto or enacted from time to time, then as to every default or breach, except non-payment of rent, the Landlord may give the Tenant_____days' written notice thereof, and if such default has not been cured within such _____ -day period, then the Landlord may give the Tenant_____days' notice of the termination of this lease, and this lease shall expire accordingly and the Tenant shall surrender possession to the Landlord, but the Tenant shall remain liable as hereinafter provided. In case of default by the Tenant in the payment of rent, the notice shall be a three-day notice provided by Statutes of the State of_____, and the Landlord shall have such rights as is provided by such statutes. If the apartment becomes vacant or abandoned, this lease shall expire and terminate and the Landlord may re-enter and take possession or may take possession in the manner provided by law. In case the Landlord shall recover possession of the apartment, the landlord may, but shall not be required to remove the property of the Tenant and store the same at the Tenant's expense, or he may dispose of said property, and the Tenant agrees that in no respect shall the Landlord be responsible in damages for any action in entering said apartment or removing and disposing of Tenant's property, with or without process of law. Notwithstanding anything stated herein, the Tenant agrees that whether possession is taken or this lease is cancelled by the Landlord, the entire unpaid balance of rent shall accelerate and immediately become due and payable and the Tenant shall be responsible for all costs, including attorneys fees incurred by the Landlord in and about enforcing this and any other provision of this lease.

In the event of a default by Tenant, Landlord shall not be required to return any part or portion of the security deposit, but the landlord may either retain the security deposit as liquidated damages or retain the security deposit and apply it against actual damage sustained by Landlord by reason of Tenant's default. The retention of the security deposit shall not be the only remedy to which Landlord is entitled but Landlord shall have all recourse against the Tenant provided by this lease and by law, and all remedies shall be cumulative and non-exclusive. Tenant agrees to pay Landlord's reasonable attorneys fees and expenses incurred in and about enforcing any of the terms of this lease, in collecting past due rent, and in and about recovering possession from Tenant, should the services of an attorney be retained by Landlord in so doing.

ABANDONMENT: In the event any installment of rent shall not have been paid within _____ days of its due date and the Tenant shall not have been physically present in the apartment during such period of time, it shall be conclusively deemed (and the Tenant so agrees) that the apartment has been abandoned regardless of whether or not any of Tenant's possessions remain in the apartment, and in such event, the Landlord may take possession without process of law, without in any way being responsible to Tenant for damages, trespass, unlawful entry, or any matter or thing whatever by reason thereof, and the Landlord may, at Landlord's option, in the event of such abandonment, declare this lease terminated. This right on the part of the Landlord shall be in addition to and not exclusive of all other rights and remedies provided by this lease and by law.

QUIET ENJOYMENT: In the event that Tenant pays the rent as provided for herein and otherwise performs all of the covenants and conditions to be performed by the Tenant and abides by all of the rules and regulations as set forth herein and referred to, Tenant shall have peaceful and quiet enjoyment of all the demised premises for the term of this lease.

IN WITNESS WHEREOF, the Landlord and Tenant have executed this lease the day and year first above written

By _____

Witness: LANDLORD

_____   _____

_____   _____

                                                                TENANT

No. 13–2
DWELLING HOUSE LEASE

This agreement, entered into this _____ day of _____, A.D. 19_____ between _____ hereinafter called the Lessor, and _____ hereinafter called the Lessee, and _____ hereinafter called the Rental Agent.

Witnesseth, that in consideration of the covenants herein contained, on the part of the said Lessee to be kept and performed, the said Lessor does hereby demise and lease to the said Lessee that certain

(Here describe property)

To hold the said premises hereby demised unto the said Lessee from the _____ _____ day of _____, A.D. 19_____, to the _____ day of _____, A.D. 19_____, the said Lessee paying therefor the rent of _____ dollars as follows:

(Here include how rents are to be paid, security deposits held and any other special terms and conditions).

The Lessor covenants with the Lessee that the Lessee paying the rent when due as aforesaid, shall peaceably and quietly use, occupy and possess the said premises for the full term of this lease without let, hindrance, eviction, molestation or interruption whatever, except as provided below, and the said Lessee covenants with the Lessor:

1. To pay said rent hereinbefore reserved at the times at which the same is made payable.

2. To pay all water, electric, gas, and telephone charges which may be assessed upon the demised premises during the term hereof.

3. Not to suffer or commit any waste of the premises, nor make any unlawful, improper or offensive use of same.

4. Not to assign this lease or underlet the said premises or any part thereof without the previous consent of the said Lessor being first obtained in writing.

5. That this lease shall terminate when the Lessee vacates the said premises, providing all payments have been made hereunder or a sub-lease agreement has been executed.

6. At the termination of said tenancy to quietly yield up the said buildings and grounds in as good and tenantable condition in all respects (reasonable wear and use and damage by fire and other unavoidable causes excepted) as the same now are:

It is hereby agreed that all expenses in connection with upkeep of the grounds including all water used for irrigation purposes will be paid for by _____.

Provided always that if the rent hereby reserved, or any part thereof, shall be in arrears, or in event of any breach of any of the covenants and agreements on the part of the Lessee herein contained, the Lessor may at his option declare the entire rent for the term for which said premises are leased, due and payable, and/or may declare this lease terminated and re-enter upon the said demised premises.

Provided always that if the premises or any part thereof shall at any time during the said term be destroyed or rendered uninhabitable by fire or storm then the payment of the rent hereby reserved, or a proportionate part thereof, according to the extent of the damage incurred, shall be suspended until the premises shall have been reinstated and rendered fit for habitation.

I. COMMISSION AGREEMENT:

Lessor acknowledges that Lessee was procured by _____
_____ and agrees to recognize said Rental Agent the Standard Board of Realtors Commission on such extensions or renewal when made. On month-to-month extensions, commission shall be paid monthly or quarterly.

If the property of which the premises are a part is sold by Lessor to Lessee during the term of this lease, or during the term of any further extension or renewal agreement, (any continued occupancy of the premises by the Lessee after the expiration of this lease shall be considered a further extension or renewal agreement), the Lessor will pay said Rental Agent a commission on the selling price, said commission to be based upon the Board of Realtors Commission Schedule in effect at the time of sale, deducting from such sales commission any unearned leasing commission previously paid by Lessor from date of expiration of lease.

Witness our hands and seals, in triplicate, on the day and year first above written.
Signed, Sealed and Delivered in the presence of

_____   _____ (Seal)

_____   _____ (Seal)
(Witnesses to Lessor)

_____   _____ (Seal)

_____   _____ (Seal)
(Witnesses to Lessee)

_____   By: _____ (Seal)

_____
(Witness to Rental Agent)

No. 13–3

BUSINESS PROPERTY LEASE

General Form Suitable for, Stores, Offices, Lofts, Warehouses, Etc.

THIS AGREEMENT, entered into this_____ day of_____
_____, 19____ between _____
_____, hereinafter called the lessor,
party of the first part, and_____
of the County of_____ and State of_____
hereinafter called the lessee or tenant, party of the second part:_____
WITNESSETH, That the said lessor does this day lease unto said lessee, and said lessee
does hereby hire and take as tenant_____under said lessor Room_____
or Space
NO. _____
situate in_____Florida, to be used and occupied by the lessee as
_____ and for no other purposes or uses whatsoever,
for the term of_____, subject and conditioned on the
provisions of clause ten of this lease beginning the_____ day of_____
_____, 19____, and ending the_____day of_____
_____, 19____, at and for the agreed total rental of_____
_____dollars, payable as follows:

all payments to be made to the lessor on the first day of each and every month in advance
without demand at the office of _____
in the City of _____ or at such other place and to such
other person, as the lessor may from time to time designate in writing.

The following express stipulations and conditions are made a part of this lease and are
hereby assented to by the lessee:

FIRST:The lessee shall not assign this lease, nor sub-let the premises, or any part thereof
nor use the same, or any part thereof, nor permit the same, or any part thereof, to be used for

any other purpose than as above stipulated, nor make any alterations therein, and all additions thereto, without the written consent of the lessor, and all additions, fixtures or improvements which may be made by lessee, except movable office furniture, shall become the property of the lessor and remain upon the premises as a part thereof, and be surrendered with the premises at the termination of this lease.

SECOND: All personal property placed or moved in the premises above described shall be at the risk of the lessee or owner thereof, and lessor shall not be liable for any damage to said personal property, or to the lessee arising from the bursting or leaking of water pipes, or from any act of negligence of any co-tenant or occupants of the building or of any other person whomsoever.

THIRD: That the tenant _____ shall promptly execute and comply with all statutes, ordinances, rules, orders, regulations and requirements of the Federal, State and City Government and of any and all their Departments and Bureaus applicable to said premises, for the correction, prevention, and abatement of nuisances or other grievances, in, upon, or connected with said premises during said term; and shall also promptly comply with and execute all rules, orders and regulations of the Southeastern Underwriters Association for the prevention of fires, at _____ own cost and expense.

FOURTH: In the event the premises shall be destroyed or so damaged or injured by fire or other casualty during the life of this agreement, whereby the same shall be rendered untenantable, then the lessor shall have the right to render said premises tenantable by repairs within ninety days therefrom. If said premises are not rendered tenantable within said time, it shall be optional with either party hereto to cancel this lease, and in the event of such cancellation the rent shall be paid only to the date of such fire or casualty. The cancellation herein mentioned shall be evidenced in writing.

FIFTH: The prompt payment of the rent for said premises upon the dates named, and the faithful observance of the rules and regulations printed upon this lease, and which are hereby made a part of this covenant, and of such other and further rules or regulations as may be hereafter made by the lessor, are the conditions upon which the lease is made and accepted and any failure on the part of the lessee to comply with the terms of said lease, or any of said rules and regulations now in existence, or which may be hereafter prescribed by the lessor, shall at the option of the lessor, work a forfeiture of this contract, and all of the rights of the lessee hereunder, and thereupon the lessor, his agents or attorneys, shall have the right to enter said premises, and remove all persons therefrom forcibly or otherwise, and the lessee thereby expressly waives any and all notice required by law to terminate tenancy, and also waives any and all legal proceedings to recover possession of said premises, and expressly agrees that in the event of a violation of any of the terms of this lease, or of said rules and regulations, now in existence, or which may hereafter be made, said lessor, his agent or attorneys, may immediately re-enter said premises and dispossess lessee without legal notice or the institution of any legal proceedings whatsoever.

SIXTH: If the lessee shall abandon or vacate said premises before the end of the term of this lease, or shall suffer the rent to be in arrears, the lessor may, at his option, forthwith cancel this lease or he may enter said premises as the agent of the lessee, by force or otherwise, without being liable in any way therefor, and relet the premises with or without any furniture that may be therein, as the agent of the lessee, at such price and upon such terms and for such duration of time as the lessor may determine, and receive the rent therefor, applying the same to the payment of the rent due by these presents, and if the full rental herein provided shall not be realized by lessor over and above the expenses to lessor in such re-letting, the said lessee shall pay any deficiency, and if more than the full rental is realized lessor will pay over to said lessee the excess of demand.

SEVENTH: Lessee agrees to pay the cost of collection and ten per cent attorney's fee on any part of said rental that may be collected by suit or by attorney, after the same is past due.

EIGHTH: The lessee agrees that he will pay all charges for rent, gas, electricity or other illumination, and for all water used on said premises, and should said charges for rent, light or water herein provided for at any time remain due and unpaid for the space of five days after the same shall have become due, the lessor may at its option consider the said lessee tenant at sufferance and immediately re-enter upon said premises and the entire rent for the rental period then next ensuing shall at once be due and payable and may forthwith be collected by distress or otherwise.

NINTH: The said lessee hereby pledges and assigns to the lessor all the furniture, fixtures, goods and chattels of said lessee, which shall or may be brought or put on said premises as security for the payment of the rent herein reserved, and the lessee agrees that the said lien may be enforced by distress foreclosure or otherwise at the election of the said lessor, and does hereby agree to pay attorney's fees of ten percent of the amount so collected or found to be due, together with all costs and charges therefore incurred or paid by the lessor.

TENTH: It is hereby agreed and understood between lessor and lessee that in the event the lessor decides to remodel, alter or demolish all or any part of the premises leased hereunder, or in the event of the sale or long term lease of all or any part of the_____ ; requiring this space, the lessee hereby agrees to vacate same upon receipt of sixty (60) days' written notice and the return of any advance rental paid on account of this lease.

It being further understood and agreed that the lessee will not be required to vacate said premises during the winter season: namely, November first to May first, by reason of the above paragraph.

ELEVENTH: The lessor, or any of his agents, shall have the right to enter said premises during all reasonable hours, to examine the same to make such repairs, additions or alterations as may be deemed necessary for the safety, comfort, or preservation thereof, or of said building, or to exhibit said premises, and to put or keep upon the doors or windows thereof a notice "FOR RENT" at any time within thirty (30) days before the expiration of this lease. The right of entry shall likewise exist for the purpose of removing placards, signs, fixtures, alterations, or additions, which do not conform to this agreement, or to the rules and regulations of the building.

TWELFTH: Lessee hereby accepts the premises in the condition they are in at the beginning of this lease and agrees to maintain said premises in the same condition, order and repair as they are at the commencement of said term, excepting only reasonable wear and tear arising from the use thereof under this agreement, and to make good to said lessor immediately upon demand, any damage to water apparatus, or electric lights or any fixture, appliances or appurtenances of said premises, or of the building, caused by any act or neglect of lessee, or of any person or persons in the employ or under the control of the lessee.

THIRTEENTH: It is expressly agreed and understood by and between the parties to this agreement, that the landlord shall not be liable for any damage or injury by water, which may be sustained by the said tenant or other person or for any other damage or injury resulting from the carelessness, negligence, or improper conduct on the part of any other tenant or agents, or employees, or by reason of the breakage, leakage, or obstruction of the water, sewer or soil pipes, or other leakage in or about the said building.

FOURTEENTH: If the lessee shall become insolvent or if bankruptcy proceedings shall be begun by or against the lessee, before the end of said term the lessor is hereby irrevocably authorized at its option, to forthwith cancel this lease, as for a default. Lessor may elect to accept rent from such receiver, trustee, or other judicial officer during the term of their occupancy in their fiduciary capacity without effecting lessor's rights as contained in this contract, but no receiver, trustee or other judicial officer shall ever have any right, title or interest in or to the above described property by virtue of this contract.

FIFTEENTH: Lessee hereby waives and renounces for himself and family any and all homestead and exemption rights he may have now, or hereafter, under or by virtue of the constitution and laws of the State of Florida, or of any other State, or of the United States, as against the payment of said rental or any portion hereof, or any other obligation or damage that may accrue under the terms of this agreement.

SIXTEENTH: This contract shall bind the lessor and its assigns or successors, and the heirs, assigns, administrators, legal representatives, executors or successors as the case may be, of the lessee.

SEVENTEENTH: It is understood and agreed between the parties hereto that time is of the essence of this contract and this applies to all terms and conditions contained herein.

EIGHTEENTH: It is understood and agreed between the parties hereto that written notice mailed or delivered to the premises leased hereunder shall constitute sufficient notice to the lessee and written notice mailed or delivered to the office of the lessor shall constitute sufficient notice to the Lessor, to comply with the terms of this contract.

NINETEENTH: The rights of the lessor under the foregoing shall be cumulative, and failure on the part of the lessor to exercise promptly any rights given hereunder shall not operate to forfeit any of the said rights.

TWENTIETH: It is further understood and agreed between the parties hereto that any charges against the lessee by the lessor for services or for work done on the premises by order of the lessee or otherwise accruing under this contract shall be considered as rent due and shall be included in any lien for rent due and unpaid.

TWENTY-FIRST: It is hereby understood and agreed that any signs or advertising to be used, including awnings, in connection with the premises leased hereunder shall be first submitted to the lessor for approval before installation of same.

IN WITNESS WHEREOF, the parties hereto have hereunto executed this instrument for the purpose herein expressed, the day and year above written.

Signed, sealed and delivered in the presence of:

_____   _____ (Seal)
                                        _____ (Seal)
          As to Lessor   Lessor

_____   _____ (Seal)
                                        _____ (Seal)
          As to Lessee   Lessee

STATE OF FLORIDA,   ⎫
County of_____ ⎭

    Before me, a Notary Public in and for said State and County, personally came_____

_____ to me

well known and known to be the person_____named in the foregoing lease, and_____

_____ acknowledged that_____executed the same for the purpose

therein expressed.

    IN WITNESS WHEREOF, I have hereunto set my hand and affixed my official seal

the_____ day of_____ , 19_____

                                                   _____

My commission expires_____   _____
                                         Notary Public, State of Florida at Large.

This Instrument prepared by:
Address

        (Reproduced with permission of Official Legal Forms, Hialeah, Fla.)

No. 13–4
STORE OR OFFICE
LEASE

THIS AGREEMENT, made this_____ day of_____ ,

19_____ , by and between_____

_____ ,

as Landlord, and_____a corporation of the State of

_____ , with its principal office and place of business in_____

_____ as Tenant:

WITNESSETH: That the said Landlord does hereby demise and lease to Tenant and Tenant does hereby hire from Landlord the following described premises:

together with all appurtenances thereto and with easements of ingress and egress necessary and adequate for the conduct of Tenant's business as hereinafter described, for the term of_____years, running from and including the_____

day of_____ , 19_____up to and including the_____

day of_____ , 19_____ , for use in Tenant's regular business of

_____

_____

or in any other legitimate business, subject to the terms and conditions of this lease.

AMOUNT OF RENTAL

Tenant covenants to pay to Landlord at Landlord's office at_____

_____

or such other place in_____

as Landlord shall designate in writing as rent for said premises, the sum of $_____

per month, payable in advance commencing _____ .

In addition to the above, Landlord and Tenant mutually covenant and agree as follows:

TENANT'S MAINTENANCE AND REPAIR OF PREMISES

1. Except as hereinafter provided, Tenant shall maintain and keep the interior of the premises in good repair, free of refuse and rubbish and shall return the same at the expiration or termination of this lease in as good condition as received by Tenant, ordinary wear and tear, damage or destruction by fire, flood storm, civil commotion or other unavoidable cause excepted; provided, however, that if alterations, additions and/or installations shall have been made by Tenant as provided for in this lease, Tenant shall not be required to restore the premises to the condition in which they were prior to such alterations, additions and/or installations except as hereinafter provided.

TENANT'S ALTERATIONS, ADDITIONS, INSTALLATIONS, AND REMOVAL THEREOF

2. Tenant may, at its own expense, either at the commencement of or during the term of this lease, make such alterations in and/or additions to the leased premises including, without prejudice to the generality of the foregoing, alterations in the water, gas, and the electric wiring system, as may be necessary to fit the same for its business, upon first obtaining the written approval of Landlord as to the materials to be used and the manner of making such alterations and/or additions. Landlord covenants not to unreasonably withhold approval of alterations and/or additions proposed to be made by Tenant. Tenant may also, at its own expense, install such counters, racks, shelving, fixtures, fittings, machinery and equipment upon or within the leased premises as Tenant may consider to the conduct of its business. At any time prior to the expiration or earlier termination of the lease, Tenant may remove any or all such alterations, additions or installations in such a manner as will not substantially injure the leased premises. In the event Tenant shall elect to make any such removal, Tenant shall restore the premises, or the portion or portions affected by such removal, to the same condition as existed prior to the making of such alteration, addition or installation, ordinary wear and tear, damage or destruction by fire, flood, storm, civil commotion or other unavoidable cause excepted.

All alterations, additions or installations not so removed by Tenant shall become the property of Landlord without liability on Landlord's part to pay for the same.

LANDLORD'S MAINTENANCE AND REPAIR OF PREMISES

3. Landlord shall, without expenses to Tenant, maintain and make all necessary repairs to the foundations, load bearing walls, roof, gutters, downspouts, heating system, air

conditioning, elevators, water mains, gas and sewer lines, sidewalks, private roadways, parking areas, railroad spurs or sidings, and loading docks, if any, on or appurtenant to the leased premises.

UTILITIES

4. Tenant shall pay all charges for water, gas and electricity consumed by Tenant upon the leased premises.

OBSERVANCE OF LAWS

5. Tenant shall duly obey and comply with all public laws, ordinances, rules or regulations relating to the use of the leased premises; provided, however, that any installation of fire prevention apparatus, electric rewiring, plumbing changes or structural changes in the building on the leased premises, required by any such law, ordinance, rule, or regulation shall be made by Landlord without expense to Tenant.

DAMAGE BY FIRE, ETC.

Damage Repairable Within One Hundred Twenty (120) Days

6. In the event the said premises shall be damaged by fire, flood, storm, civil commotion, or other unavoidable cause, to an extent repairable within one hundred twenty (120) days from the date of such damage, Landlord shall forthwith proceed to repair such damage. If such repair shall not have been completed within one hundred twenty (120) days from the date of such damage, delays occasioned by causes beyond the control of Landlord excepted, this lease may, at the option of Tenant, be terminated. During the period of repair, Tenant's rent shall abate in whole or in part depending upon the extent to which such damage and/or such repair shall deprive Tenant of the use of said premises for the normal purposes of Tenant's business. In the event that Landlord shall fail to promptly commence repair of such damage, or, having commenced the same shall fail to prosecute such repair to completion with due diligence, Tenant may at Tenant's option upon five (5) days' written notice to Landlord, make or complete such repair and deduct the cost thereof from the next ensuing installment or installments of rent payable under this lease.

Damage Not Repairable Within One Hundred Twenty (120) Days

7. In the event the said premises shall be damaged by fire, flood, storm, civil commotion, or other unavoidable cause, to an extent not repairable within one hundred twenty (120) days from the date of such damage, this lease shall terminate as of the date of such damage.

SIDEWALK ENCUMBRANCES

8. Tenant shall neither encumber nor obstruct the sidewalk in front of, or any entrance to, the building on the leased premises.

SIGNS

9. Tenant shall have the right to erect, affix or display on the roof, exterior or interior walls, doors and windows of the building on the leased premises, such sign or sign advertis-

ing its business as Tenant may consider necessary or desirable, subject to all applicable municipal ordinances and regulations with respect thereto.

TERMINATION BY REASON OF DEFAULT

10. In the event that either of the parties hereto shall fail to perform any covenant required to be performed by such party under the terms and provisions of this lease, including Tenant's covenant to pay rent, and such failure shall continue unremedied or uncorrected for a period of fifteen (15) days after the service of written notice upon such party by the other party hereto, specifying such failure, this lease may be terminated, at the option of the party serving such notice, at the expiration of such period of fifteen (15) days; provided, however, that such termination shall not relieve the party so failing from liability to the other party for such damages as may be suffered by reason of such failure.

CONDEMNATION

11. In the event that the leased premises shall be taken for public use by the city, state, federal government, public authority or other corporation having the power of eminent domain, then this lease shall terminate as of the date on which possession thereof shall be taken for such public use, or, at the option of Tenant, as of the date on which the premises shall become unsuitable for Tenant's regular business by reason of such taking; provided, however, that if only a part of the leased premises shall be so taken, such termination shall be at the option of Tenant only. If such a taking of only a part of the leased premises occurs, and Tenant elects not to terminate the lease, there shall be a proportionate reduction of the rent to be paid under this lease from and after the date such possession is taken for public use. Tenant shall have the right to participate, directly or indirectly, in any award for such public taking to the extent that it may have suffered compensable damage as a Tenant on account of such public taking.

ASSIGNMENT

12. Tenant may assign this lease or sub-let the premises or any part thereof for any legitimate use, either with or without the consent of Landlord. If any assignment or sub-lease is made by Tenant without Landlord's consent, Tenant shall remain liable as surety under the terms hereof notwithstanding such assignment or sub-lease.

TAXES

13. Landlord shall pay all taxes, assessments, and charges which shall be assessed and levied upon the leased premises or any part thereof during the said term as they shall become due.

TENANT'S LIABILITY INSURANCE

14. During the term of this lease, Tenant at his own expense shall carry public liability insurance in not less than the following limits:
bodily injury $100,000/$300,000
property damage $50,000

LANDLORD'S RIGHT TO ENTER PREMISES

15. Tenant shall permit Landlord and Landlord's agents to enter at all reasonable times to view the state and condition of the premises or to make such alterations or repairs therein as may be necessary for the safety and preservation thereof, or for any other reasonable purposes. Tenant shall also permit Landlord or Landlord's agents, on or after sixty (60) days next preceding the expiration of the term of this lease, to show the premises to prospective tenants at reasonable times, and to place notices on the front of said premises, or on any part thereof, offering the premises for lease or for sale.

RENEWAL OF LEASE

16. Tenant shall have the option to take a renewal lease of the demised premises for the further term of_____( ) years from and after the expiration of the term herein granted at a monthly rent of_____
_____dollars ($_____) and under and subject to the same covenants, provisos and agreements as are herein contained. In the event Tenant desires to exercise the option herein provided, Tenant shall notify Landlord of such desire in writing not less than sixty (60) days prior to the expiration of the term hereby granted.

AND IT IS MUTUALLY UNDERSTOOD AND AGREED that the covenants and agreements herein contained shall insure to the benefit of and be equally binding upon the respective executors, administrators, heirs, successors and assigns of the parties hereto.

IN WITNESS WHEREOF, the parties hereto have executed this lease the day and year first above written.

_____ (L. S.)

_____ (L. S.)

Signed, Sealed and   _____ (L. S.)

Delivered in the   _____ (L. S.)

presence of   Landlord (s)

_____

_____

Attest:

_____   _____
     Assistant Secretary   Vice President

(Tenant)

(Reproduced with permission of PPG Industries, Inc., Pittsburgh, Pa.)

No. 13–5
LEASE OF MOBILE HOME LOT

THIS LEASE AND AGREEMENT made and entered into at_____
this the_____day of_____, 19_____, by and between_____,
and Mobile Home Park of_____ St.,_____, State of_____.

WITNESSETH:

THAT WHEREAS, the landlord is engaged in the business of operating a mobile home park at_____, and

WHEREAS, tenant is desirous of renting a mobile home lot from the landlord for the purpose of locating thereon a mobile home for residence purposes only, and

WHEREAS, it is necessary and desirable in the conduct and operation of the mobile home park to establish rules and regulations for the operation of said park for the benefit of all persons now residing or who may hereafter reside in the mobile home park so that the mobile home park may be conducted and maintained in a clean, safe, wholesome and proper manner for the benefit of all the tenants of the mobile home park.

NOW, THEREFORE, in consideration of the tenant being permitted to use said mobile home park, they agree to abide by and strictly conform to the following rules and regulations and to such further rules and regulations as may hereafter be prescribed by the landlord for the occupants thereof or by County Ordinance or other proper authority:

The landlord reserves the right and it is clearly understood by the occupants and they agree to remove their mobile home within five days time if asked to do so by the landlord. Any advance payment of rent upon the actual rent of occupancy may be returned to the occupant when asked to leave. It shall not be necessary for the landlord to specify any reasons for asking any occupant to leave and when requested to leave, the occupants are to voluntarily leave the mobile home park and to leave the area occupied by their mobile home in clean and proper condition.

All mobile home lots are rented on monthly basis, and the tenant agrees to pay $_____ per month in advance for his lot. Rental payments are to be paid at_____, due the first day of each month. Rent will be prorated for tenant moving in before end of month.

Occupants having additional persons in the mobile home must register them at the office.

If rent is not paid within_____ days after due date there will be a $_____ per day penalty.

For the mutual benefit of the landlord and tenants, the following regulations shall remain in effect at all times:

1. Each mobile home must be connected with the park's sewer, gas/oil system at each lot.
2. Water lines connected with the mobile home shall be of metal and shall be insulated or fitted with electric wire setup.
3. All garbage must be in cans, presentable, with tops on, and located in the rear.
4. No shrubbery, flowers, etc. can be removed upon termination of occupancy.
5. No awnings, shelters, etc. of any kind are to be erected without consent of the landlord. Only the umbrella type clothesline will be permitted. No Sunday drying.
6. Swimming pool is for tenants and their children only. Others must have permission from the Office to use pool. Anyone using pool does so at his own risk and assumes all responsibility.
7. Speed limit will be rigidly enforced at 10 miles per hour. Cars are to be parked on parking pads. Any damage done to lot or street will be repaired at tenant's expense. No loud mufflers. No repairing of cars in the park.

8. Residents of this park shall be responsible for all guests and their conduct while in the park.

9. Pets are allowed outside only if kept on a leash.

10. Lots must be kept free and clean of rubbish and bottles. No storage under mobile homes. Grass must be kept cut regularly. We do not furnish mowers or tools of any kind. All improvements must meet with park requirements.

11. All mobile homes must be properly winterized by (date) of each year. Running of water in the wintertime to keep pipes from freezing will not be allowed. If caught running water, there will be a $_____ charge imposed. Park management reserves the right to shut off all utilities when found to be necessary.

12. Any damage or stoppage to sewer line before it reaches the main line shall be repaired at tenant's expense and promptly. Sewer lines must be kept tight and free from leaks.

13. No selling or soliciting in this park without first receiving consent of landlord.

14. The tenants are cautioned and urged to be careful of electric wires, objects left on the ground and the condition of walks, drives and steps. The mobile home park will not be responsible for injuries to persons or to property or for property lost by park tenants, invitees, or guests, fire, windstorm or other casualty. The tenants assume the risks or hazards which may be created by other occupants in the park.

15. The tenants further agree to abide by any additional rules and regulations which may be shown in a conspicuous place in the mobile home park and which may, in the opinion of the landlord of the park be necessary in the operation of the mobile home park so that the same may be a desirable, attractive and proper place for persons to live.

16. No rebates will be made on prepaid rent except when paid over one (1) month in advance.

17. Tenant agrees to furnish the mobile home park_____ weeks notice prior to departure.

18. All mobile home spaces are rented to persons signing contracts. Any resident making sale of his mobile home must have new tenant previously approved by office, otherwise on the sale of the mobile home, the lot must be vacated. Tenants agree that no mobile home will be rented, all tenants must be owners.

19. There will be an additional charge for more than two automobiles, and for trucks. Cars not being used daily must be removed from the park.

20. Any boats, campers, or other large objects must be stored in storage area provided by the park.

21. All mobile homes must be under-pinned with approved material within_____ months after entering park.

22. Tenants must go direct to_____Gas & Electric Company to sign up for electric service. You will receive your electric bill direct from them.

23. All fences must be of metal chain-link type and shall not extend beyond_____ feet from street thus leaving parking area and yard beside it free of fencing material.

IN TESTIMONY WHEREOF, witness the hands of the parties hereto in duplicate, this the day and year first above written.

By: _____

_____   Occupant's Signature
Street & No.   _____
                                             Occupant's Signature

_____
Lot No.

No. 13-6

Iowa Farm Lease
Cash or Crop-Share

This agreement is made this .... day of .... 19........, between ....
.... hereinafter called the landlord and ....
.... hereinafter called the tenant.

SECTION I. DESCRIPTION OF FARM

In consideration of the rental specified below, the landlord hereby leases to the tenant his farm of .... acres, more or less, known as the .... farm, located in .... County, State of ...., together with all the buildings and improvements upon it, subject to easements now existing or which the landlord may grant in the future.

The description of the farm is as follows:
....
....
Easements now in effect are as follows: ....
....

SECTION II. LENGTH OF LEASE

Option 1. The length of this lease is from March 1, 19........, to the last day of February, 19........, and continuing thereafter from year to year unless either party gives written notice to the other, in a form in accordance with Iowa law, to terminate the lease. Such notice shall be given prior to .... of the lease year, or of the final year of the lease term in the event this lease is for a term longer than one year, to terminate the lease on the last day of the next February whereupon this lease shall terminate on said last day of February.

Option 2. This lease shall extend from .... to ....

SECTION III. AMOUNT OF RENTAL

1. The tenant shall pay to the landlord as rental for part or all of the above described farm, as the case may be, an annual cash rent totaling $........................, or $........................ per acre for all land in .... and $........................ per acre for all land in .... and a share of the crops as hereinafter provided. In the event that this lease provides for a cash rental for the entire farm, the farm shall be taken as containing .... acres for the purpose of computing the cash rental. The cash rental shall be due and payable as follows: .... $........................; ....
                                                                                                    (Date)   (Amount)   (Date)
$........................; .... $........................; .... $........................ of each lease year and shall be payable at ....
(Amount)   (Date)   (Amount)   (Date)   (Amount)
....

IOWA STATE UNIVERSITY of Science and Technology
COOPERATIVE EXTENSION SERVICE
Ames, Iowa . . . November, 1967 . . . FM-1538

2. In the event that this lease shall be in part or in total a crop-share lease, the tenant agrees to pay to the landlord as rental the following shares of crop and the landlord agrees to pay the shares of crop expenses as shown in the following schedule.

Crops	Landlord's share of crops	Landlord's share of crop expense				
		Seed	Combining, shelling, delivery, etc.	Commercial fertilizers	(Other)	(Other)
Corn						
Soybeans						
Oats						
Hay						

3. The landlord reserves storage facilities proportionate to his share of the crop as indicated in schedule above (item 2) unless otherwise provided (state exception, if any): ....
....
The tenant agrees to store as much of the landlord's share of the crops as possible in the storage space hereinbefore reserved.

4. The tenant further agrees to deliver the landlord's share of the grain to an elevator, purchaser, or dealer at ....
.... or at any other place, at a time and place specified by the landlord, provided the cost to the tenant of so doing shall not exceed the cost of delivering said grain to the elevator at the aforementioned place.

5. Other: ....
....

SECTION IV. THE SYSTEM OF FARMING

The parties to this lease agree that in general the crop rotation shall consist as nearly as practicable of .... acres in corn or soybeans or other row crops, ... acres in small grain, and .... acres of the rotated land in some soil conserving crop such as hay or pasture crops; not less than .... acres shall be in permanent pasture. Insofar as practicable approximately .... acres of the cropped land shall be annually seeded to some soil conserving crop such as
....

SECTION V. FARM OPERATION

A. The landlord agrees:

1. To pay the share of expenses indicated in the schedule shown in paragraph 2 of Section III above.

2. To make the following improvements and repairs, which shall be completed and ready for use on or before the date specified, barring delays due to unavoidable causes:
....
....
....

3. To furnish materials reasonably necessary for repair and upkeep of the fixed improvements on the farm, including dwelling, water systems, tiling systems and fences.

4. To furnish necessary skilled labor employed in making permanent improvements.

5. To repair or replace as soon as practicable buildings or other improvements essential to the operation of the farm that may be destroyed by fire, accident or other casualty; or to provide comparable facilities within a reasonable time except as may be agreed upon (state exceptions, if any): ....
....

6. To assist in the control of noxious weeds as herein agreed: ....

7. In applying lime and constructing terraces and grassed waterways, to furnish the following: ....
....

8. To warrant and defend the tenant's possession against any and all persons as long as this lease remains in effect.

9. Other: ....
....

B. The tenant agrees:

1. To manage and operate the farm in an efficient and husbandmanlike manner, following the cropping system and land-use practices indicated in Section IV, and other tillage and husbandry recognized as the best in the community, and provide such labor, machinery and equipment as shall be reasonably required for such management and operation, and $\begin{cases} \text{to occupy} \\ \text{not to occupy} \end{cases}$ the premises himself during the full lease term.

2. To keep the premises in as good condition as their reasonable use will permit.

3. To perform the unskilled labor necessary in making minor repairs and minor improvements on the farm.

4. To plow or otherwise break up no permanent pasture, drainageways, grassed waterways, terraces or ditches without the consent of the landlord, and undertake no operations that will injure the land.

5. To be aggressive in the control of noxious weeds and to keep fence rows and roadsides cut or sprayed.

6. To sell or burn no hay, straw or crop residues grown on the farm, except by permission of the landlord.

7. At least once a year to haul out and spread upon appropriate fields all manure on the premises.

8. In applying lime and fertilizer, to furnish the following: ....

....

9. To account for the rental share of any corn left in the field after harvest in excess of .... bushels per acre either in corn or cash settlement at the option of the landlord.

10. To participate in and fully comply with any program offered by the United States Department of Agriculture or any other government agency if such participation is elected by the landlord.

11. To take reasonable care of all trees, vines, and shrubs and to take reasonable care to prevent injury to same.

12. Avoid pasturing new seeding of grass and legumes beyond ....

13. Not to cut or pasture perennial legumes after .... of each year this lease continues in force, providing the field is not to be cultivated the following year.

14. Avoid pasturing rotation field crops when the soil is very wet or muddy and damage hereto is likely to occur; keep swine weighing over 30 pounds rung when running on pasture; and not over graze pastures.

15. Peaceably to surrender possession and occupancy of the premises at the termination of the lease and leave them in as good condition as he found them, reasonable allowance being made for ordinary wear and depreciation.

16. Other (spray equipment, labor and materials for spraying insects, noxious weeds, etc.) : ....

....

17. Other (such as fencing, handling new seeding, moving baled straw, buying landlord's share of crops) : ....

....

18. To assist in the establishment and maintenance of grassed waterways and terraces on the farm as follows: ....

....

19. Not to sell or exchange any sand or gravel except by permission of the landlord.

20. Other: ....

SECTION VI. COMPENSATION FOR IMPROVEMENTS AND REMOVAL OF FIXTURES

1. Emergency repairs costing less than $........................ for each such repair and totaling no more than $........................ annually may be made without consent of the landlord. Provided the tenant keeps all receipts for such expenditure and presents same to the landlord at the next rent-paying date, these items shall be deducted from rental payments due.

2. The tenant may apply limestone or commercial fertilizers, establish meadows and pastures, seed legumes for soil improvement and make repairs or improvements upon buildings, fences and water supply systems at his own expense and consistent with the terms of this lease. Provided written consent of the landlord shall have been obtained thereto in advance and provided these are improvements which cannot be removed when the tenant leaves the farm, the tenant shall receive from the landlord compensation for the unexhausted value of the improvements. To be eligible for such compensation the value of the tenant's contribution, date of completion and rate of depreciation must have been agreed upon and entered in the schedule in paragraph 4 below, or in another written agreement signed by the landlord.

3. The tenant shall receive from the landlord compensation for the unexhausted value of other improvements provided the landlord's approval has been obtained prior to making the improvements and the method of determining such compensation has been properly entered in the schedule in paragraph 4 below, or in another written agreement signed by the landlord.

4. A value shall be placed on the tenant's contribution to improvements specified in paragraphs 2 and 3 above and entered in column 6 of the schedule. The rate of depreciation shall be entered in column 7. If the tenant leaves the farm before the end of the depreciation period, the landlord agrees to compensate the tenant for the unexhausted value of the improvement according to that part of the depreciation period not elapsed at the time the tenant leaves the farm.

(1) Type and location of improvement	(2) Date to be completed	Percent to be furnished by landlord and by tenant						(6) Value placed on tenant's contribution	(7) Rate of annual depreciation (percent)	(8) Signatures
		(3) Materials		(4) Labor		(5) Machinery or trucking				
		L	T	L	T	L	T			

(Note: There is available from Iowa State University a larger form for this purpose. It is entitled "A Lease Supplement for Making Improvements on a Rented Farm.")

5. The tenant shall have the right to take away from the farm any movable buildings and fixtures which he has placed upon the farm at his own expense. Such moving must be done within 60 days after the termination of the lease. The tenant must leave the premises from which such improvements are removed in as good a condition as they were before said removal or compensate the landlord for damages.

6. Each party shall present to the other all such claims for compensation in writing at the termination of the lease.

SECTION VII. COMPENSATION FOR DAMAGES TO THE FARM

At the end of the tenancy the landlord shall receive from the tenant a reasonable compensation for any damage to property for which the tenant is legally responsible. Damage caused by ordinary wear and depreciation or by forces beyond the tenant's control, such as, but not limited to fire, tornado, windstorm and hail, shall not be recoverable.

SECTION VIII. RIGHT OF ENTRY AND NONFULFILLMENT

1. The landlord hereby reserves the right to enter the premises at any reasonable time to inspect the property, and to work and make improvements as he shall deem expedient, provided such entry and work on the part of the landlord or his agent does not interfere with the tenant in carrying out the regular farming operations.

2. If either party shall fail in any respect to carry out any of the provisions of this lease, then the other shall serve notice demanding redress within a specified period of time, and if redress is not given may hire the same done and the cost shall be paid by the party failing to carry out said provisions.

3. If the tenant fails to pay the landlord his cash rent or rental share or commits any act of gross negligence or waste which he is unable or unwilling to redress, a receiver may be appointed, at the request of either party, to take possession of the premises and all the property co-owned, and care for same until settlement can be made, which shall be done according to the terms of this lease.

SECTION IX. ARBITRATION

Any differences between the landlord and the tenant may be submitted to arbitration by one disinterested person agreeable to both, or by three disinterested persons, one of whom shall be selected by the tenant, one by the landlord and the third by the two thus appointed. If and when disputes are thus submitted, the decision of the arbitrator(s) shall be binding upon the parties to this contract.

SECTION X. TRANSFER OF INTEREST

1. The parties agree not to assign, sublease or sublet any part of the premises without written consent of the other, provided that nothing herein contained shall bar or prevent sale or exchange of the premises by the landlord.

2. This lease shall be binding upon the heirs, legatees, devisees, representatives, assignees and successors in interest of the respective parties hereto.

SECTION XI. OTHER PROVISIONS

It is particularly understood and agreed that this is not a partnership agreement, nor is the relation a partnership. Neither party hereto shall mortgage or otherwise encumber the jointly owned or co-owned property, nor pledge the credit of the other party hereto for any purpose whatsoever without the consent of the other party.

....

....

....

....

....

....

Executed in duplicate on the date first above written:

....
                        Tenant   Landlord
....
                         Wife   Wife

State of Iowa, ... County ss:

On this .... day of ...., A. D. 19........ before me, the undersigned, a Notary Public in and for said County, in said State, personally appeared ....

....

....

to me known to be the identical persons named in and who executed the foregoing instrument, and acknowledged that they executed the same as their voluntary act and deed.

....

...., Notary Public in and for said County

No. 13-7

Iowa Stock-Share Farm Lease

(Non-Partnership)

This agreement is made this .... day of .... 19........, between .... hereinafter called the landlord and .... hereinafter called the tenant.

SECTION I. DESCRIPTION OF FARM

In consideration of the rental specified below, the landlord hereby leases to the tenant his farm of .... acres, more or less, known as the .... farm, located in .... County, State of ...., together with all the buildings and improvements upon it, subject to easements now existing or which the landlord may grant in the future.

The description of the farm is as follows: ....

....

Easements now in effect are as follows: ....

....

SECTION II. LENGTH OF LEASE

Option 1. The length of this lease is from March 1, 19........, to the last day of February, 19........, and continuing thereafter from year to year unless either party gives written notice to the other, in a form in accordance with Iowa law, to terminate the lease. Such notice shall be given prior to .... of the lease year, or of the final year of the lease term in the event this lease is for a term longer than one year, to terminate the lease on the last day of the next February, whereupon this lease shall terminate on said last day of February.

Option 2. This lease shall extend from .... to ....

SECTION III. DIVISION OF INCOME AND EXPENSES

1. The tenant shall set aside and pay to the landlord as rent for the leased premises and as payment for the use of the landlord's share of the co-owned property, an amount equal to .... percent of the gross income from the leased premises, except as otherwise provided in this lease. The gross income shall be understood to consist of the proceeds from the sale or exchange of all grain, livestock and other products produced upon the leased premises, except ....

2. The tenant may take from the undivided products sufficient milk, cream, eggs, poultry, up to .... lbs. of hogs and the produce of garden crops not exceeding .... acres for consumption as needed by the farm family. If the poultry is not co-owned, the tenant shall be permitted to have for his own use and disposal, no more than .... chicks each year with no more than .... hens, all such poultry to be fed from the undivided crop to the extent of farm-produced grains.

3. Expenses, including investments in personal property, shall be supplied by the landlord and tenant as follows: except as indicated in Section VII:

Investments in Personal Property	Furnished by Landlord	Tenant
Beef cow herd	....	....
Feeder cattle	....	....
Hogs	....	....
Sheep	....	....
Dairy cattle	....	....
Poultry	....	....
....	....	....
....	....	....
Machinery and equipment as follows:		
....	....	....
....	....	....
....	....	....
....	....	....
Expenses		
Crop Expense		
Fertilizer	....	....
Lime	....	....
Seed	....	....
Insecticides	....	....
Custom work		
Trucking crops, feed, livestock	....	....
Shelling - corn	....	....
Combining - oats	....	....
Combining - soybeans	....	....
Other	....	....
....	....	....

	Furnished by Landlord	Tenant
Herbicides	....	....
Crop insurance	....	....
Other crop supplies		
Fuel - tractor	....	....
Fuel - truck	....	....
Fuel - crop drying	....	....
Fuel - other	....	....
Electricity	....	....
Telephone	....	....
Livestock expense		
Feed purchased	....	....
Veterinary fees	....	....
Breeding fees	....	....
Medicines	....	....
Feed grinding and mixing	....	....
Other livestock supplies	....	....
General hired labor	....	....
Labor for maintenance - buildings	....	....
Labor for maintenance - fences	....	....
Materials for building maintenance	....	....
Materials for fence maintenance	....	....
Insurance - buildings	....	....
Insurance - co-owned property	....	....
Taxes - co-owned property	....	....
Taxes - real estate	....	....
Interest - co-owned property	....	....
Other	....	....
....	....	....

Neither landlord nor tenant shall have authority to bind the other in any contract with third parties. All expenses, costs and charges not listed in the above schedule shall be the responsibility of the tenant, except for charges and expenses relating to the real property.

SECTION IV. OWNERSHIP OF LIVESTOCK, FEED AND SUPPLIES

1. All livestock (except ....) shall be owned in tenancy in common in equal undivided shares by landlord and tenant. Except as otherwise agreed in writing no other livestock shall be kept on the farm. All feed and other supplies on hand at the beginning and during the terms of the lease shall likewise be owned in tenancy in common and in equal shares. This co-ownership shall be arranged by appraisal, prior to the beginning of the lease term, of the property contributed by each party. The party furnishing property of higher value shall be compensated by the other party to an amount sufficient to give equal co-ownership. If either party purchases any property to be added to the co-owned property, he shall purchase it in his own name and upon his own account, and if the other party later approves, it is agreed that the purchaser will then resell a one-half interest therein to the other party.

2. In all matters involving the sale, mortgage or encumbrance of co-owned property, and incurring of expenses as described in paragraph 3 of Section III, neither party is authorized to act without the consent of the other. Except as otherwise specifically provided neither party shall purchase anything, nor make any contract, except in his own name and on his own account. It is particularly understood and agreed that this is not a partnership agreement, nor is the relationship a partnership.

3. At the termination of the lease the co-owned property shall be divided as follows:

a. All hay, grain, silage and other feeds and all supplies co-owned including straw and other bedding materials shall be divided by measure or value, whichever is more equitable, with the landlord and tenant each receiving title to his respective share.

b. The tenant shall divide each class of livestock, as cows, steers, calves, hogs and poultry, etc., into two groups and the landlord shall take his choice of the two groups of each. In case the groupings cannot be made of nearly equal value, a difference in monetary value shall be assigned before the choice is made and added to the choice.

c. If in connection with any of the co-owned classes of property the parties mutually agree to set aside the above described plan of division, it is agreed that the tenant shall set a value on the entire amount of the respective co-owned classes of property on the basis of which he will either sell his undivided one-half interest or buy that of the landlord, at the option of the landlord.

d. If the parties mutually agree, the co-owned property may be disposed of by private or public sale arranged for that purpose at a reasonable time and place.

SECTION V. THE SYSTEM OF FARMING

A. Cropping Plan

The parties to this lease agree that in general the cropping program shall consist as nearly as is practicable of ....
acres in corn, soybeans or other row crops, ... acres in small grain and .... acres of tillable land in some soil conserving crop such as hay or pasture crops; not less than .... acres shall be in permanent pasture. Insofar as is practicable .... percent of land in small grain each year shall be seeded to some soil conserving crop such as ....
....

B. Livestock Plan

The parties agree that as nearly as possible the plan will be to produce, maintain or feed as the case may be, the following numbers and classes of livestock: ....
....

C. Other
....

SECTION VI. SYSTEM OF RECORDS, BANK ACCOUNTS, REPORTS AND SETTLEMENT

....

....

....

....

SECTION VII. FARM OPERATION

A. The tenant agrees

1. To manage and operate the farm in an efficient and husbandmanlike manner, following the cropping system, land-use practices and livestock program, indicated in Section V, and other tillage and husbandry recognized as the best in the community, and to provide such labor, machinery and equipment as shall be reasonably required for such management and operation, except as specified in Section III.

2. Personally to reside on the farm for the full period of the lease, unless the landlord gives written permission to move or to reside elsewhere.

3. To keep the premises in as good condition as their reasonable use will permit.

4. To plow or otherwise break up no permanent pasture, drainageways, grassed waterways, terraces or ditches without consent of the landlord.

5. To be aggressive in the control of noxious weeds, and to keep fence rows and roadsides cut or sprayed.

6. Not to sell, burn or otherwise destroy or remove from farm any hay, straw, crop residues grown on the farm except by permission of the landlord.

7. To haul out and spread upon appropriate fields on the farm all manure and compost at least once a year.

8. To take reasonable care of trees, vines and shrubs and use ordinary care to prevent injury to the same.

9. Not to cut or pasture perennial legumes after .... of each year this lease continues in force, providing the field is not to be cultivated the following year.

10. To avoid pasturing new seedings of grass and legumes beyond ....

11. To avoid pasturing rotation field crops when the soil is very wet or muddy and damage hereto is likely to occur; keep swine weighing over 30 pounds rung when running on pasture; and not over graze pastures.

12. To keep a full account of all transactions in the matters that are mutually agreed upon by both parties as outlined in Section VI of this lease and to make those records available to the landlord at the intervals agreed upon. The records shall include full information on income, expense, inventory, feed, crop and livestock production on the farm. Settlement shall be made in the manner described in Section VI of the lease.

13. To assist in the establishment of grassed waterways as follows: ....

....

14. To assist in terracing the land as follows: ....

....

15. Peaceably to surrender possession and occupancy of the premises at the termination of the lease leaving premises in as good condition as he found them at beginning of the lease, reasonable allowance being made for ordinary wear and depreciation.

16. To participate in and fully comply with any program offered by the United States Department of Agriculture or any other government agency if such participation is elected by the landlord.

17. Not to sell or exchange any sand or gravel except by permission of the landlord.

18. Other ....

....

B. The landlord agrees

1. To warrant and defend tenant's possession against any and all persons during the period of the lease.

2. To furnish the following amounts and types of equipment in addition to that specified in Section III: ....

....

3. To make the following improvements and repairs, which shall be completed and ready for use on or before the date specified, barring delays due to unavoidable causes: ....

....

....

4. To furnish materials reasonably necessary for repair and upkeep of buildings and improvements, including dwelling, barns, granaries, water systems, tiling systems and fences unless specified otherwise in Section III.

5. To repair or replace as soon as practicable buildings or other improvements essential to the operation of the farm that may be destroyed by fire, accident or other casualty; or to provide comparable facilities within a reasonable time except as may be agreed upon (state exceptions, if any): ....

....

6. To assist in the control of noxious weeds as herein agreed: ....

....

7. To assist in establishing grassed waterways as follows: ....

....

8. To assist in terracing land as follows: ....

....

9. Other ....

....

SECTION VIII. COMPENSATION FOR IMPROVEMENTS AND REMOVAL OF FIXTURES

1. Emergency repairs costing less than $................ for each such repair and totaling no more than $................ annually may be made without consent of the landlord. Provided the tenant keeps all receipts for such expenditure and presents same to the landlord at the next rent-paying date, these items shall be deducted from rental payments due.

2. The tenant may apply limestone or commercial fertilizers, establish meadows and pastures, seed legumes for soil improvement and make repairs or improvements upon buildings, fences and water supply systems at his own expense and consistent with the terms of this lease. Provided written consent of the landlord shall have been obtained thereto in advance and provided these are improvements which cannot be removed when the tenant leaves the farm, the tenant shall receive from the landlord compensation for the unexhausted value of the improvements. To be eligible for such compensation, the value of the tenant's contribution, date of completion and rate of depreciation must have been agreed upon and entered in the schedule in paragraph 4 below, or in another written agreement signed by the landlord.

3. The tenant shall receive from the landlord compensation for the unexhausted value of other improvements provided the landlord's approval has been obtained prior to making the improvements and the method of determining such compensation has been properly entered in the schedule in paragraph 4 below, or in another written agreement signed by the landlord.

4. A value shall be placed on the tenant's contribution to improvements specified in paragraphs 2 and 3 above and entered in column 6 of the schedule. The rate of depreciation shall be entered in column 7. If the tenant leaves the farm before the end of the depreciation period, the landlord agrees to compensate the tenant for the unexhausted value of the improvement according to that part of the depreciation period not elapsed at the time the tenant leaves the farm.

(1) Type and location of improvement	(2) Date to be completed	Percent to be furnished by landlord and by tenant						(6) Value placed on tenant's contribution	(7) Rate of annual depreciation (percent)	(8) Signatures
		(3) Materials		(4) Labor		(5) Machinery or trucking				
		L	T	L	T	L	T			

(Note: There is available from Iowa State University a larger form for this purpose. It is entitled "A Lease Supplement for Making Improvements on a Rented Farm.")

5. The tenant shall have the right to take away from the farm any movable buildings and fixtures which he has placed upon the farm at his own expense. Such moving must be done within 60 days after the termination of the lease. The tenant must leave the premises from which such improvements are removed in as good a condition as they were before said removal or compensate the landlord for damages.

6. Each party shall present to the other all such claims for compensation in writing at the termination of the lease.

SECTION IX. COMPENSATION FOR DAMAGES TO THE FARM

At the end of the tenancy the landlord shall receive from the tenant a reasonable compensation for any damage to property for which the tenant is legally responsible. Damage caused by ordinary wear and depreciation or by forces beyond the tenant's control, such as but not limited to fire, tornado, windstorm and hail, shall not be recoverable.

SECTION X. RIGHT OF ENTRY AND NON-FULFILLMENT

1. The landlord hereby reserves the right to enter the premises at any reasonable time to inspect the property, and to work and make improvements as he shall deem expedient, provided such entry and work on the part of the landlord or his agent does not interfere with the tenant in carrying out the regular farming operations.

2. If either party shall fail in any respect to carry out any of the provisions of this lease, then the other shall serve notice demanding redress within a specified period of time, and if redress is not given may hire the same done and the cost shall be paid by the party failing to carry out said provisions.

3. If the tenant fails to pay the landlord his rental share or commits any act of gross negligence or waste which he is unable or unwilling to redress, a receiver may be appointed, at the request of either party, to take possession of the premises and all the property co-owned, and care for same until settlement can be made, which shall be done according to the terms of this lease.

SECTION XI. ARBITRATION

Any differences between the landlord and the tenant may be submitted to arbitration by one disinterested person agreeable to both, or by three disinterested persons, one of whom shall be selected by the tenant, one by the landlord and the third by the two thus appointed. If and when disputes are thus submitted, the decision of the arbitrator(s) shall be binding upon the parties to this contract.

SECTION XII. TRANSFER OF INTEREST

1. The parties agree not to assign, sublease or sublet any part of the premises without written consent of the other, provided that nothing herein contained shall bar or prevent sale or exchange of the premises by the landlord.

2. This lease shall be binding upon the heirs, legatees, devisees, representatives, assignees and successors in interest of the respective parties hereto.

SECTION XIII. OTHER PROVISIONS

....

....

....

....

....

....

Executed in duplicate on the date first above written:

....
             Tenant   Landlord

....
             Wife   Wife

STATE OF IOWA .... COUNTY, ss:

On this .... day of ...., A.D. 19........, before me, the undersigned, a Notary Public in and for said County, in said State, personally appeared ....

to me known to be the identical persons named in and who executed the foregoing instrument, and acknowledged that they executed the same as their voluntary act and deed.

....

...., Notary Public in and for said County

No. 13–8
LEASE FOR GRAZING OF CATTLE

State of_____

County of_____

    KNOW ALL MEN BY THESE PRESENTS, that this lease is made by and between _____ , known herein as the Lessor, and _____ _____ Ranch, known herein as the Lessee,

    WITNESSETH:

    That the Lessor, for and in consideration of the sum of_____ _____dollars ($_____), to them cash in hand paid, the receipt of which is hereby acknowledged, does by these presents lease and demise unto Lessee the following property:

(Here include legal description)

for the term of_____years, commencing the_____day of_____, 19_____ , and ending the_____day of_____, 19_____ , upon the following conditions and covenants:

GRAZING PURPOSES

    1. Lessee shall use said property for grazing purposes only.

SUBLETTING

    2. Lessee shall not sub-let said premises or any part thereof to any person or persons whomsoever without having first obtained the written consent of the Lessor.

MAINTAINING THE PROPERTY

    3. The Lessee shall quietly deliver up said property on the expiration date of this lease in as good condition as the same were in when received, reasonable use and wear and tear thereof excepted.

LESSOR'S REMEDY IF LEASE IS VIOLATED

    4. In the event the Lessee should fail to comply with any of the foregoing conditions or should violate any of the foregoing covenants, the Lessor may declare this lease forfeited at his discretion and in such event his agent or attorney shall have the right to enter and hold,

occupy and repossess the entire property hereinbefore described, as before the execution of this property.

SUBJECT TO EXISTING GAS, OIL, MINERAL LEASE

5. This lease is subject to the terms and conditions of any gas, oil and/or mineral lease now on said premises.

In witness whereof, the Lessor and Lessee have executed this lease this_____ day of_____, 19_____. Witness:

_____
Lessor

_____
Lessee

No. 13–9
OIL, GAS AND MINERAL LEASE

THIS AGREEMENT, dated the_____day of_____, 19_____

between_____

_____

_____

_____Lessor (whether one or more)

and_____ , Lessee,

WITNESSETH:

1. Lessor, in consideration_____DOLLARS ($_____) in hand paid, and of the agreements of Lessee herein contained, hereby grants, lets and leases exclusively unto Lessee the land hereinafter described, for the purpose of prospecting, exploring, investigating, drilling and mining for and producing, taking, saving, storing, treating, processing and owning oil, gas and all other minerals together with all privileges, rights and easements useful or convenient for Lessee's operations hereunder on said land and on nearby lands, including particularly the following rights (but not excluding others): to lay pipe lines; to dig canals; and to construct tanks, docks, pump stations, power stations, repressuring plants, recycling plants, telephone, telegraph and power lines, roads, railroads, bridges, warehouses,

houses for its employees and other structures. The said land included in this lease is situated in _____ County, Mississippi, and is described as follows, to wit:

containing_____acres of land more or less; including all minerals underlying easements and rights-of-way which traverse or adjoin said land; and also, in addition to the above described land, all land adjoining the same and owned or claimed by Lessor.

This lease shall cover all the interest actually owned or claimed by Lessor, even though incorrectly stated above. For the purpose of calculating any payments based on acreage, said land and its constituent parcels shall be deemed to contain the acreage above stated, whether they actually contain more or less.

2. Subject to the other provisions herein contained, this lease shall remain in force for a term of ten years from the date hereof, "primary term," and, after the expiration of the primary term, shall remain in force so long as either or both of the following conditions shall prevail without cessation or interruption of more than three consecutive months: (a) so long as oil, gas or other mineral, or any one or more of them, is produced from said land hereunder; (b) so long as Lessee is engaged in drilling, mining or reworking operations on said land hereunder.

3. This is a PAID-UP LEASE. In consideration of the down cash payment, Lessor agrees that Lessee shall not be obligated except as otherwise provided herein, to commence or continue any operations during the primary term. Lessee may at any time or times surrender this lease as to all or any portion of said land by delivering to Lessor or by filing for record a release or releases, and be relieved of all obligation thereafter accruing as to the acreage surrendered.

4. If during the last three months of the primary term, after Lessee has commenced drilling, mining or reworking operations or has secured production of oil, gas or other mineral, all such operations and all such production shall cease for any cause, this lease shall not terminate if Lessee, within three months after such cessation, shall commence or resume any of such operations, or production of any such mineral.

5. Royalties to be paid by Lessee are: (a) on oil, one-eighth (1/8) of that produced and saved from said land, to be delivered at the wells or to the credit of Lessor into the pipe line to which the wells may be connected or into storage furnished by Lessor; Lessee may from time to time purchase any royalty oil, paying therefor the market price prevailing for the field where produced on the day it is run to the pipe lines or storage tanks, or if no such market price is established, the price for which Lessee sells its share of such oil, less the costs of handling and transportation to the point of sale; (b) on gas, including casinghead gas or other gaseous substance, produced from said land and sold or used, the market value at the well of one-eighth (1/8) of the gas so sold or used, provided that on gas sold at the well the royalty shall be one-eighth (1/8) of the amount realized from such sales; (c) on sulphur, seventy-five cents (75c) per long ton mined and marketed; (d) on all other minerals, one-eighth (1/8) of that mined and marketed in kind or value at the well or mine, at Lessee's election. Where gas has been discovered on said land or on land pooled and consolidated with any of said land, Lessee at Lessee's election may at any time or times during or after the primary term pay Lessor as royalty (in addition to the royalties provided above) the sum of $1.00 per acre for each acre of said land then covered by this lease, or the gross sum of $200.00, whichever is greater, and it shall be considered that gas is being produced hereunder for a period of one year from the date on or for which any such payment is made. Any such payment may be made in cash or by Lessee's check mailed or delivered to Lessor or to any bank for Lessor's credit, and may be made jointly to all parties having any interest therein. Lessee shall notify Lessor of any such payment at Lessor's address last known to Lessee.

Lessee may use, free of royalty, oil, gas, and water from said land, except water from Lessor's wells, for all operations hereunder and for repressuring the oil and gas formations in the field.

6. Lessee shall pay for damages caused by Lessee's operations to houses, barns, growing crops and fences. Lessee shall have the right during or within one year after the life of this lease to remove all Lessee's property and fixtures, including the right to draw and remove all casing. When required by Lessor, Lessee will bury pipe lines below ordinary plow depth. No well shall be drilled closer than 200 feet to any residence or barn now on said land unless another location is impracticable. Lessee agrees to drill such wells, but only such wells, as a reasonably prudent operator would drill under the same or similar circumstances: (a) in order to prevent substantial net uncompensated drainage from said land by wells located on adjoining land not owned by Lessor; and (b), after discovery of oil on said land, in order most efficiently and economically to develop said land. No forfeiture or cancellation of this lease shall affect or include any well being drilled, worked on, or produced hereunder, or the drainage area of any such well, or any other part of this lease as to which Lessee is not in default.

7. The rights of Lessor and Lessee hereunder may be assigned in whole or in part. No change in ownership of Lessor's interest (by assignment or otherwise) shall be binding on Lessee until Lessee has been furnished with notice, consisting of certified copies of all recorded instruments or documents and other information necessary to establish a complete chain of record title from Lessor, and then only with respect to payments thereafter made. No other kind of notice, whether actual or constructive, shall be binding on Lessee. No present or future division of Lessor's ownership as to different portions or parcels of said land shall operate to enlarge the obligations or diminish the rights of Lessee, and all Lessee's operations may be conducted without regard to any such division. If all or any part of this lease is assigned, no leasehold owner shall be liable for any act or omission of any other leasehold owner.

8. Whenever any cause beyond Lessee's control (such as fire, flood, windstorm or other act of God; law, order or regulation of any governmental agency: or inability to secure men, material, or transportation as a result of the present war) prevents, interrupts or interferes with any of Lessee's operations hereunder this lease shall not be terminated, nor shall Lessee be held liable.

9. Lessee may at any time or times pool and consolidate this lease, in whole or in part, or as to any stratum or strata, with adjacent lands and leases, so as to constitute a unit or units not substantially exceeding the size required for the most efficient and economical location and spacing of wells in the field or pool, or the size (if any) approved by State or Federal authorities, by delivering to Lessor or by filing for record an instrument so declaring. Drilling, mining, or reworking operations upon, or production of any mineral from any part of any such unit shall be treated, for all purposes hereunder, as such operations upon or such production from this lease. Upon production from any part of any such unit, Lessor shall be entitled to royalties calculated as follows: there shall be allocated to the portion of this lease included in such unit a fractional part of such production, in the ratio that the number of acres of this lease included in such unit bears to the total number of acres of all lands and

leases included in such unit, and Lessor shall be entitled to the royalties in this lease provided, on such fractional part of such production, and no more. Provided, that if State or Federal authorities shall prescribe a different method of allocation, the method so prescribed shall prevail.

10. Lessor warrants and agrees to defend the title to said lands, or to the interest therein which this lease expressly purports to cover. The royalties hereinabove provided are determined with respect to the entire mineral estate, and if Lessor owns a lesser interest, the royalties to be paid Lessor shall be reduced proportionately. Lessee at its option may discharge in whole or in part any tax, mortgage or other lien upon said land, or may redeem the same from any purchaser at any tax sale or adjudication, and may reimburse itself from any royalties accruing hereunder and shall be subrogated to such lien with the right to enforce same.

11. Should any one or more of the parties hereinabove named as Lessor fail to execute this lease, it shall nevertheless be binding upon all such parties who do execute it as Lessor. The word "Lessor," as used in this lease, shall mean any one or more or all of the parties who execute this lease as Lessor. All the provisions of this lease shall be binding on the heirs, successors and assigns of Lessor and Lessee.

IN WITNESS WHEREOF, this instrument is executed as of the date first above written.

Witnesses Sign Here   Lessor Sign Here

_____)
_____)   _____

_____)
_____)   _____

_____)
_____)   _____

(Reproduced with permission of Hederman Bros., Jackson, Miss.)

No. 13–10
SIGN (BILLBOARD) LEASE

THIS LEASE AGREEMENT made the_____ day of_____ , A.D. 19_____ , between_____hereinafter called the lessor, and_____ Outdoor Advertising Corporation, hereinafter called the lessee.

WITNESSETH, that in consideration of the annual payment of the sum of $_____ _____ , payable in quarterly installments commencing the_____ day of_____ _____ , A.D. 19_____ , the lessor hereby grants to the lessee the exclusive right and permission to use and occupy the following described premises:

(Here include the exact portion of ground, roof area, side of building, etc. to be utilized as well as a description of the property).

USAGE: The use of the premises shall be for the purpose of constructing and maintaining outdoor advertising displays or devices, including necessary electrical or other equipment.

THE TERM of this agreement shall be for a period of_____years from date of a sign permit being issued with further privileges to the lessee on like terms from year to year for_____additional years unless terminated as hereinafter provided for and under the following terms and conditions:

1. The lessee may terminate this agreement should the view of the subject premises become obstructed or impaired. In this, even, a prorated adjustment will be made.

2. In the event the subject property is sold, or an addition to the existing building, or the sign permit is revoked, the lessor has the option to cancel this agreement upon giving _____days' notice. In this event all amounts paid in advance will be prorated and returned to the lessee as of the effective date of cancellation.

ALL MATERIAL and equipment used in constructing the sign on the above premises is the property of the lessee and may be removed at any time upon giving the lessee_____ _____days' notice.

IT IS AGREED that time shall be of the essence and this agreement shall be binding on both parties, their heirs, personal representatives, and/or assigns when this lease agreement shall be signed by both parties or their authorized agents.

Witness:

1. _____   By_____
                                                    As to Lessor

2. _____

1. _____   By_____
                                                    As to Lessee

2. _____

No. 13–11
NINETY-NINE YEAR LEASE

THIS LEASE, made and entered into at_____,_____,_____, by and between_____, As Trustee, and individually, joined by_____ _____, hereinafter referred to as the "Lessors," and_____, a _____corporation, hereinafter referred to as the "Lessee," which terms of Lessors and Lessee are used in a general sense and shall include the successors and assigns of the respective parties.

W I T N E S S E T H :

THAT in consideration of the covenants and agreements hereinafter mentioned and to be performed by the respective parties hereto, and the payment of rental herein designated to be paid by the Lessee in accordance with the provisions of this lease, the Lessors have leased, rented, let and demised, and by these presents do lease, rent, let and demise unto the said Lessee, its successors and assigns, the following described property, situate in_____

_____ , _____ to wit:

TO HAVE AND TO HOLD the above described premises, together with all and singular the tenements, hereditaments and appurtenances thereunto belonging, or in anywise incident or appertaining, unto the Lessee for the term of NINETY-NINE (99) YEARS, commencing on the_____day of_____, _____ .

ARTICLE I
TERM OF LEASE

THIS LEASE shall begin at _____ on the day of_____ ___, _____ , and continue for NINETY-NINE (99) YEARS thereafter unless sooner terminated as herein provided. Possession hereof shall be given simultaneously with the execution of this lease.

ARTICLE II
TITLE AND SURVEY

(a) The Lessors covenant that they have lawful title to said premises, free and clear of all liens, mortgages and encumbrances and have full authority to make this lease on the terms herein set forth. Lessors will furnish to the Lessee an abstract of title covering the leased premises continued to a date subsequent to the date hereof, which abstract shall show a good and marketable title to said premises, as described above, to be vested in Lessors.

(b) Lessee will, at its own expense, procure a survey of the leased premises if it desires such survey.

ARTICLE III
STAMPS

Should any Documentary Stamps be required to be affixed to this lease under the laws of the State of _____ , such stamps shall be at the expense of the Lessee.

ARTICLE IV
RENTAL

The Lessee hereby covenants with the Lessors that it will pay to the Lessors, at such place as the Lessors may designate in writing, an annual rental of_____ _____ , payable in advance on the_____day of_____of each and every year. The first year's rent, in the sum of_____shall be paid in advance upon the execution of the lease, receipt of which is herewith acknowledged with the signing of this lease.

All rents shall be payable in current legal tender of the United States of America, as the same is then, by law, constituted. The extension of any time or times for the payment of any installment or installments of rent, or the acceptance by the Lessors of any money other than of the kind herein specified, shall not be a waiver or release of the right of the Lessors to insist on having any or all of said payments of said rent made in the manner and at the time herein set forth.

ARTICLE V
LESSORS' LIEN FOR RENT

THE LESSORS SHALL HAVE THE FIRST LIEN, paramount to all others on every right and interest of the Lessee in and to this lease on any building, buildings, or improvements placed on the premises, and on any furnishings and equipment, fixtures or personal property of any kind, or the equity of the Lessee therein; which lien is granted for the purpose of securing the payment of rents, taxes, assessments, charges, liens, penalties and damages herein covenanted to be paid by the Lessee, and for the purpose of securing the performance of all and singular the covenants, conditions and obligations of this lease to be performed and observed by the Lessee, subject only to any mortgages joined in by the Lessors pursuant to the terms hereof. Such lien shall be in addition to all rights of a Landlord given under the Statutes of the State of_____which are now or might hereafter be in effect.

ARTICLE VI
ALL TAXES PAYABLE BY LESSEE

IN ADDITION TO THE RENT HEREINABOVE SPECIFIED, and as a further part of the consideration to be furnished by the Lessee, and as additional rental for the term demised, the Lessee covenants and agrees with the Lessors that the Lessee will promptly pay all taxes levied or assessed at any or all times during the term hereby demised, by any and all taxing authorities, including all taxes, charges, assessments, impositions, liens for public improvements,special charges and assessments (including specifically all special assessments and liens on the date of the presents) and, in general, all taxes, tax liens or liens in the nature of taxes which may be assessed, imposed, or levied against the premises, including the land and all buildings, fixtures and improvements which may be hereafter placed thereon, and all taxes levied upon the personal property which from time to time constitutes the furniture, furnishings, fixtures and equipment of any building or buildings placed on the demised premises, including all taxes which are assessed by any and all governmental authorities, (City, State, County, Federal, special drainage, school, or other taxing agencies, authorities, or districts, or otherwise), together with any interest, penalties or other charges which may accrue thereon; PROVIDED that in the event any of said taxes or assessments are payable according to the terms of their impositions, in installments, then the Lessee shall have the right to pay the same as such installments fall due.

NOTHING IN THIS ARTICLE CONTAINED SHALL OBLIGATE THE LESSEE to pay any income, inheritance, estate or succession tax, or any tax in the nature of such described taxes, or any other tax which may be levied or assessed against the Lessors; with respect to, or because of the income derived from this lease; nor shall the Lessee be deemed obligated hereby to pay any corporation, franchise or excise taxes which may be assessed or levied against the Lessors, any corporate successor or transferee of, or claiming under, the Lessors.

THE PARTIES UNDERSTAND AND AGREE THAT THE LESSEE SHALL PAY taxes and other charges as enumerated in this numbered section of the lease, and shall deliver official receipts evidencing such payments unto the Lessors at the place at which rental payments are required to be made, which payment of taxes shall be made and said receipts delivered at least_____(_____) days before the said tax itself would become delinquent in accordance with the law then in force governing the payment of such tax or taxes. If, however, the Lessee desires to contest the validity of any tax or tax claim, the Lessee may do so without being in default hereunder as to its obligation to pay said taxes; provided the Lessee gives the Lessors notice of its intention to do so and furnishes the Lessors with a bond with surety made by a surety company qualified to do business in_____, in one-and-one half times the amount the tax item or items intended to be contested conditioned to pay the tax item or items in such time as when the validity thereof shall finally have been determined, which said written notice and bond shall be given by the Lessee unto the Lessors not later than a day which is_____ (_____) days before the tax item or items proposed to be contested would otherwise beome as enumerated in this Article, and furnish the receipts therefore, or to furnish the written notice and bond just herein referred to, not later than_____(_____) days before the said taxes or tax, or any item of them would become delinquent, shall constitute the Lessee in default under this lease.

IN CASE THE LESSEE SHALL FAIL, REFUSE OR NEGLECT TO MAKE any or either of the payments in and by this Article required, then the Lessors, at their option, may, and without constituting a waiver of the default thus occurring in the lease, pay the same, and the amount or amounts of money so paid, including reasonable attorney's fees and expenses which might have been reasonably incurred because of, or in connection with, such payments together with interest on all of such amounts at the rate of_____percent per annum, shall be repaid by the Lessee unto the Lessors upon demand of the Lessors and the payment thereof may be collected or enforced by the Lessors in the same manner as though said amount were an installment of rent specifically required by the terms of this lease to be paid by the Lessee unto the Lessors upon the day when the Lessors demand the repayment thereof or the rightful reimbursement therefor of and from the Lessee.

THE PARTIES INTEND THAT ANY TEMPORARY EXTENSION BY TAX COLLECTING AUTHORITIES, or by ordinances, or by statute, of the due or delinquency date of taxes shall not accrue to the benefit of the Lessee, but the Lessee shall, in any event, pay taxes at least thirty (30) days before the same become delinquent under the general law governing payment of same.

ARTICLE VII
FIRE AND WINDSTORM PROVISIONS

THE LESSEE DOES HEREBY COVENANT AND AGREE WITH THE LESSORS that it will, at all times during the term of this lease, keep insured any and all buildings and/or improvements that may be built or placed upon said demised premises and all personal property which may be subject to the Lessors' lien hereunder, in good and responsible insurance companies authorized to do business in the State of and approved by the Lessors, or any mortgagee then holding a mortgage encumbering the demised premises, for protection against all losses or damage by windstorm, fire and other casualty and against damage resulting from the use of any boilers situated on said premises, to an amount that will be sufficient to prevent co-insurance on the part of the Lessors, and all such policies issued and the renewals thereof shall be payable in the event of loss, jointly to the Lessors and the Lessee, as their interest may appear. In the event of destruction of said buildings and/or improvements, or said personal property by fire, windstorm or any other casualty for which insurance money shall be payable, and such insurance money shall have been paid to the Lessors and the Lessee, said sums so paid shall be deposited to the joint account of the Lessors and the Lessee in a bank in the City of Miami, designated by the Lessors, and shall be available to the Lessee for the reconstruction or repair, as the case may be, of any building or buildings damaged or destroyed by fire, windstorm or other cause herein set forth for which insurance money shall be payable, and shall be by the Lessors and the Lessee paid out from said joint account from time to time on the estimates of any architect licensed in the State of _____having supervision of such reconstruction and repair, certifying that the amount of each estimate is being applied to the payment of the reconstruction or repair, and at a reasonable cost therefor; provided, however, that it first be made to appear to the satisfaction of the Lessors that the amount of money necessary to provide for the reconstruction or repair and refurnishing of any building or buildings destroyed or injured, as aforesaid, according to the plans adopted therefor, which may be in excess of the amount received upon such policies, has been provided by the Lessee for such purpose and its application for such purpose assured; and the Lessee covenants and agrees that in the event of the destruction or damage of the said buildings and improvements, or any part thereof, and as often as any building or improvement on said premises shall be destroyed or damaged by fire, windstorm or other casualty, that the said Lessee shall at its expense rebuild and repair the same upon the same general plans and dimensions as before the said fire, windstorm or other casualty, or other plan to be agreed upon, in writing, by the Lessors and Lessee, respectively, the reconstruction so rebuilt and repaired and the personal property as so replaced to be of the same value as the buildings and improvements upon the demised property prior to such damage or destruction, and shall have the same rebuilt and ready for occupancy within_____(_____) months from the time when the loss or destruction occurred, and this obligation to rebuild, renovate or repair, shall exist irrespective of the availability of insurance funds with which to accomplish such repair, renovation or rebuilding.

If, at any time, any such insurance money comes into the possession of the Lessors and the Lessee after destruction or damage by fire and windstorm or other casualty, and the Lessee is in default in the payment of any rent, tax, assessment, lien or other damage which, by the terms of this lease, has been agreed to be paid by the Lessee, or if such default shall occur during the time said insurance money or any part thereof, is in the joint bank account, as aforesaid, then the Lessors shall be entitled to receive so much of the insurance money as may be necessary fully to pay or discharge any such sums of money in the payment of which the Lessee is in default, as aforesaid, and this shall be done whenever and as often as any such default shall occur on the part of the Lessee. Nothing herein contained, however, shall be construed as permitting the Lessee to default in the payment of the rentals or other charges herein stipulated to be paid or in the performance of the other covenants of this lease, and the Lessors may, at their option, in case of default in the performance of any other covenant in this lease, proceed against the Lessee for the collection of such rentals and charges hereby accrued and recover and take possession of the premises herein described, in accordance with the provisions of this lease herein set forth, and without prejudice to their rights to the benefit of such insurance money as security for the payment of such rentals and other charges. Lessee will forthwith reimburse such joint bank account and deposit therein, for the purpose of reconstruction or repair any amount so paid thereout on account of default of the Lessee; and if the fact that the Lessors have utilized the fund to pay unto the Lessee's rent which would otherwise be in default, diminishes the fund to the point where there are insufficient funds therein to accomplish the work or repair, renovation or rebuilding, the failure of the Lessee forthwith to reimburse such joint bank account for a sufficient and proper amount to give effect to the terms of this paragraph shall constitute a default in the lease, nor shall the fact that the Lessors utilized a portion of the funds to pay then maturing and past due rent, constitute a waiver of the Lessee's default arising by reason of the Lessee's failure to reimburse said joint bank account accordingly.

IT IS AGREED BY AND BETWEEN THE LESSORS AND THE LESSEE that any excess of money received from insurance remaining in the joint bank account, after the reconstruction or repair of such building or buildings, if there be no default on the part of the Lessee in the performance of the covenants herein, shall be paid to the said Lessee; but in case of the Lessee's not commencing the reconstruction or repair of said buildings and prosecuting them continuously to completion and causing such completion to be accomplished within_____ (_____) months after the occurrence of such damage or loss occasioned, as aforesaid, then the amount so collected or the balance thereof remaining in the joint account, as the case may be, shall be paid to the Lessors, and it will be at its option to terminate this lease and retain such amount as liquidated damages resulting from the failure upon the part of the Lessee promptly, within the time specified, to complete such work of reconstruction or repair.

PROVIDED, HOWEVER, that it is hereby agreed by and between the Lessors and the Lessee that should any claim for damages to the premises, such claim being covered by the insurance provided for herein, be made, and such claim is in the amount of_____ _____, or less, the Lessors do hereby agree to endorse over to the Lessee said proceeds for use in repair to the premises without conforming to those provisions set forth in this section as may regard the joint account provided herein.

ARTICLE VIII
MORTGAGEE'S INTEREST IN INSURANCE PROCEEDS

THE LESSEE LIKEWISE COVENANTS AND AGREES THAT IN THE EVENT any mortgage has been placed against the demised premises, the Lessee shall be permitted to attach the necessary mortgage and loss payable clauses, making loss payable under such insurance policies payable to the holder of such mortgage, as well as to the Lessors and the Lessee, as their interests may appear. In the event any mortgagee, having the right to collect and apply upon the mortgage any amount as a result of loss under the said policies of insurance, shall so collect any such sums and shall apply it in the payment or in reduction of the mortgage debt owned to such mortgagee, and, in such case, the Lessors agree that they will join with the Lessee in the execution of a mortgage to be obtained by Lessee at Lessee's sole expense, in the amount so credited from the collection by the mortgagee of the said insurance funds and the sum procured by the execution of the mortgage by the Lessors and the Lessee shall be delivered in escrow to a duly established_____, _____, bank for the purpose of repairing, rebuilding and reconstructing the improvements then located upon the demised premises in accordance with and in the manner as provided herein for the rebuilding and reconstruction thereof. In no case, however, shall such new mortgage exceed in the amount the mortgage outstanding against the property at the time of such loss or destruction, and then only to the extent that such mortgage is in conformity with the requirements of this lease defining the limitation upon the principal amortization, rate of interest and time for a final installment to mature in determining the propriety of the original mortgage contemplated and authorized hereby.

ARTICLE IX
PAYMENT OF INSURANCE PREMIUMS

IT IS FURTHER UNDERSTOOD AND AGREED THAT THE LESSORS SHALL, in no way, be or become liable for the payment of any of the premiums required to be paid for any of the policies of insurance required in and by this instrument to be procured by the Lessee, nor shall the Lessors, in any way, be and become liable for the collection or non-collection of any of the proceeds from any of the policies of insurance.

IT IS FURTHER COVENANTED AND AGREED THAT IN CASE, at any time, during the continuance of this indenture, the Lessee shall fail, refuse or neglect, after being given_____ (_____) days' notice required in and by this instrument to be procured by the Lessee, or to keep and maintain the same in full force and effect, the Lessors, at their option (and without such act constituting a waiver of the default by the Lessee thus occurring) may procure or renew such insurance and thereupon, the amount or amounts of money paid as the premium or premiums thereon, plus interest at the rate of_____per cent per annum shall be collectible as though it were rent then matured hereunder and shall be due and payable within thirty (30) days after written demand for reimbursement therefor shall have been made by the Lessors upon the Lessee and the Lessee's failure to effect such reimbursement within such time thereafter, such demand shall constitute a default herein.

ARTICLE X
PREMISES TO BE USED FOR LEGAL PURPOSES ONLY

THE LESSEE COVENANTS AND AGREES that during the term hereof, it will conform to, and observe all ordinances, rules, laws and regulations of the County of_____ _____and State of_____ , and the UNITED STATES OF AMERICA, and all public authorities, boards, or officers, relating to said premises, or improvements upon the same, or use thereof, and will not, during such term, permit the same to be used for any illegal or immoral purpose, business or occupation; PROVIDED, that a violation of this section shall operate as a breach of this lease only in the event that the property herein shall be closed or abated by the proper legal authorities for any illegal or immoral purpose, business or occupation. Lessee covenants through the entire term of the lease at the Lessee's sole cost and expense to make all repairs, alterations and/or additions, whether ordinary or extraordinary, that may be required by any present or future law, ordinances, regulations or statutes in connection with the occupation and use of the demised premises and all repairs which may be necessary to prevent the building or buildings and/or furniture, and furnishings from falling into a state of ill repair; and the term "ill repair" means such a state of repair that the failure to cure it would constitute legal waste.

ARTICLE XI
ASSIGNMENT

THE LESSORS AND LESSEE COVENANT AND AGREE that this lease shall be freely assignable upon the following terms and conditions:

(a) That the Lessors may be notified in writing of the assignment and the name and address of the assignee, and that such notice to the Lessors from the Lessee must be sent by registered mail; further, that said notice described herein must be received at least five (5) days prior to the execution of any assignment of lease as contemplated herein.

(b) That at the time of the assignment, the lease is in good standing and shall not be in default.

(c) That the original executed assignment shall be field of record in the Public Records of_____County,_____, and that an executed copy thereof shall be delivered to the Lessors within ten (10) days from the recording of the original thereof.

(d) The Lessors agree that upon written request of the Lessee, the Lessors will furnish a written statement to any proposed assignee, setting forth that the lease is or is not in good standing, as the case may be, which written statement will be furnished within five (5) days from such written request, then it shall be presumed that the Lessors will have acknowledged that this lease is at that time in good standing and not in default.

ARTICLE XII
LESSORS' INTEREST NOT SUBJECT TO MECHANICS' LIENS

IT IS HEREBY STIPULATED AND AGREED BY AND BETWEEN THE PARTIES HERETO that during the demised term, there shall be no mechanics' liens upon the Lessors' interest in the demised land and in the buildings and improvements located thereon, or against the furnishings which constitute the equipment thereof, arising through the act of the Lessee, or any person claiming under, by or through the Lessee; and that no person who furnishes work, labor, services or materials, to the demised premises, or to the furniture, furnishings, fixtures and equipment thereof, and claiming directly or indirectly through or under the Lessee, or through or under any act or omission of the Lessee, shall ever become entitled to a lien which is superior in rank and dignity to that of this indenture reserved unto the Lessors upon the lands hereby demised or upon any improvements now or hereafter situate thereon, or upon any insurance policies or insurance money aforesaid, or on account of any labor or materials furnished for any such improvements, or for or on account of any other material or thing whatsoever, and nothing in this indenture shall be construed in such a way as to contradict this provision in this indenture. All persons furnishing any such labor or material to the Lessee, or to the premises, at Lessee's order, or at the order of any person dealing directly or indirectly with the Lessee, as well as all other persons whomsoever, shall be bound by this provisions and by notice thereof from and after the date of this indenture, and all materialmen, contractors, mechanics and laborers are hereby charged with notice that they must look to the Lessee and the Lessee's interest in all buildings and improvements thereon situate, to secure the payment of any and all bills for work done, or materials furnished or performed during the term hereby granted.

THE LESSEE SHALL HAVE NO AUTHORITY TO CREATE ANY LIEN for

labor or material upon the Lessors' interest in the demised premises, and neither the Lessee nor anyone claiming by, through or under the Lessee shall have any right to file and place any labor or material lien of any kind or character whatsoever upon the demised premises, and the building and improvements thereon located so as to encumber or affect the title of the Lessors in said land and the buildings and improvements thereon located, and all persons contracting with the Lessee, directly or indirectly, or with any person who in turn is contracting with the Lessee, for the erection, construction, installation, alteration or repair of any building, buildings or other improvements or for the destruction or removal of any building or buildings upon the demised premises, including furnishings and fixtures, and all materialmen, contractors, mechanics and laborers, as heretofore stated, are hereby charged with notice that as and from the date of this instrument they must look to the Lessee and the Lessee's interest only in and to the demised premises to secure the payment of any bill for work done or materials furnished or performed during the term hereby granted.

THE MERE FACT OF THE EXISTENCE OF A MECHANICS' OR MATERIALMEN'S LIEN OR LIENS, however, shall not, of itself, operate as a forfeiture or termination of this indenture, PROVIDED, the Lessee, within_____ (_____) days after the recording of such notice of lien among the Public Records of_____ _____County,_____, in the event notice of lien is not served upon the Lessee, shall cause the same to be cancelled, released and extinguished or the premises released therefrom by the posting of bond, or by any other method prescribed by law, and proper evidence thereof be furnished to the Lessors, and if such lien or liens appear of record, the Lessee shall cause the same to be cancelled, satisfied and discharged of record. If, however, the Lessee shall dispute the amount or validity of any mechanical or materialmen's lien claimed, or any other claim asserted, and shall, with all due diligence institute or defend an appropriate action or proceeding in a court or courts of competent jurisidiction upon the cause of action and shall, by injunction, due defense of the suit, or otherwise prevent any sale or impairment of the title of the Lessors, and shall prosecute or defend such action or proceeding with reasonable diligence to a final determination, and if such suit or defense shall be instituted within said period of_____ (_____) days after the time when said lien shall have been filed, then, in such case, the time reasonably required in the litigation of such cause of action shall be added to the above_____ (_____) days time; PROVIDED, HOWEVER, that in any event it shall be the duty of the Lessee, after contesting such lien, to cause said lien to be cancelled, released, extinguished or adjudicated not to exist, or to cause the premises to be released therefrom by the posting of bond or by any other method prescribed by law, at least_____(_____) days before the time when the premises or any interests therein, or the Lessee's interest therein, might otherwise be offered for sale by reason of the said lien, or any court decree or order arising by reason thereof or in connection with the enforcement of said lien; and promtply upon relieving the premises of such claim, the Lessee shall then have the duty of furnishing the evidence thereof unto the Lessors.

ARTICLE XIII
LESSORS' JOINDER IN PERMANENT MORTGAGE

FOR THE PURPOSE OF ENABLING THE LESSEE TO CONSTRUCT a building

or buildings, if it decides to do so, the Lessors will, at the request of the Lessee, join in the execution of a mortgage which will encumber the leased premises and the interest of the Lessors therein. Such mortgage shall be made to a bank, trust company, life insurance company, a federal savings and loan association, or other leader of an institutional nature making mortgages or doing a mortgage lending business in _____
County,_____ , and shall be conditioned upon the following:

(a) That said mortgage and note or notes secured thereby shall set forth the fact that the execution thereof by the Lessors shall not render them personally responsible for the payment of the debts which the said mortgage secures.

(b) That the total cost of securing such mortgage and all expenses incurred thereby shall be borne by the Lessee.

(c) That the proceeds of such permanent mortgage shall be disbursed through an institutional lender in a manner to assure completion of said improvements and the payment of all bills incurred in connection therewith.

(d) That should the Lessee desire a construction loan to aid in financing the construction of a building or buildings upon said property, the Lessors will join in the execution of a construction mortgage providing that a commitment for the permanent mortgage loan as aforesaid has been procured and an executed copy thereof delivered to the Lessors.

(e) That the Lessors shall be required under the provisions of this Article to join in the execution of one or more permanent mortgages which will encumber the leased premises with the following qualifications:

In the event the Lessee elects to improve only a portion of the leasehold, then and in that event the Lessors shall join in the execution of a mortgage encumbering that portion of the leasehold so improved, but shall not thereafter by required to join in the execution of any mortgage which encumbers that portion previously encumbered. Thereafter, if the Lessee shall elect to improve that portion of the leasehold not previsouly encumbered, the Lessors will join in the execution of a mortgage encumbering that portion of the leasehold not previously encumbered, but thereafter shall not be required to join in the execution of any further encumbrances. In the event the Lessee elects to improve the entire leasheold at one time, the Lessors shall join only in the execution of one mortgage encumbering said leasehold, and shall thereafter not be required to join in the execution of any mortgage encumbering said leasehold.

However, in either event, whether the Lessee elects to improve a portion of said leasehold or all of said leasehold at any time, the agreement of the Lessors to join in the execution of said mortgage or mortgages, as the case may be, shall cease and terminate_____
_____ , and thereafter the Lessors shall not be required to join in the execution of any mortgage or mortgages encumbering said leasehold.

Lessors shall pay off all existing encumbrances on the property prior to Lessee's obtaining its construction money mortgage and permanent mortgage.

ARTICLE XIV
LESSEE'S OBLIGATION TO PAY MORTGAGE

IT IS FURTHER UNDERSTOOD AND AGREED by and between the parties that the obligation to pay any mortgage hereinafter made by the Lessors, at the request of the

Lessee, and of keeping it in good standing is the duty of the Lessee herein, and the Lessee covenants and agrees with the Lessors that the Lessee will keep said mortgage in good standing and will not suffer or permit the said mortgage to be in default and will deliver unto the Lessors a receipt evidencing the payment of principal and interest due under said mortgage or mortgages, as such payments mature. The Lessors, on their part, agree that they will execute all papers necessary to give effect to an undertaking to obtain the mortgage or mortgages herein referred to, including the application papers which may be required by the proposed mortgagee; but such application papers shall contain the statement that the Lessors shall never be rendered liable personally for the payment of the debt proposed to be secured by the mortgage. If the Lessee should default in its undertaking to keep the said mortgage or mortgages in good standing in the manner herein set forth, and then the Lessors may, at their option, make such payments as are necessary to restore the mortgage or mortgages to good standing, and all payments thus made by the Lessors shall bear interest at the rate of _____ per cent per annum from the date upon which they are made and shall be considered so much additional rent as may be collected in the same manner as rent could be collected; but the election of the Lessors to make payment of such sums and to collect them as rent shall not be deemed to cure the default thus committed by the Lessee and said sums so advanced shall be deemed thus due and payable unto the Lessors by the Lessee immediately as though they were installments of rent then currently maturing; but nothing herein contained shall be construed as preventing the Lessors from treating the Lessee's failure to keep the said mortgage in good standing as a default in the lease, enforceable according to the terms hereof.

ARTICLE XV
LESSEE TO CARRY LIABILITY INSURANCE

THE LESSEE COVENANTS AND AGREES THAT IT WILL, AT ALL TIMES, and at its own expense, keep the building and improvements situated on the demised premises at any time, and all property which is subject to the Lessors' lien hereunder, during the term of this lease, in good order, condition and repair, and shall, at all times, save and keep the Lessors free and harmless from any and all damage and liability occasioned by the use of the said premises, and shall indeminify and keep harmless the Lessors from and against any loss, cost, damage and expense arising out of and in connection with any accident causing injury to any person or property whomsoever or whatsoever and due directly or indirectly to the use or occupancy of said premises; and the Lessee covenants and agrees to provide policies of insurance generally known as public liability and/or owners', landlord and tenant policies, boiler policies, and elevator policies, insuring the Lessee and the Lessors against all claims and demands made by any person or persons whatsoever for injuries received in connection with the operation and maintenance of the improvements and building or buildings located therein, to the extent of not less than _____ _____ to cover the claim or damage from any single or specific cause, by any one person, and to the extent of not less than _____ _____ to cover, in connection with any one particular accident or occurrence, the total aggregate of any claims that may arise or be claimed to have arisen against the Lessors or the

Lessee, as aforesaid. Said policies, as aforesaid, shall be taken with insurance companies authorized to do business in the State of_____.

ARTICLE XVI
DEFAULT CLAUSE

IF THE LESSEE SHOULD FAIL TO KEEP AND PERFORM ANY OF THE TERMS, covenants, conditions or provisions in this lease contained by the Lessee to be kept and performed, then it shall and may be lawful for the Lessors, at the Lessors' option, to declare said demised term ended and to re-enter upon the demised premises and the buildings and improvements situated thereon, or any part thereof, and to retake possession of the said leased premises, buildings thereon, and the furniture and equipment contained therein, either with or without process of law, the said Lessee hereby waiving any demand for possession of said premises and any and all buildings and improvements then situated thereon, or the Lessors may have such other remedy as the law and this instrument afford. And the Lessee covenants and agrees that upon termination of the said demised term, at such election of the Lessors, or in any other way, it, the Lessee, will surrender and deliver up said premises and property, real and personal, peaceably to the Lessors, their agents and attorneys, immediately upon the termination of the said demised term; and if the Lessee, its agents, attorneys and tenants shall hold the said premises or any part thereof one (1) day after the same should be surrendered according to the terms of this lease, it shall be deemed guilty of forcible detainer of said premises under the Statute of and shall be subject to eviction or removal forcibly or otherwise, with or without process of law. Nothing herein contained shall be construed as authorizing the Lessors to declare this lease in default; however, where the default consists in the non-payment of rent or taxes, until such non-payment, in violation of the terms of this lease shall have continued for a period of_____ (_____) days beyond the time when such items should have been paid by the Lessee, and where the alleged default consists in some violation other than the non-payment of rent or taxes, Lessors shall not declare this lease in default until such violation shall have continued uncured for_____
_____(_____) days after the Lessors shall have given the Lessee written notice of such violation, and Lessee shall have failed within said period of notice to cure such default, or shall have commenced or taken such steps as are necessary to cure such default, which once commenced the Lessee agrees and shall pursue continuously until the default is finally cured.

ARTICLE XVII
RECEIVERSHIP CLAUSE

In addition to the other security for the performance of the lease, the Lessee pledges with the Lessors all of the rents, issues and profits which might otherwise secure unto the Lessee for the use, enjoyment and operation of the demised premises; and in connection with such pledging of the rents, the Lessee covenants and agrees with the Lessors that if the Lessors, upon default of the Lessee, elect to file a suit in chancery to enforce the lease and protect the Lessors' rights thereunder, the Lessors may as ancillary to such suit apply to any court having jurisdiction, for the appointment of a Receiver of all and singular the demised premises, the improvements and buildings located thereon, and the personal property located therein, and thereupon it is expressly covenanted and agreed that the court shall without notice forthwith appoint a Receiver with the usual powers and duties of receivers in like cases, and such appointment shall be made by such court as a matter of strict right to the Lessors, and without reference to the adequacy or inadequacy of the value of the property which is subject to the Landlord's lien, or to the solvency or insolvency of the Lessee; and without reference to the commission of waste.

ARTICLE XVIII
RELATION THAT OF LANDLORD AND TENANT

THOUGH THIS BE A LONG TERM LEASE, the parties understand and agree that the relationship between them is that of landlord and tenant, and the Lessee specifically acknowledges that all statutory proceedings in the State of_____ regulating the relationship of landlord and tenant and the remedies accruing to the landlord upon default of the tenant, respecting collection of rent or repossession of the premises accrue to the landlord hereunder.

ARTICLE XIX
EFFECT OF TERMINATION

IT IS FURTHER COVENANTED AND AGREED BY AND BETWEEN THE PARTIES HERETO, in the event of the termination of this lease, at any time before the expiration of the term hereof for the breach of any of the covenants herein contained, then, in such case, all of the rights, estate and interest of the Lessee in and under this indenture and in the demised premises hereinabove described, and all improvements, buildings and the Lessee's interest in all furniture, furnishings, fixtures and equipment then situate in said demised premises, together with all rents, issues and profits of said premises and the improvements thereon, whether then accrued or to accrue, and all insurance policies, and all insurance moneys paid or payable thereunder shall, without any compensation made therefor unto the Lessee, at once pass to and become the property of the Lessor, not as a penalty or forfeiture, but as liquidated damages to the Lessors because of such default by the Lessee hereby fixed and agreed upon between the parties hereto, all of the parties hereto recognizing the impossibility of precisely ascertaining the amount of damages that will be sustained by the Lessors in consequence of such default, and all parties desiring to obviate any question or dispute, concerning the amount of such damage and the cost and effect of such default in consequence of such forfeiture, have taken these elements into consideration in fixing and agreeing upon the amount of rent to be paid by the Lessee to the Lessors.

ARTICLE XX
LESSORS' ELECTION OF REMEDY NOT EXCLUSIVE

IT IS MUTUALLY COVENANTED AND AGREED THAT THE VARIOUS RIGHTS, powers, elections, privileges and remedies of the Lessors contained in this lease shall be construed as cumulative, and no one of them as exclusive of the other, or exculsive of any rights or priorities allowed by law.

AND IT IS FURTHER AGREED BY AND BETWEEN THE PARTIES HERETO

that the right given to the Lessors in this lease to collect the rent that may be due under the terms of this lease by additional rent, money or payments due under the terms of this lease by any proceedings under the same, or the right given to the Lessors to enforce any of the terms and provisions of this lease, shall not in any way affect the right of such Lessors to declare this lease void, and the term created thereby ended, as herein provided, when default is made in the payment of said rent, or when default is made by the Lessee in any of the terms and provisions of this lease.

ARTICLE XXI
LESSEE TO PAY COSTS AND FEES

AND IT IS MUTUALLY COVENANTED AND AGREED BY THE PARTIES HERETO THAT in case the Lessors shall without fault on their part, be made parties to any litigation commenced by or against the Lessee, then the Lessee shall pay all costs and reasonable attorneys' fees incurred by or against the Lessors, or in connection with such litigation, and the Lessee shall and will also pay all costs and reasonable attorneys' fees incurred by, or against the said Lessors in enforcing the covenants, agreements, terms and provisions of this lease, and/or in terminating this lease by reason of the Lessee's default; and that all such costs and reasonable attorneys' fees, if paid by the Lessors, and the rent reserved in this lease, and all taxes and assessments, and the payment of all money provided in this lease, to be made by the Lessors, shall be, and they are hereby declared to be a first lien upon any building and improvement placed upon said demised premises at any time during said term, subject to the provisions of this lease respecting the existence or creation of liens which are, or will be, prior to the lien for rent.

ARTICLE XXII
HOW NOTICE GIVEN

IT IS FURTHER AGREED, AS A CONDITION OF THIS LEASE, that in every case where, in the option of the Lessors, or under the conditions of this lease, it shall be deemed necessary for the interest of the Lessors to serve a notice or demand on the Lessee concerning this lease, or any of the provisions or conditions thereof, it shall be sufficient service of said notice or demand, or declaration to deliver a copy thereof to the Lessee or mail a copy thereof by registered mail, addressed to the Lessee at the demised premises. Correspondingly, the Lessee may serve notice upon the Lessors by delivering or mailing the same to the Lessors at the place last designated by the Lessors as the place for the payment of rent, or, in the absence of such designation, at the last place at which rent was paid to the Lessors, or, if said place was not an actual address, then to the last known address of the Lessors. When the parties hereto consist of more than one Lessee or more than one Lessor, then the default of one shall be the default of all and notice to one shall be notice to all.

ARTICLE XXIII
CONDEMNATION CLAUSE

IT IS FURTHER COVENANTED AND AGREED THAT IF AT ANY TIME DURING the term of this lease the demised real estate or the improvements or buildings located thereon or any portion thereof be taken or appropriated or condemned by reason of eminent domain, that there shall be such division of the proceeds and awards in such condemnation proceedings and such abatement of rent and other adjustments made as shall be just and equitable under the circumstances. If the Lessors and the Lessee are unable to agree upon what division, annual abatement of rent or other adjustments are just and equitable within thirty (30) days after such award has been made, then the matters in dispute shall, by appropriate proceedings, be submitted to a court then having jurisdiction of the subject matter in_____County,_____, for its decision and determination of the matters in dispute. If the premises be wholly taken by condemnation, the lease shall be cancelled. Although the title to the buildings and improvements placed by the Lessee upon the demised premises will pass to the Lessors, nevertheless, for the purpose of condemnation, the fact that the Lessee placed such building on the demised premises shall be taken into account and the deprivation by the Lessee of the use of such building shall pro tanto be an item of damage in determining the portion of the condemnation award to which the Lessee is entitled. In general, it is the intent of this paragraph that upon condemnation, the parties hereto shall share in their award to the extent that their interests, respectively, are depreciated, damaged or destroyed by the exercise of the rights of eminent domain, provided, however, it is understood and agreed that the taking of a portion of the demised property for street and/or sidewalk purposes, exclusive of any portion of building, shall not warrant any abatement or entitle the Lessee to any abatement of annual rental hereunder.

ARTICLE XXIV
LEASE NOT AFFECTED BY DAMAGE TO PROPERTY

NO DESTRUCTION OR DAMAGE TO ANY BUILDING OR IMPROVEMENTS by fire, windstorm or other casualty of any kind, character, or nature, shall be deemed to entitle the Lessee to surrender possession of the demised premises or to terminate this lease, or to violate any of its provisions, or to cause any rebate or abatement in rent then due, or thereafter becoming due under the terms hereof.

ARTICLE XXV
RETURN OF PREMISES TO THE LESSORS

THE LESSEE COVENANTS, STIPULATES AND AGREES THAT UPON the termination of this indenture, whether by lapse of time or otherwise, it will, at once, peaceably and quietly deliver up to the Lessors all of the demised premises, including the buildings and improvements situated thereon, and all of the furnishings and equipment thereunto belonging, in as good a state and condition as reasonable use and wear thereof will have permitted, and that all buildings, improvements, fixtures and equipment then situate upon the described premises and belonging to the Lessors, and that no compensation shall be allowed or paid to the Lessee therefor.

ARTICLE XXVI
LESSEE GIVEN OPTION TO PURCHASE DEMISED PREMISES

IT IS HEREBY AGREED BY AND BETWEEN THE LESSORS AND LESSEE that the Lessors do hereby grant to the Lessee an option to purchase the demised premises, said option to become effective_____ , and under no circumstances is this provision intended by the Lessors and the Lessee to grant said option at any date prior to that as aforesaid. Said option to purchase shall terminate_____ ____. The purchase price shall be the sum of_____ , in cash, payable in legal tender at the time of the closing.

CLOSING OF THIS TRANSACTION shall take place within_____(___) days of the receipt of notice from the Lessee to the Lessors of Lessee's intention to exercise said option, provided that said notice is given to the Lessors sufficiently prior to the expiration of the option period to close said transaction within_____(___) days, and in all events prior to the expiration of the option period. The closing of the purchase and sale shall follow customary procedure in commencing and consummating the transaction.

IN THE EVENT THE LESSEE shall not desire to exercise the option to purchase, then and in that event the terms and conditions of this lease shall be binding on the parties hereto for the remainder of the life of the lease, as though no such option had ever been made a part thereof.

ARTICLE XXVII
MISCELLANEOUS PROVISIONS

(a) It is COVENANTED AND AGREED that no waiver of a breach of any of the covenants of this lease contained shall be construed to be a waiver of any succeeding breach of the same covenant.

(b) TIME IS OF THE ESSENCE IN EVERY PARTICULAR, and particularly where the obligation to pay money is involved.

(c) ALL ARREARAGES IN THE PAYMENT OF RENT shall bear interest from the date when due and payable at the rate of_____per cent per annum, until paid.

(d) IT IS FURTHER UNDERSTOOD AND AGREED that no modification, release, discharge, or waiver of any provisions hereof, shall be of any force, value or effect unless in writing, signed by the Lessors, or their duly authorized agent.

(e) ALL COVENANTS, PROMISES, CONDITIONS, AND OBLIGATIONS herein contained, or implied by law, are covenants running with the land and shall be attached to and binding upon the heirs, executors, administrators, successors, legal representatives, and assigns, of each of the parties to this lease.

(f) IT IS MUTUALLY STIPULATED AND AGREED by and between the parties hereto that this instrument contains the whole agreement between them as of this date, and that the execution thereof has not been induced by either party by any representations, promises or understandings not expressed herein, and that there are no collateral agreements, stipulations, promises or undertakings whatsoever upon the respective parties in any way touching the subject matter of this contract which are not expressly contained in this instrument.

(g) ALL USES OF PRONOUNS IN REFERENCE TO THE LESSORS AND LESSEE respectively, mean such Lessors and Lessee respectively, whether the personal or impersonal, singular or plural pronoun is used.

IN WITNESS WHEREOF, the Lessors herein have hereunto affixed their hands and seals, and the Lessee herein has caused these presents to be signed and executed in its corporate name by its President, and its seal affixed and attested to by its Secretary, at_____ _____County,_____, this_____ day of_____,_____ .

Signed, sealed and delivered
in the presence of:

_____   _____ (SEAL)

_____
As to "LESSORS"

_____ (SEAL)
"LESSORS"

_____   By: _____
                                                                    President

_____
As to "LESSEE"   Attest: _____
                                                        Secretary

(Reproduced with permission of Attorney Seymour J. Simon, Miami, Fla.)

No. 13–12
RECEIPT FOR DEPOSIT AND CONTRACT TO LEASE

RECEIPT is hereby acknowledged by_____, Realtor, hereinafter called AGENT, of the sum of_____ dollars ($_____), from_____, hereinafter called LESSEE, as an earnest money deposit and as a part of the rental price on account of offer to rent the property of_____, hereinafter called LESSOR, said property being situated in the County of_____, State of Florida to wit:

upon the terms and conditions, as follows:

1. PROPERTY TO BE USED FOR:_____
   Term of Proposed Lease:_____
   Total rent to be paid:_____ .
   Monthly Payments:_____
   Prepayments, if any:_____

2. TAXES. Lessee agrees to pay Florida sales tax as required by law in addition to monthly rent payments. Taxes on real property to be paid by:_____. Taxes on

personal property to be paid by: _____

3. UTILITIES: Water to be paid by: _____
                   Sewer to be paid by: _____
                   Refuse collection to be paid by: _____
                   Electricity to be paid by: _____
                   Heat to be paid by: _____
                   Air-conditioning to be paid by: _____

4. INSURANCE: Plate glass insurance to be paid by: _____
                   Public Liability to be paid by: _____
                   Personal property to be paid by: _____
                   Fire and extended coverage on building (not contents) to be paid by:

5. ZONING. RESTRICTIONS. It is understood and agreed that the above mentioned property is being rented subject to the zoning ordinances and restrictions and limitations of record and subject to any easements for public utilities which may be of record; provided, however, final acceptance is contingent on there being no zoning or deed restrictions which will prohibit the intended use as above stated.

6. DEFAULT BY LESSEE. If Lessee fails to perform any of the covenants of this contract, at the option of Lessor, the deposit made pursuant to this contract by the Lessee shall be retained by or for the account of Lessor, as consideration for the execution of this contract and in full settlement of any claims for damages, and the Lessor and the Lessee shall be relieved of all obligations to each other under this contract.

7. DEFAULT BY LESSOR. If Lessor fails to perform any of the covenants of this contract, the aforesaid deposit shall, at the option of the Lessee, be returned to Lessee on demand, and Lessee shall not thereby waive any right or remedy he may have because of such default of Lessor.

8. TIME is of the essence of this contract and of each of the covenants and provisions hereof.

9. APPLICATION OF DEPOSIT ON DEFAULT. In the event Lessee fails to perform and the deposit aforesaid is retained, the amount of such deposit shall be divided equally between the Broker and the Lessor, provided however, that the amount to be retained or received by the Broker shall not exceed the full amount of the commission and any excess shall be paid to the Lessor.

10. SPECIAL CLAUSES.

11. FORMAL CLOSING. The _____
_____ shall have prepared at his expense a Lease Agreement in general standard form incorporating the provisions of this offer and the same shall be executed by all parties hereto on or before _____ days after the effective date of this Agreement.

12. THIS INSTRUMENT shall become effective as a contract when signed by Agent, Lessor and Lessee. If not executed by all parties on or before _____
_____ any money deposited shall be refunded and the proposed transaction shall terminate.

13. PERSONS BOUND. The covenants herein contained shall bind, and the benefits and advantages shall inure to, the respective heirs, executors, administrators and successors of the parties hereto. Whenever used the singular number shall include the plural, the plural the singular, and the use of any gender shall include all genders. This contract shall not be assigned by either Lessor or Lessee without the written consent of the other.

14. OTHER AGREEMENTS. No agreements, unless incorporated in this contract, shall be binding upon any of the parties.

Date executed:

_____   _____ (SEAL)
                                            BROKER AND AGENT

I, or we, agree to execute and accept a Lease to the above described property on the above stated terms and conditions.

                                            _____ (SEAL)

Date executed: _____ (SEAL)

_____   _____ (SEAL)
                                            LESSEE

I, or we, agree to execute a lease to the above described property on the above stated 'erms and conditions, and further agree to pay to the Broker/Agent, a commission of__
_____Dollars, ($_____), upon the formal closing and delivery of the Lease Agreement, or in the event of default by Lessor. Lessor further agrees to pay a commission to Broker in accordance with the commissions on sales as established by rates, rules and customs of the Board of Realtors in the County or area where said property is located in the event said property is sold to the Lessee during the term of said Lease. This provision shall carry over and be binding upon the Lessor whether the same is incorporated in the Lease Agreement or not.

                                            _____ (SEAL)

Date executed: _____ (SEAL)

_____   _____ (SEAL)
                                            LESSOR
(Copyrighted form of Florida Association of Realtors used with
its permission in this publication and not for reprinting)

In some states a condensed form called a "memorandum of lease" may be taken from the full lease for purposes of recording. In this manner, with the omission of confidential information such as the rental amount (or any other term which the parties desire to remain private), the remaining covenants of the agreement can be recorded.

No. 13–13
LEASE MEMORANDUM
(With Rental Amount Omitted for Recording)

A LEASE between _____(Name)_____ of ____(Address)____ _____ , herein called the Lessor and _____(Name)_____ _____ of _____(Address)_____ , herein called the Lessee was made regarding the following described premises:

(Here include description of the premises)

The date of execution of the lease was _____ , A.D., 19_____ .
Subject lease is for a term of_____years and shall commence on the_____ day of_____ , A.D., 19_____ , and shall terminate on the_____ day of_____ , A.D., 19_____ .
Other Provisions:
In Witness Whereof the parties hereto have respectively executed this memorandum this _____day of_____ , A.D., 19_____ .

_____   _____ (Seal)
Witness as to Lessor   Lessor

_____   _____ (Seal)
Witness as to Lessee   Lessee

No. 13–14
MONTH TO MONTH LEASE

THIS MONTH TO MONTH lease agreement made the_____day of_____ _____ , A.D. 19_____ , between_____ _____hereinafter called the Lessor and_____ _____hereinafter called the Lessee.

WITNESSETH that the said Lessor has let to the said Lessee the following described premises:

(Here follows a description of the demised premises)

for a term of_____commencing on the_____day of_____ _____ , A.D. 19_____ and ending on the_____day of_____ _____ , A.D. 19_____ , at the rent of $_____per month, payable on the_____ _____day of each month in advance. It is hereby agreed between the Lessor and Lessee that the term of this lease shall be for_____ only, and if renewed it shall be from month to month thereafter.

THE SUBJECT PREMISES shall be used only as_____ _____ , and at the termination of this month to month lease agreement the Lessee shall vacate and surrender the demised premises, leaving it in the same condition as the Lessee received it, normal wear and tear excepted.

Witness:

1. _____   By _____
                                                              Lessor

2. _____

1. _____   By _____
                                                              Lessee

2. _____

No.13–15
SUB-LEASE

This Sub-Lease *made the_____ day of_____ , 19_____ , between*

hereinafter referred to as Lessor, and

hereinafter referred to as Lessee

WITNESSETH, *that the Lessor hereby leases to the Lessee, and the Lessee hereby hires and takes from the Lessor, the following premises, to wit;*
in the building known as

to be used and occupied by the Lessee for

and for no other purpose, for a term to commence on the_____ day of_____ ,
19_____ , and to end on the_____ day of_____ , 19_____ , unless
sooner terminated as hereinafter provided, at the ANNUAL RENT as hereinafter provided,
payable in equal monthly installments in advance on the _____ day of each and every
calendar month during said term, except the first installment, which shall be paid upon the
execution hereof.

The said premises are the same premises, or a part or the premises, referred to in a lease
between

as the landlord and the Lessor herein as the tenant therein, dated the_____ day
of_____ , 19_____

The Lessee represents that the Lessee has read the said lease *(an exact copy thereof is
attached hereto).

The terms, covenants, provisions and conditions of said lease are hereby incorporated
herein and shall be binding upon both parties hereto, those applying to the landlord therein shall
apply to the Lessor herein and those applying to the tenant therein shall apply to the Lessee
herein with the following exceptions:

_____

* Strike out words within parenthesis if they do not apply.

a. *The annual rent payable hereunder shall be $*

b. *The security, if any, to be deposited hereunder shall be $*

c. *The following numbered paragraphs of said lease shall not apply to this sub-lease:*

The following numbered paragraphs of said lease are amended to read as follows:

IN WITNESS WHEREOF, *the parties have executed this sub-lease in duplicate the day and year first above written.*

Signed, sealed and delivered in the presence of

_____

_____

_____

(Form courtesy of Julius Blumberg, Inc., 80 Exchange Pl., New York, N. Y.)

No. 13–16
ASSIGNMENT OF LEASE
With Consent

THIS ASSIGNMENT made the_____day of_____, 19_____.

That _____hereinafter known as the Assignor, for and in consideration of Ten ($10.00) Dollars and other good and valuable consideration to the Assignor, paid by_____ _____hereinafter known as the Assignee, the receipt of which is hereby acknowledged, do by these presents, grant, convey, assign, transfer and set over unto the Assignee, his successors and assigns, that certain lease agreement dated_____, 19_____ _____, executed by_____as Lessor, and_____ _____as Lessee for Suite #'s _____ and_____ on the_____floor of an office building commonly known as_____ _____located at # _____ _____ Street,_____City, State of _____, for a term commencing on the_____day of_____ _____, 19_____, and ending on the_____day of_____, 19_____, at the agreed monthly rental of $_____. A copy of the subject office lease is hereto attached and made a part of this agreement. Said assignment is subject to obtaining the written consent of the lessor.

The security deposit in the amount of $_____now being held by the Lessor is hereby assigned to the Assignee. If said security deposit is returnable under the lease agreement, then same shall be returned to the Assignee at the conclusion of the term of the lease.

The Assignor shall at all times remain fully liable with the Assignee for the performance of all the provisions and covenants of the lease.

Witness:

1. _____   _____
                                                              Assignor

2. _____

1. _____   _____
                                                              Assignee

2. _____

CONSENT

_____, 19_____

    The Lessor hereby consents to the foregoing assignment. The assigned premises has been inspected by us and we are satisfied with its general condition.
Witness:

1. _____   _____
                                                              Lessor

2. _____

No. 13–17
LEASE RENEWAL ENDORSEMENT

    THIS ENDORSEMENT is to be attached to and made a part of that certain lease agreement dated the_____ day of_____, 19_____, between _____ as Lessor and_____ _____ as Lessee, covering demised premises known as Apartment #_____, at #_____ _____Avenue, City of_____, County of_____, State of_____ .

    For value received and by mutual consent, the aforesaid lease is hereby extended and renewed for a term of_____year(s) beginning the_____day of_____ _____, 19_____and ending the_____ day of_____, 19_____, for a total renewal of $_____, payable in equal monthly installments of $_____, in advance, plus any and all other payments required to be made by the Lessee as rent or otherwise in accordance with the terms and conditions of the original lease.

    All of the terms, provisions, covenants, covenants and stipulations contained in the original lease, of which this renewal forms a part, and hereby made a part of this renewal, shall be binding on the parties and remain in full force and effect.

    In addition, the Lessee has the option for a further renewal for_____year(s) from the_____ day of_____, 19_____.

    IN WITNESS WHEREOF, the parties hereto set their hands and seals this_____ _____day of_____, 19_____.

Witness:

_____   _____
                                                          Lessor
_____

_____   _____
                                                          Lessee
_____

No. 13–18
SURRENDER OF LEASE

THIS INDENTURE, made the_____day of_____ _____, in the year one thousand nine hundred and_____ _____BETWEEN_____

_____ of the second part. WHEREAS, the said part_____of the second part, by a certain indenture of Lease bearing date the_____day of_____, 19_____ did demise and let unto_____ _____of the first part.

NOW THESE PRESENTS WITNESS, that for and in consideration of the sum of

_____ _____dollars, paid by the said part_____of the second part_____of the first part at the sealing and delivery of these presents, the receipt whereof is hereby acknow- ledged, and to the intent and purpose that the said term in the said land and premises may be wholly merged and extinguished, the said part_____of the first part ha____given, granted, and surrendered, and by these presents do____give, grant and surrender unto the said part_____of the second part and_____heirs, all the said lands and pre- mises in the said Indenture of Lease contained and demised as aforesaid, and all the estate, right, title, interest, term of years, property, claim and demand whatsoever of the said part _____of the first part, of, in, to or out of the same, or any part or parcel thereof.

TO HAVE AND TO HOLD, the said land and premises to the said part_____of the second part,_____heirs and assigns, to_____their own proper use and behoof.

AND THE SAID part_____of the first part do_____hereby, for _____heirs, executors and administrators, covenant and agree to and with the said part of the second part,_____heirs and assigns, that the said part_____ of the first part ha_____not at any time heretofore made, done, committed, executed, permitted or suffered any act, deed, matter or thing whatsoever, whereby or wherewith, or by reason or means whereof the said lands and premises hereby assigned or surrendered, or any part or parcel thereof are, or is, or may, can or shall be in any wise impeached, charged, effected or encumbered.

IN WITNESS WHEREOF, the said parties have hereunto set their hands and seals the day and year first above written.

In the presence of

(Form courtesy of Julius Blumberg, Inc., 80 Exchange Pl., New York, N. Y.)

No. 13–19
TIMBER LEASE

LEASE AGREEMENT made this＿＿＿＿＿＿＿day of＿＿＿＿＿＿＿, 19＿＿＿＿
＿＿＿＿, between＿＿＿＿＿＿＿＿＿＿＿＿＿＿＿＿＿, party of the first part and＿＿＿＿＿＿
＿＿＿＿＿＿＿＿＿＿＿＿＿, party of the second part.

PURPOSE

Witnesseth, that the said party of the first part, for and in consideration of certain agreements hereinafter contained does grant, bargain, demise, sell and lease to said party of the second part, his heirs and assigns the right to enter on the land hereinafter described to cut, box and haul all the timber growing on the following described land.

(Here describe property)

AMOUNT AND TERM

The party of the second part paying the party of the first part the sum of＿＿＿＿＿＿
＿＿＿＿＿＿＿＿＿＿＿＿＿＿＿＿＿＿Dollars ($＿＿＿＿＿＿＿) for said right to cut, box and haul the timber commencing the＿＿＿＿＿＿ day of＿＿＿＿＿＿＿, 19＿＿＿＿, and ending the＿＿＿＿＿＿day of＿＿＿＿＿＿＿＿＿, 19＿＿＿ .

LIMITATION

It is understood and agreed that the party of the second part shall not cut, remove or destroy timber measuring＿＿＿＿＿＿＿inches in diameter or less.

RESEEDING

Further, it is expressly understood that the party of the first part shall have and hereby reserve the right to reseed all areas of the property that have already been cut or have been damaged by fire or blight or other causes.

INGRESS AND EGRESS

The party of the second part is hereby given the right of ingress to and egress from the said land and the right to construct necessary logging roads, tramways or other contrivance for transporting cut timber.

RIGHT TO ASSIGN

It is further covenanted and agreed that the party of the second part has the right, at any time, to assign this lease in whole or part and that the assignee shall have the same right of assignment and all the rights and privileges of the party of the second part shall vest in whomsoever may succeed to the interest hereby conveyed to said party of the second part.

SUCCESSORS

It is further agreed and understood between the parties that all of the conditions, covenants, limitations, reservations, etc., are binding, not only on the party of the second part, but also upon the successors and assigns; and it is further agreed that on the performance of the agreements and covenants on the part of the party of the second part, the successors and assigns, shall have and hold free and uninterrupted use and enjoyment of the timber for the time aforesaid unto the said party of the second part, the successors and assigns.

In witness whereof the parties have hereunto set their hands and seal the day and year first above written.

Done in presence of

_____   _____

_____   _____

No. 13–20
NOTICE TO TENANT

THIS NOTICE made this_____ day of _____, 19_____.

To:_____
          (Name of Tenant)

_____
          (Address of Premises)

_____
          (City & State)

YOU ARE HEREBY notified that you are indebted to the Landlord of the demised premises above mentioned in the amount of_____
_____dollars ($_____) for unpaid rent of said premises from the_____day of_____, 19_____ to the_____ day of _____, 19_____, which you are required to pay within_____ days of receiving this notice or vacate said premises. If payment is not made or premises are not vacated, the Landlord will take appropriate legal action to recover possession of the premises.

Witness:

_____   _____
                                                                            Landlord

_____

No. 13–21
NOTICE TO TENANT
Another Form

_____ , 19_____

To_____, tenant of premises

_____

  This is to notify you that the Landlord elects to terminate your tenancy of the above described premises now held by you, and unless you vacate the said premises on or before the_____day of_____, 19_____, the day on which your term expires, the Landlord will commence summary proceedings under the Statute to remove you from said premises for the holding over after the expiration of your term.

_____

(Landlord)

_____

(Agent)

No. 13–22
EXTENSION AND MODIFICATION AGREEMENT
Of Lease

  THIS AGREEMENT made between _____
_____, as Landlord, and_____, as Tenant, extending and modifying the lease of the entire_____floor in the_____ Building, No._____Avenue,_____City,_____ .

  NOW, in consideration of the premises and of the sum of one dollar ($1.00) paid by each of the parties to the other, which is acknowledged, said lease is hereby extended and modified to_____, 19_____, at the monthly rental of_____ _____dollars ($_____), due and payable on the first of each and every month commencing_____ , 19_____.

  IT IS expressly understood that in all other respects, said terms and conditions of the lease shall be in full force and effect.

  THIS extension and modification agreement shall bind the heirs, executors, administrators and assigns of the respective parties.

  IN WITNESS WHEREOF, the parties hereto set their hands and seals this_____ _____ day of_____ , 19_____ .

Witness:_____   _____

                Lessor

_____   _____

                Lessee

CLAUSES IN LEASES

Percentage Lease Provision

Lessee agrees to pay lessor a sum of money equal to_____ % of the sales in excess of $_____, hereinafter referred to as the minimum sales base, made from the leased premises during each lease year. A report of sales made from the leased premises shall be given to the lessor by the lessee within_____ days after the close of the lease year, and if sales disclosed thereby are sufficient to require a payment hereunder, such payment shall accompany such report. For the purpose of this paragraph "sales" shall not include rebates, refunds, allowances to customers, sales taxes imposed by any governmental authority, cash discounts, discounts to customers, discount sales to employees, or any excise tax. The words "lease year" shall mean a period of twelve successive months. The first lease year shall begin on the commencement date of this lease agreement, provided, however, that it shall include any period of time preceding the defined lease year during which lessee is open for business prior to the commencement date and further provided, that the minimum sales base shall be increased pro rata for any such additional period, but shall not be decreased should lessee open for business after said commencement date.

Percentage Lease Provision—Another form

The lessee agrees to pay the lessor a minimum rental of $_____per annum, payable in monthly installments commencing the_____day of_____, 19_____. Lessee further agrees to pay lessor as additional rental a sum equal to_____ % of the gross sales in excess of $_____, plus an additional_____ % of the gross sales in excess of $_____that are consummated on the leased premises during each lease year. The lessee shall not unreasonably withhold permission to the lessor or his agent to examine the company's books and records of sales.

Gas Station Rent Based On Gallonage

Lessee agrees to pay lessor_____¢(_____cents) per gallon on all gasoline pumped from said station as the agreed rental, to be paid on the first of each and every month during the term of this lease. It is understood that the payment shall be on all gasoline delivered to the lessee by_____Oil Company, or from any other company, during each month of this lease in accordance with the records of_____Oil Company, or any other company delivering gasoline to lessee.

Light And Air Provision

The purpose of this provision is to insure light and air to the north side of the demised premises. The lessor agrees that, during the term of this lease, he will not construct an adjoining building or any other structure on his property over_____feet tall. The lessor Agrees that said light and air restriction shall not become subject or subordinate to any other lien or encumbrance affecting the demised premises.

Lease of Concession In Department Store

The lessor agrees to lease a space at the northwest corner of the main (street level) floor of_____ Department store measuring_____ feet by_____ feet, plus _____ square feet of basement storage space, to_____ _____ , as lessee for a term commencing on the_____ day of _____ , 19_____, and ending on the_____ day of _____ , 19_____, at the monthly rental of $_____ _____. In addition, a security deposit of $_____ shall be given the lessor upon signing this agreement. Said security deposit shall be refunded to the lessor at the expiration of the agreement, less damages, if any. A floor plan depicting the leased space and aisle access in relation to the rest of the main (street level) floor area is attached to and made a part of this agreement. During the term of the lease the lessor shall engage in selling only the products herein designated:

(Itemize list of products)

The lessee agrees to spend_____% of his monthly gross sales for newspaper and other forms of advertising. Said advertising shall be contracted through, and copy and art work prepared in cooperation with the lessor's Advertising Department. The "bulk" advertising space rate savings thus obtained shall be the rate charged the lessor.

Increase Tax Adjustment

The lessee shall pay a proportionate share of any increase in city, county and personal property taxes paid by the lessor over the amount of taxes paid during the initial year of the lease. The lessee's proportionate share shall be in the ratio which the number of square feet leased bears to the total number of square feet of the total rentable area of the building. The lessor agrees to pay all taxes before delinquency, and the lessee shall not be obligated to pay any portion of any penalty for delinquent payment. Any payment due hereinafter shall be pro-rated as of the termination or expiration date of this lease agreement. Any payments made by lessee to lessor under this clause shall be a non-cumulative credit against any percentage payments due under this lease agreement during its term or any renewals thereof.

Option To Renew

The lessee shall have the right to renew this lease agreement for a further period of _____ years commencing on the_____ day of_____ , 19_____, provided he:

1. Has kept all of the terms and conditions of this lease agreement, and
2. He shall notify the lessor in writing on or before the_____ day of_____ _____ , 19_____ that desires such a renewal, and agrees to sign a new lease upon the same terms and conditions as contained in this lease, except as to the duration dates and the exclusion of any further option to renew.

In the event of the extension of the lease under the terms of this option, the security deposit heretofore posted shall be retained by the Lessor to the expiration of the additional term, under the same terms and conditions as originally set out in said lease agreement.

Transfer Clause

If, during the term of this lease, the lessee is transferred to an area beyond_____ miles of_____city, this lease agreement may be cancelled if the following terms and conditions are met:

1. That the lessor receives_____days' notice of the transfer.
2. The lessor is furnished written proof of such a transfer by the lessee's employer. (In case of military personnel, a letter from the Commanding Officer).
3. The lessee's rental payments are current and no terms and conditions of this lease have been violated.

Covenant To Vacate Lease Upon Sale

In the event the premises is sold prior to the termination of this lease agreement and the purchaser shall desire possession of the premises, the lessee shall cancel this lease and surrender possession, executing any documents deemed necessary to evidence complete cancellation of the lease; provided the lessor gives the lessee_____days written notice of said sale and evidence purchases desire to actually occupy the premises.

Increase Operating Costs Provision

In the event of an increase in the wages paid to employees who maintain the building (janitors, repair men, painters, elevator operators, engineers, etc.), the tenant, in addition to the fixed rental amount shall pay a proportionate increase in rent. The said proportionate share shall be calculated by the total amount of square feet of the above ground rented area in the building, divided by the amount of square feet contained in the demised premises. Conversely, if the labor cost for any subsequent year is less, then the foregoing formula shall apply in the tenants favor and the tenant shall receive a similarly calculated proportionate reduction.

Air Conditioning Clause

The lessee will not install or use an air conditioning unit or any other cooling mechanism without obtaining written consent of the lessor.

Landlord's Entry

The lessor or his agent may enter, at all reasonable hours of the day, to inspect and make such repairs to the leased premises as the lessor may reasonably desire. Further, that_____days prior to the expiration of this lease agreement, prospective tenants, at all reasonable hours of the day, shall be admitted to view the premises until it is rented. If lessor is not present to permit entry, the lessor or his agent may enter the premises without rendering him liable. The lessor shall at all times accord reasonable care to the lessee's property.

Quiet Enjoyment

As long as the lessee pays the rent as provided herein and otherwise performs all of the covenants and conditions to be performed by the lessee and abides by all of the rules and regulations as set forth herein, lessee shall have peaceful and quiet enjoyment of the demised premises for the term of this lease.

No Broker Clause

The lessor and the lessee agree that this lease was directly negotiated between them and that no broker was involved in bringing about this agreement. No claim of a broker's fee shall be made against either party.

Broker's Commission (With further provision if tenant exercises option)

It is agreed that_____Realty, Inc. is the real estate brokerage office that negotiated and completed this lease. That they are the only ones entitled to the commission. Said commission, which shall be in the amount of $_____ _____, is payable by the lessor at the time of execution of this lease agreement. It is also agreed that if, as and when the lessee exercises the option contained herein to renew the lease or to purchase the premises, an additional commission in accordance with the recommendated rates of the_____City Real Estate Board will be paid to them by the lessor.

Attorney's Fees

Lessee agrees to pay all court costs and other expenses of collection as well as reasonable attorney's fees on any matter pertaining to rental collection, distress or foreclosure suit.

Extension Clause

In the event the lessee occupies said premises after the expiration date of this lease with the consent of the lessor, expressly or implied, such possession shall be considered to be a tenancy from month to month. Said lessee shall pay lessor for occupancy of the premises the sum of $_____ per month for such period as lessee may remain in possession thereof.

Subordination Of Lease To Mortgages

This lease shall be subject and subordinate to any mortgage or mortgages now on the premises or ones hereinafter placed upon it and to any and all future improvements made to the land comprising the demised premises. The lessee agrees to execute, upon request, any document or documents the lessor finds necessary to accomplish such subordination of this lease to the liens of any such mortgage or mortgages. Further, the lessor is designated as attorney in fact to execute such a document or documents in the name of the lessee as his act and deed.

Payment Of Taxes

The lessor shall be responsible for the payment of all real estate taxes assessed against the demised premises during the term of this lease.

Payment of Utilities

During the term of this lease the lessee shall pay all utility charges on the leased premises and will make such payments when they become due. In the event the lessee fails to make a payment when due the lessor may make said payment and the charges shall be added to and become a part of the lessee's regular rent. It shall be considered as an additional rent payment by the lessee to the lessor, payable at the time the regular rent payment is due. Utilities in this paragraph refers to gas, electricity, telephone and water.

Payment of Utilities (Another form)

The lessee shall be responsible for the prompt payment of the following utilities: Gas, electricity, water, telephone.

Giving Notice By Registered Mail

It is understood and agreed between the parties hereto, that in the event of it becoming necessary for either party to give the other written notice, the party giving such notice shall do so by U. S. Registered Mail, postage paid. If the lessee is to be the recipient of said notice it shall be addressed to him at the demised premises, and if the lessor, to the following address, to wit:_____Street,_____City, State of_____.

Assignment

The lessee shall not assign, transfer, sub-lease, mortgage, pledge or otherwise encumber or dispose of this lease or any portion thereof without written permission of the lessor. If any assignment is made without said specific written permission, it shall be declared void and the lessor, at his option, may cancel this lease and the lessee shall become liable for the balance of the entire remaining rental due. However, such consent shall not be unreasonably withheld by the lessor to a financially and morally responsible person.

Signs

The lessee agrees not to affix, exhibit, attach or allow any sign, writing or printed matter to be placed in any window, door or wall of the demised premises without first obtaining the lessor's written consent.

Agreement To Pay Increase In Insurance Rate

If the lessee by reason of his use of the demised premises either by improper, increased or excessive usage or for any reason whatsoever cause an increase in insurance rates, then the lessee shall compensate the lessor by paying additional rent to equal the increased rate, payable on the first day of the month following such increase. However, the lessee shall be given the opportunity to attempt to remove said rate increase by complying with recommendations made by the lessor, his insurance company or any other government authorized regulatory body.

Time Is Of The Essence

The lessor and lessee understand and agree that time is of the essence of all of the terms and provisions of this lease agreement.

14

Liens

14

Liens

A Lien is a charge or claim upon property which encumbers it until the obligation is satisfied. The property serves as the security, but it does not give the holder title to the property itself.

The most frequently used form of lien in real estate is the Mechanic's Lien. Its purpose is to establish a priority of payment for work and/or materials furnished a particular property. It attaches to the land as well as the improvements upon it.

Mechanic's Liens fall into two distinct categories: a) Those in which the subcontractor's or materialman's lien is dependent upon and limited by the amount due the contractor. This is referred to as the "New York" system. b) Mechanic's Liens in which the subcontractor's or materialman's lien is not dependent upon the existence of any indebtedness due the contractor, but rather is a direct lien against the owner. This is known as the "Pennsylvania" system of liens.

Various jurisdictions in the United States require special wording to legally comply with local requirements. The right to acquire and enforce a mechanic's lien depends almost wholly on these statutes. Specific area requirements should be carefully studied and proper reference made to them when applying the following forms.

No. 14–1
CLAIM OF LIEN
Affidavit Form

State of_____

County of_____

The_____ Corporation of_____Street, City of

_____, State of_____, being duly sworn says that in pursuance of a

contract with_____, that they furnished parts and

materials and performed labor and service work to the air conditioning system consisting

of numerous checking of wiring, pressure points, switches, fuses, etc., and the replacement

of numerous parts to the value of_____ dollars

($_____) on the following described real property:

(Here include legal description)

They further state that the last items of service and material performed and furnished was on the_____day of_____, 19_____, and of the contract price consisting of many service calls, there is unpaid the amount of_____ _____dollars ($_____), for which amount they claim a lien on the real property herein described.

                                                    _____
                                                    President,_____Corp.
Subscribed and Sworn to Before Me This _____
_____ day of_____, 19_____.

No. 14–2
CLAIM OF LIEN
Notice Form

Notice is hereby given that_____has and claims a lien for and on the property located at_____
_____
owned by_____, for labor and materi-als expended between_____, 19_____, and_____, 19_____, in the amount of_____
_____dollars ($_____).

                                                    _____
                                                                    Claimant

An Owner's Affidavit Of No Liens or Mechanic's Lien Affidavit as it is also called is a required form when transferring real estate in many jurisdictions. It states that there are no liens, unpaid bills, judgements or other encumbrances upon the property.

No. 14–3
OWNER'S AFFIDAVIT OF NO LIENS

STATE OF_____)
COUNTY OF_____)

_____ of_____County, State of _____, being duly sworn, upon oath deposes and says:
That he is the owner of a certain tract of land and the improvement thereon in_____
_____County, containing_____acres legally described as_____

That all bills, claims, and demands due, laborers, contractors, furnishers for labor or material entering into the improvements on the above described property, are fully paid for.

That no judgements have been rendered and no suits are now pending which might impair or involve title to said property. That there are no vendor's liens or any other liens of any kind or character now outstanding against said property.

That no petition of bankruptcy has been filed by or against the above named owner within the past_____months in any federal court in the United States.

This affidavit is made for the purpose of inducing_____
_____to purchase said land and to assure him that no liens against the property exist whatsoever.

Sworn to before me this_____
_____day of_____, 19_____.

_____
Notary

No. 14—4
SATISFACTION AND DISCHARGE OF LIEN

This is to certify that a certain lien owned and held by the undersigned bearing date of the_____day of_____, 19_____, was executed by_____
_____against_____and was recorded in the County Clerk's Office, County of_____, State of_____, on the_____day of _____, 19_____, _____in Plat Book #_____, Page # _____, is fully paid and has been satisfied. The undersigned therefore consents that the aforesaid lien may be discharged on the records thereof, according to the statutes in such case provided.
In Witness Whereof:

_____   _____

_____

No. 14—5
ASSIGNMENT OF LIEN

Know All Men By These Presents, That _____, party of the first part, in consideration of_____ dollars ($_____), to him in hand paid by_____, party of the second part, does hereby sell, assign and transfer unto the party of the second part and assigns, a lien bearing date of the_____day of_____, 19_____. Said lien was executed by_____against_____, and was recorded in the County Clerk's Office, County of_____, State of_____, on the_____day of_____, 19_____, in Plat Book #_____, Page_____, together with all right and interest in and to the debt hereby secured; and hereby appoints the party of the second part irrevocably to collect and receive said debt, and to foreclose, enforce and satisfy said lien the same as the assignor might or could have done were this assignment not executed, but at the cost and expense of the party of the second part.

In testimony whereof, the said party of the first part has hereunto set his hand this _____ day of _____ , 19_____ .

_____

Witness:

_____

_____

15

Mortgages

15

Mortgages

A mortgage is an instrument that pledges property as security for the payment of a debt or the performance of an obligation.

Two distinct premises exist as to who retains legal title to mortgaged property. Thirty states hold that the title remains with the owner (mortgagor), and the mortgage creates only a lien upon the property. These states are referred to as *lien theory states*.[1] The remaining states are under the common law or *title theory,* holding that the mortgage acts as a deed, conveying the entire estate to the lender (mortgagee). This conveyance becomes void only upon satisfying the terms of the mortgage.[2]

Statutes in several states regulate real estate mortgages and the foreclosure thereof. In some states the statute permits the filing of a master mortgage and the incorporation of it by reference in subsequent short statement filings. (See Mortgage—Statutory Long Form on page 317, and Mortgage—Short Form on page 320.

The states also vary as to the type of evidence of debt which accompany the mortgage. As an example, the bond form is used in New York, while a note is the instrument in use in Florida. Each state's requisites should be studied before preparing a mortgage and its accompanying instruments.

The various divisions of a sample mortgage form follow.

    a. (DATE)

THIS INDENTURE, made and entered into this_____day of_____, in the year of our Lord One Thousand Nine Hundred and_____.

    b. (PARTIES)

BETWEEN_____, hereinafter called the Mortgagor, which term as used in every instance shall include Mortgagor's heirs, executors,

---

1. Lien theory states include: Alaska, Arizona, California, Colorado, Florida, Georgia, Hawaii, Idaho, Indiana, Iowa, Kansas, Kentucky, Lousiana, Michigan, Minnesota, Montana, Nebraska, Nevada, New Mexico, New York, North Dakota, Oklahoma, Oregon, South Carolina, South Dakota, Texas, Utah, Washington, Wisconson, and Wyoming.
2. Title theory states include: Alabama, Arkansas, Connecticut, Delaware, Illinois, Maine, Maryland, Massachusetts, Mississippi, Missouri, New Hampshire, New Jersey, North Carolina, Ohio, Pennsylvania, Rhode Island, Tennessee, Vermont, Virginia, and West Virginia.

administrators, successors, legal representatives and assigns, and shall denote the singular and/or plural and the masculine and/or feminine and natural and/or artificial persons whenever and wherever the context so requires or admits, party of the first part, and_____ _____, hereinafter called the Mortgagee, which term as used in every instance shall include Mortgagee's heirs, executors, administrators, successors, legal representatives and assigns and shall denote the singular and/or plural and the masculine and/or feminine and natural and/or artificial persons whenever and wherever the contest so requires or admits, party of the second part;

c. (AMOUNT OF INDEBTEDNESS, INTEREST RATE, MANNER OF PAYMENT)

WHEREAS, the said Mortgagor is justly indebted to the said mortgagee in the aggregate sum of_____Dollars, lawful money of the United States, for money actually loaned to the Mortgagor, with interest thereon to be computed from the_____day of_____, 19_____, at the rate of_____% per annum, and to be paid_____

according to a certain bond, note or obligation bearing even date herewith.

d. (DESCRIPTION OF PROPERTY)

The mortgagor hereby mortgages to the mortgagee, ALL that certain

(Here include description)

e. (CONVEYANCE OF PROPERTY[1])

NOW, THEREFORE, for and in consideration of the sum of one dollar in hand paid by the mortgagee, receipt whereof by the mortgagor is hereby acknowledged, and also for the better securing of the payment of the said sum of money and interest thereon, and for the better securing of the performance of the covenants and agreements hereinafter contained, the said mortgagor has granted, bargained, sold and conveyed, and by these presents does grant, bargain, sell and convey unto the said mortgagee, that certain lot, piece or parcel of land above described

f. (SIGNED, SEALED, WITNESSED)

IN WITNESS WHEREOF, the Mortgagor on the day and year first written, has executed these presents under seal.
In Presence Of:

_____   _____

_____   _____

_____

---

1. This paragraph can be omitted in lien theory states.

g. (ACKNOWLEDGED OF MORTGAGE)

State of_____)

County of_____)ss

I, an officer authorized to take acknowledgements according to the laws of the State of
_____, duly qualified and acting, HEREBY CERTIFY that_____
_____to me personally known, this day personally
appeared and **acknowledged** before me that_____executed the fore-
going Mortgage, and I further certify that I know the said person (s) making said acknowledgement to be the individual(s) described in and who executed the said Mortgage.

No. 1–51
MORTGAGE
Statutory Long Form

THIS MORTGAGE, made the_____day of_____, nineteen hundred and
_____BETWEEN_____,
herein referred to as the mortgagor, and_____
_____,
herein referred to as the mortgagee,

WITNESSETH, that to secure the payment of an indebtedness in the sum of_____
_____

_____dollars, lawful money of the United States, to be paid_____
_____

with interest thereon to be computed from_____day of_____,
19_____, at the rate of_____per centum per annum, and to be paid_____
_____

according to a certain bond, note or obligation bearing even date herewith, the mortgagor
hereby mortgages to the mortgagee, ALL_____
_____

TOGETHER with all right, title and interest, if any, of the mortgagor of, in and to any
streets and roads abutting the above-described premises to the center lines thereof.

TOGETHER with all fixtures and articles of personal property now or hereafter attached
to, or contained in and used in connection with, said premises, including but not limited
to all apparatus, machinery, plumbing, heating, lighting and cooling fixtures, fittings, gas
ranges, bathroom and kitchen cabinets, ice boxes, refrigerators, food freezer, air-conditioning fixtures, pumps, awnings, shades, screens, storm sashes, aerials, plants and shrubbery.

TOGETHER with any and all awards heretofore and hereafter made to the present and
all subsequent owners of the mortgaged premises by any governmental or other lawful
authorities for taking by eminent domain the whole or any part of said premises or any
easement therein, including any awards for any changes of grade of streets, which said
awards are hereby assigned to the holder of this mortgage, who is hereby authorized to

collect and receive the proceeds of any such award from such authorities and to give proper receipts and acquittances therefor, and to apply the same toward the payment of the amount owing on account of this mortgage and its accompanying bond or note, notwithstanding the fact that the amount owing thereon may not then be due and payable; and the said mortgagor hereby covenants and agrees, upon request, to make, execute and deliver any and all assignments and other instruments sufficient for the purpose of assigning the aforesaid award to the holder of this mortgage, free clear and discharged of any and all encumbrances of any kind or nature whatsoever.

AND the mortgagor covenants with the mortgagee as follows:

1. That the mortgagor will pay the indebtedness as hereinbefore provided.

2. That the mortgagor will keep the buildings on the premises insured against loss by fire for the benefit of the mortgagee; that he will assign and deliver the policies to the mortgagee; and that he will reimburse the mortgagee for any premiums paid for insurance made by the mortgagee on the mortgagor's default in so insuring the buildings or in so assigning and delivering the policies.

3. That no building on the premises shall be removed or demolished without the consent of the mortgagee.

4. That the whole of said principal sum and interest shall become due at the option of the mortgagee: after default in the payment of any installment of principal or of interest for _____ days, or after default in the payment of any tax, water rate, sewer rent or assessment for_____days after notice and demand; or after default after notice and demand either in assigning and delivering the policies insuring the buildings against loss by fire or in reimbursing the mortgagee for premiums paid on such insurance, as hereinbefore provided; or after default upon request in furnishing a statement of the amount due on the mortgage and whether any offsets or defenses exist against the mortgage debt, as hereinafter provided.

5. That the holder of this mortgage, in any action to foreclose it, shall be entitled to the appointment of a receiver.

6. That the mortgagor will pay all taxes, assessments, sewer rents or water rates, and in default thereof, the mortgagee may pay the same.

7. That the mortgagor within six days upon request in person or within fifteen days upon request by mail will furnish a written statement duly acknowledged of the amount due on this mortgage and whether any offsets or defenses exist against the mortgage debt.

8. That notice and demand or request may be in writing and may be served in person or by mail.

9. That the mortgagor warrants the title to the premises.

10. That the mortgagor will, in compliance with Section 13 of the Lien Law, receive the advances secured hereby and will hold the right to receive such advances as a trust fund to be applied first for the purpose of paying the cost of the improvement and will apply the same first to the payment of the cost of the improvement before using any part of the total of the same for any other purpose.

11. That fire insurance policies which are required by paragraph No. 2 above shall contain the usual extended coverage endorsement; in addition thereto the mortgagor, within thirty days after notice and demand, will keep the buildings on the premises insured

against loss by other insurable hazards including war damage for the benefit of the mortgagee, as may reasonably be required by the mortgagee; that he will assign and deliver the policies to the mortgagee; and that he will reimburse the mortgagee for any premiums paid for insurance made by the mortgagee on the mortgagor's default in so insuring or in so assigning and delivering the policies. The provisions of subdivision 4, of Section 254 of the Real Property Law, with reference to the construction of the fire insurance clause, shall govern the construction of this clause so far as applicable.

12. That in case of a sale, said premises, or so much thereof as may be affected by this mortgage, may be sold in one parcel.

13. That in the event of any default in the performance of any of the terms, covenants or agreements herein contained, it is agreed that the then owner of the mortgaged premises, if he is the occupant of said premises or any part thereof, shall immediately surrender possession of the premises so occupied to the holder of this mortgage, and if such occupant is permitted to remain in possession, the possession shall be as tenant of the holder of this mortgage and such occupant shall, on demand, pay monthly in advance to the holder of this mortgage a reasonable rental for the space so occupied and in default thereof, such occupant may be dispossessed by the usual summary proceedings. In case of foreclosure and the appointment of a receiver of rents, the covenants herein contained may be enforced by such receiver.

14. That the whole of said principal sum shall become due at the option of the mortgagee after default for thirty days after notice and demand, in the payment of any installment of any assessment for local improvements heretofore or hereafter laid, which is or may become payable in annual installments and which has affected, not affects or hereafter may affect the said premises, notwithstanding that such installment be not due and payable at the time of such notice and demand, or upon the failure to exhibit to the mortgagee, within thirty days after demand, receipts showing payment of all taxes, assessments, water rates, sewer rents and any other charges which may have become a prior lien on the mortgaged premises.

15. That the whole of said principal sum shall become due at the option of the mortgagee, if the buildings on said premises are not maintained in reasonably good repair, or upon the actual or threatened alteration, removal or demolition of any building on said premises or of any building to be erected upon the mortgaged premises, or upon the failure of any owner of said premises to comply with the requirement of any governmental department claiming jurisdiction within three months after an order making such requirement has been issued by any such department.

16. That in the event of the passage after the date of this mortgage of any law of the state of_____, deducting from the value of land for the purposes of taxation any lien thereon, or changing in any way the laws for the taxation of mortgages or debts secured by mortgage for state or local purposes, or the manner of the collection of any such taxes, so as to affect this mortgage, the holder of this mortgage and of the debt which it secures, shall have the right to give thirty days' written notice to the owner of the mortgaged premises requiring the payment of the mortgage debt. If such notice be given the said debt shall become due, payable and collectible at the expiration of said thirty days.

17. That the whole of said principal sum shall immediately become due at the option

of the mortgagee, if the mortgagor shall assign the rents or any part of the rents of the mortgaged premises without first obtaining the written consent of the mortgagee to such assignment.

18. That if any action or proceeding be commenced (except an action to foreclose this mortgage or to collect the debt secured thereby), to which action or proceeding the holder of this mortgage is made a party, or in which it becomes necessary to defend or uphold the lien of this mortgage, all sums paid by the holder of this mortgage for the expense of any litigation to prosecute or defend the rights and lien created by this mortgage (including reasonable counsel fees), shall be paid by the mortgagor, together with interest thereon at the rate of_____percent. per annum, and any such sum and the interest thereon shall be a lien on said premises, prior to any right, or title to, interest in or claim upon said premises attaching or accruing subsequent to the lien of this mortgage, and shall be deemed to be secured by this mortgage and by the bond or note which it secures. In any action or proceeding to foreclose this mortgage, or to recover or collect the debt secured thereby, the provisions of law respecting the recovering of costs, disbursements and allowances shall prevail unaffected by this covenant.

19. That the whole of said principal sum shall immediately become due at the option of the mortgagee upon any default in keeping the buildings on said premises insured as required by paragraph No. 2 or paragraph No. 11 hereof, or if after application by any holder of this mortgage to two or more fire insurance companies lawfully doing business in the state of_____and issuing policies of fire insurance upon buildings situate in the place where the mortgaged premises are situate, the companies to which such application has been made shall refuse to issue such policies, or upon default in complying with the provisions of paragraph No. 11 hereof, or upon default for five days after notice and demand, either in assigning and delivering to the mortgagee the policies of fire insurance or in reimbursing the mortgagee for premiums paid on such fire insurance as hereinbefore provided in paragraph No. 2 hereof. If more than one person joins in the execution of this mortgage, and if any be of the feminine sex, or if this mortgage is executed by a corporation, the relative words herein shall be read as if written in the plural, or in the feminine or neuter gender, as the case may be, and the words "Mortgagor" and "Mortgagee" where used herein shall be construed to include their and each of their heirs, executors, administrators, successors and assigns.

This mortgage may not be changed orally.

IN WITNESS WHEREOF, this mortgage has been duly executed by the mortgagor.

IN PRESENCE OF:

_____   _____

_____   _____

(Form by courtesy of Julius Blumberg, Inc., 80 Exchange Place, New York, N.Y.)

No. 15–2
MORTGAGE
Short Form

THIS INDENTURE, made this_____day of_____, A.D. 19_____,

BETWEEN_____
hereinafter called the Mortgagor, and_____
_____hereinafter called the Mortgagee,
WITNESSETH, That the said Mortgagor, for and in consideration of the sum of One
Dollar, to_____in hand paid by the said Mortgagee,
the receipt whereof is hereby acknowledged,_____granted, bargained and sold to
the said Mortgagee,_____
heirs and assigns forever, the following described land situate, lying and being in the
County of_____, State of_____to wit:

and the said Mortgagor do hereby fully warrant the title to said land, and will defend the
same against the lawful claims of all persons whomsoever.

    PROVIDED ALWAYS, That if said Mortgagor,_____
heirs, legal representatives or assigns shall pay unto the said Mortgagee,_____
_____legal representatives or assigns, certain promissory note dated the_____
____day of_____, A.D. 19_____, for the sum of_____
_____dollars, payable_____with interest
at_____percent from_____signed by
_____and shall perform, comply
with and abide by each this mortgage, and shall pay all taxes which may accrue on said land
and all costs and expenses said Mortgagee may be put to in collecting said promissory note
by foreclosure of this mortgage or otherwise, including a reasonable attorney's fee, then this
mortgage and the estate hereby created shall cease and be null and void.

    IN WITNESS WHEREOF, the said Mortgagor hereunto set_____
hand and seal_____the day and year first above written.
Signed, sealed and delivered in presence of us:

_____) _____(SEAL)
)
_____) _____(SEAL)

    A Deed of Trust is the instrument used in some areas of the country as a mortgage.[1]
The document is placed in escrow with a third party who holds it until the obligation is
satisfied. When the debt is cleared the third party delivers the deed of trust to the purchaser,
freeing him of further responsibilities. It is also referred to as a Long Term Escrow or Trust
Indenture.

No. 15–3
DEED IN TRUST

    THIS DEED made this_____day of_____, 19_____, by and between
_____ , grantor, party of the first part, and_____
_____ , trustee, party of the second part, and_____

---

1. Notably California, Illinois, Missouri, Virginia and Washington, D.C., as well as in certain other jurisdictions.

_____, party of the third part,

WITNESSETH:

The party of the first part does hereby grant unto the party of the second part, the following described property

(Here include description)

in trust, however, to secure the balance only of the purchase price of the above described premises, evidenced by the following described obligation:

(Here describe notes or other indebtedness to be secured, and insert name of party for whose benefit same is made)

IN WITNESS WHEREOF, the party of the first part has hereunto set his hand and seal this the day and year first above written.

_____
                                                    (SEAL)

Acknowledgement

This Deed of Trust accepted this_____day of_____, 19_____.

_____
                                                    Trustee

A convenient feature of the following quit claim Deed In Trust form is its completeness on a single page. Margin space is provided for document numbering and for the affixing of riders and revenue stamps. For recording it requires a single frame of microfilm.

No. 15–4
DEED IN TRUST

Another Form

THIS INDENTURE WITNESSETH, That the Grantor

of the County of_____ and State of_____ for and in consideration of_____Dollars, and other good and valuable considerations in hand paid, Convey_____ and Quit Claim_____ unto the CHICAGO TITLE AND TRUST COMPANY, a corporation of Illinois, as Trustee under the provisions of a trust agreement dated the_____day of_____, 19_____, known as Trust Number_____, the following described real estate in the County of_____ and State of Illinois, to-wit:

TO HAVE AND TO HOLD the said premises with the appurtenances upon the trusts and for the uses and purposes herein and in said trust agreement set forth.

Full power and authority is hereby granted to said trustee to improve, manage, protect and subdivide said premises or any part thereof, to dedicate parks, streets, highways or alleys and to vacate any subdivision or part thereof, and to resubdivide said property as often as desired, to contract to sell, to grant options to purchase, to sell on any terms, to convey either with or without consideration, to convey said premises or any part thereof to a successor or successors in trust and to grant to such successor or successors in trust all of the title, estate, powers and authorities vested in said trustee, to donate, to dedicate, to mortgage, pledge or otherwise encumber said property, or any part thereof, to lease said property, or any part thereof, from time to time, in possession or reversion, by leases to commence in praesenti or futuro, and upon any terms and for any period or periods of time, not exceeding in the case of any single demise the term of 198 years, and to renew or extend leases upon any terms and for any period or periods of time and to amend, change or modify leases and the terms and provisions thereof at any time or times hereafter, to contract to make leases and to grant options to lease and options to renew leases and options to purchase the whole or any part of the reversion and to contract respecting the manner of fixing the amount of present or future rentals, to partition or to exchange said property, or any part thereof, for other real or personal property, to grant easements or charges of any kind, to release, convey or assign any right, title or interest in or about or easement appurtenant to said premises or any part thereof, and to deal with said property and every part thereof in all other ways and for such other considerations as it would be lawful for any person owning the same to deal with the same, whether similar to or different from the ways above specified, at any time or times hereafter.

In no case shall any party dealing with said trustee in relation to said premises, or to whom said premises or any part thereof shall be conveyed, contracted to be sold, leased or mortgaged by said trustee, be obliged to see to the application of any purchase money, rent, or money borrowed or advanced on said premises, or be obliged to see that the terms of this trust have been complied with, or be obliged to inquire into the necessity or expediency of any act of said trustee, or be obliged or privileged to inquire into any of the terms of said trust agreement; and every deed, trust deed, mortgage, lease or other instrument executed by said trustee in relation to said real estate shall be conclusive evidence in favor of every person relying upon or claiming under any such conveyance, lease or other instrument, (a) that at the time of the delivery thereof the trust created by this indenture and by said trust agreement was in full force and effect, (b) that such conveyance or other instrument was executed in accordance with the trusts, conditions and limitations contained in this indenture and in said trust agreement or in some amendment thereof and binding upon all beneficiaries thereunder, (c) that said trustee was duly authorized and empowered to execute and deliver every such deed, trust deed, lease, mortgage or other instrument and (d) if the conveyance is made to a successor or successors in trust, that such successor or successors in trust have been properly appointed and are fully vested with all the title, estate, rights, powers, authorities, duties and obligations of its, his or their predecessor in trust.

The interest of each and every beneficiary hereunder and of all persons claiming under them or any of them shall be only in the earnings, avails and proceeds arising from the sale or other disposition of said real estate, and such interest is hereby declared to be personal property, and no beneficiary hereunder shall have any title or interest, legal or equitable, in or to said real estate as such, but only an interest in the earnings, avails and proceeds thereof as aforesaid.

If the title to any of the above lands is now or hereafter registered, the Registrar of Titles is hereby directed not to register or note in the certificate of title or duplicate thereof, or memorial, the words "in trust", or "upon condition", or "with limitations", or words of similar import, in accordance with the statute in such case made and provided.

And the said grantor_____hereby expressly waive_____and release_____ any and all right or benefit under and by virtue of any and all statutes of the State of Illinois, providing for the exemption of homesteads from sale on execution or otherwise.

In Witness Whereof, the grantor_____aforesaid ha_____hereunto set_____

_____hand_____and seal_____this_____
day of_____, 19_____.

_____ (Seal)   _____ (Seal)
_____ (Seal)   _____(Seal)

State of_____ }   I,_____a Notary Public
County of_____ } SS.   in and for said County, in the state aforesaid, do hereby
                                         certify that_____
_____

_____

personally known to me to be the same person_____ whose name_____subscribed to the foregoing instrument, appeared before me this day in person and acknowledged that_____signed, sealed and delivered the said instrument as_____free and voluntary act, for the uses and purposes therein set forth, including the release and waiver of the right of homestead.
Given under my hand and notarial seal this_____day of
_____, 19_____

_____
Notary Public

For information only insert street address of above described property.

No. 15–5
SUBORDINATE MORTGAGE

When a mortgage is second, third, etc., in rank to another, it is called a subordinate or junior mortgage. The instrument used is worded the same as a first mortgage with the additional clauses as follows:

In the event the mortgagor fails to pay any installment of principal or interest on any prior mortgage when the same becomes due, the mortgagee may pay the same, and the mortgagor on demand will repay the amount paid with interest thereon at the legal rate and the same shall be added to the mortgage indebtedness and be secured by this mortgage.

This mortgage is subject and subordinate nevertheless to that certain mortgage.

(Here describe mortgage or mortgages that are superior in rank)

No. 15–6
SUBORDINATION AGREEMENT
Of Mortgage

KNOW ALL MEN BY THESE PRESENTS THAT:

_____, as present legal holder and owner of that certain mortgage dated_____executed by_____ _____, as Mortgagors, to _____, as Mortgagee, recorded _____in Docket_____, page_____, records of_____ _____County, _____ and concerning the real property in_____ _____described as follows:

_____

for and in consideration of the sum of Ten Dollars and Other Valuable Consideration to him in hand paid, the receipt of which is hereby acknowledged, has, and by these presents does waive the priority of the lien of the said mortgage insofar as the following described mortgage is concerned, but not otherwise:

That certain Mortgage dated_____, by_____ _____, as Mortgagor to_____, as Mortgagee securing payment of a note in the amount of $_____dated_____ _____, with interest from the date hereof on unpaid principal at the rate of_____ _____% per annum; principal and interest payable in installments of $_____ _____on the_____day of every month beginning_____ _____and continuing until_____on which date the entire balance of principal and interest remaining unpaid shall be due and payable.

The undersigned, _____, hereby consenting that the lien of the mortgage first above described be taken as second and inferior to the mortgage last above described.

WITNESS his hand this_____day of_____, 19_____.

_____   _____(Seal)

_____   _____ (Seal)

_____   _____ (Seal)

_____   _____ (Seal)

No. 15–7
PURCHASE MONEY MORTGAGE

A Purchase Money Mortgage is one that is taken back by the seller in lieu of cash. The wording is the same as in any other mortgage with the addition of the following line after the description of the property:

Said property is the same premises conveyed to the mortgagee by the mortgagor by a deed bearing even date with these presents, which are given to secure the (payment) (part payment) of the purchase money of the said property.

A lease creates valuable rights in real estate. Although it is considered personal property, it covers an estate. In most jurisdictions a lease may be mortgaged. All of the rights the lessee possesses can be conveyed to the mortgagee.

No. 15–8
MORTGAGE OF LEASE

This mortgage, made the_____ day of_____, 19_____, BETWEEN_____ _____ of_____ St._____ City, State of_____ , party of the first part, and_____ _____ of_____ Ave._____ City, State of_____ , party of the second part.

WHEREAS_____ of_____ did by a certain indenture of lease, bearing date of_____ day of_____ , 19_____, demise, lease, and let unto_____ and to his executors, administrators and assigns, all of singular the premises hereinafter mentioned and described, together with their appurtenances:

To have and to hold the same unto_____ and to his executors, administrators, and assigns, for and during and until the full end and termination of_____ ____ years from_____ day of_____ , 19_____ fully to be completed and ended, yielding and paying therefore unto_____ and to his heirs, executors, administrators or assigns (or, if the lessor be a corporation, paying to its successors or assigns) the yearly rental of $_____ .

(Here set forth the terms of the lease)

and WHEREAS, party of first part is justly indebted to party of second part, in the sum of $_____ , lawful money of the United States, secured to be paid by his certain bond or obligation bearing even date with these presents, in the penal sum of $_____ , lawful money as aforesaid, conditioned for the payment of first mentioned sum of $_____ as by said bond or obligation and the condition thereof, reference being thereunto had, will more fully appear:

Now, indenture witnesseth: That party of first part, for the better securing the payment of the sum of money mentioned in the consideration of said bond or obligation, with interest thereon, according to the true interest and meaning thereof, and also, for and in consideration of the sum of $1.00, to him in hand paid, by party of second part, at or before the ensealing and delivery of these presents, the receipt whereof is hereby acknowledged, has granted, bargained and sold, assigned, transferred, and set over, and by these presents does grant, bargain and sell, assign, and transfer and set over unto party of the second part all _____ (Here insert description of premises as in lease.)

Together with all and singular the edifices, buildings, rights, members, privileges, and appurtenances thereunto belonging or in anywise appertaining, and also, all the estate, rights, title, interest, term of years yet to come and unexpired, property, possession, claim and demand whatsoever, as well in law as in equity, of party of first part, of, in and to said demised premises, and every part and parcel thereof with the appurtenances, and also, said indenture of lease, and every clause, article, and condition therein expressed and contained:

To have and to hold said indenture of lease, and other hereby granted premises, unto party of second part, his executors, administrators, and assigns to his and their only proper use, benefit and behoof, for and during all the rest, residue and remainder of said term of years yet to come and unexpired, subject nevertheless, to the rents, covenants, conditions and provisions in said indenture of lease mentioned. Provided always, and these presents are upon this express condition, that if the party of the first part shall well and truly pay unto party of the second part, the sum of money mentioned in the condition of the said bond or obligation, and the interest thereon, at the time and in the manner mentioned in the condition, according to the true intent and meaning thereof, that then and from thenceforth these presents and the estate hereby granted shall cease, determine and be utterly null and void, anything therein before contained to the contrary in anywise notwithstanding. And party of the first part does hereby covenant, grant, promise and agree to and with party of the second part, that he shall well and truly pay unto party of the second part the sum of money mentioned in the condition of said bond and obligation, and the interest thereon, according to the condition of said bond or obligation, and that said premises hereby conveyed now are free and clear of all encumbrances whatsoever, and that he has good right and lawful authority to convey the same in manner and form hereby conveyed. If default shall be made in the payment of the sum of money or interest above mentioned, or any part of either, then and from thenceforth it shall be lawful for party of the second part and his assigns to sell, transfer and set over all the rest, residue and remainder of said term of years then yet to come, and all other right, title and interest of party of the first part, of and to the same, at public auction according to the act in such case made and provided; and as the attorney of the party of the first part, for that purpose for these presents duly authorized, constituted and appointed to make, seal, execute and deliver to the purchaser or purchasers thereof, a good and sufficient assignment, transfer or other conveyance in the law, for the same premises with the appurtenances; and out of the money arising from such sale to retain the principal and interest which shall then be due on said bond or obligation, together with the costs and charges of advertisement and sale of said premises, rendering the overplus of the purchase money (if any there shall be), unto the party of the first part, or his assigns, which sale, so to be made, shall be a perpetual bar, both in law and equity, against the party of the first part, and against all persons claiming or to claim the premises, or any part thereof, by, from, or under him, them, or any of them.

In witness whereof, I hereunto set my hand, the_____day of_____, 19_____.

Signed and delivered in the presents of:

_____ (SEAL)

(ACKNOWLEDGEMENT)

A Supplemental Mortgage is one that is given as additional Security for paying an obligation. It can be for furniture, equipment or other chattels,[1] as well as for a leasehold interest, as long as it has tangible value.

No. 15–9
SUPPLEMENTAL MORTGAGE

THIS SUPPLEMENTAL MORTGAGE made between the parties hereto covering the premises hereinbefore described is given as further, additional and collateral security by the party of the first part to the party of the second part covering a leasehold interest of the party of the first part in and to the certain premises located at

(Here insert address of leasehold interest)

It is understood and agreed that any and all sums paid on the prior existing mortgage, shall be credited to and applied to the payment of this supplemental mortgage. It is further understood and agreed that on the payment by the party of the first part or owner of either the prior existing mortgage or this supplemental mortgage of the sum of $_____

_____together with any accrued interest on the entire principal sum that may remain due on the date of the payment of said sum of $_____ , then and in that event the party of the second part or the holder of the prior existing mortgage shall and will cancel and discharge the prior existing mortgage, together with the appurtenances and all the estate and rights of the mortgagor in and to said premises, and also all personal property appurtenant to the building erected on said premises and now contained therein or which may hereinafter be contained therein.

Witness:

_____

1. See also Chattel Mortgage, page 329, and Mortgage Of Lease, page 326.

_____   _____(Seal)

_____   _____(Seal)

_____   _____(Seal)

_____   _____(Seal)

No. 15–10
CHATTEL MORTGAGE

$_____ 19_____

ON OR BEFORE, the_____day of_____, 19_____,_____

_____promise to pay to_____

or order,_____Dollars with interest at the rate of

_____percent, per annum from date until paid. Value received.

WITNESS:

_____   _____(SEAL)

_____   _____(SEAL)

_____   _____(SEAL)

And said_____as mortgagor for the purpose of securing
the prompt and full payment of the same at maturity, do give unto the mortgagee,_____
_____, heirs, successors and assigns, a mortgage lien upon the
following property, now in _____possession, custody
and control, in the County of_____ and State of_____
_____, to wit:

And said mortgagor_____do_____hereby warrant
and represent that_____has_____full rights and power
to encumber said property as above set forth, and that the same is free and clear of all other
mortgages, liens or encumbrances, of any kind or nature whatsoever.
And the said mortgagor_____do_____hereby agree
that if said note or any part thereof remains unpaid at maturity, to pay all costs, charges
and expenses together with an attorney's fee of_____per cent, on the amount of
the claim that the said_____heirs, successors, or assigns, may
incur or be put to in collecting said money by law or otherwise.
And the said mortgagor_____hereby waive the benefit of the
Homestead and Exemption Laws of the State of_____ upon the above
described property.
IN WITNESS WHEREOF,_____have hereunto set_____

hand-and-seal this_____day of_____, A.D., 19_____.

_____   _____(SEAL)

_____   _____(SEAL)

_____   _____(SEAL)

_____   _____(SEAL)

No. 15–11
MORTGAGEE'S CERTIFICATE OF REDUCTION

THE UNDERSIGNED, the owner_____and holder_____of the following mortgage
_____and of the bond_____or note secured thereby:

Mortgage dated the_____day of_____, 19_____, made by

_____

to _____
in the principal sum of $_____and recorded in_____of section
_____of Mortgages, page_____in the office of the_____
County of_____, State of_____.

covering premises situate

(Here include legal description)

in consideration of the sum of one dollar, the receipt of which is hereby acknowledged, DO
HEREBY CERTIFY, that there is now owing and unpaid upon said bond_____or
note_____and mortgage_____is_____now a lien
_____on the premises covered thereby only to the extent of the said last mentioned
principal sum and interest.

DATED, the_____day of_____, 19_____.

IN PRESENCE OF:

_____   _____(SEAL)

_____   _____(SEAL)

TRUTH IN LENDING ACT

In order to protect the unsophisticated buyer, the federal government has enacted the
Truth In Lending Act and Federal Reserve Regulation Z. This act and regulation requires
professional lenders to give notice of interest rates and detailed finance charges to individuals
in all loans under $25,000.

As further protection, the individual has the right to rescind the entire transaction within three business days after the required finance charges and interest rates have been disclosed to him. If he elects to rescind the transaction, he is not liable for finance charges. All deposits given by him must be returned within 10 days.

The forms used to effect these regulations follow.

No. 15–12

NOTICE TO CUSTOMER REQUIRED BY FEDERAL LAW

FEDERAL RESERVE REGULATION Z

(To Be Executed in Duplicate)

REAL PROPERTY TRANSACTION   Loan No._____

OTHER THAN PURCHASE SECURED

BY FIRST LIEN ON A DWELLING

The FINANCE CHARGE on this transaction will begin to accrue on_____

_____

The AMOUNT OF THE LOAN in this transaction is $_____Less the

PREPAID FINANCE CHARGE on this transaction which includes:

1. Closing points	$_____
2. Inspection fee	$_____
3. Interest to date of first payment	$_____
4. Mortgage insurance premium	$_____
5. Life insurance premium	$_____
6. _____	$_____
7. _____	$_____
	TOTAL $_____

Equals the AMOUNT FINANCED in this

transaction $_____

This amount includes the following charges:

1. Recording mortgage	$_____
2. Recording deed	$_____
3. Recordings satisfaction	$_____
4. Mortgage tax	$_____
5. Stamps on note	$_____
6. Abstract	
a. Cont. to date	$_____
b. Cont. to show mtg.	$_____
7. Attorney fee for title opinion	$_____
8. Title insurance	$_____
9. Survey (a) Lot	$_____
(b) Final	$_____

10. Appraisal fee $_____
11. Notice of Commencement $_____
12. Tax and inurance escrow $_____
13. _____ $_____
14. _____ $_____

TOTAL $_____

NET PROCEEDS $_____

The FINANCE CHARGE on this transaction totals $_____
The ANNUAL PERCENTAGE Rate on this transaction is   _____%

Payment of principal and interest on this transaction shall be_____monthly installments of $_____beginning on the_____day of_____, 19_____and due on the_____day of each month thereafter. The TOTAL OF PAYMENTS on this transaction will be $_____.

The institution's security interest in this transaction is a Mortgage on property located at_____also specifically described in the documents furnished for this loan. The documents executed in connection with this transaction cover all after-acquired property and also stand as security for future advances, the terms for which are described in the documents.

Describe late payment formula, if any, in accordance with Section 226.8 (b) (4)_____

_____

Describe prepayment formula, if any, in accordance with Section 226.8 (b) (6)_____

_____

Describe rebate formula, if any, in accordance with Section 226.8 (b) (7)_____

_____

Miscellaneous disclosures, or explanations, if any,_____

_____

Fire and other hazard insurance protecting the property, if written in connection with this loan, may be obtained by borrower through any person of his choice, provided, however, the association may, for reasonable cause, refuse to accept an insurer or agency on any such insurance which is required.

I hereby acknowledge receipt of the disclosures made in this notice

BY_____ CUSTOMER_____

TITLE_____ CUSTOMER_____

DATE_____ DATE_____

LOAN No._____

No. 15–13
NOTICE OF RIGHT OF RESCISSION

Name of Borrower(s)

Amount of Loan

Property Address

Notice To Customer Required By Federal Law:

You have entered into a transaction on (date) which may result in a lien, mortgage, or other security interest on your home. You have a legal right under federal law to cancel this transaction, if you desire to do so, without any penalty or obligation within three business days from the above date or any later date on which all material disclosures required under the Truth in Lending Act have been given to you. If you so cancel the transaction, any lien, mortgage, or other security interest on your home arising from this transaction is automatically void. You are also entitled to receive a refund of any down payment or other consideration if you cancel. If you decide to cancel this transaction, you may do so by notifying

by mail or telegram sent not later than midnight of (date). You may also use any other form of written notice identifying the transaction if it is delivered to the above address not later than that time. This notice may be used for that purpose by dating and signing below.

I hereby cancel this transaction.

_____   _____
(Date)   (Customer's Signature)

                                            _____
                                            (Customer's Signature)

* * * * * *

EFFECT OF RESCISSION. When a customer exercises his right to rescind under paragraph (a) of this section, he is not liable for any finance or other charge, and any security interest becomes void upon such a rescission. Within 10 days after receipt of a notice of rescission, the creditor shall return to the customer any money or property given as earnest money, down payment, or otherwise, and shall take any action necessary or appropriate to reflect the termination of any security interest created under the transaction. If the creditor has delivered any property to the customer, the customer may retain possession of it. Upon the performance of the creditor's obligations under this section, the customer shall tender the property to the creditor, except that if return of the property in kind would be impracticable or inequitable, the customer shall tender its reasonable value. Tender shall be made at the location of the property or at the residence of the customer, at the option of the customer. If the creditor does not take possession of the property within 10 days after tender by the customer, ownership of the property vests in the customer without obligation on his part to pay for it.

Loan No._____

16

Options

16

Options

An option is a right or privilege given by an owner to another person to purchase or lease property at some time in the future[1] for a stated price and terms. In most jurisdictions, a valuable consideration must accompany the option agreement for it to be considered valid. The consideration is generally forfeited if the option is not exercised. This, however, is the optionee's only obligation. His loss of the consideration terminates the agreement. If the option is exercised, the amount of the consideration is frequently (but not necessarily) applied as a credit toward completing the transaction. If the option is not exercised, the payment is taxable as rental income received by the seller.

A contract may be in the form of an option, but in reality it is a sales contract with a provision for forfeiture.

An option to purchase property is recordable if acknowledged and otherwise meets recording requirements.

No. 16–1
OPTION
General Form

AGREEMENT made this_____day of_____, 19_____, by and between_____, herein called the first party, and _____, herein called the second party.

IN CONSIDERATION of_____dollars ($_____), the receipt of which is hereby acknowledged, the second party agrees to convey by_____ _____deed to first party or his designates, for the purchase price of_____ _____Dollars ($_____), payments to be made in the following manner:_____ _____, for the real property described as

(Here include legal description)

---

1. An option unlimited as to time of execution violates the rule of law against perpetuities.

Second party agrees to furnish first party a good and marketable title to said property on or before the_____day of_____, 19_____.

Possession of the premises is to be given the first party at any time he may demand on or before the_____day of_____, 19_____.

Witness:

_____   _____

_____

No. 16–2
OPTION
With The Consideration Applied Toward Price

In consideration of_____dollars ($_____

_____) paid to me, the receipt of which is hereby acknowledged, I hereby give to_____, his heirs and assigns, the exclusive option of buying, for the price of_____ dollars ($_____), the following described real estate with the improvements thereon, situated in the County of_____, State of_____, to-wit:

(Here include legal description)

_____ shall have the right to close title on or before the_____day of_____, 19_____, at which time I will execute to him, his heirs or assigns, a good and sufficient_____deed. Upon the delivery of said deed, I am to be paid the further sum of_____ dollars ($_____), which shall be payment in full for the above described property. If the option is not exercised on or before the above specified date, I am to retain the said consideration as liquidated damages. If the option is closed within the specified time, the said consideration is to be applied toward the purchase price.

Date this_____day of_____, 19_____.

Witness:

_____   _____

_____

No. 16–3
OPTION
Another Form

AGREEMENT made this_____day of_____, 19_____between_____

_____hereinafter described as the Seller, and_____
_____hereinafter described as the Purchaser.

WITNESSETH, that for and in consideration of the sum of_____

_____dollars ($_____), paid by the Purchaser, the receipt of which is hereby acknowledged by the Seller, the Seller hereby gives and grants to the Purchaser the exclusive option, right and priviledge of purchasing_____

ALL THAT TRACT OR PARCEL OF LAND with the buildings and improvements thereon, situate in the_____of_____, County of _____, State of_____, briefly described as follows:_____

_____

_____for the sum of_____

dollars ($_____) payable as follows: $_____upon the execution and delivery of this option as hereinbefore provided, which amount Seller agrees to apply on the purchase price if Purchaser elects to exercise the option; $_____upon the acceptance of this option by the Purchaser as hereinafter provided; and the balance of the purchase price, to wit, $_____, in the following manner:_____

_____

Notice of election to purchase hereunder shall be given by the Purchaser in writing by registered mail, addressed to the Seller, at_____

_____on or before_____, 19_____, which said notice shall be accompanied by the payment of $_____hereinbefore specified, and title shall close and the deed shall be delivered at the office of_____

_____at_____o'clock_____.M. on_____

_____, 19_____, following the giving of such notice, or at such time and upon such other date as shall be mutually agreed upon by the parties hereto.

Seller shall convey said premises to Purchaser in fee simple, free and clear of all liens, rights of dower or other encumbrances (unless herein otherwise specified), by a good and sufficient deed of conveyance, in the usual form of a warranty deed, except that if Seller conveys as executor, trustee, administrator or guardian, or in any trust capacity, the usual deed given in such cases shall be accepted. Said conveyance shall also be made subject to all restrictions, easements and conditions of record, if any.

If Purchaser gives a mortgage on the herein referred to premises, to secure to Seller any of the purchase money therefor, it shall be designated therein as being given for that purpose; it shall be accompanied by the usual bond; both shall contain the usual statutory interest, insurance, tax, assessment and receivership clauses, if Seller so requires. The mortgage recording tax, recording fee for the mortgage and the revenue stamps on the bond accompanying the same, shall be paid by the Purchaser as part of the consideration of the said purchase.

Purchaser is to have possession of the premises on the day of transfer of title, except

All rentals, insurance premiums, interest and all matters affecting the property herein referred to, not herein otherwise provided for, shall be adjusted pro rata to the day of the transfer of title.

The transfer is to include, without further consideration and unless herein otherwise stated, all fixtures and appurtenances now in said premises, including the heating plant and all appliances connected therewith, ranges, service hot water heaters, gas and electric chandeliers and fixtures (excepting portable lamps), bathroom fixtures attached, outside shades, screens, awnings, storm sash and storm doors.

The buildings on said premises shall be kept insured by Seller against loss by fire for a sum not less than $_____ until the time of transfer, and any insurance, in case of loss, shall be allowed to Purchaser who shall take the property in accordance with this contract notwithstanding any injury or destruction of the said buildings by fire.

The Seller agrees that_____brought about this sale and agrees to pay the broker's commission therefor, if this option is duly accepted and exercised by the Purchaser.

The stipulations aforesaid are to apply to and bind the heirs, executors and administrators of the respective parties hereto. This instrument may not be changed orally.

WITNESS the signatures and seals of the above parties.

_____ L.S.

_____ L.S.

_____ L.S.

No. 16–4
OPTION
With Purchase Money Mortgage
As Part Of The Consideration

I,_____, of_____
_____County, State of_____, for and in consideration of the
sum of_____dollars ($_____),
do hereby give the said_____, heirs
and assigns, the privilege of purchasing on or before the_____day of_____,
19_____, the following described real estate, to-wit:

(Here include legal description)

at and for the price of_____dollars ($_____),
to be paid as follows, viz:

_____dollars ($_____) in cash and the
sum of_____dollars ($_____) to be secured

by a mortgage[1] or a trust deed on said real estate, in form to be satisfactory to_____
_____; said cash payment to be made and
securities delivered on or before the_____day of_____, 19_____ to_____
_____.

    I also agree to furnish an abstract of title showing good title to said real estate. In case
the privilege of purchase hereby given is executed, the price above named paid and secured,
and the securities accepted, as above provided, I agree to convey and assure the said real
estate to said_____, heirs or assigns, by a good
and sufficient_____deed, reciting a consideration of _____dollars ($_____
_____) free and clear of all liens or encumbrances whatsoever, except as to taxes,
assessments or impositions levied, assessed, or imposed upon said real estate subsequent to
_____.

    This instrument shall not be recorded, but is deposited by the said_____
_____, by mutual agreement, with_____
_____; and in case the privilege of purchase hereby given is not
exercised and the conditions hereof fully performed by said_____
_____, heirs or assigns, and written notice of such exercise and
performance given by _____to said
_____on or before the_____day of
_____, 19_____, said privilege shall thereupon wholly cease (but no
liability to refund money paid therefor shall arise) said abstract of title be returned in good
order and said_____shall at once surren-
der this instrument to _____for
cancellation. During the existence of said privilege of purchase, this instrument shall be
binding on_____heirs, executors, administrators, and assigns, who may
exercise the rights herein reserved by_____and receive the surrender above mentioned.
    Witness my hand and seal this_____day of_____, 19_____.

_____   _____ (Seal)

_____   _____ (Seal)

No. 16–5
OPTION TO LEASE

    THIS AGREEMENT, made in duplicate this_____day of_____

---

1.   The basic terms and conditions of the mortgage are sometimes stated in the option agreement. Sample phraseology follows: "Said mortgage shall be payable $_____per month, including_____% interest per annum until paid in full."

___, 19_____, by and between_____, herein called the Optionor, and_____, herein called the Optionee.

In consideration of_____ dollars ($_____ _____), the Optionor hereby grants the Optionee the exclusive right to lease, on or before the_____day of_____, 19_____, the building and grounds located at _____Street,_____City, State of_____, upon the terms and conditions of the proposed lease agreement that shall be attached to and made a part of this option, and initialed by both the parties hereto for purposes of identification.

In the event the Optionee exercises his option within the specified time, the consideration hereinbefore stated shall be credited him by applying the sum toward the payment of the initial month's rent. If the Optionee fails to exercise the option, the amount of the consideration shall be retained by the Optionor as satisfaction in full for holding the property for the Optionee. However, the Optionor shall make no additional demands upon the Optionee and the agreement shall be declared null and void and of no further affect.

This option to lease may be exercised at any time prior to the_____day of____ _____, A.D. 19_____, at the law offices of_____ _____,_____Avenue,_____City,_____ _____State, upon the Optionee giving written notice to the Optinor of his intention to exercise the option.

Time is of the essence of this agreement.

Exercised in the presence of:

_____   _____
                                                                                Optionor

_____

                                                            _____
                                                                                Optionee

(Attach copy of proposed lease)

No. 16–6
OPTION
To Repurchase Property

Agreement made this_____day of_____, 19_____.

KNOW ALL MEN that_____, of_____Street,_____City,_____State, herein called the first party, purchased on_____, 19_____, from_____ _____, of_____Street,_____City, _____State, herein called the second party, for the purchase price of _____ ($_____) dollars, the below described land, to wit:

(Here include legal description)

It is mutually agreed that the second party has the option to repurchase the subject land from the first party, or his assigns, on or before the_____day of_____, 19_____, for the price of _____ ($_____) dollars. If this option is not exercised on or before the aforesaid date, it shall automatically be declared null and void and of no further effect whatsoever.

Witness: _____(L.S.)
                                                           First Party

_____

                                              _____(L.S.)
                                                          Second Party

_____

No. 16–7
EXERCISE OF OPTION

                                              _____, 19_____

To _____ :
    This is to inform you that pursuant to the option agreement executed by us on the _____day of_____, 19_____, I hereby signify my intention to proceed with the purchase of the property therein described.
    I am ready, willing and able to perform all of the terms and conditions of the agreement and at such time and place designated by you, I will deposit the sum of_____ _____dollars ($_____), in the form of a certified check, as payment in full of the purchase price. At that time I am to receive a properly executed _____ deed of said property, along with all other necessary instruments and closing statements to consummate this transaction.

                                              _____
                                                            Optionee

No. 16–8
EXERCISE OF OPTION
Another Form

                                              _____, 19_____

    You are hereby notified that I elect to exercise my option to purchase your real property located at_____in accordance with the terms and conditions of our option agreement dated_____ _____, 19_____.

                                              _____
                                                            Optionee

OPTION CLAUSES[1]

First Refusal

The Tenant shall have the right of first refusal to purchase the property at the price and terms of any bona fide written offer made for it. Said right to be exercised by notifying the Landlord by registered mail within_____days of his receiving written notice that such a bona fide offer has been made.

Right To Test The Land

The Optionee has the right to take percolation tests and other borings, make surveys and otherwise investigate the land to determine its composition and suitability for his purposes. Upon completing such investigations, the Optionee shall restore the property to its former state, or if any crops or other plantings are thereby damaged, the Optionor shall be reinbursed for its reasonable value.

Option To Renew Lease

On or before_____days prior to the completion of this lease, the Lessee shall have the option to renew same for an additional period of_____years (s), on the same terms and conditions, by giving written notice to the Lessor.

Option To Renew Lease—Another Clause

Tenant shall have the option to take a renewal lease of the demised premises for a further term of_____year (s) from and after the expiration of the term herein granted at a monthly rent of_____ dollars ($_____), and under and subject to the same covenants, provisions and agreements as are herein contained. In the event the Tenant desires to exercise the option herein provided, Tenant shall notify Landlord of such desire in writing not less than_____days prior to the expiration of the term hereby granted.

Applying Part Of Rent Toward Purchase Price

If the Tenant, during the term of his lease, decides to purchase the demised premises, it is mutually agreed that the selling price shall be_____
_____dollars ($_____), payable as follows: (Here include terms and conditions).

It is further mutually agreed that_____% of the total rental payments made shall be applied toward reducing the purchase price.

Mortgagee's Option Upon Default

Any deficiency in the amount of monthly payments shall, unless made good by the Mortgagor prior to the due date of the next such payment, constitute an event of default under this mortgage. At Mortgagee's option, Mortgagor will pay a late charge not exceeding

---

1.   Option clauses shown here appear in contracts, leases, mortgages, as well as other legal instruments.

_____% of any installment when paid more than_____days after the due date thereof to cover the extra expense involved in handling delinquent payments, but such late charge shall not be payable out of the proceeds of any sale made to satisfy the indebtedness secured hereby, unless such proceeds are sufficient to discharge the entire indebtedness and all proper costs and expenses secured thereby.

Second Mortgagee's Option Upon Default Of First Mortgage

Said second mortgage shall provide that a default under the first mortgage is a default under the second mortgage. Should payment of principal and interest remain in arrears for _____days, or should any suit be filed to foreclose the first mortgage, then the entire remaining balance of the second mortgage may become due and payable at any time thereafter at the option of the second mortgagee.

Landlord's Option To Terminate Lease

In the event of a bona fide contract to sell the property, or its condemnation for public use, or due to insolvency of the Tenant, the Landlord reserves the right to terminate this lease by giving the Tenant_____days' written notice, by registered mail, of his intention to regain possession of the demised premises. At the expiration of_____days of Tenants receipt of said written notice, the lease shall be terminated and the demised premises vacated.

Tenant's Option To Terminate Lease

It is agreed that the Tenant shall have the right to terminate this lease in the event that he is transferred to an area beyond_____miles of this city. However, before such cancellation becomes effective, the following conditions must be met. 1. The Landlord be given_____days' written notice of such transfer. 2. The Landlord is furnished bona fide proof that such a transfer is being made by Tenant's employer. 3. The Tenant's rent is current.

Prepayment Right

The Optionee shall have the right to prepay said mortgage, in whole or in part, at any time without penalty after_____year(s).

Assignment By Optionee

The Optionee has the right to sell, assign and transfer all his interest in and to this option agreement.

Option To Terminate An Agreement

Either party shall have the option to terminate this agreement by giving_____ days' written notice to the other, but all the rights and benefits of the parties which accrued prior to giving said notice shall in no way be lost or dissipated by termination of this agreement.

17

Promissory Notes

17

Promissory Notes

A Promissory Note is a person's written promise to pay another, or to the bearer, a certain sum of money, at some specified time in the future. It is written proof of an obligation to repay. In real estate transactions, many states use the Promissory Note as evidence of the debt secured by the mortgage.

A note need not be negotiable for it to be considered valid.

No. 17–1
PROMISSORY NOTE
General Form

$_____ City of_____, State of_____ Date_____

    FOR VALUE RECEIVED, I (or we, jointly, jointly and severally) promise to pay to the order of_____ the principal sum of_____ dollars ($_____) in lawful money of the United States, with interest thereon from _____ at the rate of_____ % per annum until paid, payable on_____ and_____ thereafter, and if not paid as it becomes due, to be added to the principal and become a part thereof and to bear interest at the same rate.

                _____ (Seal)

                _____ (Seal)

No. 17–2
PROMISSORY NOTE
Interest Bearing, Jointly And Severally

$_____ _____(Place)_____ _____, 19_____

    FOR VALUE RECEIVED the undersigned promises to pay to the order of_____ _____ the principal sum of_____ _____ dollars ($_____), together with interest thereon from date at the rate of_____ % per annum until maturity, said interest being payable _____ on the_____ day of_____ and_____ each year; both

principal and interest being payable in lawful money of the United States at_____
_____. Said principal sum to be payable
on the dates and in the amounts specified below, to-wit:

(Here detail the specific terms and any special conditions of the note)

Each maker and endorser severally waives demand, protest and notice of maturity,
non-payment or protest and all requirements necessary to hold each of them liable as
makers and endorsers.

Each maker and endorser further agrees, jointly and severally, to pay all costs of collection, including a reasonable attorney's fee in case the principal of this note or any payment on the principal or any interest thereon is not paid at the respective maturity thereof,
or in case it becomes necessary to protect the security hereof, whether suit be brought
or not.

Deferred principal and interest payments shall bear interest at the rate of_____ %
per annum from their respective maturities until paid.

This note is to be construed and enforced according to the State of_____.

_____ (Seal)

_____ (Seal)

No. 17–3
PROMISSORY NOTE
Interest Bearing, Single Liability

$_____ _____(Place)_____ __ _____, 19_____
_____months after date, I promise to pay to the order of_____
_____ dollars ($_____) at_____
____(Place)____, with interest at_____per cent (_____ %) per annum.
The interest charge is_____dollars
($_____). The total payment is_____
dollars ($_____).

_____ (Seal)

No. 17–4
PROMISSORY NOTE
Installment Payments

$_____   _____,_____
                                     _____day of_____, 19_____

For value received, the undersigned, jointly and severally promise to pay in lawful
money of the United States of America to the order of_____

_____, at_____the sum of_____
_____ ($_____) Dollars, to-
gether with interest at the rate of_____per cent per annum on the deferred balances
until paid; said principal and interest shall be paid in_____installments of
not less than_____ ($_____) each; the first said
installment shall be paid on or before the_____day of_____, 19_____,
and thereafter on the_____day of each and every_____during the continuance of this loan.

Said payments shall be credited first to the payment of accrued interest, and the balance of such payment in excess of said interest shall be credited upon the principal of this note, and thereafter interest shall be charged only upon the remaining unpaid part of the principal. Said payments to continue until the aggregate amount paid on account of principal shall equal to the amount of the total principal promised herein.

If default be made in the payment of any installment under this note and if such default is not made good within thirty days, the entire principal sum and accrued interest shall at once become due and payable without notice at the option of the holder of this note. Failure to exercise this option shall not constitute a waiver of the right to exercise the same in the event of any subsequent default.

This note and deferred interest payments shall bear interest at the rate of_____ per cent per annum from maturity until paid. This note is secured by a_____ mortgage.

Now, should it become necessary to collect this note through an attorney each of us, whether maker or endorser, hereby agrees to pay all costs of collection, including a reasonable attorney's fee and hereby waives presentment for payment, protest, and notice of protest and nonpayment of this note.

_____ (SEAL)

_____ (SEAL)

No. 17–5
PROMISSORY NOTE
Secured By A Mortgage

$_____ _____(Place)____ Date_____

FOR VALUE RECEIVED the undersigned jointly and severally promise to pay to the order of_____ the principal sum of_____ dollars ($____ _____) together with interest thereon from this date at the rate of_____per cent per annum until maturity. The said principal and interest being payable at_____ _____, or at such other place as the holder hereof may designate in writing. The said principal and interest being payable as follows:

(Here include the specific terms of the note)

This note may be prepaid in whole or in part at any time without penalty.

This note is secured by a mortgage of even date herewith and is to be construed and enforced according to the laws of the State of_____. Upon the makers' failure to pay any sum required to be paid by the terms of this note or the securing mortgage, promptly when they severally become, or upon the breach of any stipulation, agreement or covenant of this note or of the securing mortgage, the entire sum of principal and interest remaining unpaid shall, at the option of the holder hereof, become immediately due and payable. Failure to exercise said option shall not constitute a waiver of the right to exercise the same at any subsequent time.

This note, including any installment payment of principal and/or interest, shall bear interest at the rate of_____% per annum from the respective maturity dates thereof until paid.

Each maker and endorser agrees, jointly and severally, to pay all cost of collection, including a reasonable attorney's fee, if this note, including any installment payment, is not paid promptly when due, and the same is given to any attorney for collection, whether suit be brought or not.

Each maker and endorser severally waives demand, protest and notice of maturity, non-payment or protest and notice of maturity, non-payment or protest and all other requirements necessary to hold each of them liable as makers and endorsers.

_____(Seal)

_____(Seal)

No 17–6
PROMISSORY NOTE
Secured By A Mortgage
Another Form

_____ City_____ 19_____

$_____

FOR VALUE RECEIVED,

promise to pay to

or order, at

or at such other place as may be designated in writing by the holder of this note, the principal sum of_____ dollars, with interest thereon to be computed from the date hereof, at the rate of_____per centum per annum and to be paid on the_____ day of_____, 19_____, next ensuing and_____thereafter.

IT IS HEREBY EXPRESSLY AGREED, that the said principal sum secured by this note shall become due at the option of the holder thereof on the happening of any default or event by which, under the terms of the mortgage securing this note, said principal sum may or shall become due and payable; also, that all of the covenants, conditions and agreements contained in said mortgage are hereby made part of this instrument.

Presentment for payment, notice of dishonor, protest and notice of protest are hereby waived.

This note is secured by a mortgage made by the maker to the payee of even date herewith, on property situate in the

This note may not be changed orally.

STATE OF_____, COUNTY OF_____ ss:

On the_____day of_____, 19_____, before me personally came _____to me known to be the individual described in and who executed the foregoing instrument, and acknowledged that _____executed the same.

STATE OF_____, COUNTY OF_____ ss:

On the_____day of_____, 19_____, before me personally came _____the subscribing witness to the foregoing instrument, with whom I am personally acquainted, who being by me duly sworn, did depose and say that_____he resides at No._____; that_____he knows_____ _____to be the individual described in and who executed the foregoing instrument; that_____he, said subscribing witness, was present and saw_____ _____execute the same; and that_____he, said witness, at the same time subscribed_____ name as witness thereto.

THE UNDERSIGNED, the owner_____and holder_____of the following mortgage _____and of the bond_____or note secured thereby:

Mortgage dated the_____day of_____, 19_____, made

by

to

in the principal sum of $_____ and recorded in liber_____

of section_____of Mortgages, page_____, in the office of the _____ of the covering premises situate

in consideration of the sum of one dollar, the receipt of which is hereby acknowledged, DO _____HEREBY CERTIFY, that there is now owing and unpaid upon said bond_____or note_____and mortgage_____the principal sum of_____dollars, with interest thereon at the rate of _____per centum per annum from the_____day of_____, 19_____; and that said mortgage_____is_____ now a lien_____on the premises covered thereby only to the extent of the said last mentioned principal sum and interest.

DATED, the_____day of_____, 19_____.

IN PRESENCE OF:

STATE OF_____, COUNTY OF_____ ss:

On the_____day of_____, 19_____, before me personally came_____
_____to me known to be the individual described in and who executed the
foregoing instrument, and acknowledged that_____executed the same.

No. 17–7
BUILDING LOAN MORTGAGE NOTE

_____ City, 19_____

FOR VALUE RECEIVED,_____
promise to pay to_____
or order to pay to_____
or order, at_____
or at such other place as may be designated in writing by the holder of this note, the principal sum of_____dollars, or so much thereof as
may be advanced, on_____
with interest thereon to be computed from the date of each advance, at the rate of_____
_____per centum per annum and to be paid on the_____day of_____,
19_____, next ensuing and_____thereafter.
IT IS HEREBY EXPRESSLY AGREED, that the said principal sum secured by this note
shall at the option of the holder thereof become due on the happening of any default or
event by which, under the terms of the mortgage securing this note or of the building loan
contract mentioned in said mortgage, principal sum may or shall become due and payable;
also, that all of the covenants, conditions and agreements contained in said mortgage and
building loan contract are hereby made part of this instrument.
Presentment for payment, notice of dishonor, protest and notice of protest are hereby
waived.
This note is secured by a mortgage made by the maker to the payee of even date herewith,
on property situate in the_____.
This note may not be changed or terminated orally.

_____

CLAUSES IN PROMISSORY NOTES

Note Being One Of A Series

This note is number one of a series of_____similar notes. Upon the default of
any one, all unpaid notes in the series shall automatically and without notice become due
and payable at once.

Payment Of Attorney's Fees

In the event of delinquency of principal or interest payment of this note, and it becomes
necessary to retain an attorney for collection, we agree to pay reasonable attorney's fees,
whether suit be brought or not.

Prepayment Privilege

This note may be prepaid at any time before maturity, in whole or in part, without penalty.

Grace Period

There shall be a_____day grace period allowed before any installment shall be deemed in default.

Balloon Mortgage[1]

This is a balloon mortgage and the final payment of the balance due upon maturity is $_____, together with accrued interest, if any, and all advancement made by the mortgagee under the terms of this mortgage.

Penalty for Default

It is hereby expressly agreed that should any default be made in the payment of any installment of principal or interest on any day whereon the same is payable, or if any default be made, and should not be corrected within_____days, the balance of said principal sum, with all arrearages of interest thereon, shall, at the option of the holder of this note, become due and payable immediately.

---

1. Some states require that mortgage payments calling for a larger final payment be clearly identified on the instrument. The balloon clause given here is required by Florida statutes.

18

Property Management

18

Property Management

The management of income producing properties encompasses leasing, service to tenants, maintenance and repairs, hiring personnel, collecting rents, purchasing and accounting. Income and commercial properties such as office buildings, apartment houses, factories, shopping centers, stores, warehouses, hotels and motels are frequently managed by trained individuals and firms specializing in this field of real estate.

Profitable management requires professional know how. Utilizing and maintaining the property so that it will bring the highest income for the longest period of time is the prime objective of good management.

In some states a property manager must be licensed if he is to receive a commission for effecting rentals. The real estate license laws of the state concerned should be studied.

Harmonious owner-manager relationship is of first importance. Each has certain duties and obligations to the other. To avoid misunderstandings it is wise to have a written agreement outlining all areas of responsibilities as well as what the compensation will be. A letter of agreement will often serve this purpose, or a more formal, comprehensive contract may be used. Examples of both are presented in this chapter, along with other forms of value in the operation of a property management department.

No. 18–1
MANAGEMENT AGREEMENT CONTRACT

PARTIES

In consideration of the covenants herein contained _____

_____

(hereinafter called "Owner"), and_____

_____

(hereinafter called "Agent"), agree as follows:

EXCLUSIVE AGENCY

1. The Owner hereby employs the Agent exclusively to rent, lease, operate and manage the property known as_____

upon the terms hereinafter set forth for the period of_____beginning on the

359

_____day of_____, 19_____, and ending on the_____ day of_____, 19_____, and thereafter for annual periods unless on or before sixty (60) days prior to the date last above mentioned, or on or before thirty (30) days prior to the expiration of any such renewal period, either party hereto shall notify the other in writing of an intention to terminate this agreement in which case this agreement may be terminated prior to the last mentioned date. Either party may terminate this agreement upon thirty (30) days' written notice after the expiration of_____ months of the original term.

RENTING OF PREMISES AGENT TO NEGOTIATE LEASE

2. The Agent accepts the employment and agrees:

a. To use due diligence in the management of the premises for the period and upon the terms herein provided, and agrees to furnish the services of his/its organization for the renting, leasing, operating and managing of the herein described premises.

MONTHLY STATEMENTS

b. To render monthly statements of receipts, expenses and charges and to remit to Owner receipts less disbursements. In the event the disbursements shall be in excess of the rents collected by the Agent, the Owner hereby agrees to pay such excess promptly upon demand of the Agent.

SEPARATE OWNERS' FUNDS

c. To deposit all receipts collected for Owner (less any sums properly deducted or otherwise provided herein) in a Trust account in a national or state institution qualified to engage in the banking or trust business, separate from Agent's personal account. However, Agent will not be held liable in event of bankruptcy or failure of a depository.

BONDED EMPLOYEES

d. Agent's employees who handle or are responsible for Owner's monies shall be bonded by a fidelity bond in adequate amount.

AGENT'S AUTHORITY

3. The owner hereby gives to the Agent the following authority and powers and agrees to assume the expenses in connection herewith:

a. To advertise the availability for rental of the herein described premises or any thereof, and to display "for rent" signs thereon; to sign, renew and/or cancel leases for the premises or any part thereof; to collect rents due or to become due and give receipts therefor; to terminate tenancies and to sign and serve in the name of the Owner such notices as are appropriate; to institute and prosecute actions; to evict tenants and to recover possession of said premises; to sue for in the name of the Owner and recover rents and other sums due; and when expedient, to settle, compromise, and release such actions or suits or reinstate such tenancies. Any lease executed for the Owner by the agent shall not exceed_____ years.

REPAIRS

b. To make or cause to be made and supervise repairs and alterations, and to do decorating on said premises; to purchase supplies and pay all bills therefor. The Agent agrees to secure the prior approval of the Owner on all expenditures in excess of $_____

____for any one item, except monthly or recurring operating charges and/or emergency repairs in excess of the maximum, if in the opinion of the Agent such repairs are necessary to protect the property from damage or to maintain services to the tenants as called for in their leases.

EMPLOYEES

c. To hire, discharge and supervise all labor and employees required for the operation and maintenance of the premises; it being agreed that all employees shall be deemed employees of the Owner and not the Agent, and that the Agent may perform any of its duties through owner's attorneys, agents or employees and shall not be responsible for their acts, defaults or negligence if reasonable care has been exercised in their appointment and retention.

SERVICE CONTRACTS

d. To make contracts for electricity, gas, fuel, water, telephone, window cleaning, ash or rubbish hauling and other services or such of them as the Agent shall deem advisable; the Owner to assume the obligation of any contract so entered into at the termination of this agreement.

SAVE HARMLESS

4. The Owner further agrees:

a. To save the Agent harmless from all damage suits in connection with the management of the herein described property and from liability from injury suffered by any employee or any other person whomsoever, and to carry, at his own expense necessary public liability and workmen's compensation insurance adequate to protect the interests of the parties hereto, which policies shall be so written as to protect the Agent as co-insured. The Agent also shall not be liable for any error of judgement or for any mistake of fact of law, or for anything which it may do or refrain from doing hereinafter, except in cases of willful misconduct or gross negligence.

b. The agent is hereby instructed and authorized to pay mortgage indebtedness, property and employee taxes, special assessments, and to place fire, liability, steam boiler, pressure vessel, or any other insurance required, and the agent is hereby directed to accrue and pay for same from the Owner's funds, with the following exceptions:_____

_____

c. Upon and after the termination of this agreement pursuant to the method described in Paragraph 1 hereof, Owner shall recognize Agent as the broker in any pending negotiations of said premises, or any part thereof, and in the event of the consummation thereof Owner shall pay to Agent a commission therefor at the rate prescribed on Paragraph 4 d. hereof.

d. To pay the agent:
   (1) For Management _____
   (2) For Leasing _____
   (3) For Modernization _____
   (4) For Refinancing _____
   (5) For Sale _____
   (6) For Fire Restoration _____
   (7) Other _____

   _____
   _____
   _____
   _____

e. Other Items of Mutual Agreement. _____
_____

This Agreement shall be binding upon the successors and assigns of the Agent, and the heirs, administrators, executors, successors and assigns of the Owner.

IN WITNESS WHEREOF the parties hereto have affixed or caused to be affixed their respective signatures this_____day of_____, 19_____.

WITNESS:

_____   _____
                                                                          Owner

_____   _____
                                                                          Agent

(Reproduced with permission of the Institute of Real Estate Management, Chicago, Ill.)

No. 18–2
MANAGEMENT AGREEMENT CONTRACT
Another Form

AGREEMENT made this_____day of_____, 19_____, by and between_____
_____
(hereinafter called the "Owner"), and_____Management Corporation, a corporation organized and existing under the laws of the State of_____.

WITNESSETH:

In consideration of the premises and mutual covenants herein set forth, the parties agree as follows:

1. Owner hereby appoints_____Management Corporation as its exclusive agent for the care and management of_____
_____
hereinafter called "the property," located at_____
_____in the City of_____, County of_____
_____in the State of_____.

2. _____Management Corporation shall be authorized and required to establish

and maintain in effect, operating policies and procedures for the Property to assure its most favorable operation from the viewpoint of the Owner's interest. This shall cover all aspects of management such as leasing, tenant relationships, public relationships, maintenance and accounting.

_____Management Corporation shall be authorized and required to take all action necessary in order to assure that such policies and procedures are correctly followed.

_____Management Corporation is hereby appointed the owner's exclusive agent and attorney-in-fact with full power and authority in Owner's name and under seal to advertise the availability for rental of the herein described premises or any part thereof, and to display "for rent" signs thereon; to execute, renew, modify, and/or cancel leases for the premises or any part thereof; to collect rents due or to become due and give receipts therefore; to terminate tenancies and to sign and serve in the name of the Owner such notices as are appropriate; to institute and prosecute actions; to evict tenants and to recover possession of said premises; to sue for in the name of the Owner and recover rents and other sums due; and when expedient, to settle, compromise, and release such actions or suits or reinstate such tenancies. Any lease executed for the Owner by the agent shall not exceed _____years without written approval of Owner.

3. _____Management Corporation shall be responsible for the leasing of available space in the Property to desirable tenants under terms most advantageous to the Owner.

Standards and procedures for negotiation of leases and renewals shall be established and controlled by_____Management Corporation and approved by the Owner.

_____Management Corporation may employ outside brokers or locators to augment the efforts of on-site employees, and pay the commission currently prevailing in the locality. In order to promote such leasing, newspaper advertising, renting signs, circulars, and other forms of advertising may be utilized at Owner's expense.

4. _____Management Corporation shall establish procedures for the collection of rentals and other income from the Property promptly when such amounts become due, and the deposit of all such amounts in a special bank account maintained by_____Management Corporation for the benefit of Owner as set forth in Paragraph 7.

5. *Maintenance and Operation:*

_____Management Corporation shall direct the purchase of necessary supplies; the making of contracts for electricity, gas, water, telephone, refuse disposal, vermin extermination, and for any other utility or service which_____Management Corporation shall reasonably consider advisable. _____Management Corporation will also direct the making of necessary repairs and alterations.

6. *Employees:*

_____Management Corporation shall employ, supervise and control the employment, discharge and salary administration of all servants, employees, resident manager, or contractors, including attorneys and accountants, at Owner's expense, considered by _____Management Corporation to be necessary for the efficient management of the property, and shall be reimbursed by the Owner out of the income from the Property for the wages and salaries of such employees, including payroll taxes and workmen's compensation premiums. _____Management Corporation shall not be liable to the Owner or to others for any act or omission on the part of such employees if_____Management

Corporation has taken reasonable care of their employment.

Owner shall not reimburse_____Management Corporation for salaries or expenses of its executive, supervisors or office personnel.

7. _____Management Corporation shall establish a separate bank account known as the_____Operating Account, and the funds in such account shall be and remain at all time the property of the Owner.

Owner shall advance to_____Management Corporation the sum of $_____, which shall be deposited in said account, and which represents the estimated disbursements to be made in the first_____days following the effective date of this Agreement. Within _____working days after the end of each month,_____Management Corporation shall submit to the Owner an accounting for the expenditures for that period, the balance in the Operating Account and an estimate of the expenditures to be made within the next month._____Management Corporation shall accompany such accounts with a check on the said account for the balance therein less estimated expenses for the next_____days. In the event such estimated expenses exceed the said balance, Owner agrees to pay such excess to_____Management Corporation promptly on demand.

From the Operating Account,_____Management Corporation shall pay all expenses of operating the Property, including but not limited to: salaries of resident manager, maintenance personnel, janitors, maids and security guards, supplies and materials necessary for maintenance and operation, outside contracts such as trash disposal, exterminators, elevator maintenance and landscaping._____Management Corporation shall also, if required by law or contract, maintain an escrow account for tenants' security deposits and advance rentals.

(Other expenses such as Real Estate Taxes, insurance, legal fees, mortgage payments, etc., may be paid by_____Management Corporation or Owner, as may be agreed upon.)

The Owner further agrees to carry, at his own expense, necessary public liability insurance adequate to protect the interests of the parties hereto, which policies shall be so written as to protect_____Management Corporation in the same manner and to the same extent they protect the Owner, and will name_____Management Corporation as co-insured.

As full compensation for_____Management Corporation's services under this Agreement, Owner shall pay to_____Management Corporation the sum of_____ _____percent of the gross income from the Property, which_____Management Corporation may pay to itself monthly out of the Operating Account.

9. *Terms:*

This Agreement shall become effective on the date first written above, and unless sooner terminated as provided below, shall continue in effect until one year from the date hereof. Thereafter, it shall continue in effect unless either party shall serve written notice of cancellation to the other party, in which case this Agreement shall terminate_____days after the service of such notice.

10. *Early Termination:*

This Agreement may be terminated at any time upon the occurrence of any of the following circumstances:

(a) In the event of a bona fide sale or demolition of the property, the Owner may terminate this Agreement on not less than_____days' written notice.

(b) If a Petition in Bankruptcy is filed by either the Owner or_____Management Corporation, or if either shall make an assignment for the benefit of creditors, either party may terminate this Agreement forthwith upon written notice.

(c) Owner may terminate this agreement at any time without cause on_____(____) days' notice to_____Management Corporation.

11. *Assignment:*

This Agreement shall be binding upon the parties hereto and their respective successors and assigns, provided however, that no assignment of any of the rights or obligations of _____Management Corporation hereunder shall be made without the prior written consent of the Owner.

12. *This Agreement:*

This Agreement contains the entire agreement between the parties, and may not be altered or amended except in writing signed by the parties against whom enforcement of the amendment is sought.

Attest: _____Management Corporation

_____   By:_____(Corp. Seal)
            Secretary

Attest: _____(Seal)

_____   By:_____(Corp. Seal)
            Secretary

No. 18–3
MANAGEMENT AGREEMENT LETTER

_____, 19_____

To:_____

_____

_____

                                        Re: Management of Your
                                             Property Known As
                                             _____, Located
                                             At_____

Dear Sir:

This is to confirm our agreement to manage the above described property owned by you for a period of_____commencing_____, 19_____, and ending _____, 19_____.

Our duties as your authorized managing agents shall include a) Overall operation and maintenance of the premises; b) hiring, discharging and supervising resident manager and all other personnel; c) collecting rents; and d) leasing and renewing existing leases.

Monthly statements showing itemized income and expenses shall be rendered to you on or before the_____day of each month. We will maintain a bank account in the name of the property and shall forward you a monthly check if and when the account exceeds $_____.

Expenses for alterations, maintenance and repairs may be made without your consent if the expenditures do not exceed $_____per month. Except in an emergency, all other expenditures exceeding this amount must first be approved by you.

It is agreed that our payment for these services shall be_____% of the gross income per month.

It is understood that this management agreement can be terminated by either party giving the other_____written notice.

Yours truly,

_____
                              Signature

Accepted and Approved:

_____
Property Owner

Management companies have devised a variety of forms to aid them in their day to day duties. Some larger companies have complex bookkeeping systems and daily rent collection and disbursement forms to be submitted by their resident managers. Those presented here should prove helpful in carrying out the business of property management.

No. 18–4
RENTAL APPLICATION

Name_____

Home Address_____

Present Address In_____City Area_____

_____

Years at present address_____Tel No._____

Firm Name or Employer_____Nature of Business_____

Address_____

Position_____Yrs. with Firm_____

Business Tel. No._____

Bank Reference 1._____

         2._____

Personal Reference 1._____

                           Name   Address

_____2._____

Tel. No.   Name   Address

_____ 3. _____

Tel. No.   Name   Address

_____ .

Tel. No.

Marital Status_____ No. of Children_____

Ages_____ Children's Names_____

Type of Apt. Wanted_____ Bed Room Furn.   Unfurn.

Deposit $_____Rental Rate $_____

Next of Kin_____Relationship_____

                         Name

Street_____City_____

State_____ Their Tel._____

                                              _____
                                                        Signature
                                     Date _____

No. 18–5
RENTAL APPLICATION
Another Form

ALL RENTS ARE DUE AND PAYABLE FIRST DAY OF EACH AND EVERY MONTH

Date_____ , 19   No. _____

Applicant_____

Address_____Tel. _____

Employed By_____Tel. _____

Position_____How Long?_____

Present Landlord_____

Present Residence_____Tel. _____

How Long at Present Residence_____Rent _____

Business References (Name and Address)

_____

_____

Banking Account with_____Checking_____Savings_____

Does Applicant Own Real Estate?_____Where?_____

PREMISES APPLIED FOR

Apartment⎤ at_____
House   ⎦

Number to Occupy_____Adults_____Children_____Pets_____

Ages of Children_____

Rent per Month $_____Payment on Account_____

Term of Lease_____Rent Begins_____Will Occupy_____

Signature _____

Remarks _____
_____
_____

(Reproduced with permission of the Real Estate Forms Institute, Boston, Mass.)

No. 18–6
RENT REMINDER

Premises # _____ Rent for month of_____, 19_____
    A rental payment of $_____was due on_____.
    According to our records, a payment has not been received. Kindly arrange to make payment at your earliest convenience. If you have already mailed your check, please disregard this notice.

The Management

No. 18–7
RENT RECEIPT

RECEIPT is hereby acknowledged from_____
_____ the sum of_____
_____ dollars, being one month's rent in advance
for Premises # _____commencing_____
_____, 19_____and ending_____ , 19_____.

$ _____   By_____
                                        Authorized Agent

No. 18–8
INVENTORY FORM
For Furnished Apartment

_____ Apartment No._____
Name of Building

LIVING ROOM	DINING ROOM	KITCHEN
____ Tables	____ Dining Tables	____ Carpet Sweepers
____ Desk	____ Dining Chairs	____ Shades
____ Mirror	____ Buffet	____ Brooms
____ Chairs	____ Rugs	____ Oil Mops
____ Smoking Stands	____ Pictures	____ Wet Mops
____ Lamps	____ Drapes	____ Dust Pans
____ Settee	____ Shades	____ Ironing Boards
____ Ash Trays	____ Scarfs	____ Waste Baskets
____ End Tables	____ Curtains	____ Garbage Cans
____ Rugs	____ Venetian Blinds	____ Water Buckets
____ Drapes	_____	____ Refrigerators
____ Shades	_____	____ Range

_____ Waste Baskets
_____ Pictures
_____ Vases
_____ Table Scarfs
_____ Curtains
_____ Venetian Blinds
_____ Statues

_____
_____
_____

BED ROOM
1   2

_____ _____ Bed, Spring, Mattresses
_____ _____ Bed Pads
_____ _____ Bed Spreads
_____ _____ Rugs
_____ _____ Lamps
_____ _____ Tables
_____ _____ Dressers
_____ _____ Chests
_____ _____ Vanity
_____ _____ Blankets
_____ _____ Chairs
_____ _____ Pillows
_____ _____ Dresser Scarfs
_____ _____ Shades
_____ _____ Curtains
_____ _____ Night Stands

_____
_____
_____

DISHES

_____ Dinner Plates
_____ Bread and Butter Plates
_____ Soup Plates
_____ Pie Plates
_____ Cups
_____ Saucers
_____ Sauce Dishes
_____ Cereal Dishes
_____ Vegetable Dishes
_____ Platters

_____
_____
_____

_____
_____

LINEN
_____ Sheets
_____ Pillow Slips
_____ Face Towels
_____ Bath Towels
_____ Table Cloths
_____ Napkins
_____ Kitchen Towels
_____ Bath Mats
_____ Shower Curtains
_____ Bed Spreads
_____ Blankets

_____
_____
_____
_____

SILVER
_____ Knives
_____ Forks
_____ Small Spoons
_____ Soup Spoons
_____ Sugar Shell
_____ Salad Forks
_____ Butter Knives
_____ Sugar Spoons

_____
_____
_____

_____ Sugar Bowls
_____ Cream Pitchers
_____ Salt Shakers
_____ Pepper Shakers
_____ Ice Tea Glasses
_____ Water Pitchers
_____ Glass Dishes
_____ Water Glasses

_____
_____
_____
_____
_____

_____ Chairs
_____ Towel Rack
_____ Pc. Canister Set
_____ Frying Pans
_____ Grater
_____ 6-cup Muffin Pans
_____ Roasters
_____ Cake Pans
_____ Pie Pans
_____ Bread Pans
_____ Tea Pots
_____ Coffee Pots
_____ Tea Kettles
_____ Stew Kettles
_____ Sauce Pans
_____ Egg Beater
_____ Fruit Squeezer
_____ Pancake Turner
_____ Dish Pans
_____ Double Boiler
_____ Mixing Bowls
_____ Drip Pans
_____ Dippers
_____ Colander
_____ Flour Sifter
_____ Sink Strainer
_____ Strainers
_____ Potato Masher
_____ Bread Box
_____ Bread Board
_____ Rolling Pin
_____ Can Opener
_____ Large Spoons
_____ Large Forks
_____ Carving Knife
_____ Paring Knife
_____ Bread Knife
_____ Bulbs
_____ Stools
_____ Venetian Blinds

_____
_____
_____
_____
_____

I have this date checked the above inventory and assume full responsibility for same. Upon termination of my lease I will return the contents in as good condition as when received, ordinary wear and tear excepted. Any broken or lost articles will be replaced, and the linens, drapes and curtains will be cleaned. If I fail to leave the premises in satisfactory condition, the necessary cleaning and replacement may be done by you, the cost of which may be deducted from my security deposit.

Tenant

Date _____

No. 18–9

RULES AND REGULATIONS FOR_____APARTMENTS

1. The tenants, their family and guests shall have due regard for the comfort and enjoyment of the other tenants, their family and guests in the building. No musical instruments, radio, television or record players shall be played after 11:00 P.M. in such a manner as to create an annoyance or disturbance.

2. No materials, bicycles, garbage, trash or other paraphernalia shall be allowed in the halls, passageways or court areas of the buildings.

3. No pets or children shall be allowed to occupy the premises.

4. No clothing or other materials are to be washed or dried in such a manner so as to be conspicuous to other tenants or other persons in the area. Laundry room is available for the use of the tenants or laundry may be done by hand in the tenant's apartment. Nothing shall be placed upon the outer windowsills or patio and hallway railings and dustmops, clothing, rugs, etc. shall not be shaken, cleaned or placed in any part of the halls or from any of the windows, doors or railings.

5. The management reserves the right to enter any apartment to protect its property at any time, upon notifying the tenant if at home, otherwise without notice.

6. The management shall not be liable for any damages to tenant's property arising from the leaking or overflowing of plumbing installed in the buildings or resulting from the acts of negligence of other occupants of the buildings nor for any personal property stolen from the tenant, occupant or guest of tenant, whether stolen from the apartment, or any other part of the buildings, pool or cabana area, automobiles, etc.

7. No painting shall be done or shall any alterations be made, nor outside television or radio antennas be installed, without the consent of the management. There shall be no nailing, boring or screwing into the woodwork, walls or ceiling without the written consent of the management.

8. Additional locks shall not be put upon any door without the written consent of the management. If permission is granted, tenant shall provide the management with an additional key for right of entry when necessary.

9. Tenants shall not damage or remove furniture, rugs, floors, walls, ceilings, window glass, decorations, locks, plumbing, heating, refrigeration equipment or other equipment and they will be required to pay for any such damage over and above reasonable allowance for normal wear and tear; whether such damage is caused by negligence, abuse or carelessness or whether willfully or accidentally damaged.

10. The management reserves the right to make such other rules and regulations from time to time as may be deemed needful for the safety, care and cleanliness of the premises and for securing the comfort and convenience of all the tenants.

11. The pool and cabana area is provided for the use and pleasure of the tenants and is specifically subject to the rules and regulations posted in the pool area.

12. Visiting guests of the tenants of a temporary nature shall be allowed. However, no tenants shall have guests for a period of time exceeding two days without the specific written consent of the management, and the management reserves the right to make such charges for said additional guests as the management may feel reasonable under the circumstances.

13. Please feel free to discuss any problems with the manager. We will also welcome any suggestions you have to offer.

The Management

No. 18–10
MONTHLY RECEIPTS AND DISBURSEMENTS

Building _____ Month ending _____, 19__

			411	Linen & Laundry	
			470	Telephone	
300	INCOME		412	Legal & Accounting	
300.1	Apartments		416	Office Expense	
300.2	Extra Service Income		400	Advertising	
300.3	Washer Commission		406	Garbage	
300.4	Maid Service		414	Management	
300.5	Miscellaneous		220/21	Payroll Taxes	
300.6	Other			TOTAL	
303	Sales Tax Commission			TOTAL OPERATING EXPENSES	
	TOTAL			Net Opertaing Income	
430	MAINTENANCE				
430.1	Building			Fixed Expenses	
430.2	Lawn & Landscaping		407	Insurance	
430.3	Furniture		420.1	Taxes	
430.4	Pool		420.2	License & Permits	
430.5	Carpets		408	Interest	
430.6	Cleaning			Depreciation	
430.7	Exterminating			Amortization	
430.8	Miscellaneous			TOTAL FIXED EXPENSES	
430.9	Elevator				
	TOTAL			Net Income	
440	REPAIRS				
440.1	Building			Add. Sec. Dep. Rec'd	
440.2	Furniture & Fixtures			Sales Tax Received	
440.3	Pool			TOTAL	
440.4	Plumbing				
440.5	Electric		200	Less Sec. Dep. Paid	
440.6	Painting			Sales Tax Paid	
440.7	Air Condition			TOTAL	
440.8	Mech. Equipment				
440.9	Miscellaneous			DEDUCTIONS FROM NET INC.	
	TOTAL		210	Principal Payment Mtg.	
460	UTILITIES		140	Escrow Fund	
460.1	Electric		150.1	Purchase of Furniture	
460.2	Gas		150.2	Rugs & Carpets	
460.3	Water		150.3	Purchase of Mech. Equip.	
460.4	Sewer		150.4	Grounds Furniture & Furnish.	
460.5	Fuel		150.5	Master METER Deposits	
460.6	Other		150.6	Air Conditioner	
	TOTAL		150.7	Miscellaneous	
450	SALARIES		150.8	New Const. & Remodeling	
450.1	Res. Mgr.			TOTAL DEDUCTIONS	
450.2	Maid			Total Fixed Expenses & Deductions from Net Inc.	
450.3	Maintenance			Net Loss or Gain for Month	
450.4	Other				
	TOTAL				

_____ Management Co.

By _____

19

Real Estate Office Forms

19

Real Estate Office Forms

All real estate offices perform their day to day duties with certain printed forms to more effectively operate their businesses. To keep track of prospects and listings in the most efficient manner possible, many set forms have been devised. A broker's inventory is his listings. Without complete and accurate details of the properties he has for sale or lease, his task would be ten-fold more difficult. Indeed, he could hardly expect to succeed.

Detailed facts of the buyer's needs and the listed properties he has to offer often are the difference between making or losing the sale. Everything about a property must become known to him and then accurately written down. To accomplish this in a proper, logical and orderly manner, printed listing forms and work sheets are in constant use by brokers for every type of real estate transaction. They serve as a check list to assure that nothing of significance is omitted when a presentation is made.

Real estate investors, attorneys, appraisers, mortgage men, accountants, etc. may also find these forms and work sheets valuable tools when obtaining facts in their respective fields.

Few real estate offices use the same information forms. Many devise their own to suit area and individual needs. Those presented here will serve either as a model to use as they appear, or as a guide for setting up one's own.

No. 19–1
ACREAGE

Total Acreage_____   Total Price $_____

Size_____   Price per Acre $_____

Zoned_____   Terms_____

Location_____

Legal Description_____

_____

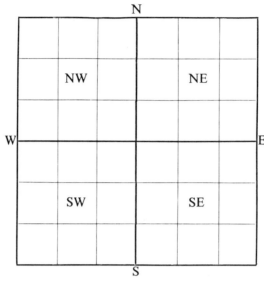

Mortgage Information_____

_____

Taxes $_____ Paved Streets_____ Water_____

Electricity_____ Topography_____

Income $_____

Existing Building (s)_____

Additional Information_____

_____

_____

Owner_____ Listing Salesman_____

Address_____ Exclusive_____ Open_____

Telephone_____ Date_____ 19_____

No. 19–2
APARTMENT HOUSE

Name of Apartment_____

Address_____

Units_____ Stories_____ Type of Construction_____

Age_____ Pool_____ ×_____ Lot size_____

Total Units_____ Number Furnished_____ Number Unfurnished_____

   Efficiencies   _____

   One Bedroom   _____

   Two Bedrooms_____

   Hotel Rooms   _____

   Other   _____

Roof_____ Windows_____ Floors_____ Shopping_____

Bus_____ Children Allowed_____ Pets Allowed_____

Elevator_____Parking_____Carpeting_____

Air Conditioning_____Heating_____Laundry Facilities_____

Recreation Area_____Utilities_____

Miscellaneous_____

Square ft. rentable area and size of each apartment:

Efficiencies _____ _____

One Bedroom _____ _____

Two Bedrooms _____ _____

Hotel Rooms _____ _____

Other _____ _____

First Mortgagee_____

Second Mortgagee_____

Other Lienholders_____

Ground Lease Information_____

Insurance Company_____

Legal Description_____

_____

Remarks _____

_____

_____

Mortgage Information:

Balance 1st Mtg. $_____Payable $_____Int.____% Yrs. to pay out_____

Balance 2nd Mtg. $_____Payable $_____Int.____% Yrs. to pay out_____

Other Liens $_____Payable $_____Int.____% Yrs. to pay out_____

Total $_____Payable $_____

Ground Lease $_____per_____

Recapture between_____and_____@ $_____

Commitments _____

Purchase Money Mortgage Terms_____

Expenses		Income		
County RE Taxes	_____	Eff. Furn.	@ $	$_____
City RE Taxes	_____	Eff. Unfurn.	@ $	$_____
County PP Taxes	_____	1 Bdrm. Furn.	@ $	$_____
City PP Taxes	_____	1 Bdrm. Unfurn.	@ $	$_____
Electricity	_____	2 Bdrm. Furn.	@ $	$_____
Water	_____	2 Bdrm.Unfurn	@ $	$_____
Gas	_____		@ $	$_____
Oil	_____		@ $	$_____
Pool	_____		@ $	$_____
Elevator	_____	Gross Total		$_____
Exterminator	_____	Less Vacancy Factor(___%)	$	$_____
Licenses	_____	Balance		$_____

Management	_____	Misc. Income	$_____
Air Cond.	_____	Grand Total	$_____
Advertising	_____	Less Cash Out	$_____
Insurance	_____	Net Cash Income	$_____
Repairs	_____		
Maintenance	_____	Total Mortgages	$_____
Supplies	_____	Owner's Equity	$_____
Accounting	_____	PURCHASE PRICE	$_____
Garbage	_____		
Landscaping	_____	Cash Required	$_____
Ground Rent	_____	Balance as purchase	
Other	_____	money mtg. @____% with	_____
Mortgage Payments	_____	payments of $____per____	$_____
Total Cash Out	_____	Owner's Equity	$_____

Owner _____   Listing Salesman _____

Address _____ Tel. _____   Exclusive _____ Open _____

Manager _____   Date _____ , 19 _____

Manager's Tel. _____   To Show _____

No. 19–3
APARTMENT HOUSE
Short Form

LISTING _____

PRICE $ _____   Vicinity _____

CASH $ _____   Assessment _____

Construction _____

No. OF SUITES _____   Fireproof _____ Age _____

Lot _____ Laundry _____

Amount $____ At ____% Due _____   No. Storeys _____ Refrig. _____

Payable $_____   Brick _____ Stoves _____

1st Mortgagee _____   Incinerator _____ Inter-Com. _____

Heating _____ Lobby _____

Amount $____ At ____% Due _____   Floor Suite _____ Rec. Pl. G. _____

Payable $_____   Floor Hall _____ Air-cond. _____

2nd Mortgagee _____   Elevator _____ Balconies _____

SUITE	MONTHLY	ANNUALLY	OPERATING EXPENSES
____ Bachelor	_____	_____	Fuel _____
____ 1 Bedroom	_____	_____	Taxes _____
____ 2 Bedroom	_____	_____	Insurance _____
____	_____	_____	Superintendent _____
____ Spaces	_____	_____	Maintenance _____

_____ Garages   _____   _____   Water_____
Sundry Income   _____   _____   Hydro_____
                                                           _____
                                                           _____

        GROSS ANNUAL INCOME $_____
                                                     ANNUAL
        Less Annual Expenses   _____   EXPENSES $_____

        Income Before Debt Charges $_____

MORTGAGE PAYMENTS
        1st mortgage   _____
        2nd mortgage   _____

        Total Payments   _____

PRINCIPAL PAYMENTS (Average___years) $_____   Net Cash Surplus
        Principal on 1st mortgage_____
        Principal on 2nd mortgage_____

        Total Principal   _____

              GROSS RETURN $_____ % of investment

Remarks_____
_____
_____
_____

Apt. Name_____ Address_____
All information furnished regarding property for sale, rental or financing is from sources
deemed reliable, but no warranty or representation is made as to the accuracy thereof and
same is submitted subject to errors, omissions, change of price, rental or other conditions,
prior sale, lease or financing or withdrawal without notice.
                (Reproduced with permission of Lennox Real Estate Ltd., Toronto, Canada)

No. 19–4
BUSINESS OPPORTUNITY

Type of Business_____
Main Location_____
Company Name_____
Total Annual Income_____ $_____
Annual Expenses
Taxes $_____
Insurance $_____

Electricity $_____
Gas & Fuel $_____
Water & Sewer $_____
Rent $_____
Payroll $_____
Payroll Tax $_____
Supplies $_____
Maintenance $_____
Supplies $_____
Advertising $_____
Travel $_____
Entertainment $_____
Other (Itemize)

_____ $_____
_____ $_____
_____ $_____
_____ $_____
_____ $_____
_____ $_____
_____ $_____

Total Expenses ....$_____
Net Income ....$_____

General Information—Replacement Value _____
Income Value_____Good Will Value_____
Mortgage(s)_____
Cash Required $_____PRICE $_____Terms_____
Lease Information_____
Additional Information_____
_____
_____

Owner_____   Listing Salesman_____
Address_____   Exclusive_____Open_____
Telephone_____   Date_____19_____

No. 19–5
COMMERCIAL AND INDUSTRIAL PROPERTY

LOCATION _____   SIZE _____

                                                DATE _____
FOR SALE FOR LEASE DALLAS COUNTY OUT OF DALLAS COUNTY
INVESTMENT VACANT LEASED OWNER-OCCUPANT UNDER CONSTRUCTION
BRIEF DESCRIPTION: _____

LAND DIMENSIONS
LAND AREA   SQ. FT.   ACRES
IN CITY OF   COUNTY   LOT & BLOCK #
OTHER LEGAL

FRONTAGE ON   CORNER OF
ZONING
BUILDING DIMENSIONS:
BUILDING AREA
AMOUNT OFFICE
DISTRICT   YEAR BUILT
CONDITION   CONSTRUCTION
PARKING   OFFICE A/C& HEAT
WHSE. HEAT   CEILING HT. (CLEAR)
TOILETS   RAIL
CAR SPOTS   TRUCK SPOTS
DOCK HIGH   DRIVE-IN DOOR
HEAVY WIRING   SPRINKLERED
OTHER:

LEASE LEASE PRICE$ ANNUAL SQ. FT. RATE
LEASE TERM   DATE AVAILABLE
USE RESTRICTIONS
LANDLORD WILL PROVIDE
TENANT TO PROVIDE

SALE SALE PRICE$ CASH REQUIRED
EXISTING MORTGAGES

1st	$	%INT.	TERM	EXPIRES	PER MO.$
2nd	$	%INT.	TERM	EXPIRES	PER MO.$
OWNER TAKE BACK$		%INT.	TERM	EXPIRES	PER MO.$

PRESENT TENANT   LEASE EXPIRES
PRESENT INCOME   TAXES   INS.
LESS EXPENSES   UTILITIES   MAINT.
NET OPERATING INCOME   MGMT.   REPAIR
DEBT SERVICE   MISC.
GROSS SPENDABLE INCOME   % RETURN ON CASH
LISTED BY   EXCLUSIVE OPEN EXPIRES   SIGN
DATE   EXCLUSIVE RESERVED YES NO EXPIRES
IN FILE (CIRCLE) LEGAL-PLOT PLAN-SURVEY-FLOOR PLAN-MAPS
   OWNER (NAME, ADDRESS, PHONE) OTHER (DESCRIBE)

(Reproduced with permission of Harold Collum Company, Dallas, Texas)

No. 19–6
COMMERCIAL AND INDUSTRIAL PROPERTY
Another Form

Type Building_____   Price $_____
Total Sq. Ft._____   Cash Required_____

Sq. Ft. Rentable_____ Terms_____

No. of Units_____ _____

Location _____

Legal Description _____

Age_____ Lot Size ___ × ___ Zoned_____ Type Const. _____

No. Stories_____ RR Siding_____ Paved Street_____ Sidewalks_____

Floors_____ Roof_____ Heat_____ Air Cond._____ Water_____

Sewage_____ City Taxes_____ County Taxes_____ Insurance_____

Parking Facilities_____ Sprinkler System_____ Windows_____

Other Features_____

Unit	Tenant	Sq.Ft.	Rental	Lease Expires	Remarks

First Mortgage $_____, Held By_____ _____

   Payable Monthly $_____. Including interest of____ %, Until 19_____

Second Mortgage $_____, Held By_____

   Payable Monthly $_____, Including interest of____ %, Until 19_____

Ground Lease or other _____

Listed by_____ Date_____ Exclusive_____ Sign_____

Owner_____ Address_____ Phone_____

No. 19–7
DUPLEX

	I	II
BEDROOMS		
BATHS		

PRICE $_____

DOWN PAY. $_____

LOCATION_____

LOT_____ BLOCK_____ SUBDIVISION_____

LOT SIZE____ × ____ZONED_____ CITY_____ COUNTY_____

DESCRIPTION:

	I	II		
LIVING ROOM			NO. STORIES	
FLORIDA ROOM			SWIM POOL	
KITCHEN			FLOORS	
DINING ROOM			ROOF	
UTILITY ROOM			TYPE CONST.	
GARAGE			SQUARE FT.	
CARPORT			WATER	
PORCH			SEWAGE	
FURNISHED			PAVED ST.	
STOVE			SIDEWALKS	
REFRIG.			TYPE WINDOWS	
AIR COND.			CITY TAXES	
HEAT			COUNTY TAXES	
FIREPLACE			INSURANCE	
AWNINGS			BUILDER	
H.W. SYSTEM			YEAR BUILT	
MONTHLY RENT			KEY AT	
OCCUPANT			WILL TRADE FOR	
OTHER FEATURES				

TERMS:

FIRST MORTGAGE $_____ HELD BY _____

PAYABLE $_____ PER MO., INTEREST _____ %

SECOND MORTGAGE $_____ HELD BY _____

PAYABLE $_____ PER MO., INTEREST _____ %

OWNER_____ LISTED BY_____

ADDRESS_____ DATE LISTED_____

TELEPHONE_____ EXCLUSIVE_____

APPROVED BY_____

(OWNER)

No. 19–8
MOTEL AND HOTEL
Suitable For Sales, Leases, Leasebacks
And Appraisals

The answers to these questions and information attached hereto are to be used for a review appraisal report. It is understood that you have retained us for this purpose and once our staff has completed its analysis of this information, a detailed report will be submitted to you. Answer yes or no, unless otherwise indicated.

1. Name of property_____
2. Date opened_____
3. Address of property_____

4. City and state where located_____
5. Land area_____ __
6. Plot plan (indicate dimensions or attach copy of same)

7. Location map (attach area map indicating location)
8. Plans and specifications (attach basic layout plans and preliminary specifications)
9. Type of construction_____

10. Physical description_____

Number of units_____	Television_____
Number of rooms_____	in all rooms_____
with one double bed_____	Swimming pool_____
with two double beds_____	size_____
with twin beds_____	heated_____
Number of studio rooms_____	type of heating fuel_____
Number of suites_____	enclosed_____
Average room size_____	Children's pool_____
(not including bath)_____	Playground_____
Number of kitchenettes_____	Room telephones_____
Number of baths_____	manual_____
with tubs_____	direct dial_____
with showers_____	message lights_____
with tubs and showers_____	Meeting facilities_____
Type heating_____	describe_____
Type fuel_____	_____
Air conditioning_____	
in all rooms_____	Age of furniture and fixtures_____
type of system_____	Valet and laundry service_____
Height of building_____	Hat check_____
Number of elevators_____	Gift shop_____
Type of elevators_____	Barber shop_____
Radios_____	Beauty parlor_____
in all rooms_____	News stand_____

Baby sitter service_____
Bellman service_____
Airport limousine service_____
Automobile room registration service
_____
Other guest facilities:_____
_____
_____

11. Food and beverage facilities
Is there any food and/or beverage
served on premises?_____
If not, what and where is nearest food
facility?_____
_____
Do you operate or lease_____
If lease give basic terms_____
_____
_____
_____
Hours of operation_____
Do you give a free continental break-
fast?_____
Check if available on premises and
number of seats
Main dining room_____
Coffee shop or diner_____
Banquet facilities_____
Bar/cocktail lounge_____
Meeting facilities_____
Hours of room service_____
Entertainment offered (dancing,etc.):
_____
_____
_____

12. Automobile storage
Type of parking_____
_____
_____
_____
Number of cars accommodated_____
Do you manage parking facilities?____
If not, how are services operated?____
_____

_____
_____

13. Other sources of income
Do you have store space for lease?___
If so, describe in detail and give annual
income
_____
_____
_____
Do you have office or other commer-
cial income?_____
If so, describe in detail and give annual
income_____
_____
_____

14. Real estate appraisal (attach copy of
latest appraisal of the project).
15. Feasibility survey or certified operating
statement (attach copy of latest feasibility survey of this project or certified
operating statements for past 2–3
years).
16. Local tax information
Land assessment $_____
Building assessment $_____
Annual real estate taxes $_____
Annual personal property taxes $____
Other local taxes_____
_____
_____
17. Land cost $_____
Construction cost $_____
Furnishings, fixtures and
equipment cost $_____
18. Do you own your land?_____
If not, give expiration date of land
lease_____
_____
Describe any options (terms, etc.)
_____
_____
_____
_____

If rental not fixed amount, describe

_____

_____

_____

_____

State annual ground rent $_____

State annual ground rent called for in

   option $ _____

Do leases allow subordination?_____

Do you pay land taxes?_____

If not, state amount of taxes $_____

Can land be purchased?_____

   at what price $_____

   when?_____

19. Insurance_____

   Amount of fire and extended coverage

   $ _____

   per annum premium $_____

   Amount of personal liability $_____

   per annum premium $_____

Other insurance policies:

Type of coverage	Amount of coverage	Per annum premium
_____	$_____	$_____
_____	$_____	$_____
_____	$_____	$_____
_____	$_____	$_____

20. Financial data

How much of the project cost is/is to be supplied by a first mortgage?_____ %

What are the terms of this mortgage:

Length_____   Interest rate_____ % per annum

	Monthly	Quarterly	Annually
Constant payment	($)	($)	($)
Constant amortization	($)	($)	($)

If there is/is to be any other type of financing such as equipment leases, chattel mort-gages, etc., attach a separate sheet and give the following information: type of loan; amount of loan ($); length of loan and expiration date; interest rate (% per annum); whether interest payable annually or whether it is an Add-On Interest Loan; amount of monthly payments covering both interest and amortization ($).

21. Name of owner_____

22. Address of owner_____

23. Telephone number of owner_____

24. What franchise, management contract, or other affiliation do you have/plan to have and what are the costs to you for this (both one-time charge and annual fees)_____

_____

_____

_____

25. In addition to answering all the foregoing questions, we require a detailed rate register (schedule) and pictures or renderings of your property (postcards will do). Be sure to attach all information requested herein to this form before mailing same back to us.

(Reproduced with permission of Stephen W. Brener, Sr. Vice President, Hemsley-Spear, Inc., New York, N. Y.)

No. 19–9
ORANGE GROVE LISTING

GROVE LISTING

OWNER _____ DATE _____

LOCATION _____

LEGAL DESCRIPTION _____

ACRES GROVE _____ ACRES LAND _____ TAXES _____

PRICE _____ TERMS _____ IRRIGATION _____

SALESMAN _____

Number Acres	Number Trees	Variety	Age	Root Stock	Production						Gross Income		
					19	19	19	19	19	19	19	19	19
		Valencia											
		Pope Summer											
		Hamlin											
		Pineapple											
		Parson Brown											
		Temple											
		Tangerine											
		Tangelo											
		Marsh Seedless											
		Seeded											
		Pink Grapefruit											
		Red Grapefruit											
		TOTAL											

PRODUCTION COSTS   19 _____   19 _____   19 _____   19 _____   19 _____   19 _____

REMARKS

_____ County_____ Acres File No. _____

Section _____Township _____ Range_____

Legal Desc. _____

N

W   E

S

Location _____

Size _____ Utilities _____

Residence _____ Mortgage $_____

Price $ _____ Taxes $_____

Terms_____

Owner _____

Address _____

Phone _____

Listed By _____

Date _____

Exclusive _____

No. 19–10
OFFICE BUILDING
LISTING FORM

	3
	OFFICE

LOCATION   SIZE

NAME   DATE

FOR SALE FOR LEASE DALLAS COUNTY OUT OF DALLAS COUNTY

INVESTMENT VACANT LEASED OWNER-OCCUPANT UNDER CONSTRUCTION

BRIEF DESCRIPTION

LAND DIMENSIONS

LAND AREA   SQ. FT.   ACRES

IN CITY OF   COUNTY OF   LOT&BLOCK #

OTHER LEGAL

ZONING

FRONTAGE ON   CORNER OF

BUILDING OR OFFICE DIMENSIONS

BUILDING OR OFFICE AREA

NO. STORIES   YEAR BUILT

PARKING   ELEVATOR

FLOOR   CONSTRUCTION

WALLS   LIGHTING

A/C   HEATING

FLOOR LOAD CAPACITY

PARTITIONING

OTHER

TENANT DATA	SQ.FT.	RENT	LEASE EXPIRES	REMARKS
#1				
#2				
#3				

NAMES OF OTHERS

% OCCUPIED   VACANT SPACE   SQ. FT. @ $ POT. RENT

LEASE LEASE PRICE   MO. ANN. SQ. F.T. RATE   LEASE TERM

DATE AVAILABLE   USE RESTRICTIONS

LANDLORD WILL PROVIDE

TENANT TO PROVIDE

SALE   SALE PRICE   REQUIRED

EXISTING MORTGAGES

1ST	$	%INT.	TERM	EXPIRES	PER MO. $
2ND	$	%INT.	TERM	EXPIRES	PER MO. $
OWNER TAKE BACK	$	%INT.	TERM	EXPIRES	PER MO. $

GROSS SCHEDULED INCOME   TAXES

-VACANCY   INS.

GROSS OPERATING INCOME   UTIL.

OPERATING EXPENSES   MAINT. &REPAIR

NET OPERATING INCOME	MGMT.	
DEBT SERVICE	MISC.	
GROSS SPENDABLE INCOME	RETURN ON CASH	
LISTED BY	EXCLUSIVE OPEN EXPIRES	SIGN
DATE	EXCLUSIVE RESERVED YES NO	EXPIRES

IN FILE(CIRCLE) LEGAL-PLOT PLAN-FLOOR PLAN-TENANT DATA-MAPS-
PHOTOS-
OWNER'S (NAME, ADDRESS, PHONE) OTHER (DESCRIBE)

(Reproduced with permission of Harold Collum Company, Dallas, Texas)

No. 19–11
RANCH

Name of Ranch_____ Estab. Since_____

Owner_____ Telephone_____

Address_____

PRICE_____ Cash Required_____

Terms_____

Grazing Acreage_____ Plowed Acreage_____ Fenced Acreage_____

Irrigated Acreage_____ TOTAL ACREAGE_____

Cattle Capacity_____

Crop Production (Type)_____

General Topography_____

Elevations_____

Types of Grasses_____

Oil & Mineral Rights_____ Water Rights_____

Easements_____ Restrictions_____

Dwelling House Details: Age_____ Bedrooms_____ Baths_____

    Dining Rm._____ Kitchen_____ Patio_____ Garage_____ Heat_____

    Air Cond._____ Floors_____ Roof_____ Style Const._____

Other Buildings:_____

_____

Livestock Included In Sale (Give details such as number, breed, age, classification, physical
conditions, etc.)_____

_____

Inventory of Implements, Tools, furnishings, vehicles, etc. _____

_____

Expenses: Taxes_____ Electricity_____ Fuel_____ Materials_____

    Veterinarian_____ Wages & Salary_____ Others_____ TOTAL_____

Income: Cattle Sale_____ Crops_____ Others_____ TOTAL_____

Mortgage Information-

  First Mortgage_____

  Second Mortgage_____

No. 19–12
RENTAL
Residential

BEDROOMS_____ RENT PER MO. $_____

BATHS_____ RENT PER SEASON $_____

FURNISHED_____ COND. OF FURN._____

LOCATION_____

_____

DESCRIPTION:

LIVING ROOM_____GARAGE_____SEWAGE_____

FLA. ROOM_____CARPORT_____TYPE HEAT_____

KITCHEN_____FLOORS_____STOVE_____

DINING ROOM_____TYPE CONST._____REFRIG._____

UTIL. ROOM_____WATER_____LOT SIZE_____×_____

DISTANCE TO SHOPPING CENTER_____

DISTANCE TO BUS STOP_____

DISTANCE TO GRADE SCHOOL_____

DISTANCE TO HIGH SCHOOL_____

LEASE REQUIRED_____SECURITY REQUIRED_____

NO. CHILDREN ALLOWED_____PETS ALLOWED_____

UTILITIES PAID BY:

WATER_____ELEC._____GAS_____GARBAGE_____

INSTRUCTIONS OF OWNER_____

_____

OWNER_____DATE LISTED_____

ADDRESS_____LISTED BY_____

PHONE_____

No. 19–13
RESIDENTIAL

ML	Section Address		BR	Baths	Pool	WATER FRONT	Furn.	PRICE
Listing		**Will**	CONST.		GARAGE		CASH	
Office		**Exchange**	LOT SIZE		CARPORT		FIRST MTG.	
		Yes ☐	ZONING		AWNINGS		HELD BY	
		No ☐	YR. BUILT		AIR COND.		PAYMENT	

ROOF	HEAT	INT.
FLOORS	REFRIG.	SECOND MTG.
WINDOWS	RANGE	HELD BY
LIVING ROOM	WATER HTR.	PAYMENT
DINING ROOM	SPRINKLER SYSTEM	INT.
KITCHEN	PUMP	COMMIT.
FLA. ROOM	WATER SUPPLY	ISSUED BY
PORCH/PATIO	SEWER	PAYMENT

OWNER	ADDRESS	PHONE	DEN	TAXES–CITY	INT.
REMARKS			UTILITY ROOM	TAXES–COUNTY	POSSESSION
			LEGAL		TO SHOW

(Reproduced with permission of the Miami Board of Realtors, Miami, Fla.)

No. 19–14
RESIDENTIAL
Another Form

PRICE $_____

OWNER: _____ TEL.: _____

STREET: _____ BUS. TEL.: _____

CITY–TOWN: _____ AGE: ____

OWNER'S ADDRESS: _____

TYPE: _____ FINISH: _____ COND.: _____

COLOR: _____ NO. ROOMS _____ NO. BED ROOMS _____

LAND AREA: _____ FRONT: _____ DEPTH: _____

LANDSCAPING: _____

1ST FLOOR: _____

_____ _____

_____

2ND FLOOR:

KITCHEN:	RANGE:
BATHS:	OVEN:
FIREPLACE:	LAUNDRY:
TYPE FLOORS:	INSULATION:
TYPE HEAT:	YEARLY COST:
DOMESTIC HOT WATER:	OCCUPANCY:
SCREENS:	STORM WINDOWS:
GARAGE:	OTHER BLDGS.:
MORTGAGE: $	BANK:
ASSESSMENT: $	MONTHLY TAX: $
BETTERMENTS:	ZONING:

BASEMENT:

APPLIANCES INCLUDED:

TYPE SEWAGE:	GAS:	WATER:
SCHOOLS:	STORES:	TRANS.:

STAMPS: BOOKS: PAGE: DATE:

WHY MOVING?   WILL YOU SELL F.H.A.?

F.H.A. APPROVED: $ MAY G.I. BUY?

IF G.I., WILL YOU ASSIGN PRESENT MORTGAGE?

DATE LISTED: BY: SIGN:

SOURCE: EXCLUSIVE: EXPIRES:

KEYS OR ENTRY:

SPECIAL REMARKS:

LISTING AUTHORIZED BY:

For residential sales, some real estate offices find "listing slips" the most convenient way of keeping information concerning a great many houses readily at hand. For use with a loose-leaf notebook, a typical such form provides space for all the necessary basic information, yet need only be about the size of a 3″ × 5″ index card. In this way, a salesman can carry hundreds of listings with him in one compact, interchangeable book. If a house is sold or taken off the market, it is simply removed. New listings are just as easily inserted.

No. 19–15
LISTING SLIP

OWNER_____ DATE_____

ADDRESS_____ PHONE_____

STORIES	WATER	TAXES	OCCUPANCY	EXTRAS
				REFRIGERATORS ☐
ATT.-SEMI-DET.	INSULATED	ATTIC	AGE	WASH. MACH. ☐
GARAGE	HEAT	MATERIAL		SCREENS ☐
LOT	BATHROOM	BASEMENT		STORM WIND. ☐
				VEN. BLIND ☐
1ST MTGE.	HELD BY	INT. & AM.	DUE	FIRE PLACE ☐
ROOMS				FRONT TERRACE ☐
				REAR TERRACE ☐
				RAD. COVERS ☐
LOCATION			PRICE	COMB SCR. ST. ☐
				CARPETING ☐
				STAIR PADS ☐
				FENCE ☐

(Reproduced with permission of National Advertising Co., New York, N. Y.)

No. 19–16
STORES
LISTING FORM

LOCATION_____ SIZE_____

NAME_____ DATE_____

FOR SALE FOR LEASE DALLAS COUNTY OUT OF DALLAS COUNTY

INVESTMENT VACANT LEASED OWNER-OCCUPANT UNDER CONSTRUCTION

BRIEF DESCRIPTION:

LAND DIMENSIONS

LAND AREA		SQ. FT.		ACRES
IN CITY OF	COUNTY OF		LOT&BLOCK#	

OTHER LEGAL

		ZONING	
FRONTAGE ON		CORNER OF	

BUILDING DIMENSIONS

BUILDING AREA

YEAR BUILT		PARKING
CONDITION		CONSTRUCTION
FLOOR		LIGHTING
CEILING		FRONT
A/C		HEATING
WIRING CAPACITY		LOADING AREA

OTHER

TENANT DATA	SQ. FT.	RENT	LEASE EXPIRES	REMARKS
#1				
#2				
#3				

NAMES OF OTHERS

% OCCUPIED	VACANT SPACE	SQ. FT. @$	POT. RENT
LEASE LEASE PRICE$	MO. ANN. SQ. FT. RATE		LEASE TERM
DATE AVAILABLE	USE RESTRICTIONS		

LANDLORD WILL PROVIDE

TENANT TO PROVIDE

SALE SALE PRICE		CASH REQUIRED			
EXISTING MORTGAGES					
1ST	$	%INT.	TERM	EXPIRES	PER MO. $
2ND	$	%INT.	TERM	EXPIRES	PER MO. $
OWNER TAKE BACK$		%INT.	TERM	EXPIRES	PER MO. $

GROSS SCHEDULED INCOME	TAXES
-VACANCY	INS.
GROSS OPERATING INCOME	UTIL.
OPERATING EXPENSES	MAINT. &REPAIR
NET OPERATING INCOME	MGMT.
DEBT SERVICE	MISC.
GROSS SPENDABLE INCOME	RETURN ON CASH
LISTED BY	EXCLUSIVE OPEN EXPIRES SIGN
DATE	EXCLUSIVE RESERVED YES NO EXPIRES

IN FILE (CIRCLE) LEGAL-PLOT PLAN-FLOOR PLAN-TENANT DATA-MAPS-
PHOTOS- OWNER'S (NAME, ADDRESS, PHONE) OTHER (DESCRIBE)

(Reproduced with permission of Harold Collum Co., Dallas, Texas)

No. 19–17
UNIMPROVED LOT

Total Size_____	Price $_____
No. of Lots_____	Price per sq. ft. $_____

Address of Property_____   Price per front ft. $_____
_____   Terms_____
Legal Description _____
_____

```
      N
      |
W—●—E
      |
      S
```

Mortgage Information_____
_____

Taxes–City $_____   County $_____   Total $_____
Paved Streets_____   Sidewalks_____   Water_____
Sewage_____   Electricity_____   Gas_____
Topography_____   Zoning_____
Remarks_____
_____
_____

Owner_____   Listing Salesman_____
Address_____   Exclusive_____   Open_____
Telephone_____   Date_____   19_____

No. 19–18
UNIMPROVED LOT
Another Form

Date Listed_____   Checked_____

Location (est. add.)_____

LEGAL: Lot_____   Block_____

Sub._____

Zone_____   Size_____

Pav. St._____ Easement_____
Sidewalks_____ Elev. _____
Cleared_____ Transp._____
Water_____ To Schools_____
Sewer_____ To Churches_____
Put Up Sign?_____ Tax_____
Building Restrictions _____

PRICE $_____ TERMS:_____

REMARKS:_____

NORTH

WEST

EAST

SOUTH

Listed By:

In amassing information when listing income properties, particularly the large ones, some brokers prefer to use work sheets to be sure of having all of the income and expense facts, cash flow, mortgage costs, capitalization rates, etc. clearly at hand. Unlike regular listing forms, they deal more with the "arithmetic" of the property, rather than the land and the improvements. Four such forms follow:

No. 19–19
SALE-LEASEBACK
(Work Sheet)

Date_____   Listed Property #_____
Owner's Name_____ Company Name_____
Address _____Zip_____
Phone_____
Name of Property_____
Location of Property (City, State)_____

CASH FLOW

Gross Income	$_____	Type (Garden, Hi-rise)	_____
Less: Vacancy_____%	_____	Year Built	_____
		Total Units	_____
Net Income	$_____	Total Furnished	_____
Less: Expenses_____%	_____	Carpeting Furnished?	_____
		Drapes Furnished?	_____
Operating Net	$_____	Utilities Paid By:	_____
Less: Mortgage Servicing	_____	Mortgage Balance	_____
Cash Flow	$_____		

Equity Value (Comp. at 12%) $_____

TOTAL PURCHASE PRICE		PERCENT	CUSHION	
Cash	$_____ ____%		Cash Flow	$_____
1st Mortgage	_____ ____%		Less: Rent	
Purchase Money Mortgage	_____ ____%		(on cash only)	_____
Total Purchase Price	$_____	100%	Cushion	$_____

RENT PAYMENT

RENT: CASH	$_____ × ____%	$_____	(A)
Add: P. M. Morgtage	$_____ × ____%	$_____	(B)
	Total Rent to Investor	$_____	

(A) Seller-lessee will also pay, as inflationary protection to the investor, an additional amount of 25% of the increase in gross rents (less any tax increases off the top) above an agreed-upon figure.

(B) This amount is paid by the seller-lessee to the investor, who in turn pays it back to the seller-lessee. The net effect is to make it a "wash" transaction.

FINANCIAL ADVANTAGES TO SELLER	LEASEHOLD VALUE
	TO SELLER

1. Cash at Closing $_____
2. Total Cash Flow $_____
    Less: Lease Rent   _____
        Excess to Seller $_____ × 20 yrs. ⟶ Excess of $_____

3. Add: Management   capitalized at 10%
   Gross Income $_____ × 5% × 20 yrs. _____   equals leasehold value
4. Add: Inflationary increases in rent   of $ _____ .
        (not computed) $_____   (Item No. 2 below)
   Total to Seller Over 20-Year Period $_____

(Reproduced with permission of Keyes National Investors, Miami, Fla.)

No. 19–20
SHOPPING CENTER
(Work Sheet)

Date_____   Listed Propery # _____
Owner:_____Phone_____
Name of Center_____City_____State_____
Gross Leaseable Area (G.L.A.)_____Year Built_____Mall_____
Total Stores_____ Number Vacant_____Sq. Ft. Vacant_____
Major Tenants_____
Amount of % overage paid for last 3 years:
    Last year $_____Two years ago $_____Three years ago $_____
Do tenants share in real estate taxes, common area maintenance,

                                        Merchants Association?_____

_____
Number of AAA-1 Tenants_____ Total Area Occupied_____
What % is AAA-1 tenants of gross leaseable area_____

INCOME
    Minimum Rents (National & Rated) $_____
    Minimum Rents (Locals)
      Less 5% vacancy   _____ $_____
                          $_____ $_____
    Percentage Rents $_____
      Total Percentage Rents   _____ × 50%
        50% Percentage Rents   _____ $_____
    Other Charges (tax escalation
      common area, Merchants Ass'n)   _____
                        GROSS INCOME $_____ $_____

                         Cents
EXPENSES   G.L.A.   Sq. Ft.
    Northeast   _____ × .58 $_____
    Southeast   _____ × .50   _____
    North Cent. _____ × .78   _____
    Southwest   _____ × .53   _____
    Far West   _____ × .76   _____

Total Expenses $_____

Operating Net   _____
Less: Mortgage Service   _____
PROJECTED CASH FLOW $_____

Existing Mortgage Balance as at_____ $_____
Equity Cash Flow Capitalization at_____%   _____

OUR ESTIMATED PRICE $_____
OWNER'S PRICE $_____

(Reproduced with permission of Keyes National Investors, Miami, Fla.)

No. 19–21
GARDEN APARTMENTS
(Work Sheet)

Date_____   Listed Property #_____

Owner:_____   Phone:_____

Name of Property_____   City_____State_____

Total Units_____Units Furnished_____Units Vacant_____

Year Built:_____   Landlord Provides: Heat (___) Air Cond. (___) Elect. (___)
                         Gas (___) Water (___) Carpeting (___) Drapes (___)

OWNER's figures of actual gross income for last year: $_____

GROSS RENTS (If 100% rented on present rent schedule): $_____

EXPENSES (strike out non-applicable %'s)	% of Gross Income		
Operating Expenses and Vacancy Allowance:	30%		
If Landlord provides Heat:	4%		
If Landlord provides Air Conditioning:	3%		
If Landlord provides Electricity:	2%		
If Landlord provides Gas:	1%		
Furniture Replacement:			
20% furn., add 1% of gross rents			
40% furn., add 2% of gross rents			
60% furn., add 3% of gross rents			
80% furn., add 4% of gross rents			
100% furn., add 5% of gross rents	____%		
Add %'s and Multiply by Gross Income:	____%	$_____	
Actual Real Estate Taxes:	____%	$_____	
TOTAL EXPENSES:	____%	$_____	$_____
	____%		$_____
OPERATING NET:			
LESS:	____%	$_____	
Mortgage Service:	____%	$_____	
Mtg. Participation:	____%	$_____	$_____
TOTAL DEBT SERVICE:	____%		$_____

PROJECTED CASH FLOW: % of Total
                                                      Price

Existing Mortgage Balance as at_____ : _____% $_____
Existing Interest Rate:_____%
Equity: Cash Flow Capitalization at 12%   _____% $_____
                OUR ESTIMATED PRICE: _____% $_____
                OWNER'S EQUITY PRICE: _____% $_____

Note: Do not attempt to present your estimated price over the
       phone or by letter *before you have seen the property*. If
       the property has a good cash flow and the owner wants to
       sell, make an appointment to see *both him and the property*.

(Reproduced with permission of Keyes National Investors, Miami, Fla.)

No. 19–22

MOBILE HOME PARK
(Work Sheet)

Date_____   Listed Property #_____
Owner_____Phone No._____
Name of Property_____City_____State_____
Total Spaces_____Room for Additional Spaces_____
Acres Used_____Available for Expansion_____Total Acres_____
Year Built_____Additions_____
Type Park: Residential_____Transient_____

INCOME
    Space_____ $_____per month $_____
    Vacancy: 5% $_____
    Add: Vending and Utility Income $_____
                    Total Income $_____

EXPENSES
    Taxes $_____
    Operating Expenses at $40 per
        space per year $_____
                    Total Expenses $_____ $_____
                    Operating Income $_____

MORTGAGES
    Interest $_____
    Principal $_____
                    Total Payment $_____
                    CASH FLOW $_____
    Existing Mortgage Balance as at_____ $_____
    Equity: Cash Flow Capitalization at_____% $_____
                            Our Estimated Price $_____
                            Owner's Price $_____

(Reproduced with permission of Keyes National Investors, Miami, Fla.)

Keeping track of active prospects and their real estate requirements can be simplified by the use of prospect record forms or a card file system.

No. 19–23
PROSPECT RECORD

Name_____

Address_____

City_____State_____Phone_____

Prospect Desires:

Date	Property Showed	Reaction

SALESMAN_____   DATE:_____

No. 19–24
PROSPECT RECORD
Another Form

Real Estate Prospected Record   REAL ESTATE NOW OWNED

NAME
_____   _____
_____   _____
_____   _____
                                         _____
LOCATION   _____
Mailing Address_____   _____
_____   _____
_____   REAL ESTATE DESIRED
Phone Number_____   Size:_____
Place of Residence_____   Type:_____
_____   Price:_____
_____   Location:_____
                                             Other:_____
VOCATION   _____
_____   _____
_____   RESULTS
INCOME $_____   _____
_____   _____
_____   _____
                                         _____
FAMILY STATUS   _____
Single_____Married_____   _____
Children: Male, Ages_____   REMARKS
          Female, Ages_____   _____
_____   _____
Other "Family"_____   _____
_____   _____
_____   _____
_____   _____
_____   _____
_____   _____

              Front   Back

(Reproduced with permission of the Real Estate Forms Institute, Boston, Mass.)

No. 19–25
CUSTOMER CARD

BUYER   Section   PROPERTY
_____   _____
                                         Garage
Name _____   Material _____
Address _____   Stories _____
Phone _____   Rooms _____
                                         Price _____
Other Info. _____   Cash _____
_____   _____
_____   _____
                                         _____
How Interviewed _____
Salesman _____   Date _____   (over)

FRONT

Date   Property Shown   No. Fams.   If not interested, Why?

Prospect—Good   Fair   Nat. _____
Form 345—S. J. Clark's Sons, Inc., Real Estate Printing, 135 Union St., Brooklyn, N. Y.

BACK

(Reproduced with permission of S.J. Clark's Sons, Inc., Brooklyn, N. Y.)

No. 19–26
CUSTOMER CARD
Another Form

PROSPECTIVE CUSTOMER INFORMATION

NAME:	DATE:
ADDRESS:	NO. IN FAMILY
LOCATION:	TEL.:
WHEN NEEDED:	
NO. OF B'RMS:	AMT. OF LAND:
NO. OF BATHS:	G. I. OR REG.:
GARAGE:	DOWN PAYM'T:
COMMENT:	APPROX. MO.:
	PRICE:

No. 19–27
CUSTOMER CARD
Another Form

DOWN PYMT	GI ☐	TYPE OF		BASE PAY	WK
	FHA ☐	WORK:		PT OR VA	
	CONV. ☐	TOWN:		WIFE	

NAME	DATE	TOTAL NO. IN FMLY
ADDRESS	AMT. OF LAND	
TOWN		
HOME TEL. NO.	WORK TEL. NO.	
PRICE RANGE	ANY PYMTS	MO. X MO.
NO. OF ROOMS	BASEMENT	
NO. OF BEDROOMS	GARAGE	
TYPE	WHEN NEEDED	
VICINITY: 1st CHOICE	2nd CHOICE	
COMMENT		

(Reproduced with permission of the Real Estate Forms Institute, Boston, Mass.)

As a means of going on record as having shown an owner's property to a prospect, a brief, one-paragraph notice is all that is necessary. It serves the dual purpose of letting the owner know that the broker is actively working on his property, and offers protection to the broker in the event of a commission dispute.

No. 19–28
NOTICE OF PROSPECT

Date:_____

To:_____

_____

Please be advised that today we have presented your property at_____
Street,_____City,_____State, to_____
_____.
The price quoted was $_____. We will endeavor to interest them further. Should they, or anyone representing them, return or phone you directly, please notify us at once. Your cooperation may greatly assist us in satisfactorily completing the sale. You may be assured that we will be showing your property whenever the opportunity presents itself, and we will keep you advised of our progress.

_____

Once a transaction is under contract, a broker has to keep many names, addresses and telephone numbers, as well as a wealth of factual data, close at hand. The principals, their attorneys, the title company, insurance, tax receipts, cooperating office, inventory lists, the amount of the deposit, etc. all have to be held in ready reference. An information sheet for this purpose that is kept inside the file folder, serves a time-saving, useful need.

No. 19–29
SALES INFORMATION SHEET

Date_____

SELLER'S NAME_____Wife_____
   Address_____
   Phone: Bus._____Res._____
PURCHASER'S NAME_____Wife_____
   Address_____
   Phone: Bus._____Res._____
Seller's Attorney's Name_____
   Address_____
   Phone: Bus._____Res._____
Buyer's Attorney's Name_____
   Address_____
   Phone: Bus._____Res._____
PROPERTY_____PRICE_____
Placed In Trust Account: Date_____Amount_____
                Date_____Amount_____

Total In Escrow . . . . _____

Total Commission Due. . . . . _____

COOPERATING REALTOR_____His Salesman_____

  Address_____Phone_____

to receive_____% of total Commission. Paid_____

SALESMAN_____ _____% $_____

LISTING SALESMAN_____ _____% $_____

_____Realtor_____ _____% $_____

Original Source_____

Sign on Location_____yes _____no _____picked up

Expenses: Telephone_____ MLS fees_____

  Miscellaneous_____ Total $_____

Abstract at_____Phone_____

Closed_____Paid In Full_____Publicity_____

Additional Information_____

_____

_____

_____

_____

_____

_____

20

Releases and Satisfactions

20

Releases and Satisfactions

A RELEASE is the discharge or relinquishment of a right, claim or privilege. It is the liberation of a person from any further legal obligation. As it is considered a contract, it must contain a valuable consideration.

A SATISFACTION indicates fulfillment or complete payment of an obligation, while a release just discharges the indebtedeness, without "satisfaction" necessarily taking place.

Releases and satisfactions should be acknowledged in proper form to meet the varied requirements of recording statutes. Each state's provisions should be consulted. When dealing with mortgages, upon the request of the mortgagor, the mortgagee (lender) or his assigns or successors in interest must execute an instrument in proper form for recording, showing satisfaction of the mortgage obligation. With release clauses in mortgages, partial releases of lots may be granted as payments are made. (See Release of Part Mortgaged Premise form, page 413)

Releases and Satisfactions need follow no specific form. There exists, in fact, a wide variance among the states. In Massachusetts, for example, the statutory form is only four lines long. In South Carolina, payment of the debt is acknowledged by writing across the face of the instrument, dating, signing and having the signature (s) witnessed by the recording officer.

No. 20–1
RELEASE
General

To All To Whom These Presents Shall Come Or May Concern, Greeting: Know Ye, That_____, for and in consideration of the sum of_____ _____ ($_____), lawful money of the United States, to him in hand paid by _____, the receipt of which is hereby acknowledged, does by these presents release and forever discharge_____ _____, his heirs, executors, administrators, successors and assigns, of and from all, and all manner of actions and causes of actions, judgments, executions, debts, dues, claims and demands of every kind and nature whatsoever which against_____ _____he has had or now has, or which he or his heirs, executors, administrators, releases and satisfactions_____ successors and assigns have for, on, or by reason of any manner, cause or thing whatsoever from the beginning of the world to the day of the date of these presents.

This release may not be changed orally.

In Witness Whereof,_____ have hereunto set_____hand and seal the_____day of_____,19_____.

No. 20–2
RELEASE
Short Form

Know All Men By These Presents: That I_____, in consideration of the sum of_____($_____), which amount has been paid to me by_____, have remised, released and forever discharged_____ _____from all claims, demands and damages whatsoever from the beginning of the world to the day of the date of these presents.

Dated:_____,19_____.

No. 20–3
MUTUAL RELEASE
Between Buyer and Seller

This Indenture made this_____day of_____, 19_____.

Whereas, differences have arisen between_____, on the one part, and_____, on the other part, subsequent to the signing of a certain contract of sale dated_____, 19_____, covering the following described property:

(Here include legal description)

The first party does hereby release and forever discharge the second party from any claims, actions, or demands which may have heretofore existed by reason of execution of the above described contract.

And the second party does hereby release and forever discharge the first party from any claims, actions, or demands which may have heretofore existed by reason of execution of the above described contract.

Witnesseth, that on the date hereof each party has paid to the other the sum of_____ _____($_____), and each of them have cancelled and delivered up to the other the contract of sale which has been declared null and void and of no other effect.

In witness whereof, we have set our hands the day and year first above written.

_____

No 20–4
MUTUAL RELEASE
Between Buyer, Seller And Broker, Releasing Deposit

This agreement is entered into this_____day of_____, 19_____, between the undersigned buyer, seller and real estate broker who were parties to a certain contract of sale dated_____, 19_____, covering the following described property:

(Here include legal description)

Now this agreement witnesseth, that all three parties hereto, in consideration of each releasing the others from the above described contract from any and all claims, actions or demands whatsoever, which each of the parties hereto may have up to the date of this agreement against any of the other parties by reason of the said contract, do hereby forever release the others, their heirs, executors or administrators, from all claims of every kind, nature and character whatsoever from the beginning of the world to this day.

The deposit(s) being held under the terms of the said contract are hereby directed to be disbursed forthwith as follows:

In Witness Whereof we have set our hands the day and year first above written.

Witnesses:

_____   _____(L.S.)
                                       Purchaser

_____
As To Purchaser

_____   _____(L.S.)
                                       Seller

_____
As To Seller

_____   _____(L.S.)
                                       Broker

_____
As To Broker

No. 20–5
RELEASE OF PART OF MORTGAGED PREMISES

Know All Men By These Presents: Whereas,_____
_____, by Indenture of Mortgage dated_____, 19_____ and recorded at_____, County of_____, State of_____

_____, in Plat Book_____, Page_____, granted and conveyed unto_____
_____and assigns, the premises therein
particularly described, to secure the payment of the sum of_____
_____($_____), with interest as therein mentioned:

Whereas, the said_____ requested the said
_____to release the premises hereinafter
described, being part of said mortgaged premises, from the lien and operation of said
mortgage:

Now, Therefore, Know Ye, That the said_____
_____as well in consideration of the premises as of the sum of_____
_____($_____), to_____
_____, in hand paid by the said_____
_____at the time of execution hereof, the receipt whereof is hereby acknow-
ledged, does remise, release, quit-claim and discharge from the lien and operation of said
mortgage unto the said_____, his heirs
and assigns, all that piece, parcel or tract of land being a part of the premises conveyed by
said mortgage, to-wit:

(Here include legal description)

To have and to hold the same, with the appurtenances, unto the said_____
_____and assigns, forever, freed and discharged of and from the
lien of said mortgage, and every part thereof; Provided, always nevertheless, that nothing
therein contained shall in any way impair, alter or diminish the effect, lien or encumbrance
of the aforesaid mortgage on the remaining part of said mortgaged premises, not hereby
released therefrom, or any of the rights and remedies of the holder hereof.

In Witness Whereof, the said mortgagee has hereunto set his hand and seal this____
_____ day of_____, 19_____.

In The Presence Of:

_____   _____ (L.S.)

_____

No. 20–6
RELEASE OF LIEN

For and in consideration of the sum of_____
_____($_____), lawful money of the United States, to_____
_____in hand this day paid, the receipt of which is hereby acknowledged,_____
_____hereby releases the property hereinafter described from a certain lien filed by___
_____in the office of the Clerk of Circuit Court of_____
_____County, State of_____, on the_____day of_____
_____, 19_____ for the sum of_____

_____($_____) due_____for labor and materials on
said property; and_____hereby declare said lien fully satisfied. Said property is described as follows:

(Here include legal description)

In Witness Whereof,_____. has hereunto set his hand
and seal the_____day of_____, 19_____.
Signed, sealed and delivered
in the presence of:

_____   _____(L.S.)

_____

No. 20–7
RELEASE OF RENT CLAIM

For and in consideration of the sum of _____
_____($_____), lawful money of the United States, receipt of
which is hereby acknowledged, the undersigned hereby declares all present and future
rental payments due by virtue of a certain lease agreement dated the_____day of_____
_____, 19_____, between_____
as lessor, and_____as lessee, as being
fully and completely satisfied, and that the lease agreement is hereby voided, cancelled and
held for naught.

_____(L.S.)

No. 20–8
SATISFACTION OF LIEN

State of_____, County of_____ss:_____
DO_____HEREBY CERTIFY, That a certain Mechanic's Lien, filed in the office of the
Clerk of the_____, County of_____on the_____day of
_____, 19_____at_____o'clock, in the_____noon, in favor of
_____claimant against the Building
and Lot_____situate_____side
of_____Street_____

(Here include legal description)

and known as No. _____in said Street, for the sum of $_____
_____, claimed against_____
_____as owners and_____
_____as_____is paid and satisfied, and_____
_____do hereby consent that the same be discharged of record.

WITNESS the signature_____and seal_____of the above_____part _____this
_____ day of_____, nineteen hundred and
_____.

_____

_____

(Form courtesy of Julius Blumberg, Inc., 80 Exchange Place, New York, N.Y. 10004)

No. 20–9
SATISFACTION OF MORTGAGE
Individual or Corporation

KNOW ALL MEN BY THESE PRESENTS,
that

(Insert residence, if individual, or principal office,
if corporation, giving street and street number)

DO_____HEREBY CERTIFY that the following Mortgage IS PAID, and do_____
hereby consent that the same be discharged of record.
Mortgage dated the_____day of_____, 19_____, made by_____
_____to _____
_____in the principal sum of $_____
_____and recorded on the_____day of_____
_____, 19_____, in Liber_____of Section_____of Mortgages, page
_____, in the office of the_____of the_____
which mortgage has not been assigned of record. Dated the_____day of_____
_____, 19_____.
In Presence Of:

_____

_____

No. 20–10
SATISFACTION OF MORTGAGE
Another Form

KNOW ALL MEN BY THESE PRESENTS, that a certain mortgage dated the_____
_____day of_____, 19_____, made and executed by_____
_____TO _____, which mortgage
was, on the_____day of_____, recorded in Records Book #_____,
_____, page_____, in the office of the Clerk of the Circuit Court of_____

_____County, State of_____ ; given to secure the sum of_____

_____dollars, evidenced by_____certain

note (s), upon the following described property, situate, lying and being in_____

_____County, State of_____ , to wit:

have received full payment of said indebtedness, and do hereby acknowledge satisfaction of

said mortgage, and hereby direct the Clerk of the said Circuit Court to cancel the same of

record.

    WITNESS_____hand and seal this_____day of_____ , A.D.

19_____.

SIGNED, SEALED AND DELIVERED IN PRESENCE OF US:

_____   _____

_____   _____

No. 20–11
SATISFACTION OF CHATTEL MORTGAGE
Individual

KNOW ALL MEN BY THESE PRESENTS,

THAT_____ ,

DO HEREBY CERTIFY, That a certain Indenture of Mortgage bearing date the_____

_____day of_____ , nineteen hundred and_____made and

executed by_____

to _____

to secure the sum of_____ dollars and filed in the

office of the_____County of_____under file

number_____on the day of_____ , nineteen hundred and

_____at_____o'clock in the_____noon.

is PAID AND SATISFIED. And_____do hereby consent that the same be dis-

charged of Record.

    Dated the_____day of_____ , 19_____

In presence of

                                          _____

_____   _____

                                          _____

21

Sales Contracts

21

Sales Contracts

All contracts should contain certain essentials to be considered legally binding.

1. The parties to the agreement must be competent in the eyes of the law. They should be mentally capable of knowing and understanding what they are doing.

2. The contract should contain a statement of the consideration—something of value offered by the purchaser. Consideration usually takes the form of money, but personal services, merchandise, other real estate or any other benefit may be equally acceptable. Love and affection are also recognized as good consideration, as it may occur when one member of a family transfers title to property to another.

3. A valid contract must contain an offer and an acceptance. When the price, terms and conditions are acceptable to all parties, a "meeting of the minds" is said to exist. Both sides are agreeable to carrying out all of the provisions of the agreement.

4. The purpose for and the subject matter of the contract must be a lawful one. Courts refer to this as "legality of object."

5. Under the Statute of Frauds, most all jurisdictions recognize that a contract has to be in writing and signed by all principals in order to become enforceable.

In addition to the above, a contract for the sale of real estate generally includes a statement as to the amount of the deposit, an accurate legal description of the property, financial provisions, further detailed terms and conditions, type of deed to be conveyed, and a closing date and place.

Thus, in real estate, a valid, complete contract should contain the following basic divisions.

    a. (PARTIES)

    THIS CONTRACT, made and entered into this_____ day of_____

_____, . A.D., One Thousand Nine Hundred and _____

_____, by and between_____

_____, hereinafter referred to as Seller, and_____

_____, hereinafter referred to as Purchaser.

b. (OFFER AND ACCEPTANCE)

WITNESSETH, that the Seller agrees to sell and convey, and the Purchaser agrees to purchase,

c. (PROPERTY DESCRIPTION)

All that certain plot, piece or parcel of land, with the building and improvements thereon erected, situate, lying and being in the

(Here include legal description as well as common known address)

d. (CONSIDERATION)

IN CONSIDERATION THEREOF, the Purchaser agrees to pay to the said Seller the sum of_____ dollars ($_____) in the following manner, to wit:

e. (TERMS AND CONDITIONS)

(Here include cash down payment required, existing mortgages, purchase money mortgages, and their terms. Also, all subjects and conditions of the sale in detail)

f. (TYPE DEED TO BE CONVEYED)

Seller agrees to convey title free and clear of all encumbrances, except as herein set forth, by a good and sufficient_____ deed.

g. (CLOSING DATE AND PLACE)

Seller agrees to surrender possession to Purchaser on or before_____, 19_____ at_____

h. (WITNESSED SIGNATURES OF ALL PRINCIPALS)

Witness:

_____   _____ (L.S.)
                                        Seller

_____

_____   _____ (L.S.)
                                        Purchaser

_____

An *offer* is a unilateral agreement until it is accepted or rejected. Upon acceptance, it becomes a bilateral agreement creating obligations on both sides.

Contracts take various forms. Sometimes they begin as preliminary agreements, until a more formal instrument is drawn, as when Letters of Intention or Binders (Purchase Offers) are used as initial agreements. Such documents, when properly drawn, contain all the basic essentials to be found in the detailed contract that is to follow.

No. 21–1
LETTER OF INTENTION

_____ , 19_____

Mr._____

_____Street

_____City,_____

Dear Mr._____:

    The undersigned hereby offers to purchase your property at_____
_____Street, City of_____ , State of_____ , legal-
ly described as

(Here include legal description)

under the following basic terms and conditions:
    The selling price shall be $_____ , of which $_____
_____in cash is to be paid at time of closing.
    The purchase price is subject to an exisitng first mortgage of $_____
_____ , payable $_____per month, including_____% interest per
annum, until paid in full in 19_____ .
    The balance of the purchase price is to be covered by a purchase money second mort-
gage payable in_____monthly payments of $_____ ,
including_____% interest per annum.
    Included in the sale are the following items of personalty:

(Itemize)

    As a show of good faith, I have this date deposited in the trust account of_____
_____ , Realtor, the sum of $_____ .
    If this Letter of Intention is not accepted on or before_____
19_____ , it shall be declared null and void and of no further effect and the deposit shall
be immediately returned.
    The terms of this letter shall be in force and effect until a more formal and detailed
contract is drawn and signed by both parties.

Very truly yours,

_____Corporation

_____President

The above basic terms are
acceptable to me.

_____ (Owner)

No. 21–2
BINDER

THIS AGREEMENT made and entered into between_____
_____, as Seller, and the undersigned as Purchaser. Purchaser agrees to purchase
_____
at the price of $_____, with a deposit of $_____
_____, receipt of which is hereby acknowledged, and $_____
_____when a more formal contract, such as is used by Title Companies, is signed
by Seller and Purchaser, which is to be signed on or about_____,
19_____, at_____, the Purchaser agrees to
pay $_____, cash at closing, and $_____
by assuming and agreeing to pay mortgage for that amount now on subject property. The
balance of $_____is to be paid by Purchaser as follows:
_____

_____
_____. In the event the Seller is not willing to accept
the above price and terms, the deposit is to be forthwith returned. In the event the Seller
accepts and the Purchaser does not comply, the deposit shall be forfeited.

_____

_____

_____

This agreement is approved and accepted by the Seller, who agrees to pay_____
_____, licensed real estate broker, _____
% of the purchase price as commission.
Witness:

_____   Purchaser
_____

_____   Seller
_____

No. 21–3
BINDER
Another Form

_____, 19_____

Received from_____

of_____

the sum of_____

as deposit on account of purchase price of premises_____

_____

on the following terms and conditions:

TERMS

Purchase Price is $_____payable as follows:

$_____(including above deposit) on the signing of the formal
contract as hereinafter provided.

$_____by taking title subject to a first mortgage in that amount
covering said premises, bearing interest at the rate of
_____ % per annum payable_____
_____annually, principal due _____

_____

$_____by taking title subject to a second mortgage in that
amount covering said premises, bearing interest at the
rate of_____ % per annum payable_____
_____annually, principal due_____

_____

$_____the balance, in cash or certified check on delivery of
deed.

CONDITIONS

This deposit is accepted subject to owner's approval of the terms and conditions. If such approval is not obtained on or before five days from date hereof, this deposit shall be repaid to purchaser, but if obtained within such period a more formal contract in the form used by TITLE GUARANTEE AND TRUST COMPANY shall be signed by the parties at the office of_____

at No._____at_____M. on

_____, 19_____. The deed shall be delivered on the_____

day of_____, 19_____, at_____M., at the office of_____

_____

SUBJECT to rights of tenants as follows:_____

_____

SUBJECT, also, to the following:_____

_____
_____
_____

The parties agree that_____
as broker brought about this sale and the seller agrees to pay the usual brokerage commission.

This agreement may not be changed or terminated orally.

_____ Broker

The above terms and
conditions are approved
and receipt of deposit
is acknowledged.

_____ Owner

I agree to the foregoing.

_____ Purchaser

(Reproduced with permission of The Title Guarantee Company, New York, N.Y.)

A Deposit Receipt is an instrument used when submitting an offer for the purchase of real estate. In addition to serving as a receipt to the prospective purchaser, it generally is more detailed than the Binder form and becomes a valid contract in every sense upon acceptance by the seller.

No. 21–4
DEPOSIT RECEIPT
Purchase and Sales Agreement

THIS AGREEMENT made and entered into this_____day of_____
_____, 19_____.

RECEIPT IS HEREBY ACKNOWLEDGED OF THE SUM OF_____
_____dollars ($_____) from_____
_____proceeds to be held
in escrow by_____, subject to the terms hereof, as
a deposit on account of the purchase price of the following described property:

(Here include legal description)

Purchase Price:

_____ Dollars ($_____)

Terms and conditions of sale:

(Here include cash down payment required, existing mortgages and other mortgages to be put on the property, along with their terms. Also, inventory of personalty included, and any and all subjects and conditions of the sale)

Seller agrees to surrender possession of herein described premises to purchaser on _____, 19_____. Seller agrees to assume risk of any and all damage to above described premises prior to closing of this transaction, ordinary wear and tear excepted.

Taxes based on current assessments, insurance, interest assessment, rents, and other expenses or revenue of said property shall be pro-rated as of date of closing.

Certified liens, if any, shall be paid in full by the seller, and pending liens, if any, shall be assumed by the purchaser. It is understood and agreed that this property is being sold and purchased subject to the zoning restrictions, and/or reservations and limitations of record, if any. Seller agrees to convey title free and clear of all encumbrances, except as herein set forth, by a good and sufficient_____deed.

Seller agrees to deliver to purchaser within_____days from date hereof a complete abstract to said property brought up to date showing his title to be good and marketable and in event such abstract is not delivered within said time, seller hereby authorizes the undersigned broker to have an abstract made at seller's expense and delivered to purchaser, but in the event that the title shall not be found to be good and marketable, seller agrees to use reasonable diligence to make the said title good and marketable and shall have_____

_____days so to do. If after reasonable diligence on his part, said title shall not be made good and marketable within_____days, the money this day paid and all moneys that may have been paid under this contract shall be returned to purchaser, and thereupon both purchaser and seller shall be released from all obligations hereunder to each other. Or, upon request of the purchaser, the seller shall deliver the title in its existing condition.

It is mutually agreed that his transaction shall be closed and the purchaser shall pay the balance of the first payment and execute all papers necessary to be executed by him for the completion of his purchase within_____days from the delivery of the aforementioned abstract; otherwise the herein named Escrow Agent is hereby directed by both seller and purchaser to divide the moneys being held by said Escrow Agent between the seller and broker herein named as hereinafter provided. It is further agreed that in the event of such procedure, the Escrow Agent is relieved from any and all further liability. It is further agreed that in case this transaction is not completed due to any default or failure on the part of the purchaser, the said purchaser shall in that event become liable to the broker for brokerage commission as hereinafter provided. It is further agreed that in case of default by the purchaser, the seller may at his option take legal action to enforce this contract, in which event the purchaser shall pay reasonable attorney fees and court costs; or else the seller may at his option retain one-half of the deposit herein paid as consideration for the release of the purchaser by the seller from any further obligations under this contract to the seller, which release shall be implied from such act of retention by the seller.

Time shall be the essence and this contract shall be binding on both parties, their heirs, personal representatives, and/or assigns when this contract shall have been signed by both parties or their agents.

By_____
                                      Broker

    I (We) agree to purchase the above described property on the terms and conditions stated in the foregoing contract, and do hereby approve, ratify, and confirm said contract in all respects.

Witness as to purchaser:

_____   _____(Seal)

_____   _____(Seal)

    I (We) agree to sell the above described property on the terms and conditions stated in the foregoing contract, and do hereby approve, ratify, and confirm said contract in all respects. Further, I (We) acknowledge the employment of the broker named herein and agree to pay said broker_____% of the sales price of said property as a fee for finding the above signed purchaser. Brokerage fee is to be paid at closing of this transaction and shall be deducted from the deposit hereinbefore described and disbursed from the escrow account at closing. If there is not a sufficient amount of earnest money deposited to cover the brokerage fee, the balance shall be disbursed by cashier's check or cash at time of closing.

Witness as to seller:

_____   _____(Seal)

_____   _____(Seal)

(Adopted from Deposit Receipt form of the Miami Board of Realtors, Miami, Florida)

No. 21–5
DEPOSIT RECEIPT
Another Form

_____, 19_____

Received from_____herein

called Buyer, the sum of_____

Dollars ($_____) evidenced by cash ( ), personal check ( ), cashier's check ( ),

or_____

_____

as deposit on account of purchase price of_____

_____Dollars ($_____) for the pur-

chase of property, situated in_____,

County of_____, California, described as follows:

_____

_____

Buyer will deposit in escrow with_____the balance

of the purchase price within_____days from date of acceptance hereof

by Seller, as follows:

_____

_____

_____

_____

_____

_____

_____

_____

(1) If Buyer fails to pay the balance of said purchase price, or to complete said purchase as herein provided, the amounts paid hereon may be retained by Seller at his option as consideration for the execution of this agreement by Seller.

(2) Title is to be free of liens and encumbrances other than those set forth herein. Title subject to_____

_____Evidence of title shall be a California Land Title Association standard coverage form policy of title insurance issued through_____

_____

to be paid for by_____ if Seller is unable to convey a marketable title, except as herein provided, within three months after acceptance hereof by Seller, or if the improvements on said property be destroyed or materially damaged prior to transfer of title or delivery of agreement of sale, then upon demand of Buyer, said deposit and all other sums paid by Buyer shall be returned to Buyer, and this agreement as between Buyer and seller shall be of no further effect, and Seller thereupon shall become obligated to pay all expenses incurred in connection with examination of title.

(3) Taxes, premiums on insurance acceptable to Buyer, rents, interest and other expenses of said property shall be pro-rated as of the date of transfer of title or delivery of agreement of sale. The amount of any bond or assessment which is a lien shall be paid by

_____ except that the amount of any delinquency now existing shall be paid by Seller. Seller shall pay cost of revenue stamps on deed and any expenses connected with the removal of title defects.

(4) Possession of said property to be delivered to Buyer on closing escrow (   ), or not later than_____ days after closing escrow (   )

_____

(5) This offer shall be deemed revoked unless accepted in writing within_____

_____days after date hereof, and such acceptance is communicated to Buyer within said period.

(6) Time is of the essence of this contract, but Broker may, without notice, extend for a period of not to exceed one month the time for the performance of any act hereunder, except the time for the acceptance hereof by Seller and date of possession.

_____ By _____
    Real Estate Broker

Address_____Telephone_____

The undersigned Buyer offers and agrees to buy the above described property on the terms and conditions above stated and acknowledges receipt of a copy hereof.

Address_____   _____

Telephone_____   _____
                                                                    Buyer

Buyer to take title in name of_____

_____

_____Please Print_____

ACCEPTANCE

The undersigned accepts the offer on the reverse side hereof and agrees to sell the property described on the terms and conditions therein set forth.

The undersigned agrees to pay Broker therein named and employed by the undersigned to sell said property as commission the sum of_____

_____ Dollars ($_____)

or one-half of the amounts paid by Buyer in the event the same is forfeited, provided such one-half shall not exceed the full amount of said commission.

The undersigned acknowledges receipt of a copy hereof.

Dated_____, 19_____.

_____

_____

_____

Seller

Address_____

_____

Telephone_____

21–6
DEPOSIT RECEIPT
For Sale of A Business

_____, 19_____

Receipt Is Hereby Acknowledged Of The Sum Of:

_____ Dollars

($_____) from_____

as a deposit on the purchase of the following described business and all other interests sought to be conveyed, upon the terms and conditions stated herein,

DESCRIPTION OF PROPERTY:

Also, all of the seller's rights, title, interest, good will, lease and license in and to that certain business together with all the seller's personally owned equipment now situated thereon.

Also, all of the merchandise stock ordinarily carried on hand for the normal operation of said business. Inventory of equipment and merchandise shall be attached hereto:
PURCHASE PRICE:

_____Dollars ($_____)

TERMS AND CONDITIONS OF SALE:

    Taxes, insurance, interest, assessments, rents, and other expenses or revenue of said property shall be pro-rated.

    IT IS HEREBY EXPRESSLY AGREED that this transaction shall be completed and the purchaser shall pay the balance due and execute all papers necessary to be executed by _____for the completion of this transaction within_____days from the date hereof. All parties hereby agree that the Broker will retain the amount of the deposit if same does not exceed the Broker's compensation, providing the seller is ready, able and willing to comply with vendor's obligations; if Purchaser is ready, able and willing to comply and Seller for any reason fails to comply as agreed, then and in that event the Seller will become legally obligated to pay the Broker the full amount of his compensation. It is furthermore hereby distinctly and clearly understood by all parties to this transaction that there are no promises, inducements, assurances, guaranties, warranties, representations, solicitations, either expressed or implied, oral or written, except those recited and contained herein. This agreement is binding upon all parties. Seller and Purchaser hereby mutually agree to fully execute, on or before date of completion of this transaction, as hereinafter provided, such papers as deemed necessary by the Seller's and Purchaser's attorneys, conveying above described business, personal property and all interests sought to be conveyed. Each party agrees to employ a qualified attorney to represent their respective interests in this transaction and pass upon all instruments involved.

Broker BY:_____

The undersigned having carefully read the foregoing hereby represent and warrant that they are qualified to purchase and hereby agree to purchase the above described business, personal property, goods and chattels, on the terms and conditions stated in above instrument and hereby specifically certify that before execution hereof have inspected subject property, verified and investigated all oral representations heretofore made and all details heretofore set forth to our Entire satisfaction.

WITNESS_____   _____(SEAL)
                                              Purchaser

_____   _____(SEAL)
                                              Purchaser

    The undersigned having carefully read the foregoing, agree to sell the above mentioned property to the above named purchaser on the terms and conditions stated in the above instrument.

WITNESS_____   _____(SEAL)
                                              Seller

_____   _____(SEAL)
                                              Seller

The undersigned hereby agree to pay the above signed brokers in the manner heretofore set forth, full compensation for services rendered in the above transaction the sum of:

_____ DOLLARS ($_____)

WITNESS_____   _____(SEAL)

_____   _____(SEAL)

No. 21–7
PURCHASE OFFER

By_____

Through_____

_____ , 19_____

The undersigned, hereinafter called purchaser, having inspected the premises and relying entirely for its condition upon his own examination hereby agrees to purchase from the owner through you as his Realtor the real estate known as_____

_____

_____

_____

located in_____, _____County, State of

_____Purchaser hereby further agrees to pay for said property the sum of_____

_____($_____) Dollars upon the

following terms and or conditions, viz:_____

_____

_____

_____

_____

_____

No more than_____days after the acceptance of this purchase agreement shall be allowed for obtaining a favorable commitment for any financing required by this purchase agreement.

Purchaser to have complete possession_____

_____

Rents, if any, to be prorated to date of closing. Insurance to be (prorated) (cancelled) at date of closing.

All risk of loss shall be borne by seller until time of transfer of title.

Interest on encumbrances assumed by the purchaser to be prorated to date of closing. Purchaser will assume and agree to pay all installments of taxes on said real estate beginning with the installment due and payable in_____ , 19_____, and all installments subsequent thereto.

Purchaser will assume and agree to pay all assessments for municipal improvements which are completed after date of this Purchase Agreement.

Said real estate shall be conveyed in the same condition as it now is, ordinary wear and tear excepted, to purchaser by general warranty deed, and in support of title, purchaser shall be furnished at seller's expense:

(   )   Owner's policy of title   (   )   Complete and merchantable
          insurance in the amount   abstract of title continued
          of the purchase price.   to date.

Said policy or abstract to show respectively an insurable or merchantable title to said real estate in the seller, subject only to easements and restrictions of record, if any, and free and clear of all other liens and encumbrances, except as herein stated. If such abstract fails to show such merchantable title then such owner's title policy shall be furnished.

_____

_____

Provided, however, that in the event this Purchase Agreement provides for a conditional sale of said real estate, seller will execute to buyer a conditional sales contract upon standard form approved by the Indianapolis Real Estate Board.

The following clause applicable only if this agreement is contingent upon purchaser's securing an FHA insured loan. "It is expressly agreed that, notwithstanding any other provisions of this contract, the purchaser shall not be obligated to complete the purchase of the property described herein or to incur any penalty by forfeiture of earnest money deposits or otherwise unless the seller has delivered to the purchaser a written statement issued by the Federal Housing Commissioner setting forth the appraised value of not less than $_____ _____ which statement the seller hereby agrees to deliver to the purchaser promptly after such appraised value statement is made available to the seller. The purchaser shall, however, have the privilege and option of proceeding with the consummation of the contract without regard to the amount of the appraised valuation made by the Federal Housing Commissioner."

This transaction is to be closed within_____days after said binder for title insurance or abstract showing merchantable title as provided for above is delivered to purchaser. Said title work to be ordered (immediately) (immediately after loan approval).

This offer is void, if not accepted in writing on or before 12:00 o'clock noon of the_____ day of_____, 19____ . The above sales price includes all improvements permanently installed, such as electrical and/or gas fixtures, heating equipment and all attachments thereto, air-conditioning, (excluding window units), built in kitchen equipment, hot water heaters, incinerators, window shades, curtains, drapery poles and fixtures, Venetian blinds, storm doors and windows, linoleum, screens, awnings and TV antennas,_____

_____

_____

which belong to the above property and are not on the premises or elsewhere. All said items are now or will be at the date of closing fully paid for by seller. _____

_____Purchaser deposits herewith_____

_____($_____) Dollars as earnest money to apply upon the cash
payment provided herein.

The said earnest money deposit above mentioned shall be returned in full to purchaser
promptly in event this purchase agreement is not accepted. In the event this purchase
agreement is accepted, and purchaser shall, without legal cause, fail or refuse to complete the
purchase of said real estate in accordance with the terms and conditions hereof, seller may
pursue all legal or equitable remedies available to seller under the law, and said earnest
money deposit shall be retained by the broker under his listing contract with said seller and
shall be applied to the broker's and seller's damages.

It is expressly agreed that all terms and conditions are included herein, and no verbal
agreements of any kind shall be binding or recognized.

_____   _____
              Purchaser   Purchaser

As the owner(s) of the property described herein_____hereby accept this Purchase Agreement this_____day of_____, 19_____and_____agree to pay to
_____ Realtor, and licensed broker, the
total sum of_____
($_____) Dollars commission for services rendered in this transaction.

_____   _____
                Seller   Seller
(Reproduced with permission of the Indianapolis Real Estate Board, Indianapolis, Indiana)

No. 21–8
CONTRACT
General Form

THIS CONTRACT, made and entered into this_____day of_____
_____, A.D. One Thousand Nine Hundred and_____
_____, by and between_____
of the City of_____, County of_____,
State of_____, Party of the First Part, and_____
_____of_____, Party of the Second Part,

WITNESSETH: That, in consideration of the covenants and agreements hereinafter contained on the part of the said Party of the Second Part the Party of the First Part
does agree as follows:

(Here include all terms and conditions of sale)

IN CONSIDERATION THEREOF, the said Party of the Second Part agrees to pay to the said Party of the First Part, the sum of_____
_____Dollars ($_____) in the following manner, to-wit:

(Here include cash payments as well as mortgages with amounts, interest, manner of payment and duration of mortgage)

IN WITNESS WHEREOF, the above Parties have hereunto set their hands and seals on the day above written, and for themselves, their heirs, administrators and assigns, do hereby agree to do the full performance of the covenants and agreements as hereinabove set forth.

Witnessed:

_____   _____(L.S.)
_____

_____   _____(L.S.)
_____

Contracts are sometimes designed for specific real estate transactions, and are so worded to cover specialized situations. In contrast, the following contract is general in nature and may be readily adapted for house sales, office buildings, shopping centers, apartment houses, industrial properties and most other forms of real estate activity. For special wording, see Clauses In Contracts, pages 444 through 447.

No. 21–9
CONTRACT
Another Form

Agreement, made the_____ day of_____, in the year One Thousand Nine Hundred and_____BETWEEN_____

_____
_____hereinafter described as the seller, and_____

_____
_____hereinafter described as the purchaser,_____

_____
WITNESSETH, that the seller, in consideration of the sum of_____

_____
_____to be fully paid as hereinafter mentioned, hereby agrees to sell unto the purchaser,_____

_____
_____

AND THE SAID purchaser hereby agrees to purchase said premises at the said consideration of_____

_____dollars, and to pay the same as follows:

_____

_____

_____

AND THE SAID seller, on receiving such payment_____

_____

at the time and in the manner above mentioned, shall, at the seller's own proper costs and expenses, deliver to said purchaser or to the purchaser's assigns, a deed which shall be the usual_____deed in proper statutory form for record and shall be duly executed, acknowledged, and have revenue stamps in the proper amount affixed thereto by the seller, at the seller's expense, so as to convey to the purchaser the fee simple of the said premises, free of all encumbrances, except as herein stated.

If at the time of the delivery of the deed the premises or any part thereof shall be or shall have been affected by an assessment or assessments which are or may become payable in annual installments, of which the first installment is then a charge or lien or has been paid, then for the purposes of this contract all the unpaid installments of any such assessment, including those which are to become due and payable after the delivery of the deed, shall be deemed to be due and payable and to be liens upon the premises affected thereby and shall be paid and discharged by the seller upon the delivery of the deed. The following are to be apportioned:

1. Rents and interest on mortgages.
2. Insurance premiums on existing policies.
3. Taxes and water rates for the tax year.

THE RISK OF LOSS or damage by fire prior to the completion of this contract is hereby assumed by the seller.

The deed shall be delivered on the_____day of_____

_____19_____, at_____o'clock_____M., at the office of_____

_____No._____

_____ in the City of_____

AND IT IS UNDERSTOOD that the stipulations aforesaid are to apply to and bind the heirs, executors, administrators and assigns of the respective parties.

This instrument may not be changed, modified or discharged orally.

WITNESS the signatures and seals of the above parties.

In presence of

_____   _____

_____

No. 21–10
CONTRACT
Another Form[1]

STATE OF_____, County of_____ ; ss.
    I do hereby certify that the within instrument was filed and recorded at request of

_____

on_____at_____M., Docket_____
_____Page_____, Records of_____
County, State of_____
    WITNESS my hand and official seal the day and year first above written.

When recorded, mail to:

                                              _____County Recorder
                                    By_____ Deputy

AGREEMENT

THIS AGREEMENT entered into in triplicate_____
_____, 19_____, between_____
_____as Seller,
and_____as Buyer,
WITNESSETH:
    That Seller, in consideration of the covenants and agreements of Buyer hereinafter
contained, agrees to sell and convey unto Buyer, and Buyer agrees to buy, all that certain
real property, together with all and singular the rights and appurtenances thereto in anywise
belonging, situate in the County of_____, State of_____,
described as follows:

_____

_____

_____

for the sum of_____ dollars_____
($_____) lawful money of the United States, and Buyer agrees in consideration of
the premises to pay said sum in the following manner:

_____

_____

    Buyer shall pay, before they become delinquent, all installments of principal and interest
of any improvement liens against said property not deliquent at the date hereof; and_____

---

1. This form was designed to comply with the Arizona State Law. The forfeiture provisions contained herein are
allowed by Arizona Case Law and Sections 33–741 and 742 of the Arizona Revised Statutes. These provisions are
not necessarily applicable to any other state.

l

_____ ;

and all taxes and assessments on said property levied subsequent to December 31, 19_____ , together with all other assessments and charges for or on account of irrigation water or power used for furnishing irrigation water, after the date hereof. Buyer shall keep the buildings erected, and to be erected, upon said property insured against fire in the amount of the reasonable insurable value thereof, in insurance companies to be approved by Seller, for the mutual benefit and protection of the parties hereto, and to place the policy or policies representing the said fire insurance and evidence of the payment of premium thereon with the Title Insurance Company to be held by it or mortgagee.

If Buyer fails to pay any such taxes, charges, assessments, or premiums for fire insurance or to place the policies of fire insurance with the_____Title Insurance Company, or fails to pay any amount due upon or fails to perform any condition or covenant of any agreement for sale or mortgage required of Buyer, before the same shall have become delinquent, Seller shall have the right to pay or procure the same, together with necessary costs and legal fees, and the amount so advanced and such repayment thereof shall be secured hereby and shall be repaid to Seller by Buyer on demand, together with interest thereon at the rate of_____per cent per annum from date advanced by Seller until repaid, and any payment so made by Seller shall be prima facie evidence of the necessity therefor. If the_____Title Insurance Company is notified in writing by Seller of any such advances, it shall not deliver deed to Buyer until repayment thereof with interest shall have been made.

If Seller institutes suit against Buyer to enforce Seller's rights under this agreement and obtains a valid judgment against Buyer, Buyer agrees to pay all costs, expenses and attorneys' fees of Seller.

The Deed of Seller conveying the herein described property to Buyer, subject to liens, encumbrances, reservations, restrictions and exceptions affecting the title to said property has been delivered in escrow with the_____Title Insurance Company, and shall, as provided by the escrow instructions given to said Company, be delivered to Buyer upon fulfillment of Buyer's obligation to Seller under the terms of this agreement.

Buyer may enter into possession of said property and continue in such possession for and during the life of this agreement. Buyer agrees to maintain said premises and all improvements thereon in good repair, to permit no waste thereof, and to take the same care thereof that a prudent owner would take.

No transfer or assignment of any rights hereunder shall be made by anyone having an interest herein, unless made in such manner and accompanied by such deeds and other instruments as shall be required by the_____Title Insurance Company, nor until its regular escrow fee and other costs including its charge for the issuance of a new Title Insurance Policy shall have been fully paid, and all instruments deposited in escrow with it.

Seller and Buyer, and each of them, promise to pay promptly, and to indemnify and hold harmless Escrow Agent against all costs, damages, attorneys' fees, expenses and liabilities which, in good faith and without fault on its part, it may incur or sustain in connection with this agreement and in connection with any court action arising out of this agreement.

Should Buyer default in making any payment, or in fulfilling any obligation hereunder, Seller may, either elect to bring an action against Buyer for specific performance of this agreement, or enforce a forfeiture of the interest of Buyer, in any lawful manner, including but not limited to forfeiture by notice. Forfeiture may be enforced only after the expiration of the following periods after such default: where Buyer has paid on the purchase price: less than 20%–30 days; 20% or more, but less than 30%–60 days; 30% or more, but less than 50%–120 days; 50% or more–9 months. In computing said percentages, the amount of any agreement for sale or mortgage agreed to be paid by Buyer shall be treated as payment only to the extent of principal actually paid thereon by Buyer. If Seller elects to forfeit such agreement by notice, Seller shall do so through Escrow Agent by delivery to Escrow Agent a written declaration of forfeiture directed to Buyer, together with Escrow Agent's established fee for services rendered in connection with forfeitures. Said fee of Escrow Agent shall be the Buyer's obligation, shall be added to the contract balance owed by Buyer to Seller, shall be a lien upon the subject property as of the date of recording of this agreement, and shall be collected by Escrow Agent from Buyer in order for Buyer to avoid the forfeiture. Escrow Agent shall, within three days thereafter, send a copy of said declaration to Buyer at the last written address on file with Escrow Agent. If no written address has been filed, the copy of the declaration shall be sent in care of General Delivery at the city in which the office of Escrow Agent mailing the copy of the declaration is located. The copy of the declaration shall be deposited in the United States mail. The mailing of the copy of the declaration by Escrow Agent shall constitute notice of the contents of the copy of the declaration to the Buyer as of the date of such mailing and no further notice shall be required. If Buyer fails to comply with the terms of such agreement to the date of such compliance before the expiration of 10 days from the date said copy was deposited in the United States mail, Escrow Agent is authorized to deliver to Seller the documents and money deposited in the escrow or under such agreement, and/or to record a notice of completion of forfeiture. In the event a forfeiture is enforced, Buyer and anyone claiming under him shall forfeit any and all rights and interest hereunder in and to the real property hereinbefore described and appurtenances, and Buyer shall surrender to Seller, forthwith, peaceable possession of said property and shall forfeit to the Seller as liquidated damages any and all payments made hereunder, together with any and all improvements placed on or in said property. Neither the provisions of this paragraph nor any provisions of the escrow shall affect any other lawful right or remedy which the Seller may have against the Buyer.

Time is of the essence of this agreement. This agreement shall be binding upon the heirs, executors, administrators, successors, and assigns of the respective parties hereto.

IN WITNESS WHEROF, the said parties have hereunto set their hands and seals the day and year above written:

_____	_____
(Seller)	(Buyer)
_____	_____
(Seller)	(Buyer)

(Notary)

An Installment Sales Contract is the instrument used for the sale of property wherein the purchaser receives possession, but not title to it. The purchaser agrees to make periodic installment payments until the sales price is reached. Not until then does he receive the deed and lawful title to the property.

The prime reason for a contract being used instead of a mortgage is due to the relative ease in which the property can be returned to the seller in the event of a default. It precludes the necessity of any foreclosure proceedings. Large land companies as well as individuals use this form extensively for the sale of unimproved land. The essence of most Installment Sales Contracts is the complete forfeiture of all payments made if one payment is missed.[1]

Known by various names in different parts of the country, it is also referred to as a *Contract For Deed, Land Contract,* and a *Conditional Sales Contract.*

No. 21–11
INSTALLMENT SALES CONTRACT

_____ , 19_____

RECEIVED FROM _____   _____

ADDRESS _____

THE SUM OF $_____   Sales Price $_____

                                Received $_____

                                Balance $_____

The balance of $_____ is to be paid in equal monthly installments of $_____ until paid in full, on the first day of each month. This amount includes principal and interest of_____% per annum on the unpaid balance, the interest to be deducted from each payment as made.

This agreement is made betweeen _____ _____ , party of the first part, a corporation of the State of_____ , and _____ _____ , party of the second part.

WITNESSETH: That if the party of the second part shall first make the payments and perform the covenants mentioned herein on part to be performed, the party of the first part hereby covenants and agrees to convey and assure to the party of the second part, in fee simple, clear of all encumbrances whatsoever, by good and sufficient_____ _____deed, the lot_____ of ground situated in the County of_____ _____ , State of_____ , known and described as follows:

(Here include legal description)

In case of the failure of the party of the second part to make any of the payments herein designated, or any part thereof, or failure to perform any of the covenants for a period of_____ days after maturity, this agreement shall be forfeited and terminated within_____days after receipt of declaration of intent to forfeit and

---

1. Protection has been given the purchaser under the provisions of the Federal Interstate Land Sales Act as well as by many state statutes. A purchaser has the right to void a contract if false advertising, fraudulent claims, registration provisions and rules and regulations have not been complied with by the subdivider, developer, or promoter.

terminate by the Seller via registered or certified mail, and the party of the second part shall forfeit all payments made on this contract, and such payments shall be retained by the said party of the first part as due or accumulated rent on the property, and shall become liable to the party of the first part for monthly rental of $_____ per month payable on the first day of each month; and in case of nonpayment of such rent, the party of the first part shall have the right to re-enter and take possession of the premises aforesaid without being liable to any action therefor, or any costs incurred.

In addition the party of the second part agrees to pay all taxes, subsequent to year_____.

Construction shall be limited to residences built of new materials. Residences must be located at least fifteen feet from front lot line. No shacks or unsightly structures allowed. Structures of a temporary nature used during normal construction must be removed within one year. Sewage disposal systems must include septic tanks of currently acceptable design and construction.

It is further agreed by the parties hereto that this contract or any assignment thereof is not to be recorded without permission of the owners. If this contract or assignment thereto is recorded contrary to the above provision then any existing balance shall become due and payable.

It is mutually agreed by and between the parties that the time of payment shall be an essential part of this contract, and that all covenants and agreements herein contained shall extend to and be obligatory upon the heirs executors, administrators, and assigns of the respective parties.

It is agreed that the party of the second part shall have the privilege and right to examine a master abstract.

IN WITNESS WHEREOF, the parties to these presents have hereunto set their hands and seals the day and year first above written.

WITNESS OF BUYERS: BUYERS:

_____   _____ (Seal)

_____   _____ (Seal)

                                                      ACCEPTED:

ATTEST   (Seal)

_____   _____
          Assistant Secretary   President

No. 21-12
INSTALLMENT SALES CONTRACT
For Office Use Only

1 DEV. CODE	CONTRACT NUMBER	LOC.	SALESMAN	CODE	LOC.	SALESMAN	CODE
	SALESMAN'S NAME	ADV. SOURCE	STATE & CO.	☐ YES ☐ NO	PRIOR PURCHASER DEV. _____		☐ SPON. TRIP ☐ REFERRAL

PURCHASER COPY (PERMANENT)

	THIS AGREEMENT PREPARED BY:
Ⓜ	NAME
	ADDRESS

AGREEMENT OF PURCHASE & SALE
ISSUED BY
MACKLE BROS. DIVISION, THE DELTONA CORPORATION
(herein called Deltona)
TO

NAME_____
(TYPE OR PRINT)

ADDRESS_____COUNTY_____

CITY_____STATE_____ZIP CODE_____TELEPHONE_____/_____
(AREA CODE) (NUMBER)

PROPERTY DESCRIPTION { LOT _____ BLOCK _____ AT DELTONA LAKES, FLORIDA
(SUBDIVISION ACCORDING TO THE PLAT OF RECORD)

1. CASH PRICE (U.S. CURRENCY)	2. RESERVATION DEPOSIT	3. CASH DOWN PAYMENT	4. TOTAL CASH DOWN PAYMENT (BOX 2 PLUS 3)	5. UNPAID BALANCE OF CASH PRICE (BOX 1 MINUS 4)	6. ANNUAL PERCENTAGE RATE OF INTEREST (CHECK ONE ⊠)		7. FINANCE CHARGE	8. DEFERRED PAYMENT PRICE (BOX 5 PLUS 7)
					DOWN PAYMENT	INTEREST RATE		
					☐ 20% OR OVER 6½%			
					☐ 10% BUT LESS THAN 20% . . . 7%			
$	$10.00	$	$		☐ LESS THAN 10% 7½%		$	$

9. PAYMENT AMOUNT	10. FIRST PAYMENT DUE	11. PAYMENT SCHEDULE (CHECK ONE ⊠)	12. CONTRACT PERFORMANCE SCHEDULE AND NUMBER OF PAYMENTS (CHECK ONE ⊠) TERM COMMENCES UPON SIGNING OF CONTRACT BY DELTONA			
			☐ CASH PLAN	☐ PLAN 1 TERM 3 YEARS	☐ PLAN 2 TERM 4 YEARS	☐ PLAN 3 TERM 8½ YEARS
$	___/___	☐ MONTHLY ———		36 PAYMENTS	48 PAYMENTS	102 PAYMENTS
		☐ QUARTERLY ———		12 PAYMENTS	16 PAYMENTS	34 PAYMENTS
PAYABLE ON OR BEFORE 10TH OF MONTH DUE	MO. YR.	☐ SEMI-ANNUAL ———		6 PAYMENTS	8 PAYMENTS	17 PAYMENTS
		☐ ANNUAL ———		3 PAYMENTS	4 PAYMENTS	8 PAYMENTS
		☐ CASH ———		0 PAYMENTS	0 PAYMENTS	0 PAYMENTS

Payments to Deltona by the Purchaser shall be applied first to accrued interest and the balance thereof credited to the principal. Prepayment without penalty may be made at any time, however prepayment in whole or in part shall not accelerate the obligation of Deltona to deliver the Deed and Title Insurance Policy and complete the improvements before ninety days after the term of the Contract Performance Schedule has ended, as specified herein. In the event the Purchaser fails to make any required payment, then this contract may be cancelled by Deltona and prior payments may be retained by Deltona in accordance with the terms and conditions fully set forth in the Purchaser's Acknowledgment on the reverse side of this Agreement.

I acknowledge that I have read all the terms, conditions and acknowledgments above and on the reverse side hereof and that all such terms, conditions and acknowledgments are a part of this agreement and I acknowledge that the required Property Report, Public Report, Offering Statement or Prospectus has been delivered to me in advance of the signing of this Agreement of Purchase & Sale. The date of this transaction shall be the date this Agreement of Purchase & Sale is signed by Deltona.

Signed by the Purchaser(s) this_____day of_____ _____

19_____at_____O'clock___M. _____
(Purchaser's Signature)

Witnesses to The Deltona Corporation signature:	The Deltona Corporation
_____	
_____	By_____ (Authorized Signature)

I HEREBY CERTIFY that on this day, before me, a Notary Public in and for Dade County, Florida authorized to take acknowledgments, personally appeared the person indicated as authorized signer above, whom I know to be the Agent of The Deltona Corporation in the foregoing contract of sale, and acknowledged before me that he executed such contract in the name of and on behalf of The Deltona Corporation on this date and that as such Agent he is duly authorized by The Deltona Corporation to do so; and that such contract is the act and contract of The Deltona Corporation.

WITNESS my hand and seal in Dade County, Florida, this _____ day of _____ 19____

My Commission expires _____
Notary Public, State of Florida at large

PLEASE READ REVERSE SIDE — IT IS PART OF THIS AGREEMENT

Deltona Guarantees

without additional charge, that when this contract has been paid in full and the term of the contract performance schedule specified herein has ended, within ninety days thereafter —

1 WARRANTY DEED — To give you a Warranty Deed which conveys to you title to this property subject only to the matters referred to herein;

2 TITLE INSURANCE POLICY — To have issued to you a Policy of Title Insurance;

3 CENTRAL WATER MAIN — To have installed a water main in front of this property so that you may, at your expense, tap into the main and procure water service to this property;

4 PAVED STREETS — To have completed the paving of streets abutting this property.

5 NO EXTRA CHARGES — Deltona further guarantees to pay all taxes on this property until it is deeded to you, and to pay all expenses for preparing and recording your deed and for documentary stamps and that both the purchase price and the rate of interest indicated on the reverse side hereof cannot be increased on this property.

ADDITIONAL
TERMS AND CONDITIONS OF AGREEMENT
PLEASE READ CAREFULLY

1. This Agreement of Purchase & Sale will become effective and binding when signed by you in the space provided on the reverse side and also signed by Deltona and when your first payment, or its equivalent in down payment, is received by Deltona at its offices at 2818 Coral Way, Miami, Florida 33145.

2. This Agreement of Purchase & Sale is governed by the laws of Florida. It is not transferable without the written consent of Deltona, which consent shall not be unreasonably withheld.

3. This Agreement of Purchase & Sale and attached Rider(s), if any, constitute the entire agreement and the Purchaser acknowledges that no representations have been made to induce him to enter into this agreement except such as are set forth herein or in Deltona's advertising.

4. The Purchaser shall have the option to void this Agreement of Purchase & Sale (a) if he does not receive a Property Report prepared pursuant to the Rules and Regulations of the Office of Interstate Land Sales Registration, U.S. Department of Housing and Urban Development, in advance of, or at the time of, his signing the Agreement of Purchase & Sale, and (b) within 48 hours after the signing thereof, if he did not receive the Property Report at least 48 hours before the signing thereof.

5. When this contract has been paid in full, and the term of the Contract Performance Schedule specified herein has ended, Deltona will within 90 days thereafter convey title to this property free and clear, subject to applicable zoning ordinances, public utility easements, taxes for the year in which title is acquired (which taxes shall be prorated) and restrictions of record common to the neighborhood. If Deltona is unable to meet any of its obligations under this Agreement or to obtain a certificate of title insurance and after the use of reasonable diligence is unable to make the title to the property insurable as aforesaid, then it will return to you in full all money (including interest) which you have paid on this property, thus releasing both parties from any and all further obligations.

6. Notice which either party desires or is required to give to the other (except the notice requirements of Paragraph 4 of the Additional Terms and Conditions) shall only be given in writing delivered personally or by air mail addressed (with sufficient postage) as follows:

(1) to the Purchaser(s)
in care of the address as stated herein or to the last known address provided by the Purchaser in writing;

(2) to Deltona
2818 Coral Way, Miami, Florida 33145,
and said notice shall be deemed given when mailed by certified or registered air mail, return receipt requested, (with sufficient postage) to said addressee.

7. The Purchaser cannot take possession of or make improvements to the property until all amounts due Deltona have been paid and title to the property has been conveyed to such Purchaser.

8. If this Agreement is terminated, the affidavit of Deltona attesting to the default of the Purchaser and the termination of this Agreement, recorded in the official records in the office of the County Clerk, shall be conclusive proof of the default and termination in favor of any subsequent bona fide purchaser or encumbrancer for value. In such case the Purchaser irrevocably authorizes Deltona to thus attest and record such affidavit as though it were the act and deed of the Purchaser.

9. References herein to the Purchaser and any pronouns relative thereto shall include the masculine and feminine gender, and the singular and plural number wherever the context requires.

PURCHASER'S ACKNOWLEDGMENT

I understand that Deltona will grant me the following grace periods without penalty if I am unable to make any required payment (after this Agreement of Purchase & Sale becomes effective and binding) exactly on the date due; 60 days if 10% or less of the principal amount of the purchase price has been paid; 90 days if more than 10% but less than 25% of the principal amount of the purchase price has been paid; 120 days if more than 25% but less than 50% of the principal amount of the purchase price has been paid; and 150 days if more than 50% of the principal amount of the purchase price has been paid. This provision shall not prohibit the accumulation of interest for the period of time the contract may be in default. I understand that although I am under no personal liability to make any payments on this contract, since Deltona has taken this property off the real estate market and will be turning away other prospective purchasers as well as incurring development and other expenses in connection with its sale, all prior payments made by me will be retained by Deltona as agreed upon and liquidated damages in the event that I fail to make any required payment on the purchase of this property exactly on the date due or within the grace period as set forth herein or in the event this contract is not brought current within said grace period and neither party will have any further claim against the other.

No. 21–13
AGREEMENT TO TERMINATE CONTRACT

_____ , 19_____

IT IS MUTUALLY UNDERSTOOD and agreed between_____

_____and _____

_____ that in consideration of_____

_____the contract between them for the sale of the following

described property:_____

_____

is hereby rescinded, terminated, cancelled and of no further effect.

_____

_____

CLAUSES IN SALES CONTRACTS

Title Warranty

The Seller warrants and represents that it owns the fee simple title to the subject real property and owns the title to the personalty free and clear of any and all easements, reverters, limitations, covenants and restrictions which would prevent the Purchaser from utilizing the improvements for the purpose contemplated, namely the ownership and operation of the improvement now located upon the said property. The foregoing is, however, subject to the following: a) Any and all Governmental rules, regulations and ordinances. b) The first mortgage above referred to. c) The Seller represents that it has received no notices or violation of any Governmental ordinances, and if any exist at the time of closing, they shall be complied with by Seller at its sole cost and expense.

Time Of Essence

It is mutually agreed that this transaction shall be closed on or before the_____ day of_____ , 19_____ , and that time shall be of the essence. This contract shall be binding on both parties, their successors, personal representatives and/or assigns.

Representation As To Broker

The parties represent unto each other that the only real estate broker entitled to claim commission for this transaction is_____ . If a commission is claimed against the Seller as a result of acts or actions of the Purchaser by a broker other than_____ , then the Purchaser shall indemnify the Seller from any and all damages resulting from same, including reasonable attorney's fees and the cost of litigation, and will completely save the Seller harmless from such claim.

Representation As To Broker And Amount Of Commission

The Seller and Purchaser stipulate that_____
is the real estate broker of record whose services were utilized in negotiations leading to the execution of this contract and that no other real estate broker is entitled to a commission. The Seller agrees to pay_____% of the sales price as the commission in full.

Proration Agreement

At time of closing of this transaction, taxes, insurance, interest, assessments, rents and other normal expenses or revenue in connection with the operation of said property shall be prorated. Rents shall be prorated on a per diem basis.

Payment Of Liens

Certified municipal liens, if any, shall be paid in full by the Seller. In the event a pending lien has been filed against the subject property which has not been certified as of the date of closing, and the work and improvements for which the lien was filed have been completed prior to the closing, despite the fact that the pending lien has not been certified, such lien will be paid by the Seller.

Prepayment Privilege

The existing first mortgage and the purchase money mortgage are prepayable at any time, in whole or part, without penalty.

Instruments To Be Used At Closing

The Seller will convey the subject property by_____Deed and the personal property by Statutory Bill Of Sale, and will deliver unto the purchaser a Mechanics' Lien Affidavit.

Maintenance And Liability Until Closing

The Seller agrees to maintain, manage and operate the subject improvement from the date hereof through the date of closing in a manner equivalent to the Seller's prior management of the premises. Risk of loss or damage to the subject property between the date of this contract and the date of closing shall be that of the Seller, it being the understanding and agreement of the parties that at closing the improvements located on the subject property will be in the same condition as they are at the date of the signing of this contract, subject only to ordinary wear and tear. In the event of significant damage prior to the closing, the date shall be extended a reasonable length of time in order to enable Seller to repair such damage and Seller agrees that such damage will be repaired so that the subject premises will be in at least as good a condition as they were before the damage occurred.

Examination Of Title

Seller agrees to deliver to Purchaser within_____days of date hereof an abstract to said property, brought to date showing title to be good and marketable. The

Purchaser shall have_____days within which to examine the said abstract and to signify his willingness to accept same. In the event the examination of the abstract proves the title to be unmarketable, the Seller shall have_____days within which to cure the designated defects. The Seller hereby agrees to use reasonable diligence in curing said defects. Upon the defects being cured and notice of that fact being given the Purchaser, this transaction shall be closed within_____days of delivery of said notice. If the Seller, after reasonable diligence, is unable to make the title good and marketable within_____days, the money this day paid and all moneys that may have been paid under this contract shall be returned to Purchaser, and thereupon both Purchaser and Seller shall be released from all obligations hereunder to each other. Or, upon request of the Purchaser the Seller shall deliver the title in its existing condition.

Inspection Of Premises

Purchasers shall, at their expense, be allowed to have an inspection of the roof, pool, air conditioning, and the premises for termites. If defects or termite infestation are found to exist after qualified inspectors have examined the premises, they shall be corrected at the expense of the Sellers.

Approval Of New Leases

Purchaser shall have the right to approve any new leases made from the date of acceptance of this contract. Purchaser further agrees, however, that he will not unreasonably withhold his consent to any such lease, provided that the lease is on similar terms and conditions as the existing leases in the subject improvement. At time of closing, Purchaser agrees to take subject possession and assume all leases existing at time of closing.

Warranty Against Violations

Seller warrants that there are presently, to the best of his knowledge, no existing violations of any governmental codes, ordinances or zoning regulations. If notice of any such violations are received prior to closing date, Seller agrees that such violations will be corrected at Seller's expense.

Guarantees And Warranties

All guarantees and warranties in force on subject improvement, such as air conditioning, roof, elevator or other equipment, shall be delivered to Purchaser at time of closing.

Examination Of Leases

The Purchaser acknowledges that it has examined copies of leases and information concerning other tenants not on leases furnished to Purchaser by Seller and is satisfied with same. Seller represents and warrants that said copies and information are true and complete. The usual adjustments with respect to security deposits and prepaid rent, as well as any prorations, shall be made at closing; delinquent rent, if any, shall belong to Seller when collected, and all rent collected by Purchaser after closing in excess of current rent then due from that tenant shall be paid over to Seller to the extent of delinquent rent due from that tenant at closing, and Purchaser shall include such delinquent rent in any collection efforts or permit Seller to do so before evicting the tenant.

Maintenance Before Closing

The Seller agrees to maintain, manage and operate the subject improvement from the date hereof through the date of closing in a manner equivalent to the Seller's prior management of the improvement.

Liability Before Closing

Seller agrees to assume risk of loss and all damage to the subject premises prior to closing of this transaction, ordinary wear and tear excepted.

Surrendering Possession

Seller agrees to surrender possession and occupancy of the aforedescribed premises to Purchaser at time of closing, subject to the rights of tenants in possession as evidenced by leases and tenancies existing at the time of closing.

22

Other Real Estate Forms

22

Other Real Estate Forms

Forms relevant to transacting real estate and not included in the foregoing chapters are presented here.

No. 22–1
CLOSING FINANCIAL STATEMENT

As of Date_____

TITLE NO. _____ FILE OR LOAN NO._____

PREMISES_____

CLOSED_____ at _____ M. at office of_____

THE FOLLOWING PERSONS WERE PRESENT:_____

_____

_____

Title Company Closer:

_____

ITEMS	CREDIT TO BUYER	CREDIT TO SELLER

PURCHASE PRICE_____ $ _____ $ _____

    PAID ON ACCOUNT OF PURCHASE PRICE_____

1st MORTGAGE BALANCE_____

    Interest at_____ % from_____to_____

2nd MORTGAGE BALANCE _____

    Interest at_____ % from_____to_____

PURCHASE MONEY MORTGAGE_____

INSURANCE APPORTIONED (SEE SCHEDULE)_____

TAXES _____

_____

_____

WATER_____

SEWER_____

FUEL_____

RENTS (SEE SCHEDULE)_____

OTHER ADJUSTMENTS_____

_____

TOTAL CREDIT TO SELLER $_____

TOTAL CREDIT TO BUYER $_____

BALANCE DUE SELLER $_____

DISBURSEMENTS BY PURCHASER   PURCHASE PRICE PAID AS FOLLOWS

                    $ $

Mortgage Tax_____   By Cash_____

Recording Mortgage_____   By Check_____

Recording Deed_____

Title Company Fee_____

Survey_____

Drawing Bond and Mtge._____

_____

_____   DISBURSEMENTS BY SELLER

_____ $

_____   Revenue Stamps on Deed_____

_____   N. Y. C. Deed Tax_____

_____

Fee Title Insurance was obtained in the amount of $

                                     or

Purchaser was advised to obtain Fee Insurance at the time of closing and declined to do so notwithstanding such advice.

                          _____
                                           Purchaser

(Reproduced with permission of The Title Guarantee Company, New York, N. Y.)

No. 22–2
CLOSING STATEMENT
Another Form

SELLER: CLOSING DATE:

BUYER: PRORATION DATE

LEGAL   FILE NO:

ADDRESS   plat book;

Sales Price . . . .$_____

Prorate Insurance . . . .$_____

Escrow Transferred . . . .$_____

_____. . . . . _____

_____. . . . . _____

_____. . . . . _____

_____. . . . . _____

                                     $_____

LESS:

Deposit ....$_____

Broker Commission .... _____

First Mortgage Principal......................... _____

First Mortgage Interest .... _____

Second Mortgage Principal .... _____

Second Mortgage Interest .... _____

Purchase Money Mortgage....................... _____

Prorate County Real Estate Tax .... _____

Prorate City Real Estate Tax .... _____

Prorate County Pers. Prop. Tax .... _____

State Stamps on Deed .... _____

Federal Stamps on Deed......................... _____

Abstracting .... _____

Recording of Purchase Money Mtg .... _____

Recording Fee on Deed .... _____

Attorney's Fee-Preparing Instruments .... _____   _____

Amount Due (to)   (from) Seller $_____

The above tax prorations are based upon tax assessments for the year 19____ and that basis of proration is accepted by the parties to this transaction.

I (We) have read the foregoing statement, hereby approve the same and authorize disbursement in accordance therewith.

_____   _____
                Seller   Buyer

When assigning a mortgage to another, the exact amount of the remaining balance must be ascertained. An Estoppel Letter (or Certificate) is the instrument used to accomplish this. It may be signed by the mortgagor or mortgagee, but the one so doing is held responsible for the representations made. In actual practice, it is generally signed by the mortgagee.

No. 22–3
ESTOPPEL LETTER

Date_____

Re: Property at_____

Mortgage No._____

Dear Sirs:

As requested, regarding the above described property, the following estoppel information is submitted:

Balance Due on Principal ....$_____

Escrow Balance .... _____

Interest per diem $_____ from _____ .... _____

Delinquent Interest per diem $_____

    from_____ .... _____

    Total Amount Due As Of   ....$_____

    Monthly Payment of Principal and Interest ..$_____

               Taxes.................... _____

               Insurance .... _____

               Accident and Health .... _____

               Other._____

                            (itemize)

    Total Monthly Payments Due ....$_____

If we can be of further service to you regarding this mortgage, please let us know.

Yours truly,

No. 22–4
EXTENSION AGREEMENT
Endorsed On Instrument

The time for the performance of the foregoing agreement is extended to the_____ day of_____, 19_____. In all other respects said agreement shall be unmodified and in full force. Time still is of the essence of this agreement.

No. 22–5
JOINT ADVENTURE
For Acquiring Land

This agreement entered into this_____ day of_____, 19_____, by and between_____, party of the first part, and_____, party of the second part.

Witnesseth: In consideration of the agreements hereinafter expressed, the parties have become associated with each other as joint adventurers, agreeing to purchase the following described real property:

(Here include legal description)

Whereas, under date of_____, 19_____, a contract for the purchase of said land was entered into by_____, as nominee for the parties hereto.

Whereas, the parties have made equal contributions to a fund for such purpose in the total amount of $_____.

Therefore, in consideration of the sum of One Dollar ($1.00) each to the other in hand paid, and the mutual covenants herein contained, it is agreed as follows:

PURPOSE

The parties hereto have acquired said property for the purpose of investment and to share equally in all the operating and maintenance expenses and subsequent sale of the land.

BANK ACCOUNT

All funds of the said joint adventure shall be kept in a joint account at the_____ Bank,_____City, State of_____. Withdrawals from said account must bear the signatures of both the parties of the first and second part.

PAYMENTS

All payments for taxes, principal and interest, improvements and any other necessary expenses are to be paid in equal amounts by parties of the first and second part.

PROFITS

Any profits arising from the sale of all or part of said land are to be divided equally, between parties of the first and second part after deducting from the proceeds of such sale all cash advances of the first and second parties.

LOSSES

Any losses arising from the sale of the said land are likewise to be shared equally between parties of the first and second part.

DISSENTING REMEDY

In the event either party desires to sell and the other party dissents, the dissenting party agrees to buy out the other party for half of the resulting net profit from such sale and to assume title. The party selling agrees to forthwith convey his interest in said land.

DEATH OF EITHER PARTY

The death of either party shall not act to terminate the joint adventure. The estate of the deceased joint adventurer shall continue as a member thereof and shall share in any future profits or loss as hereabove provided.

In witness whereof, the party of the first part has hereunto set his hand and seal and the party of the second part has set his hand and seal, the day and year first above written. Witnesses:

_____

_____   _____
                                     Party of the First Part

_____

_____   _____
                                     Party of the Second Part

_____

No. 22–6
PARTNERSHIP AGREEMENT

THIS AGREEMENT made and entered into this the_____day of_____ _____, A.D. 19_____ BETWEEN_____ _____, of_____

_____ , of_____ _____
_____ , of_____
and_____ , of_____

WITNESSETH, as follows: The said parties above named have agreed to become copartners in business and by these presents do agree to be copartners together under the firm name and style of_____to do business together in the_____of_____
_____ , County of_____State of_____
_____ , and in such other places as the nature of their business shall require. The business to be conducted by them shall be_____

This partnership Agreement shall commence on_____

_____
day of_____ , 19_____ , and shall continue for the term or period of _____years, unless discontinued before the expiration of that period by mutual consent of the parties hereto. To the end and purpose in view, the said parties agree to contribute to said business as follows:_____

_____
_____

The sums of money or other contributions to said business are to be used and employed in common between the said partners for the support, maintenance, and management of said business, and to the mutual benefit and advantage of the said partner.

It is agreed by and between the parties to these presents that at all times during the continuance of their copartnership, they, and each of them will give their attendance and also do their, and each of their, best endeavors, and to the utmost of their skill and power, exert themselves for their joint interest, profit, benefit and advantage in the business aforesaid, and also that they shall and will, at all times during the said Copartnership, bear, pay and discharge equally between them all rents and other expenses that may be required for the support and management of the said business, shall be divided among them in the following proportion, to-wit:_____

_____

All Loss that shall happen to the said business by ill commodities, bad debts, or from any other cause, shall be borne and paid between them in like proportion.

It is agreed by and between the said parties that there shall be had and kept at all times during the continuance of their Copartnership, perfect, just and true books-of-account wherein each of the said Copartners shall enter and set down all money by them or either of them received, paid, laid out and expended in and about said business, as well as all other matters and things whatsoever to the said business and management thereof in anywise appertaining; which said books shall be used in common between the said copartners, so that either of them may have access thereto without any interruption or hinderance of the other. And also the said partners shall once in each year, or oftener if necessary, make, yield and render each to the other, a true, just and perfect inventory and account of all profits and increase by them, or either of them, made, and of all losses by them, or either of them, sustained; and also all payments, receipts, disbursements, and all other things by them made, received, disbursed, acted done or suffered by the said copartnership and business, and the said account so made, shall and will clear, adjust, pay and deliver, each to the other, at the time, their just share of the profits so made as aforesaid.

And the said parties hereby mutually covenant and agree to and with each other, that, during the continuance of the said Copartnership, neither of them shall nor will endorse any note, or otherwise become surety for any person or persons whomsoever, without the consent of the other of the said copartners. And at the end, or other sooner determination of their Copartnership, the said copartners, each to the other, shall and will make a true, just, and final account of all things relating to their said business, and in all things truly adjust the same; and all and every the stock and stocks, as well as the gains and increase thereof, which shall appear to be remaining, either in money, goods, wares, fixtures, debts, or otherwise, shall be divided between them, in the proportion aforesaid.

IN WITNESS WHEREOF, the said parties have hereunto set their hands the day and year first above written.

_____(SEAL)

_____   _____(SEAL)

_____   _____(SEAL)
(Reproduced with permission of Official Legal Forms, Hialeah, Fla.)

A Power of Attorney is a legal authorization for one to act as another's agent. The extent of the Power of Attorney is limited to that which is stated in the authorization.

No. 22–7
POWER OF ATTORNEY

KNOW ALL MEN BY THESE PRESENTS:

THAT_____ha_____made, constituted and appointed, and by these presents do make, constitute and appoint_____
_____ true and lawful attorney for_____
_____and in_____name, place and stead_____
_____
_____giving and granting unto_____
_____said attorney full power and authority to do and perform all and every act and thing whatsoever requisite and necessary to be done in and about the premises as fully, to all intents and purposes, as _____might or could do if personally present, with full power of substitution and revocation, hereby ratifying and confirming all that_____said attorney or_____

substitute shall lawfully do or cause to be done by virtue hereof.

　　IN WITNESS WHEREOF,＿＿＿＿＿＿＿have hereunto set＿＿＿＿＿＿

hand＿＿＿＿＿and seal＿＿＿＿＿＿＿＿＿the＿＿＿＿＿＿＿day of＿＿＿＿

＿＿＿＿ in the year one thousand nine hundred and＿＿＿＿＿＿＿＿＿ .

Sealed and delivered in the presence of

＿＿＿＿＿＿＿＿＿＿＿＿＿＿＿＿＿　　＿＿＿＿＿＿＿＿＿＿＿＿＿＿＿(Seal)

＿＿＿＿＿＿＿＿＿＿＿＿＿＿＿＿＿　　＿＿＿＿＿＿＿＿＿＿＿＿＿＿＿(Seal)